I0754537

Plate I

Scale ¼ inch = 1 foot.

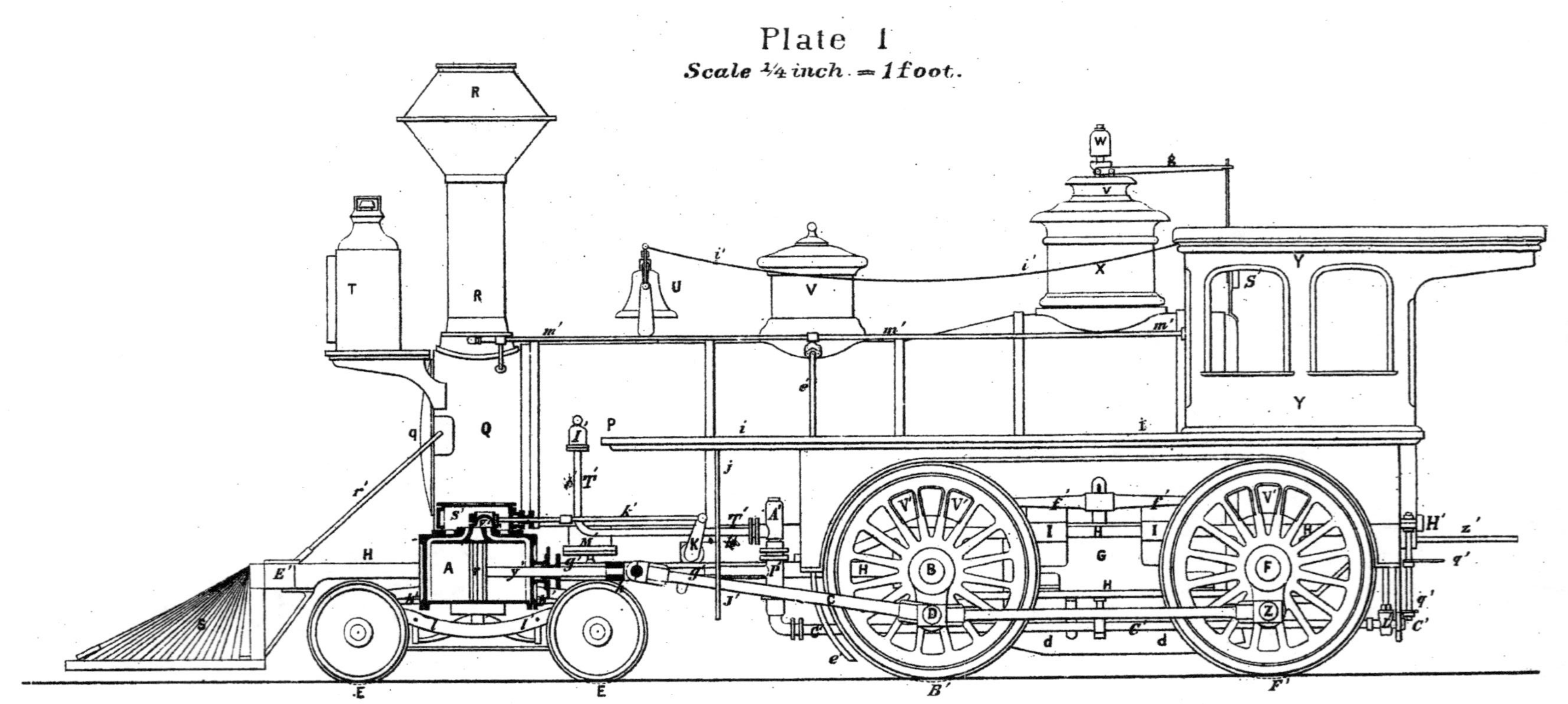

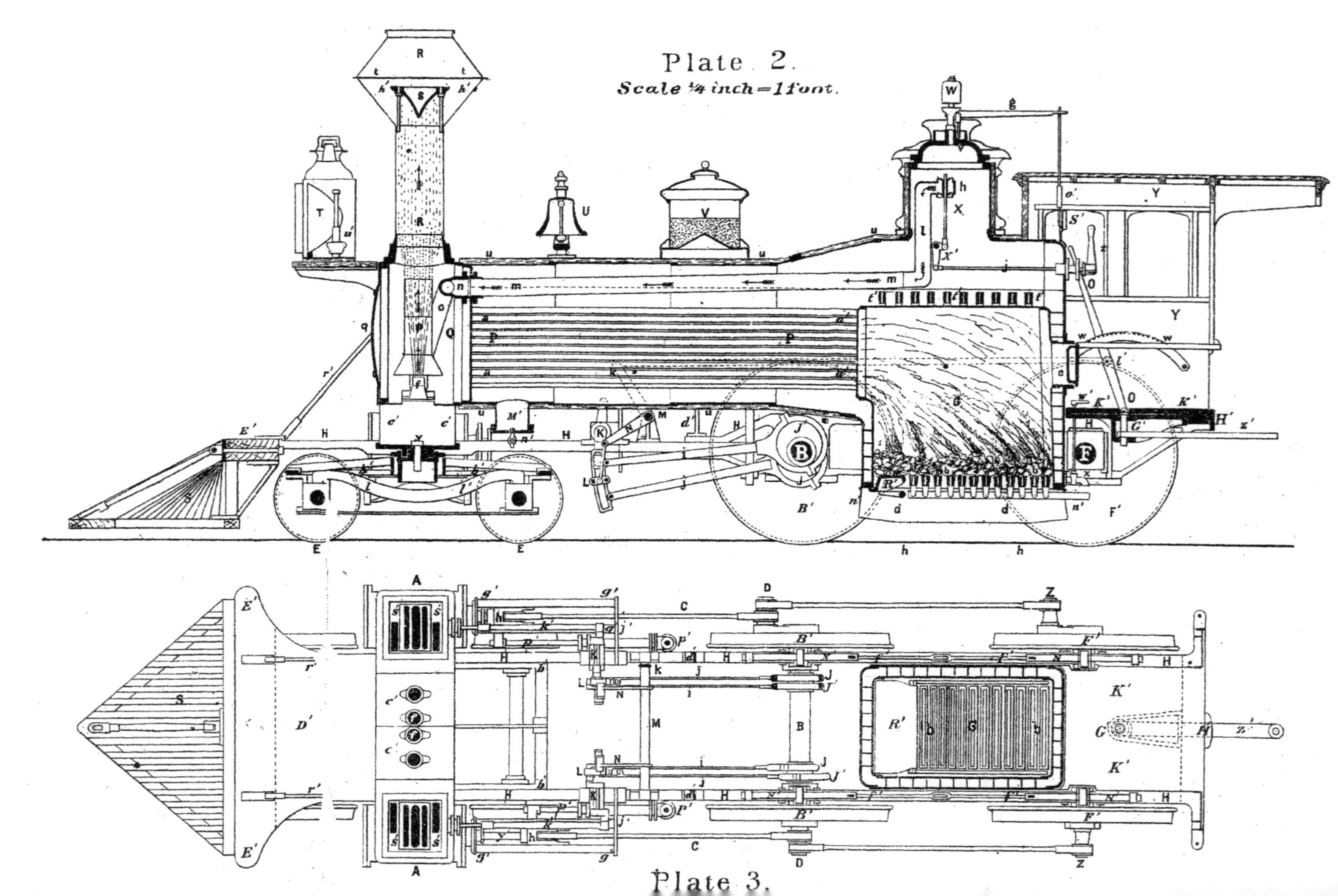
Plate 2.
Scale ¼ inch = 1 foot.
Plate 3.

CATECHISM

OF THE

LOCOMOTIVE,

BY

M. N. FORNEY,

MECHANICAL ENGINEER.

PUBLISHED BY
THE RAILROAD GAZETTE, 73 BROADWAY, NEW YORK.
1875.

CLARK W. BRYAN & CO.,
PRINTERS, ELECTROTYPERS AND PUBLISHERS,
SPRINGFIELD, MASS.

PREFACE.

Books, like individuals, have their histories, and it seems but proper that in introducing them somewhat of their ancestry should be detailed. The present book originated in this wise: the publishers of the Railroad Gazette procured a copy of the "Katechismus der Einrichtung und des Betriebes der Locomotive," by Georg Kosak. As no English translation of this excellent little book was known to be in existence, the editors of the above paper determined to translate it and adapt it to the American practice in the construction and management of locomotive steam engines, and republish it in their journal. The translation was therefore made and submitted to the writer for revision and adaptation, according to the original intention. Before the latter was entertained, however, he had commenced writing an elementary treatise on the locomotive. In revising the first part of the translation of Mr. Kosak's book, it was found that the latter occupied only to a very limited extent the ground which the writer had "staked out" in his own incomplete plan. He therefore concluded to abandon the original intention of "adapting" Mr. Kosak's work, and determined to rewrite it and make substantially a new book of it. For the "idea," however, and to some extent its plan, and for much valuable material, the author must acknowledge his indebtedness to Mr. Kosak. In some few cases the language of the translator has been employed, in part or in whole, without quotation marks, but with an acknowledgment in a foot-note. A similar plan has also been pursued in using some other books. This was done to avoid cutting up paragraphs and sentences into fragmentary parts with numerous quotation marks.

The following books have been consulted and used in writing the Catechism of the Locomotive: Heat considered as a Mode of Motion, by Prof. Tyndall; The Conservation of Energy, by Balfour Stewart; Railway Machinery, by D. K. Clark; Treatise on the Locomotive Engine, by Zerah Colburn; Treatise on the Steam Engine, by W. J. M. Rankine; Indicator Experiments on Locomotives, by Professor Bauschinger; Richards' Steam Indicator, by Charles T. Porter; Die Schule des Locomotivfuhrers, by J. Brosius and R. Koch; Mechanics, by A. Morin; The New Chemistry, by J. P. Cooke, Jr.; Combustion of Coal and the Prevention of Smoke, by C. Wye Williams; A Treatise on Steam Boilers, by Robert Wilson; Reports of the American Railway Master Mechanics' Association; Link Valve Motion, by William S. Auchincloss, and

Emergencies and How to Treat Them, by Dr. Joseph W. Howe.

For the title of the book an apology is perhaps needed, as the word Catechism is associated in nearly all persons' minds we will trust with early religious and theological instruction, and therefore a Catechism of the Locomotive is very apt to sound more ludicrous than scientific. The title of Mr. Kosak's book was adopted before it was determined to rewrite it, and it was afterwards not deemed best to change it. To those who are disposed to smile at it, the precedent of Mr. Bourne's excellent Catechism of the Steam Engine is quoted, and if they will refer to Webster's Dictionary for the definition of the word "catechism," they will find that it means "an elementary book containing a summary of principles in any science or art, but appropriately in religion, reduced to the form of questions and answers, and sometimes with notes, explanations and reference to authorities," which is exactly what the present book is intended to be.

To persons accustomed to books and study, the catechetical form is very apt to seem cumbrous and awkward, but it has some very decided advantages in writing for those who have not acquired studious habits of thought. To such the question asked presents first a distinct image of the subject to be considered, so that the explanation or instruction which follows is much more apt to be understood than it would be if no such question had been asked.

The author is indebted to Mr. D. B. Grant for the use of drawings from which most of the engravings of details of locomotives with which this book is illustrated have been made, and to other locomotive builders, whose engines are illustrated in the full-page plates, for the drawings thereof. He has also received very valuable aid from Mr. Richard H. Buel, Mechanical Engineer; Mr. William Buchanan, Master Mechanic of the Hudson River Railroad; Mr. Frank D. Child, Superintendent of the Hinkley Locomotive Works; and Mr. E. T. Jeffrey, Assistant Superintendent of Machinery of the Illinois Central Railroad.

The object in writing the book was to furnish a clear and easily understood description of the principles, construction and operation of the locomotive engine of the present day, a subject which is not concisely or adequately treated in any one similar book. If the author has succeeded in making what he has written plain to plain people, his aim will be fully accomplished.

No. 73 Broadway, NEW YORK.

CONTENTS.

APPENDIX.

INTRODUCTION.

THE Catechism of the Locomotive is intended for a large class of readers, among whom are all kinds of railroad officers and employes, consisting of locomotive runners, firemen, and the many different kinds of mechanics employed in railroad shops and in the construction of locomotive and other kinds of railroad machinery and material. Besides these there are many amateur engineers, students, and persons interested directly or indirectly in railroads, and a not inconsiderable class who are always seeking information on all subjects whatsoever. It is evident, therefore, that the only way to adapt the book to all the classes for whom it is intended, was to make it so plain that the "wayfaring man" will have no difficulty in comprehending it. It has therefore been written in as clear language as the writer could command, and the subjects presented are treated as simply and as plainly as his ability enabled him to do, and with the least possible employment of either scientific or practical technicalities. The only deviation from this plan will be found in the use of algebraic symbols to designate arithmetical calculations. This was done to save space, and because it was thought that they could be explained so that even those without any knowledge whatsoever of algebra could easily comprehend them. To such as have no such knowledge the following explanation is given:

Suppose it is necessary to add two numbers, say 1,872 and 468. The calculation, if made arithmetically, would be thus:

$$\begin{array}{r} 1{,}872 \\ 468 \\ \hline 2{,}340 \end{array}$$

This it will be seen occupies the space of several lines of print. If we want to express this calculation algebraically, it can be done by simply writing the two numbers and placing the sign +, called *plus*, between the two, which indicates that they are to be added together, thus:

$$1{,}872+468$$

To indicate what the *sum* will be, or what the two added together will amount to, the sign =, called *equal to*, or the sign of equality, is placed after the two numbers and between them and the sum, thus:

$$1{,}872+468=2{,}340,$$

which can be read as follows:

1,872 *added to* 468 *is equal to* 2,340.

Now the only use of the algebraic signs + and = is

that they save time in writing and room in printing, and when persons become accustomed to their use they make plain a number of operations at a single glance, as will be shown hereafter.

In the same way that the sign + means *added to*, the sign — means *less* or subtracted from, thus:

$$1{,}872 - 468 = 1{,}404,$$

which is the same as though it was printed as follows:

1,872 *less* 468 *is equal to* 1,404.

The sign × means *multiplied by*, or is the sign of multiplication. Thus:

$$1{,}872 \times 468 = 876{,}096;$$

that is,

1,872 *multiplied by* 468 *is equal to* 876,096.

The sign ÷ means divided by, thus:

$$1{,}872 \div 468 = 4.$$

which means:

1,872 *divided by* 468 *is equal to* 4.

The same thing is expressed by putting a line under the dividend and writing the divisor under the line, thus:

$$\frac{1{,}872}{468} = 4.$$

These signs are combined in various ways. Thus, supposing we wanted to add 1,872 to 468 and then divide the sum by 117, it would be necessary, in order to represent the arithmetical calculation, to do it as follows:

```
    1872
     468
    ----
117)2340(20
    234
    ---
      0
```

Algebraically it would be stated thus:

$$\frac{1872+468}{117}=20.$$

If you wanted to add 124 to the quotient 20 above, the calculation would be as follows:

```
    1872
     468
    ----
117)2340( 20
    234  124
    ---  ---
      0  144
```

This operation could be expressed by writing it as follows:

$$\frac{1872+468}{117}+124=144.$$

If we wanted to multiply the quotient 20 by 124 we would simply put the sign × instead of + before 124, thus:

$$\frac{1872+468}{117}\times 124=2480.$$

The sign of subtraction or division can be used in the same way.

With these explanations it is believed that any one, with nothing more than an ordinary knowledge of the four elementary rules of arithmetic, can understand all the mathematics contained in the following pages. A little explanation may also be needed of the method of representing machinery and other structures by mechanical drawings.

If we want to represent the outside of any object, say an apple, we make a drawing of it as shown at *A*.

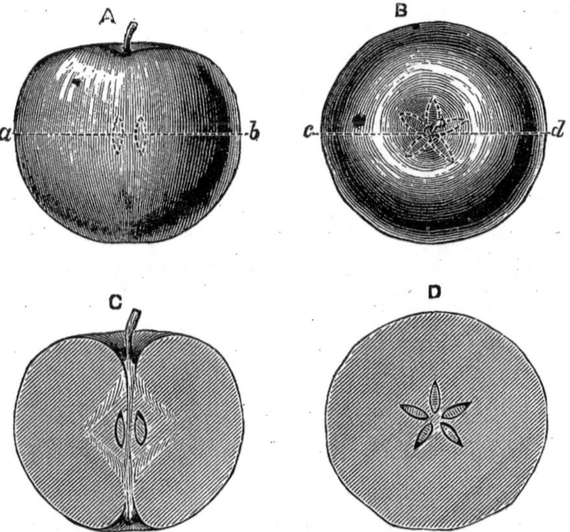

Now if we want to show the inside of the apple, say the seeds and core, we can cut it in half and represent it as shown at *C*, which is then called a ***section*** or ***sectional view*** of the apple. If we represent it as it will appear if we are above it and looking down on it as shown at *B*, it is called a ***top view*** or ***plan.***

It is evident, too, that it might be desirable to show the arrangement of the seeds in the apple as they would appear if it was cut through in the other direction, say on the line *a b*, fig. *A*, and as is shown at *D*. There are therefore two kinds of sections; one *C*, in which the object is supposed to be cut through vertically, and therefore called a ***vertical section,*** the other when the object is supposed to be cut through horizontally, and therefore called a ***horizontal section,*** as shown at *D*.

It is also evident that in looking at a locomotive or any other object, the appearance of the engine depends upon our position in relation to it. Thus, if we stand on the side of it, we see that part of the engine, and a drawing which represents the side, is therefore called a ***side view*** or ***side elevation.*** A drawing which represents a locomotive or other object as it would appear to us if we stood in front of it, is called a ***front view*** or ***front elevation,*** and a representation of the back part of any object as it would appear to us if we stood behind it is called a ***back view*** or ***back elevation.*** Plate I is a side view, Plate II a section, Plate III a top view or plan;*

* The boiler of the locomotive is supposed to be removed in Plate III.

the vignette in the title page is a front view and fig. 71 a back view of a locomotive. If the drawing is made as the object would appear if it was turned upside down, and we were looking at it from above, then it is called an *inverted plan.*

It is obvious, too, that it is possible to make a great many different sectional views of nearly any object, especially of a machine. Thus, we could suppose a locomotive cut through vertically and lengthwise, as is shown in Plate II. Such a representation is called a *longitudinal* section. A locomotive could also be cut through crosswise, as shown in fig. 40, which is called a *transverse section.* It is of course possible to represent a transverse section of a machine like a locomotive at a great many different points; for example, it could be shown as though it was cut through the smoke-stack as in fig. 40, or through the boiler farther back, as the latter is shown in fig. 42. Usually when a section is shown through a cylindrical object like a smoke-stack or boiler, it is shown through its centre. If, however, this is not apparent from the drawing or engraving, it should be stated at what point it is supposed to be taken, thus the section *D* of the apple is on the line *a b* of fig. *A*, and the section *C* is on the line *c d.*

In drawing sections, the parts which are supposed to be cut in two are usually shaded with parallel diagonal lines drawn at equal distances apart, as shown in the sections of the apple at *A* and *B*. Sections are also sometimes represented with solid black surfaces, as in Plates II and III, and in the engraving of a pump in fig. 66.

Objects which are behind others which are in front of them are often shown with dotted lines, so as to indicate their position. The seeds of the apple are thus indicated at *A*.

It is also customary, in drawings of machinery, to take great liberties with the objects represented and to show them with parts removed or broken away, if their construction can thus be made plainer. It should be remembered that the purpose of drawings of this kind is not to give a pictorial representation of the object as it appears to the eye, but to make its construction and mode of operation apparent to the mind. In such drawings therefore all perspective is disregarded. It would lead us too far were we to explain the reasons for this, and therefore readers must accept the assertion without the proof.

CATECHISM OF THE LOCOMOTIVE.

PART I.

THE STEAM ENGINE.

Question 1. *What is the motive power employed in ordinary steam engines?*

Answer. The expansive force of steam.

Question 2. *How is this expansive force of steam applied?*

Answer. It is applied by admitting it into a *cylinder*

Fig. 1.

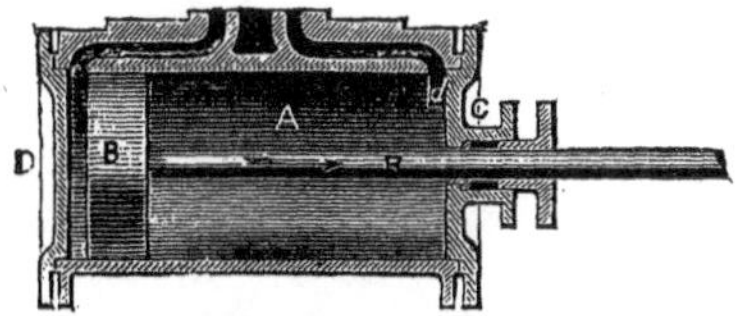

Scale ⅜ in.=1 foot.

A. Cylinder. *R.* Piston-Rod.
B. Piston. *D.* Front Cylinder-Head.
C. Back Cylinder-Head.

(*A*, fig. 1) in which a *piston*, *B*, is fitted so as to move air-tight from one end of the cylinder to the other. The steam, if admitted at *c*, will force the piston *B* to the opposite end* of the cylinder. When it has reached that end, if the steam is allowed to escape and a fresh supply is admitted to the cylinder through the opening *d*, it will move the piston back again. In this way, by alternately admitting steam at one end and exhausting it from the other, the piston receives a *reciprocating motion*, which is communicated to the outside of the cylinder by a rod, *R*, which is called the *piston-rod*, which works air-tight through an opening in one of the *cylinder-covers*, or *cylinder-heads*, as they are usually called.

* In all ordinary locomotives, the cylinders are so placed that the head *C* through which the piston-rod works is behind, and the other head *D* in front. The two ends of the cylinder are therefore designated the *front* and *back ends*, respectively.

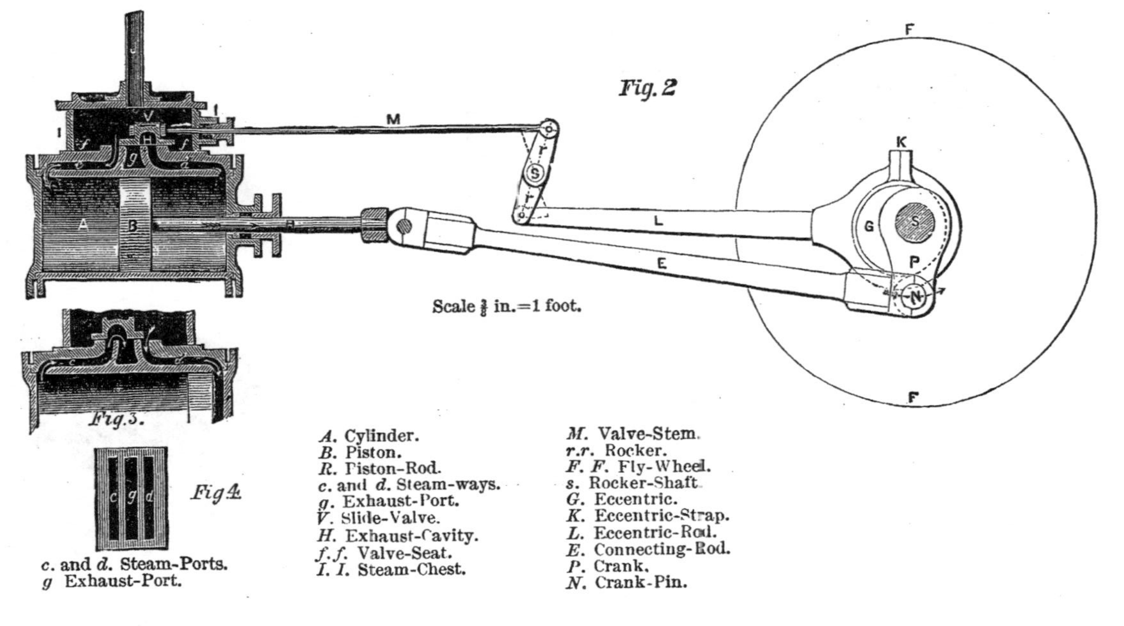
Fig. 2
M
F
K
I
V
H
f
f
g
c
d
r
S
r
A
B
R
L
G
S
P
E
N
F
Scale ⅜ in.=1 foot.
Fig. 3.
Fig 4.
c
g
d
c. and d. Steam-Ports.
g Exhaust-Port.
A. Cylinder.
B. Piston.
R. Piston-Rod.
c. and d. Steam-ways.
g. Exhaust-Port.
V. Slide-Valve.
H. Exhaust-Cavity.
f. f. Valve-Seat.
I. I. Steam-Chest.
M. Valve-Stem.
r. r. Rocker.
F. F. Fly-Wheel.
s. Rocker-Shaft.
G. Eccentric.
K. Eccentric-Strap.
L. Eccentric-Rod.
E. Connecting-Rod.
P. Crank.
N. Crank-Pin.

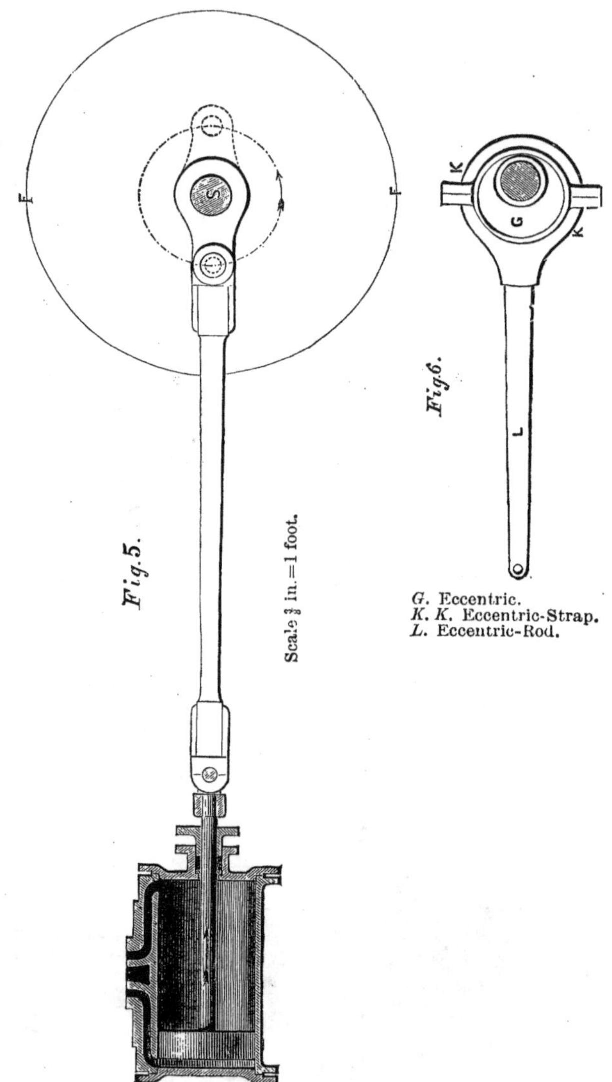

F
F
S
Fig. 5.
Scale $\frac{3}{8}$ in. = 1 foot.
K
K
G
Fig. 6.
L
G. Eccentric.
K. K. Eccentric-Strap.
L. Eccentric-Rod.

QUESTION 3. *How is this reciprocating motion of the piston converted into rotary motion?*

Answer. By connecting the end of the piston-rod *R* (fig. 2) by another rod, *E*, called a *connecting-rod*, with a crank, *P*, which is attached to a revolving shaft, *S*. It is apparent that if the piston *B* is moved in the direction shown by the dart *R*, a rotary motion will be given to the crank in the direction of the dart *N*. When, however, the crank reaches the position shown by the dotted lines in fig. 5, it is plain that a force applied to move the piston in either direction will no longer produce a rotary movement of the crank and shaft. The same thing will occur when the crank is in the opposite position, shown by the full lines. These two positions are called the *dead-points* of the crank.

QUESTION 4. *How is the crank of an ordinary steam engine carried past the dead-points?*

Answer. Stationary engines are usually provided with a large and heavy wheel, called a *fly-wheel* (*F F*, fig. 2) which is attached to the shaft *S*. This wheel receives a sufficient amount of momentum from the crank, while the latter is moving from one dead-point to the other, to carry it past those points.

QUESTION 5. *How is the steam admitted to and exhausted from the cylinder?*

Answer. It is admitted through two channels, *c*, *d*, fig. 2, called *steam-ways*, cast in the cylinder. These ways terminate in a smooth flat surface, *f f*, called the *valve-seat*. Their openings in the valve-seat are called *steam-ports*. Between them is another port or cavity, *g*, called the *exhaust-port*, which communicates with the open air. The form of these ports is long and narrow, as shown in fig. 4, which represents a plan of them. Over these ports a valve, *V,* called a ***slide-valve,*** usually made of cast iron, with a cavity, *H,* on its under side, is fitted so that by moving it backwards or forwards it will alternately cover and uncover the two steam-ports. The valve and valve-seat are inclosed in a sort of box, *I I,* fig. 2, made of cast iron, called a ***steam-chest,*** into which steam is admitted from the boiler by a pipe, *J.* When the valve is in the position represented in fig. 2, the front steam-port is uncovered and the steam is admitted to the front end of the cylinder, and thus forces the piston towards the back end. If, when the piston reaches the back end, the valve be moved into the position shown in fig. 3, the back steam-port will be uncovered and steam will be admitted to that end of the cylinder. At the same time it will be observed that the aperture of the front steam-port *c* and that of the exhaust-port are both covered by the cavity in the slide-valve, so that the steam which was admitted to the front end of the cylinder can escape through the steam-port *c* into the exhaust-port, and thus into the open air. In this way, by moving the valve alternately back and forth, steam is simultaneously admitted first to one end and exhausted from the other, and *vice versa.*

QUESTION 6. *How is the slide-valve moved so as to admit and exhaust the steam at the right time?*

Answer. This is done by what is called an ***eccentric,*** which is a circular disc, *G* (fig. 6), the axis of which is not in the centre. The outside of the eccentric is embraced by a metal ring, *K K,* made in two halves, called an ***eccentric-strap.*** The eccentric is attached to the shaft by screws or keys, and revolves with it and inside of the eccentric-strap. To the latter is also attached a rod, *L*, called an *eccentric-rod.* It is obvious from fig. 6 that if the eccentric revolves inside of the strap it will impart a reciprocating motion to the rod *L*. The eccentric, *G*, strap, *K*, and rod, *L*, are represented in fig. 2. Before describing their operation, or rather their connection with the valve *V*, it is necessary to understand that usually the valve-seat is placed on top of the cylinder, in which position it is difficult to connect the eccentric-rod with the valve. For convenience, therefore, what is called a *rocker, r r*, is placed between the cylinder and the main shaft of the engine. This rocker has two arms attached to a shaft, *s*, and the two arms have a vibratory motion about it, as indicated by the dotted lines. The eccentric-rod *L* is attached by a pin to the lower arm of the rocker, and the valve is connected to the upper arm by the rod *M*, called the *valve-stem*, or *valve-rod.* It is obvious that as the shaft *S* and eccentric *G* revolve, a reciprocating or vibratory motion will be given to the rocker, which will be communicated to the valve by the valve-stem; and it is only necessary to fix the eccentric in the proper position on the shaft, in relation to the crank and piston, to give the valve the required motion for admitting and exhausting the steam to and from the cylinder at the right time.

PART II.

THE FORCES OF AIR AND STEAM.

QUESTION 7. *What is meant by the pressure of the air?*

Answer. It is the pressure exerted by the weight of the air on every point with which it is in contact. The globe of the earth is surrounded by a layer of air about 50 miles thick, and, like every other substance, the air possesses weight, and hence presses upon every object with which it is in contact.

QUESTION 8. *How can it be shown that the air possesses weight?*

Answer. By weighing a flask when it is filled with air, and again when the air is exhausted from it. In the latter condition the weight of the flask will be found to be sensibly less than it was when full of air, showing that the air which the flask contained when it was first weighed increased its weight.

QUESTION 9. *Why do we not feel this pressure on our bodies?*

Answer. Because the air surrounds us on all sides, and presses just as much in one direction as it does in another, so that the pressures in different directions just balance each other, or are *in equilibrium;* but if you disturb this balance, for example, by sucking the air from a tube closed at one end, it will cling to your tongue; or if you take a thick piece of leather under ordinary conditions it will not adhere to anything, but if it be thoroughly wet and pressed hard against the surface of a smooth stone, so as to force out the air from under it, the stone, as nearly all school-boys know, can be lifted up if a string is attached to the leather; or if the air be sucked out of a tube, one end of which is inserted in a liquid, the latter will be forced up the tube. These phenomena are due to the pressure of the atmosphere in the first case on one side of the person's tongue, pressing it against the mouth of the tube; in the second, to the same pressure on the top of the leather, causing it to adhere to the stone; and in the last, to the weight of the air pressing on the surface of the liquid, forcing it into the vacuum in the tube.

QUESTION 10. *What is the amount of the pressure of the atmosphere, and how is it measured?*

Answer. It is usually measured by the pressure on one square inch of surface, which at the earth's surface is 15 pounds.* If, for example, we have a cylinder, *A*, fig. 7, with an air-tight piston, *B*, fitted to it whose area is just one square inch, if we exhaust the air through the tube *C* from the cylinder above the piston, the air will press against the under side of the piston so that, if no power is required to overcome its friction in the cylinder, the pressure of the air will raise a weight of 15 pounds. The pressure of the air varies, however, as you ascend or descend from the surface of the earth, because as you go up on a mountain or in a balloon the layer of air above you becomes thinner, and, therefore, its weight and consequent

*In common practice it is generally taken at 15 lbs. per square inch, but the average atmospheric pressure is more accurately 14.7 pounds.

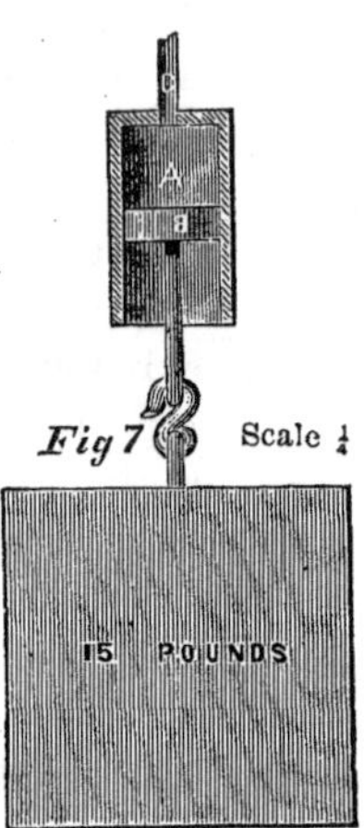

Fig 7 Scale ¼

pressure are diminished; and as you descend, as in a deep mine, the layer is thicker, and its pressure consequently greater.

QUESTION 11. *What is steam?*

Answer. Steam is water changed by means of heat into a gas. At every temperature there is formed from water, on its surface, vapor of which the clouds are formed at all seasons of the year. This change of water into vapor, or evaporation of water, takes place at low temperatures only on its surface, however. But if we heat water in a vessel to a temperature of 212 degrees Fahrenheit, then the inner particles of the mass of water (lying on the heating surface of the vessel) are changed into steam, and rise to the surface in bubbles, which is the phenomenon we call *boiling.* It must not be imagined, however, that the visible cloud which escapes from a kettle or the exhaust-pipe of a steam engine is true steam. It is rather small particles of water, into which the steam has condensed through contact with the cold air. True steam is invisible, as we may observe near the mouth of a kettle or the exhaust-pipe of an engine from which we know it is escaping.

QUESTION 12. *If water is heated in an open vessel what occurs?*

Answer. It continues for some time to increase in temperature, and the evaporation becomes more and more rapid. At length bubbles of vapor break out and reach the surface, and the process of boiling or ebullition has begun. When this takes place the temperature of the water ceases to rise, and it remains stationary until all the water has boiled away, the only difference being that if the supply of heat be very great the process is very rapid, and if the supply of heat be small the process is very slow. The point at which ebullition commences is called the *boiling-point.*

QUESTION 13. *On what does the boiling-point depend?*

Answer. Chiefly on the pressure on the surface of the water, but to some extent upon the purity of the water. Thus, boiling, which takes place at 212 degrees under the ordinary atmospheric pressure, in lighter air, as on high mountains, takes place at a much lower temperature than on lowlands, and so water boils in a glass tube from which the air has been exhausted by the warmth of the hand, that is, at 92 degrees.

QUESTION 14. *What is the pressure of steam which escapes from boiling water in an open vessel?*

Answer. It is exactly equal to the pressure of the

atmosphere in which it is boiled. Ordinarily this is 15 lbs., and the boiling-point 212 degrees; but if we go up on a mountain where the atmospheric pressure is only 10 lbs. per square inch, the water will then boil at a temperature of 193.3 degrees, and the steam which escapes will have the same pressure as the atmosphere, or 10 lbs. per square inch. On the other hand, if we could go down into a mine where the atmospheric pressure was 20 lbs. per square inch, the water would not boil until it was heated to 228 degrees, and the pressure of the escaping steam would then be 20 lbs. per square inch.

QUESTION 15. *If water is boiled in an enclosed vessel like a covered tea-kettle or a steam boiler, what occurs?*

Answer. The steam rises and fills the space above the water, and, if it cannot escape, increases in pressure. The temperature of both the water and the steam rises with the pressure, and will continue to do so as long as the heat is increased, or until the steam can escape or the vessel is exploded. The boiling point also rises as the steam pressure increases.

QUESTION 16. *Is there any pressure which corresponds to the temperature of steam and water?*

Answer. Yes. There is a fixed pressure for every temperature, when steam is in contact with water, and its pressure cannot be increased or diminished without at the same time heating or cooling the water, and the higher the temperature of the water the greater will be the corresponding steam pressure. Thus water at 212 degrees produces steam with a pressure equal to that of the atmosphere; at 240 degrees the steam will have a pressure of 25 lbs., or 10 lbs. more than the atmospheric pressure; at 281 degrees a pressure of 50 lbs.; and at 328 degrees, 100 lbs. As this relation of pressure to temperature is fixed, if we know the one we can tell the other. This is true, however, only where the steam is in contact with water, when it is called ***saturated steam.*** If it is separated from water it may be heated to a higher temperature, and is then called ***superheated steam.***

QUESTION 17. ***How is the pressure of steam measured?***

Answer. In the same way as that of the atmosphere,—that is, by the force exerted on one square inch of surface. Thus if steam is admitted into the cylinder *A*, fig. 8, under the piston *B*, whose area is equal to one square inch of surface, supposing, as we did before, that no power is required to overcome its friction in the cylinder, if the steam thus admitted would just balance the atmosphere, its pressure would be equal to 15 lbs. If, besides overcoming the pressure of the atmosphere, it would raise a weight of 15 lbs., then its pressure per square inch would be equal to 30 lbs. When the atmospheric pressure is ***included*** with that of the steam, we call it the ***absolute steam pressure.*** In ordinary engines, however, the steam must always overcome the pressure of the atmosphere, and therefore the only part of the pressure which is effective is that above, or by which it exceeds, the atmospheric pressure. For example, although the steam admitted under the piston in fig. 8 has an absolute pressure of 30 lbs. per square inch, yet it will only raise a weight of 15 lbs., because it must first overcome the pressure of the air on the other side of the piston. The pressure of the steam used in most stationary and in locomotive engines is, therefore, measured by its pressure above the atmosphere. That is, if steam introduced under the piston in fig. 8 will raise a weight of only 15 lbs., we say it has a pressure of 15 lbs. per square inch; if it will raise 50 lbs., its pressure is said to be 50 lbs. per square inch, and so on. The pressure of the atmosphere is disregarded, and all steam-gauges used on locomotives are graduated in that way. In speaking of steam pressure in future, therefore, unless otherwise specified, we shall mean *effective* and not *absolute* pressure.

QUESTION 18. *What is meant by the expansion of steam?*

Answer. In all gases a repulsion is exerted between the various particles, so that any gas, however small in quantity, will always fill the vessel in which it is held. Steam possesses this same property, and if placed in any vessel the particles in endeavoring to separate from each other will exert a force on all its sides. This force we call the steam pressure. To illustrate this we will suppose that the cylinder *A* in fig. 8 is half filled with steam of 30 lbs. pressure. If now the supply of steam is shut off, the steam in the cylinder will expand so as to push the piston upward, but with a somewhat diminishing force, the nature of which we will explain hereafter.

QUESTION 19. *What is meant by the volume of steam?*

Answer. It means the space which the steam occupies.

QUESTION 20. *What is the proportion which exists between the volume and the pressure of steam?*

Answer. If the temperatures remain the same they are INVERSELY PROPORTIONAL TO EACH OTHER; that is, the one increases in the same proportion as the other diminishes. If we admit steam of 30 lbs.

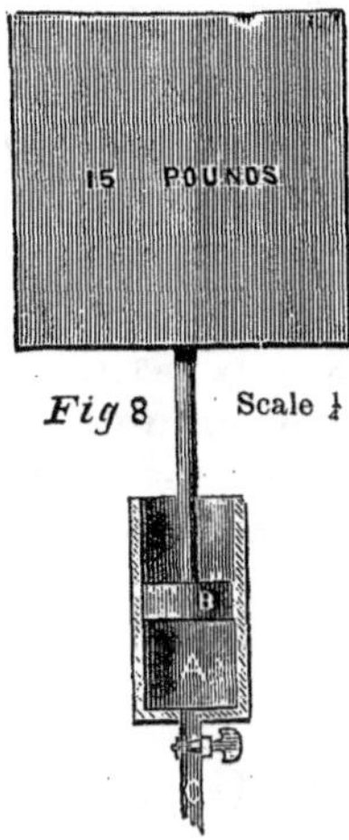

Fig 8 Scale ¼

pressure per square inch into the cylinder *A*, fig. 8, and then cut off the supply by closing the cock *C* and allow the steam in the cylinder to expand to double its volume by pushing the piston to the end of the cylinder, the steam pressure will then be only 15 lbs.; if it should expand to three times its volume its pressure would be only one-third, or 10 lbs. per square inch. This method for calculating the pressure of steam after it has expanded is correct only for the *absolute* and not for the *effective* pressures of steam. In order to ascertain the effective pressures of steam after expansion, it is only necessary to make the calculation with the absolute pressure and deduct the atmospheric pressure from the result. If, after being thus expanded, the piston be pushed down again so as to compress the steam into its original space, its pressure will again be 30 lbs., providing no heat has been lost in any way.

QUESTION 21. *With a cylinder of any given stroke* how can we determine approximately the pressure of the steam after expansion for any given point of cut-off?* †

Answer. BY MULTIPLYING THE ABSOLUTE PRESSURE PER SQUARE INCH OF THE STEAM IN THE CYLINDER BEFORE IT IS CUT OFF, BY THE DISTANCE FROM THE BEGINNING OF THE STROKE AT WHICH IT IS CUT OFF, AND DIVIDING THE PRODUCT BY THE WHOLE LENGTH OF THE STROKE. Thus, if we have a cylinder whose piston has a stroke of 24 inches, if we cut off the steam at 8 inches, and have an ABSOLUTE pressure of 90 lbs. in the cylinder, the calculation is as follows:

$$\frac{90 \times 8}{24} = 30 \text{ lbs. final pressure.}$$

If we cut off at 10, 12 and 15 inches, the final pressure would be $37\frac{1}{2}$, 50 and $56\frac{1}{4}$ lbs., respectively. To get the effective pressure deduct the atmospheric pressure from this result.

QUESTION 22. *What is the proportion between the volume of steam and that of the water from which it is formed?*

Answer. At the pressure of the atmosphere (15 lbs.) each cubic inch of water will make 1,610 cubic inches of steam. At double that pressure, or 30 lbs. absolute pressure, it will make a little more than half as much, or 838 cubic inches; at four times, or 60 lbs. absolute pressure, 437 cubic inches, or a little more than a fourth as much as at the pressure of the atmosphere.

---

* The *stroke* of a piston is the distance it moves in the cylinder, and in ordinary engines is always twice the length of the crank measured from center to center of the shaft and crank-pin.

† The steam is said to be *cut off* when the steam-port by which steam is admitted to the cylinder is closed by the valve.

Question 23. *Why is it that the quantity of steam at high pressures is somewhat greater than in inverse proportion to the pressure?*

Answer. Because the boiling-point of water, as has already been explained, is higher as the pressure increases, and therefore the temperature of the steam produced at such pressure is also higher than at lower pressures; and as all gases are expanded by heat, therefore the volume of steam at the higher pressures is somewhat greater than in inverse proportion to its pressure, on account of being somewhat expanded by its high temperature. To make this plain, if we take a cubic inch of water and convert it into steam of atmospheric pressure, its volume will be 1,610 times that of the water, and its temperature 212 degrees.* If we convert this quantity of water into steam with a pressure double that of the atmosphere, the volume of the steam will be 838 times that of the water and its temperature will be 250.4 degrees. If the volume of the steam were exactly *inversely proportional* to the pressure, the cubic inch of water at double the atmospheric pressure would make only 805 cubic inches of steam; but as the boiling-point at that pressure is 38.4 degrees higher, the steam is expanded 33 cubic inches by the increase of its heat due to the higher boiling-point.

A table in the appendix gives the pressure, temperature and volume of saturated steam up to 300 lbs. absolute pressure.

Question 24. *What is meant by the condensation of steam?*

* More accurately, 213.1 degrees, if we call the atmospheric pressure 15 lbs., as we have.

Answer. It is the reconversion of steam into water by cooling it, or depriving it of part of its heat. It has been shown that the temperature of water must be raised to a certain point to generate steam of a given pressure. If the process is reversed, and we deprive the steam of a part of its heat, some of the steam is then at once reconverted into water, or *condensed,* and the pressure of that which remains will be reduced just in proportion as the heat is lost. When the temperature gets below 212 degrees under atmospheric pressure, all the steam will be condensed. As the useful work which steam can do in an engine is due to its pressure, which in turn depends on its temperature, any loss of heat will diminish its effective power. For this reason, all waste of heat from a steam engine should, as far as possible, be prevented.

QUESTION 25. *How is the heat of the steam wasted or lost in an ordinary steam engine?*

Answer. It is wasted in three ways: first, by *conduction;* second, by *convection;* and third, by *radiation.*

QUESTION 26. *What is meant by these three terms?*

Answer. 1. By *conduction* is meant that phenomenon which is manifested when we put one end of a metal bar two or three feet long into the fire and heat it. The heat is then gradually conveyed from one particle of the metal to that next to it until finally the end of the bar farthest from the fire becomes so hot that it cannot be touched. The heat is then said to be *conducted* through the bar. In the same way the metal of the boiler, pipes, cylinders and other parts of the engine becomes heated on one side, and the heat is thus conveyed to the outside of these parts.

2. The air with which they are surrounded then becomes heated, and being then lighter than the cold air, it rises and is again replaced with air which is not heated. In this way the heat is conveyed away by the air, and this phenomena is therefore called *convection.*

3. If an iron plate be placed in front of an ordinary grate fire three or four feet from it and exposed to the rays of heat from the fire, it will soon become so hot that you cannot bear your hand on it. If you place your hand between the iron plate and the fire you will find that only the side of your hand which is exposed to the fire will become hot, showing that the air between the plate and the fire is not nearly so hot as the plate soon becomes, and therefore that the heat is not conveyed to the plate by the air between it and the fire, but by the rays from the fire. This phenomenon is called *radiation.* The same thing occurs from any hot body, as for example a coil of steam pipe for heating a room, a steam boiler or cylinder of an engine.

QUESTION 27. *Is there any difference in the conducting and radiating power of different substances?*

Answer. Yes, very great. The difference in the *conducting* power of wood and iron is shown if we place one end of a bar of each in the fire. The wood will be consumed without warming the bar more than a few inches from the fire, whereas the iron will soon become hot two or three feet from the fire. Owing to the difference in the conducting power of cotton and wool, we wear cotton clothing in summer and woolen in winter, because cotton allows the heat of the body to be conducted away from it, whereas woolen cloth prevents to a great degree this loss of heat. For the same reason, the venders of roasted chestnuts on our streets wrap them in a piece of blanket to keep them hot, that is, to keep the heat in; and in summer we wrap ice in the same way to keep it cold, that is, keep the warmth of the air out. The wool, being a very bad conductor of heat, simply prevents the heat from being transferred from the inside to the outside, and *vice versa.* It is for this reason that steam boilers, pipes and cylinders are nearly always covered with wood, and sometimes with felt.

The difference in the *radiating* power of various substances can be shown if we take a large thermometer and heat it up to the temperature of boiling water. If this thermometer is hung up in a room having the temperature of melting ice, it will lose heat in two ways,—first by heating the air which surrounds it, that is by *convection*, and also by *radiation.* In order to confine ourselves to the latter process, we will suppose that the chamber is a vacuum. If we first cover the bulb of the thermometer with a thin coating of polished silver, and then ascertain how much heat it radiates in a minute, and then coat it with lamp-black, and repeat the same experiment,—that is to say, allow the thermometer at the boiling-point to cool for one minute in a vacuum chamber at the freezing-point,—it will be found that the thermometer loses much more in a minute when coated with lamp-black than it did when coated with silver, showing that much more heat is radiated from a surface covered with lamp-black than from polished silver. Generally it may be stated that polished metals radiate much less heat than surfaces which are not polished.* For this reason, as well as for ornament, locomotive and other boilers and cylinders are usually covered with Russia iron or polished brass.

* The account of the above experiment is copied from Balfour Stewart's very excellent little book, "Lessons in Elementary Physics," of which, and the same author's "Elementary Treatise on Heat," the writer has made frequent use.

PART III.

ON WORK, ENERGY, AND THE MECHANICAL EQUIVALENT OF HEAT.

QUESTION 28. *For what purpose are all steam engines used?*

Answer. They are used to produce *motion,* which is opposed by some *resistance.* Thus, if an engine is employed to raise grain from a railroad car to the top of a warehouse, it must produce motion, which is resisted by the weight of the grain; if it is used to saw wood, it must give motion to the saw, which is resisted by the fibres of the wood; a locomotive engine must produce motion of a train of cars, which is resisted by the air, the friction of the journals and the rolling of the wheels on the track; if the locomotive is employed on a grade or incline, besides the frictional resistance referred to it must overcome that due to its own weight and that of the train, which is gradually lifted as it ascends the incline. In producing motion opposed by some resistance an engine is said to be doing "*work.*"

QUESTION 29. *Can this work be accurately measured?*

Answer. Yes; but in order to measure anything we must first establish some accurate standard or unit of measurement. Thus we say a bar of iron is so many inches long, or a road is so many miles long. In like manner we speak of so many seconds, or minutes, or hours, or days, or years, when we speak of time. So it is necessary, in order to estimate or measure "*work*" in a strictly scientific manner, for us to fix upon some accurate standard or unit. In this country and in Great Britain the unit agreed upon for this purpose is the amount of power required to raise ONE POUND ONE FOOT, and is called a *foot-pound.* If we raise one pound two feet we do two foot-pounds of work; if three feet, three foot-pounds, and so on. Again, if we raise a weight of two pounds one foot high, we likewise do two foot-pounds of work; or if we raise it two feet high, we do four foot-pounds, and so on. In order to determine the amount of work done, we must MULTIPLY THE MOTION PRODUCED (*in feet*) BY THE RESISTANCE (*in pounds*), AND THE RESULT WILL BE THE WORK DONE IN FOOT-POUNDS.

QUESTION 30. *How many foot-pounds of work are performed in a pile-driving machine in raising a weight of* 1,200 *lbs.* 24 *feet?*

Answer. 1,200×24=28,800 foot-pounds.

QUESTION 31. *When this weight is raised, is the force which was exerted in raising it annihilated or lost?*

Answer. No; because the weight has the capacity of doing an equal amount of work when it falls, from the momentum* it acquires in falling. This *power of doing work* which it acquires in falling is called *energy.* Now, although the weight has no motion-producing power when it is raised to the top of the machine, yet obviously such action is then *possible* which when it rested on the earth was not possible. It has no energy as it hangs there dead and motionless; but energy is possible to it, and we might fairly use the

* Momentum is not a very exact term, but is used here because it ordinarily conveys the idea we wish to express.

term *possible energy* to express this power of motion which the weight possesses,* and which is therefore called *potential energy.* As soon as the weight is allowed to fall it acquires a greater velocity the farther it falls, and its potential energy thus becomes and is called *actual energy.*

QUESTION 32. *How do we explain such phenomena as the heating of a car-axle while turning under a car, the heating of brake-blocks when the brakes are applied to car-wheels, the heating of an iron rod by hammering, and of a turning tool when cutting a piece of metal?*

Answer. All of these phenomena are due to the fact that the *actual energy* of motion is converted into heat, as has been repeatedly proved by many able and ingenious investigators and experiments.

QUESTION 33. *When the weight of the pile-driver falls, is its energy also converted into heat?*

Answer. A part is expended in compressing the material into which the pile is driven and in overcoming the friction of the earth against the pile, each of which efforts develops heat, and another portion is converted into heat by the impact or blow of the falling weight on the head of the pile.

QUESTION 34. *Is all energy convertible into heat and heat into energy?*

Answer. Yes. Science has demonstrated very clearly that they are mutually convertible.

QUESTION 35. *Has it been ascertained how much heat is equivalent to one foot-pound of work?*

Answer. Yes; it has been found, from the most carefully-made experiments that the amount of heat

* Tyndall's "Heat Considered as a Mode of Motion."

which is required to raise the temperature of one pound of liquid water by one degree of Fahrenheit* is equivalent to 772 foot-pounds of work. It must be remembered that this is the theoretical equivalent of heat, and that only a very small proportion of this amount of work is ever realized from the heat developed by the combustion of fuel.

QUESTION 36. ***If, then, heat is convertible into work and work into heat, can the transmutation of the heat of the steam in the cylinder of an engine into work, and the reverse process, be explained?***

Answer. Yes. Take a cylinder, fig. 9, and, in order to make the conditions of the experiment as simple as possible, imagine it to be placed in a vacuum. Now let saturated steam be admitted under the piston so as to fill the cylinder half full at an absolute pressure of 100 lbs. If we will allow this steam to expand to double its volume and raise the piston *without doing any work*, and then repeat the experiment with a load of 50 pounds on the piston, whose area is one square inch, it will be found that the temperature of the steam is sensibly less, after lifting the weight, than in the previous experiment, in which it expanded without doing work, showing that part of the heat was abstracted from the steam by doing work, or, in other words, was converted into work. If

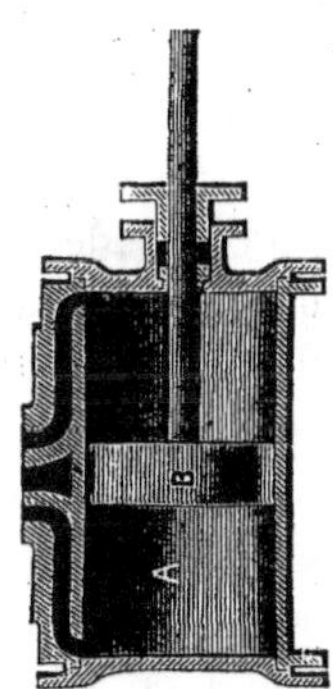

***Fig.* 9.**
Scale ⅜ in.=1 foot.

* Thermometers are divided into different scales. The one called the Fahrenheit scale, after its originator, is the one ordinarily used in this country.

then, after the steam has expanded and lifted the weight, we press the piston down so that the steam under the piston is compressed to its original volume, we shall find that its temperature is the same as before, as the work done in compressing it is converted into heat. In these experiments it is assumed that there is no friction of the piston, nor loss of heat from radiation or conduction. The same phenomena can be observed in machines used for compressing air, which is heated to so high a temperature when it is compressed that it is necessary to cool the cylinders of such machines by circulating a current of cold water around them.

QUESTION 37. *What practical relation is there between the convertibility of heat into work, and the conducting and radiating properties of different substances explained in answer to Question 27?*

Answer. The fact that heat is only another form of energy, or "the power of doing work," indicates that its loss by conduction or radiation lessens that power just as much as or more than the loss or waste of coal would, and therefore every effort should be made to protect the different parts of engines from loss of heat by covering them with substances which conduct or radiate very little heat. Care should also be taken to exclude cold air from circulating in contact with these parts, and excepting for supporting combustion, the nature of which will be explained hereafter, it should be excluded from the heating surface of boilers.

QUESTION 38. *What is meant by the term* LATENT HEAT OF EVAPORATION?

Answer. By *latent heat* is meant that heat which *apparently* disappears when water or other liquids are vaporized. Thus, it is found that if any quantity of water is converted into steam at any pressure, it is necessary not only to heat it to a temperature equivalent to that of the steam, or to the boiling-point, but after it has reached that temperature an additional amount of heat must be added in order to keep up the process of boiling. Notwithstanding this addition of heat to the water, the temperature of the steam produced will not be higher than that of the boiling water, thus showing that a considerable quantity of heat is absorbed, the only effect of which is to change the water into a gas or steam. This apparent disappearance of heat can be shown if we take a pound of boiling water whose temperature is 212 degrees and mix it with a pound of ice-cold water at 32 degrees. The result will be a mixture of two pounds of water of a mean temperature of 122 degrees. If now we convert a pound of water into steam at atmospheric pressure, the steam will heat 6.37 lbs. of ice-cold water up to 122 degrees, showing that a pound of steam at atmospheric pressure contains over six times as much heat as a pound of water of the same temperature as indicated by a thermometer. A similar apparent disappearance of heat occurs when other liquids are evaporated, and when ice or any other solid is converted into a liquid.

QUESTION 39. *What is the explanation of these phenomena?*

Answer. The exact reasons which will explain them fully are probably not yet clearly understood, but it is at least extremely probable that when any substance is changed from a solid to a liquid, or from a liquid to a gaseous condition, "a large portion of the heat is spent *in doing work* against the force of cohesion."* The particles of solid bodies, as we know, are so united that it requires more or less force, according to the nature of the substance, to tear them apart. Now we can conceive that the heat is changed into a form of energy, and in that condition resists this attraction of the particles to each other, and that being thus transformed it has lost the capacity of expanding the mercury in the thermometer. A similar effect takes place when a liquid is converted into a gas. In the former condition the particles move freely about each other and have little or no attraction for each other, but when it becomes a gas they have a *repulsion from* each other. The heat is thus converted into the energy of repulsion, and therefore is in reality no longer in the condition of heat and consequently does not affect the thermometer. We can illustrate this by supposing that by using steam heat is converted into work by raising the weight, or drop as it is called, of a pile-driving machine. When the weight is raised to the top of the guides from which it falls, although, as already explained, the heat is converted into *potential energy*, yet if we attached a thermometer to the drop we would not find that it was any warmer than before the drop was raised. If it were possible to make an instrument sufficiently sensitive to indicate an instantaneous change of temperature in the weight while falling, we would not find any increase of its temperature at the instant it had acquired its greatest momentum and just before it struck the object under it, although its potential energy would at that instant

* Balfour Stewart on the Conservation of Energy.

be converted into *actual energy* of motion. If, however, the weight should strike an unyielding object, its actual energy would at once be reconverted into heat, which our thermometer would indicate. The phenomenon of what is called latent heat of evaporation seems to be very similar to that described—the heat when the water is changed from a liquid to a gaseous condition is transformed into energy, which, as already stated, has no effect upon the mercury of the thermometer.

QUESTION 40. *What is meant by the* TOTAL HEAT *of steam?*

Answer. The "total heat of steam" is a phrase used to denote the sum of the heat required to raise the temperature of water from some given point up to the boiling-point due to a given pressure, and of the heat which disappears in evaporating one pound of water under a given pressure (or *latent heat of evaporation.*) Thus the latent heat of one pound of steam at atmospheric pressure (14.7 lbs.) is 966.1 units; and 212 units of heat are necessary to raise water from zero to the boiling-point; therefore the total heat counted from zero of steam of atmospheric pressure is 1,178.1 units. At 100 pounds absolute pressure the latent heat is 885.5 and the sensible heat 327.9 degrees; therefore the total heat measured from zero is 1,213.4 units.

PART IV.

THE SLIDE–VALVE.

QUESTION 41. *What are the essential conditions which a slide-valve must fulfill in governing the admission and exhaust of steam to and from the cylinder of an ordinary engine?*

Answer. 1. It must admit steam to one end only of the cylinders at one time. 2. It must allow the steam to escape from one end at least as soon as it is admitted to the other end; and 3, it must cover the steam-ports so as not to permit the steam to escape from the steam-chest into the exhaust-port.

QUESTION 42. *What was the first form of slide-valve used?*

Answer. That represented in fig. 10. The smallest

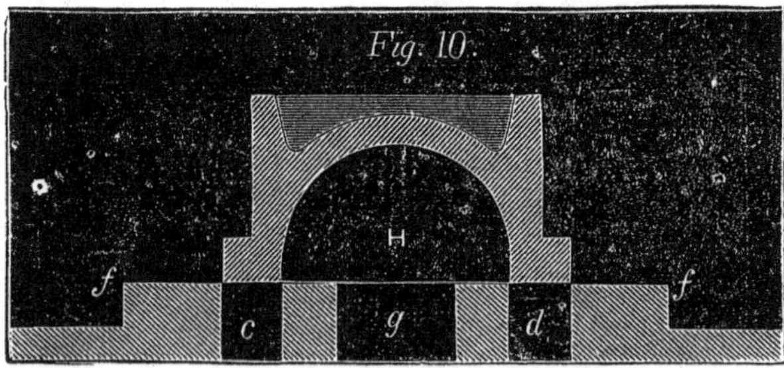

Scale 3-16 in. = 1 inch.

movement of this valve either way opens one of the

steam-ports for the admission of steam and puts the other in communication with the exhaust-port. By cutting a piece of ordinary writing paper to the form of the section of the valve, and moving it on the line *f f*, the action of the valve will be clearly shown.

QUESTION 43. *How was the admission and escape of the steam effected by this valve?*

Answer. In order to explain this clearly, a series of diagrams will be necessary. Before referring to them, however, it should be explained first that the motion of an eccentric is exactly the same as that of a small crank. It is in fact a crank with a crank-pin whose diameter is very much enlarged. In the diagrams, figs. 11 to 25, the eccentrics will therefore be represented as small cranks, and most of the other parts by their centre-lines and points only, so as to make the diagrams as simple as possible. The dimensions selected for these illustrations are for the cylinder 16 in. diameter and 24 in. stroke, and a connecting-rod 7 ft. long. The steam-ports are $1\frac{1}{4}$ in., the exhaust-port $2\frac{1}{2}$ in., and the metal or bars between them, which are called *bridges*, are $1\frac{1}{8}$ in. wide. The eccentric produces a lateral movement of 3 in., which is called its *throw*. In fig. 11 the piston is at the beginning of the backward stroke. The valve is then in the centre of the valve-face, and the eccentric is consequently at half-throw. The slightest movement of the crank in the direction of the dart *N* will move the eccentric enough to open the front steam-port to the steam and the back one to the exhaust. In fig. 12 the piston is represented as having moved 4 in. of its stroke; the valve has then partly opened the front

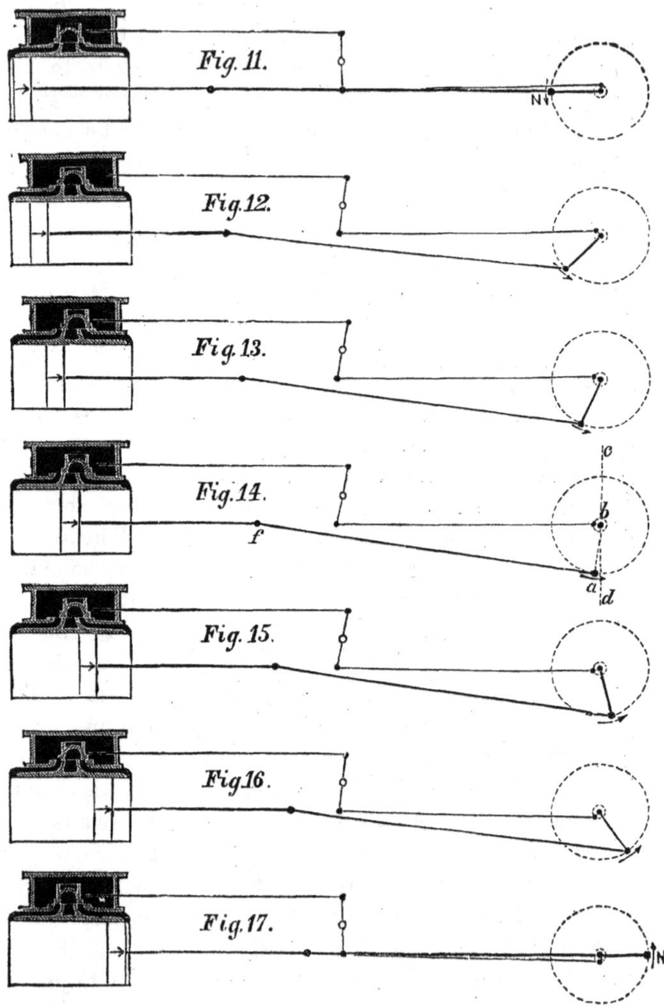

Scale ¼ in. = 1 foot.

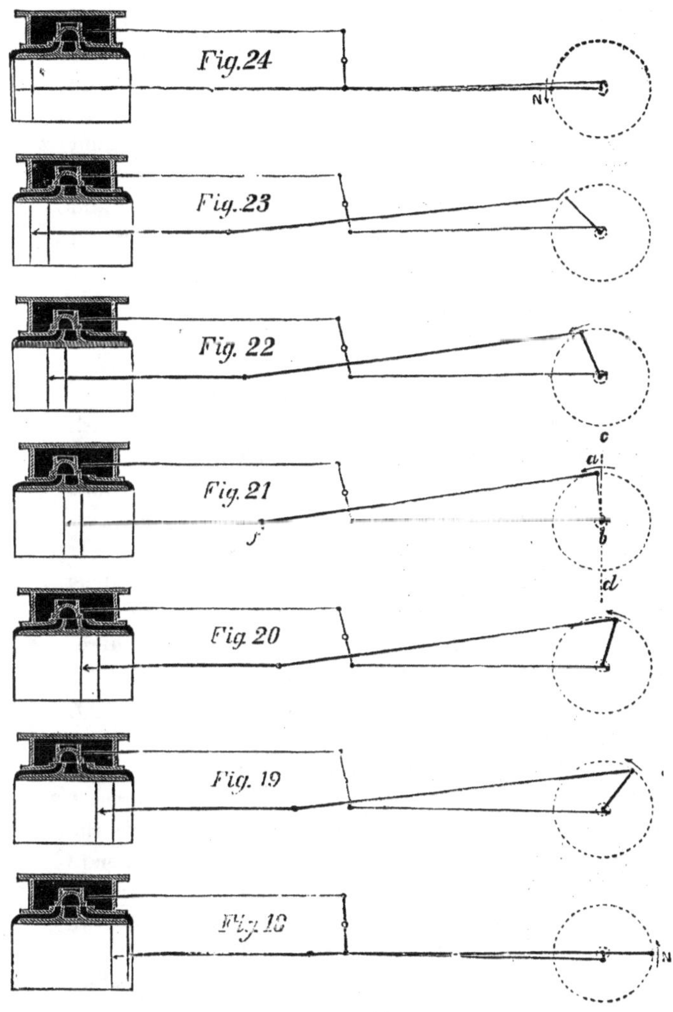

Scale ¼ in. = 1 foot.

steam-port, and the other one is open to the exhaust. In fig. 13 the piston has moved 8 in. of its stroke, and the ports are now wide open, the front one to the steam and the back one to the exhaust. In fig. 14 the piston has moved 12 in., or is at half-stroke, and the valve has then moved as far as it will in that direction. In fig. 15 the piston has moved 16 in. and the valve has begun to return. In fig. 16 the piston has moved 20 in., and the valve has nearly closed the front port to the steam and the other to the exhaust. In fig. 17 the forward stroke is completed, and both ports are closed by the valve. Figs. 18, 19, 20, 21, 22 and 23 represent the piston and the valve on the return stroke in the positions corresponding with those described for the backward stroke.

QUESTION 44. *Is there any other method by which the motion of a valve can be represented by a drawing?*

Answer. Yes, by what are called *motion-curves.* It is, however, difficult to explain these clearly, and as they are purely imaginary, it is difficult to understand their nature and purpose. Close attention will therefore be required to the following description:

We will suppose, in the first place, that the line *ff*, fig. 25, represents the valve-face, *c* and *d* the steam and *g* the exhaust-port, drawn to a larger scale than in the preceding figures. We will now draw the valve *II* in the position represented in fig. 11, where the piston is at the beginning of the stroke. In order to show the valve in the position represented in fig. 12, where the piston has moved 4 in. of the stroke, we will draw a line 4–20, four inches below and parallel to *ff*, and extend the lines, representing the edges of the ports *c*, *d* and *g*, downward. On the horizontal line 4–20 we will now draw the edges *i*, *r*, *i'*, *r*, of the valve in the same position in relation to the port *c* that it has in fig. 12. We will then draw another horizontal line, 8–16, eight inches below *ff*, and parallel to it, and on this represent the valve in the position shown in fig. 13. In the same way we will draw lines 12, 16, 20 and 24 in. below *ff*, and draw the valve on each one respectively in the positions shown in figs. 14, 15, 16 and 17. The distance between the lower line 24–0, and *ff*, will then represent the stroke of the piston, or 24 in. If now we begin from the edge *h* of the valve on the line *ff*, and draw a curve, *h i j k l m n*, through the same edge of the valve, represented on each of the parallel lines below, the curve will indicate the position of the valve in relation to the steam-port *c* at each point of the stroke. To illustrate this, suppose we draw lines 1–23, 2–22, and 3–21, one inch apart and parallel to *ff*, and between it and 4–20. They will then represent the position of the piston after it has moved 1, 2 and 3 in. from the beginning of the stroke, and where they intersect the curved line will be the position of the edge of the valve when the piston has moved 1, 2 and 3 in. of the stroke. The curved line will in fact represent the position of the valve at any point of the stroke between these lines. Other horizontal lines, 5–19, 6–18, etc., can be drawn to represent every inch of the rest of the stroke. The curve line *h i j k l m n*, or *motion-curve* as it is called, will then show the exact position of the edge of the valve and of the width of the opening of the steam-port during the whole stroke. From it we see that the valve opens the port *c* for the admission of steam simultaneously with the move-

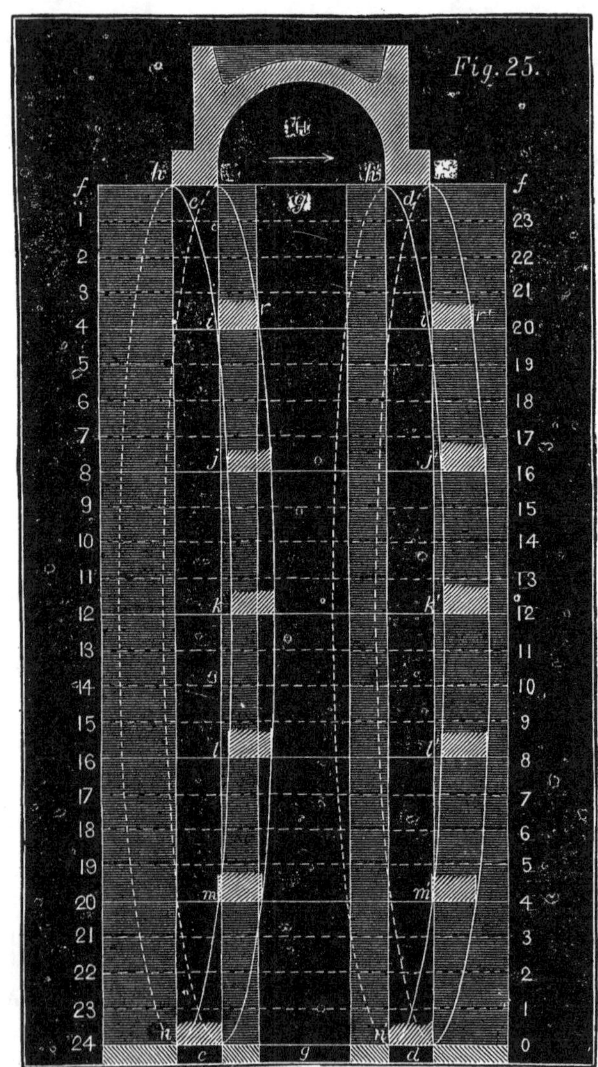

Scale 3-16 in. = 1 inch.

ment of the piston, and when the latter has made one inch of its stroke the port *c* is half open. At $4\frac{1}{2}$ inches of the stroke the port is wide open,* and at $19\frac{1}{2}$ inches it begins to be closed, but is not completely closed until the end of the stroke.

Similar motion-curves, such as *h′ i′ j′ k′ l′ m′ n′*, (represented in fig. 25) can be drawn to represent the position of the other edges of the valve, and also for the return stroke. The latter are shown in dotted lines. If we follow the curve *h′ i′ j′ k′ l′ m′ n′*, which represents the position of the edge of the valve *h′* which governs the exhaust from the back end of the cylinder, we see that the port *d* is opened and closed to the exhaust simultaneously with the opening and closing of the port *c* for the admission of steam to the front end of the cylinder, and that they both remain open until the completion of the stroke.

The width that the ports are opened by the valve is thus ascertainable from these diagrams, for any point of the stroke, and in fact can be seen at a glance. By the aid of such motion-curves, the movement of slide-valves can therefore be analyzed more perfectly than is possible without them.

QUESTION 45. *What were some of the disadvantages of valves, like that shown in fig.* 10, *and which are shown by the motion-curves in fig.* 25.

Answer. The free admission of the steam until the completion of the stroke by the piston was hurtful to the machinery, as it co-operated with the momentum of the piston and its connections in producing undue

* By cutting a paper section of the valve and placing it on the diagram in each position named, it will probably help the reader to understand the movement of the valve more and the nature of the motion-curves.

strains in the working parts. The steam then escaped from the cylinder without expansion, so that much of its useful energy was lost. The steam was not allowed to escape from one end of the cylinder until it was admitted at the opposite end, and as the process of exhausting it occupies some time, there was always more or less back pressure until all the exhaust steam was expelled from the cylinder. In practice, the imperfections of the valve-gear frequently delayed the opening of the ports, both for admitting and exhausting steam, until after the commencement of the stroke of the piston.*

QUESTION 46. *How may some of these evils be overcome?*

Answer. By moving the eccentric forward on the axle so that the motion of the valve is advanced to the same extent, and the admission and exhaust of the steam will occur a little before the completion of the stroke of the piston. In this way the steam is admitted into the cylinder so as to act as a cushion to receive the momentum of the piston, and some time is given to the exhaust steam to escape, before the return stroke.

QUESTION 47. *What is meant by lead?*

Answer. By *lead* is meant the width of the opening of the steam-ports at the beginning of the stroke of the piston. On the steam side of the valve it is called *outside lead;* on the exhaust side *inside lead.* In fig. 26 the opening h of the steam-port is the outside lead and h' the inside lead.

QUESTION 48. *What is meant by the travel of a valve?*

Answer. By the *travel* we mean the motion of the

* D. K. Clark's "Railway Machinery."

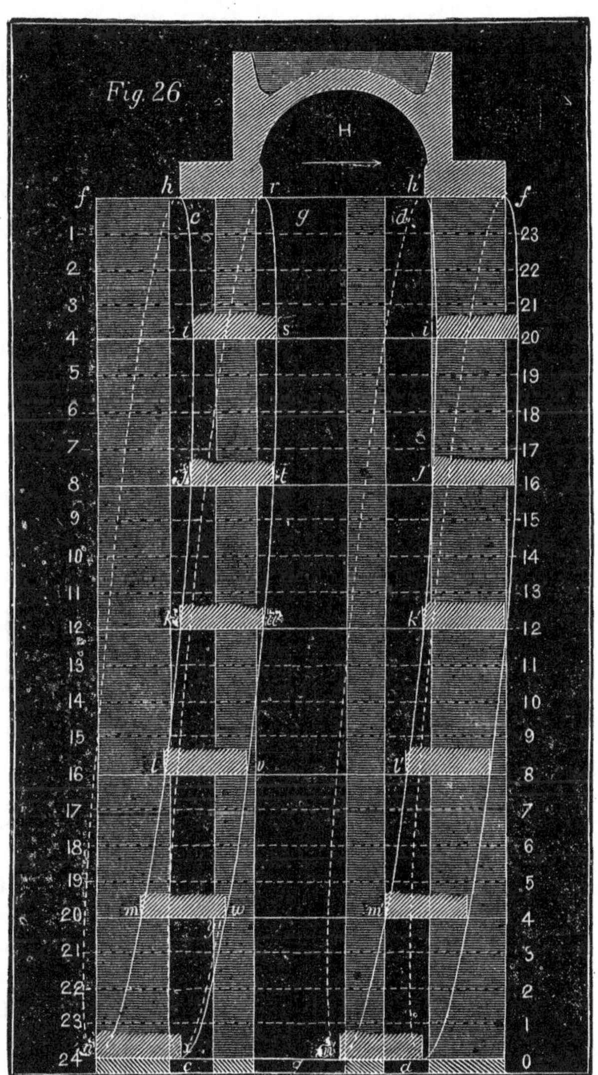

Scale 3-16 in. = 1 inch.

valve back and forth, or in other words its stroke. If the arms of the rocker are of the same length, the travel of the valve is equal to the throw of the eccentric. For the preceding illustrations we have selected an eccentric with three inches throw, which is the travel of the valve.

QUESTION 49. ***How is the steam made to work expansively with a slide-valve?***

Answer. By giving the valve what is called *lap.* That is, by allowing the edges of the valve when it is in the center of the valve-seat to overlap the edges of the steam-ports, as shown in fig. 27. Where this overlap, *L L.* is on the outside of the valve, it is called

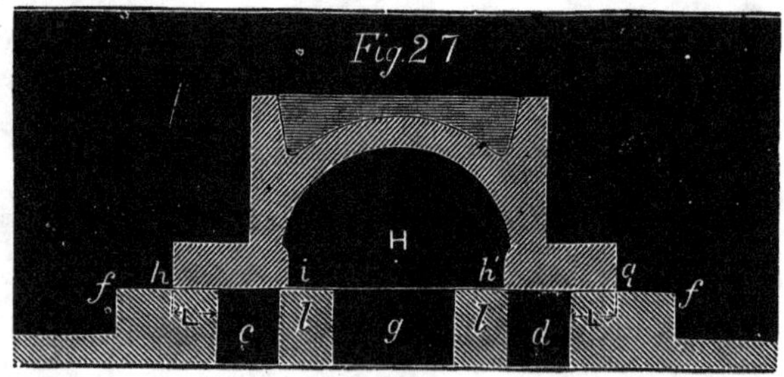

Scale 3.16 in. = 1 inch.

outside lap; when on the inside, ***l l, inside lap.*** When a valve has lap, those portions of the *face** *h, i,* and *p, q,* which cover the steam-ports, being wider than the ports, therefore occupy some time in moving over them, during which time the steam is enclosed in the end of the cylinder, as there is then no communication either with the steam-chest or the exhaust-port. This

* The valve-face is the surface of the valve in contact with the valve-seat.

action is shown very clearly by the motion-curves in fig. 26. The valve in this case has $\frac{1}{4}$ inch lead. At $4\frac{1}{2}$ inches of the stroke of the piston the valve has moved as far as it will go in that direction, and the steam-port has its maximum width of opening. From that point the valve will begin to close the steam-port, and at $14\frac{1}{2}$ inches of the stroke the port will be entirely covered, and the steam therefore be *cut off.* The port will remain closed until the piston has moved $21\frac{3}{4}$ inches, when it will be observed from the motion-curve *r s t u v w x*, that the port *c* is opened to the exhaust and the steam escapes, or, as it is technically called, the *release* takes place. From the time the steam is cut off to the time it is released, it works *expansively* in the cylinder.

QUESTION 50. *What relation is there between the amount of lap* and the degree of expansion?*

Answer. The greater the lap with any given travel, the shorter will be the period of admission of steam, and, consequently, the more time and space for expansion.

QUESTION 51. *What is the effect of inside lap?*

Answer. It delays the release of the steam. Thus in fig. 26 the valve has $\frac{1}{8}$ in. inside lap. The motion-curve *r s t u v w x* shows that the release takes place during the back stroke at $21\frac{3}{4}$ in. If now there was no inside lap, the dotted line *y, x* would represent the exhaust edges of the valve, and the release would then occur somewhat earlier, or at 21 in. For this reason no inside lap is usually given to valves for engines which run at high rates of speed, as it allows too little time for the steam to escape. In fact, in

* In speaking simply of *lap*, outside lap is always meant.

some cases, what is called ***inside clearance*** is given to the valve; that is, the valve as shown in fig. 29, when it is in the middle of the valve-face, does not entirely cover the steam-ports. The effect of this is just the reverse of that produced by inside lap; that is, it causes the release to occur earlier in the stroke.

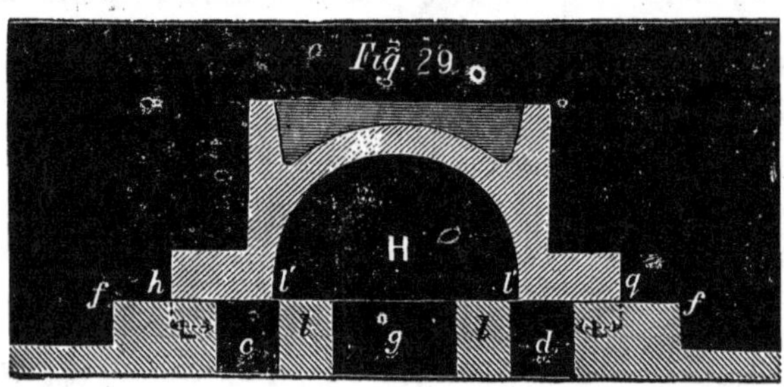

Scale 3-16 in. = 1 inch.

QUESTION 52. ***With the same outside lap, what is the effect of changing the travel of the valve?***

Answer. By increasing the travel, the period of admission is increased and that for expansion lessened; and by reducing it, the admission is lessened, and the degree of expansion is increased. This is shown by the motion-curves in fig. 28, in which the same valve and ports are represented as are shown in fig. 26, but the valve has a travel of 5 instead of 3 inches. The valve also has the same lead. By following the motion-curve *h i j k l m n*, it will be seen that the steam is thus admitted up to 20½ inches of the stroke of the piston, and the period of expansion, as compared with that in fig. 26, is correspondingly lessened. It will also be seen by comparing fig. 26 with fig. 28 that with the short travel of the valve the ports are

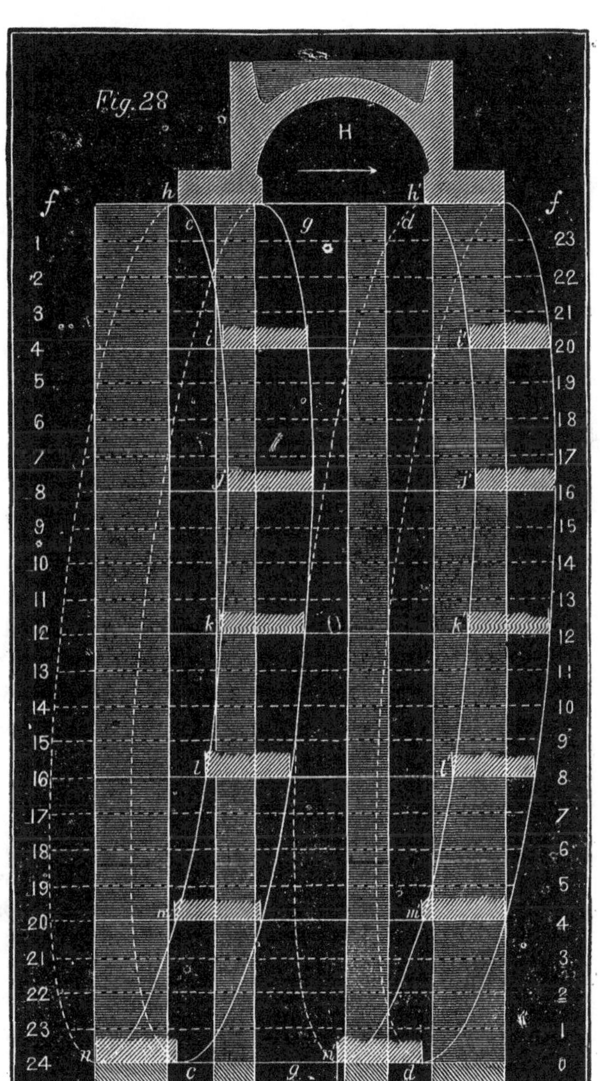

Scale 3-16 in. = 1 inch.

not opened so wide as they are when the travel is increased. This evil is practically obviated, however, by making the ports so long that with a comparatively small opening they will still have area sufficient to admit enough steam to fill the cylinders, and it is known that an opening less than the whole area of the steam-ports is sufficient to facilitate the passage of steam into the cylinder.

QUESTION 53. *How is the exhaust affected by lap and lead?*

Answer. The steam is released earlier in the stroke in proportion as the amount of outside lap and lead is increased, but the steam-port is also closed to the exhaust, or *compression,* as it is called, begins earlier with lap and lead than without. Thus, in fig. 25, it will be seen that at the beginning of the stroke both ports are entirely closed; in fig. 26, however, in which the valve has both lap and lead, the port *d* is nearly wide open at the beginning of the stroke, and by following the motion-curve *r s t u v w x,* which represents the position of the exhaust edge of the valve, it will be seen that the steam was released from the port *c* before the piston had completed its stroke, or when it had still nearly 3½ inches to move. In fig. 25 the port *c* is not opened to the exhaust until the commencement of the stroke, but it remains open to its completion, whereas in fig. 26 it is closed, or compression begins, at 18 inches of the return stroke, as shown by the dotted motion-curve.

QUESTION 54. *How does the action of the connecting-rod influence the motion of the valve in relation to the piston?*

Answer. By delaying the movement of the crank in

the backward stroke of the piston, and accelerating it in the forward stroke. This will be best explained by reference to fig. 14, in which the piston is represented in the center of the cylinder, or the middle of the backward stroke. If now we take a pair of dividers set to a length equal to that of the connecting-rod, and from the center, *f*, describe an arc of a circle, *a b*, from the center of the shaft, and through the lower half of the circle which represents the path of the crank-pin, we will find that the point of intersection, *a*, falls short of the vertical line, *c d*, and that the crank-pin has not made quite one-quarter of a revolution while the piston was moving through the first half of the backward stroke. By referring to fig. 21, in which the piston is again in the middle of its stroke, but is moving forward, and by describing another arc of a circle, *b a*, from the center of the shaft and intersecting the path of the crank-pin, it will be seen that the latter has moved *more* than a quarter revolution, while the piston has made the first half of the forward stroke. Owing to this *angularity*, as it is called, of the connecting-rod, the crank-pin is behind the piston during its backward stroke and ahead of it during the forward stroke. As the valve is moved by the eccentric, and it in turn by the shaft and crank, any irregularities of the latter are of course communicated to the valve. We therefore find, by referring to fig. 26, that the point of cut-off occurs during the backward stroke at 14½ inches, and during the forward stroke at 12 inches. A similar inequality is observable in the points of release for the front and back strokes. It is not, however, a matter of very great practical importance with stationary engines which run at comparatively slow speeds; but if it is thought desirable, the period of admission and the point of release for both strokes can be equalized, either by giving the valve more lead or lap at one end than the other, or by making the one steam-port wider than the other. The mechanism employed for moving locomotive slide-valves, however, furnishes us with the means of modifying their motion in relation to that of the piston, and of thus equalizing the periods of admission and release for the front and back strokes. The methods of doing this will be more fully explained hereafter.

PART V.

THE EXPANSION OF STEAM.

QUESTION 55. *How can we determine by experiment the pressure of the steam in the cylinder at all points of the stroke?*

Answer. By the use of an instrument made for that purpose, called an *indicator.* Its action can be best explained by supposing that we have a small cylinder and piston, *T*, fig. 30, (shown on an enlarged scale in fig. 31)

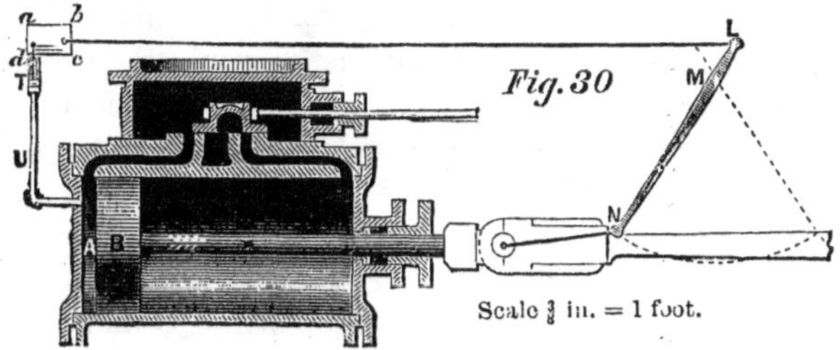

Scale ⅜ in. = 1 foot.

attached by a pipe *U* to one end of the cylinder *A*, so that when steam is admitted to the latter it will be conducted to the small cylinder *T* through the pipe *U*. Over the small piston and attached to it is a spiral spring, *s s*, fig. 31, which is compressed when the piston rises and extended when it falls. To the top of the piston-rod, *V*, a pencil, *W*, is attached. Behind this pencil we will suppose there is a card, *a b c d*, and that this card is so arranged that we can slide

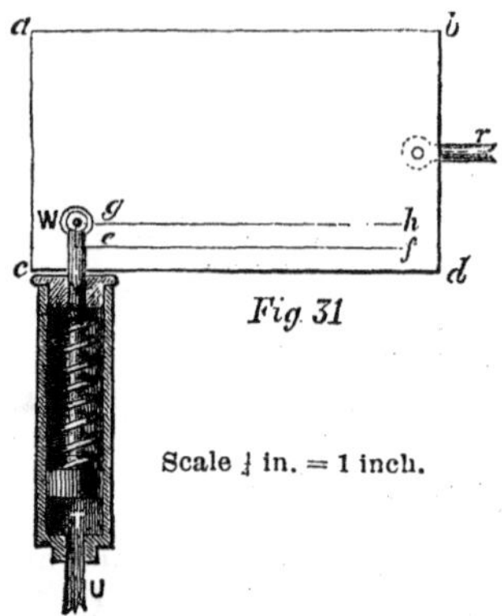

Fig. 31

it horizontally and in contact with the pencil point. With only the pressure of the atmosphere above and below the piston *T*, the spring would be neither compressed nor extended, and the piston would then stand in the position shown in fig. 31. If now we move the the card horizontally, the pencil will draw a line, *g, h,* called the *atmospheric line.* We will now suppose that the tension of the spring is such that a pressure of 10 lbs. per square inch above or below the piston will either extend or compress the spring ¼ inch. In other words, every pound of pressure per square inch in the piston will move it 1-40 of an inch. If we could produce a vacuum under the piston, it would be pressed down by the atmosphere above it 15-40, or ⅜ of an inch. If, when it is thus depressed, we again slide the card along in contact with the pencil-point, it will draw another line, *e. f,* called the *vacuum-line.* Assuming that we have drawn these two lines, and that the piston and card are in the position shown in figs. 30 and 31, we will then suppose that a reciprocating motion can be given to the card by the lever *L, M, N,* fig. 30, which is pivoted at *M* and attached at *N* to the piston-rod by a short connecting-rod. It is obvious that by connecting the upper end *L* of the lever with a rod, *L c*, to the card, the latter will be moved backwards and forwards by the motion of the piston *B*, and that the motion of the card will be simultaneous with that of the piston *B*, but of course of shorter stroke. We will assume that the stroke of the card is equal to the length of the atmospheric and vacuum lines *g h* and *e f*, fig. 31. If now, the piston being at the beginning of the stroke as shown in fig. 30, we admit steam of 85 lbs. effective pressure per square inch (which is equal to 100 lbs. absolute pressure) into the cylinder *A*, it will be conveyed through the pipe *U* to the cylinder *T*, and will force up the piston 85-40 or $2\frac{1}{8}$ inches above the atmospheric line, or 100-40 or $2\frac{1}{2}$ inches above the vacuum line, as shown in fig. 32, and the pencil will draw a vertical line, *g i*, on the card, (represented by a dotted line in fig. 32.) We will suppose that steam is admitted during 8 inches of the stroke, and is then cut off. When the piston *B*, fig. 30, has moved that distance, which is one-third of its stroke, the card will also have moved one-third of its stroke, and will stand in relation to the pencil in the position represented in fig. 33, and as the absolute steam pressure in the cylinder was maintained at 100 lbs. while the card was moving that distance, the pencil will have drawn a horizontal line, *i j*. The steam is now cut off and begins to expand, and its pressure is thereby reduced. When the piston of the engine is at half-stroke, the card will also be at half-stroke, and

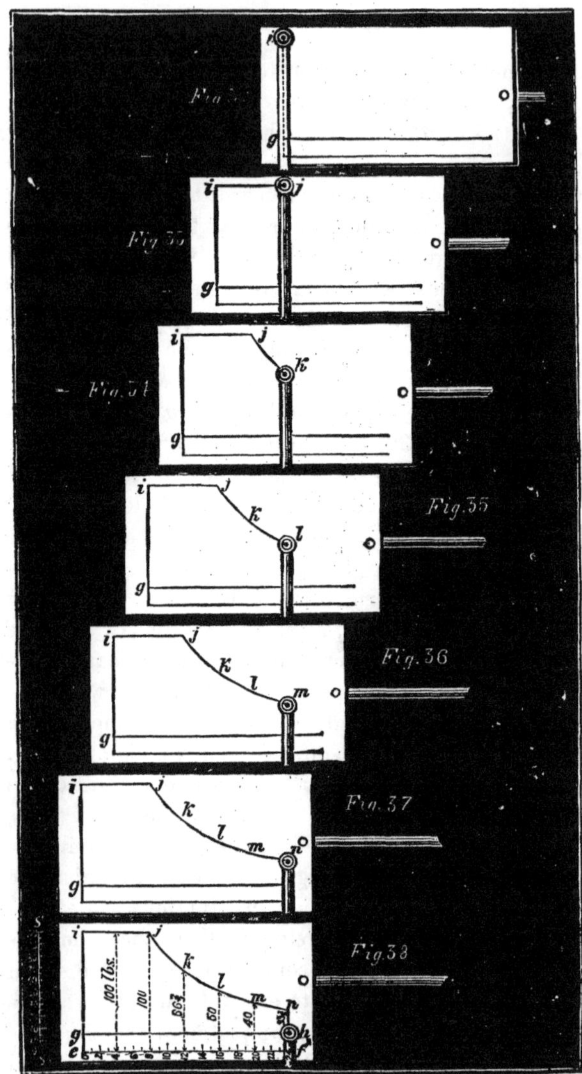

Scale ¼ in. = 1 inch.

the steam will be expanded from 8 to 12 inches of the stroke. By the rule given in the answer to question 20, its absolute pressure would then be 66⅔ lbs., and the indicator-piston will then be pressed down by the spring, so that the pencil will stand in the position shown in fig. 34, or 66⅔ fortieths of an inch above the atmospheric line. The pencil meanwhile will have drawn the curved line *j k*. When the piston has moved 16 inches, the steam will be expanded to double its volume and its absolute pressure will therefore be 50 lbs., and consequently the pencil will stand 50 fortieths or 1¼ inch above the atmospheric line as shown in fig. 35, and the pencil will have continued the curve *j k* to *l*. At 20 inches the steam will have 40 lbs., and at the completion of the stroke 33⅓ lbs. absolute pressure, and the pencil will have completed the curve *j k l m n*, as shown in figs. 36 and 37. This curve is called the *expansion curve*, and its form is that which mathematicians call a hyperbolic curve. If the steam is exhausted, the indicator-piston will descend and carry the pencil down to the atmospheric line, and the vertical line *n h*, fig. 38, will be drawn. On the return stroke, after the steam is exhausted from the main cylinder *A*, fig. 30, the pencil would draw the atmospheric line *g h*, fig. 38, thus showing that there is no steam pressure under the piston. Such a diagram is called an *indicator diagram.** In practice there are a great many influences which modify it, such as condensation, performance of work, imperfec-

---

* The indicator used in practice, to show the action of the steam in the cylinders of steam engines, differs essentially in its construction from that which we have described. The principles of operation are, however, the same in both. We will explain the construction of the Richard's indicator, the one which is now most generally used, hereafter.

tion of valve gear, etc., but for the present these are disregarded.

QUESTION 56. *How can we ascertain the pressure of the steam for any point of the stroke from such a diagram?*

Answer. By measuring the vertical distance by the expansion curve (fig. 38) from the vacuum or the atmospheric line, as for example 8 *j*, 12 *k*, 16 *l*, 20 *m*. As the indicator spring is extended or compressed one-fortieth of an inch* from every pound of pressure per square inch, either above or below the indicator piston, if we construct a scale *S*, *S*, fig. 38, with division of one-fortieth of an inch each, one of them will represent one pound of pressure per square inch if measured vertically from the atmospheric or vacuum line. If we sub-divide the vacuum line with the same number of parts as there are inches in the stroke of the piston (see fig. 39) we can draw vertical lines from these points and thus determine the pressure by comparing the length of such lines with the scale *S*, *S*. Thus the line 8 *j* measures 100 fortieths of an inch, thus showing that the absolute steam pressure at 8 inches of the stroke was 100 lbs. per square inch; the line 12 *k* measures 66⅔ fortieths of an inch, thus showing that at 12 inches of the stroke the steam pressure was 66⅔ lbs. At 16, 20 and 24 inches of the stroke the vertical lines measure 50, 40 and 33⅓ fortieths; and therefore there were that number of pounds of steam pressure when the piston was at the point of the stroke named. Similar measurements could be made from other points, such as 2, 6, 10, or any other num-

* Indicator springs are used of various degrees of tension, in proportion to the steam pressure to be indicated.

ber of inches of the stroke. Of course, if we measure from the vacuum line we will have the absolute steam pressure, or the pressure *above a vacuum*, as it is sometimes called; if we measure from the atmospheric line we will have the effective pressure, or the *pressure above the atmosphere.*

QUESTION 57. *How can we determine the average pressure during the whole stroke of steam which works expansively?*

Answer. This can be determined approximately by the following method: In the first place, divide the vacuum line (fig. 39) into any number of equal divisions, say six. From the points of division, 4, 8, 12,

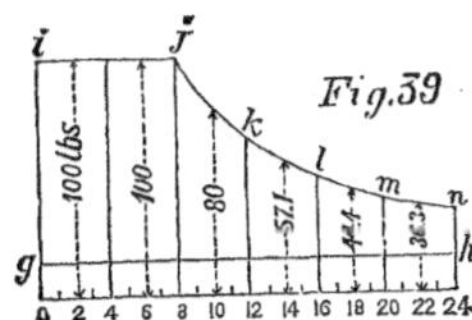

Scale ¼ in. = 1 inch.

16 and 20, which in this case correspond with the points which represent inches of the stroke, draw perpendicular lines, which will divide the indicator diagram into six divisions. It is obvious that during the time the steam is working full stroke the pressure is uniformly 100 lbs. absolute. While the piston is moving from 8 to 12 inches the pressure falls from 100 to 66⅔ lbs., so that at 10 inches we have very nearly the average pressure during the period named. So from 12 to 16, 16 to 20 and 20 to 24 the average is nearly 57.1, 44.4 and 36.3 lbs., respectively. Now, BY ADDING TOGETHER THE PRESSURES IN THE MIDDLE OF EACH ONE OF A NUMBER OF EQUAL DIVISIONS OF

THE STROKE AND DIVIDING BY THE NUMBER OF DIVISIONS, WE WILL OBTAIN APPROXIMATELY THE AVERAGE ABSOLUTE PRESSURE DURING THE WHOLE STROKE. TO GET THE AVERAGE EFFECTIVE PRESSURE, DEDUCT THE ATMOSPHERIC PRESSURE FROM THE RESULT. The calculation would in the above case be as follows:

```
  100 lbs.
  100  "
   80  "
   57.1
   44.4
   36.3
  ------
6)417.8
  ------
   69.6=Average absolute pressure.
   15
  ------
   54.6=Average effective pressure.
```

A more accurate way of calculating the average or mean pressure, as it is called, when steam is used expansively, and the one which is usually employed, is to DIVIDE THE LENGTH OF THE PISTON'S STROKE IN INCHES BY THE NUMBER OF INCHES AT WHICH THE STEAM IS CUT OFF: THE QUOTIENT IS THE RATIO OF EXPANSION. GET THE HYPERBOLIC LOGARITHM OF THE RATIO OF EXPANSION FROM THE TABLE OF LOGARITHMS IN THE APPENDIX, ADD 1 TO IT, AND DIVIDE THE SUM BY THE RATIO OF EXPANSION AND MULTIPLY THE QUOTIENT BY THE MEAN ABSOLUTE STEAM PRESSURE IN THE CYLINDER DURING ITS ADMISSION. THE RESULT WILL BE THE MEAN ABSOLUTE PRESSURE DURING THE STROKE. TO GET THE

MEAN EFFECTIVE PRESSURE, DEDUCT THE ATMOSPHERIC PRESSURE.

The calculation for the above example would be as follows:

$$\frac{24}{8}=3=\text{Ratio of expansion.}$$

$$\frac{1.0986+1}{3}\times 100=69.95=\text{Mean absolute pressure.}$$

$$69.95-15=54.95=\text{Mean effective pressure.}$$

The table of hyperbolic logarithms given in the appendix will be needed in calculating the mean pressure of steam used expansively:

QUESTION 58. *What advantages result from using steam expansively?*

Answer. There is a very important saving in the amount of steam required to do a given amount of work, and the strains and shocks which are produced by the rapid motion of the piston and other reciprocating and revolving parts of the engine are very much diminished by allowing the steam to expand, and thus become reduced in pressure during the latter part of the stroke.

QUESTION 59. *How is steam saved by using it expansively?*

Answer. Less steam is required when it is used expansively:

1. Because when steam of a high pressure is introduced into the cylinder, and allowed to expand until its pressure is comparatively low, it escapes at a lower pressure than the average pressure during the whole stroke. If steam of a pressure equal to the *average* pressure is worked full stroke, it would exert exactly the same force on the piston as the steam of

higher pressure did when working expansively, but the pressure in the latter case, when the piston reaches the end of the stroke, or the ***final pressure***, as it is called, would be considerably lower than in the other. The pressure of steam represents ***energy***, or ***capacity for doing work***, and therefore if we allow it to escape with a comparatively high pressure without doing work, it is a waste of energy. To illustrate this, we will take the same conditions which were used in the answer to Question 60, in calculating the average pressure. In that case the mean absolute pressure of the steam was 69.95 pounds per square inch, but the pressure at the end of the stroke, when the steam escaped, was only 33⅗ pounds absolute. If, therefore, steam had been used of the average pressure through the whole stroke, it would have escaped with a pressure of 69.95 pounds, or more than twice that of the expanded steam, and the work done in both cases would have been the same.

2. There is also another incidental advantage in this, because low-pressure steam can be exhausted more quickly from a cylinder than steam of a high pressure, and consequently there is less resistance, or ***back pressure***, as it is called, in the exhausted end of the cylinder to the movement of the piston.

3. The causes which produce the greatest economy when steam is used expansively cannot be fully explained without discussing principles of science more abstruse than it is desirable to introduce here. They can, however, with the aid of the table of the "Properties of Steam,"* in the appendix, be illustrated by a

* This table is copied from Colburn's Treatise on the Locomotive Engine.

few simple calculations, so that the economy of using steam expansively will be apparent.

For the basis of the calculations the same data and dimensions will be employed that were used in the previous illustration; that is, a cylinder of 16 in. diameter and piston with 24 in. stroke and steam of 100 lbs. absolute pressure cut off at 8 in. of the stroke. We will suppose, further, that the steam used is generated from water of a temperature of 60 degrees, and we will then calculate the total number of units of heat in the steam used for each stroke of the piston. The area of a piston 16 in. in diameter is 201 square inches; and as the steam is admitted until the piston moves 8 inches of its stroke, therefore the quantity of steam would be 8 times 201 cubic inches, or

$$201 \times 8 = 1608 \text{ cubic in.} = \frac{1608}{1728} \text{ cubic ft.}$$

From the table it will be seen that one cubic foot of steam of 100 lbs. pressure weighs .2307 lbs.; therefore the weight of the fraction of a cubic foot given above would be calculated as follows:

$$\frac{.2307 \times 1608}{1728} = .2146 \text{ lb.} = \text{weight of 1608 cubic in. of}$$

steam of 100 lbs. absolute pressure.

From the table it will be seen that the total heat above zero of steam of 100 lbs. absolute pressure is 1213.4 degrees. That is, as was explained in answer to Question 40,* in order to boil water under a pressure of 100 lbs. per square inch we must first heat water up to 327.9 degrees, and then, to convert it into

* In the illustration used in answer to Question 40, steam of 100 lbs. *effective* pressure was used, whereas in the above case it is *absolute* pressure.

steam, 885.5 degrees more must be added. It was also explained in the answer to Question 35 that one pound of water heated one degree is the standard of measurement or *unit of heat.* Now if we have 1 lb. of water with a temperature of zero, evidently it will take 1213.4 *units of heat* to convert it into steam of 100 lbs. absolute pressure. But as the water from which our steam was generated had a temperature of 60 degrees, we must deduct that much from 1213.4: 1213.4—60.=1153.4=units of heat in one pound of steam of 100 lbs. absolute pressure generated from water of 60 degrees temperature.

If now one pound of steam has 1153.4 units of heat, the following calculation will give the units of heat in .2146 lbs.: 1153.4×.2146=247.51=units of heat in .2146 lbs., or 1608 cubic in. of steam of 100 lbs. absolute pressure.

It was shown in answer to Question 56 that the average pressure of steam of 100 lbs. cut off at 8 in. of the stroke was 69.95 lbs. per square inch. Disregarding the small fraction, we will call it 70 lbs. Now if we admit steam of this pressure through the *whole stroke* of the piston, we will use 4,824 cubic inches. It will be found by a calculation similar to the above, that to generate this quantity of steam of 70 lbs. pressure from water of a temperature of 60 degrees would require 527 units of heat, or more than twice as many as were required to do the same work with steam of 100 lbs. pressure cut off at 8 inches when using it expansively during the rest of the stroke. The actual difference in practice is not so great as this, because the loss of heat from radiation and condensation in the cylinder and other causes is greater when steam of a high pressure is expanded than when lower pressure steam is admitted through the whole stroke. But after allowance is made for all such sources of loss and waste, there is still an enormous gain from using steam expansively.

QUESTION 60. *What is meant by wire-drawn steam?*

Answer. It is the fall which the pressure of the steam undergoes during its passage from the boiler to the cylinder,* and which is due to the contracted opening of the steam pipes or valves.

QUESTION 61. *What is the economical effect of reducing the pressure, or of wire-drawing it, by partly closing the valve by which it is admitted to the cylinders.*

Answer. By reducing the pressure of steam in this or any other way, it is necessary in doing the same amount of work to admit steam to the cylinder for a longer period, and therefore to reduce the degree of expansion. To illustrate the effect of this, we will estimate the total heat required to exert a pressure of 70 lbs. on the piston described above. It will be assumed that the steam pressure in the boiler is 100 lbs. absolute, and that this is wire-drawn down to 70 lbs. and admitted to the cylinder through the whole stroke. As was shown in the preceding answer, 4,824 cubic inches of steam are required to fill the cylinder. Now 3,376.8 cubic inches of steam of 100 lbs. pressure, if expanded to 70 lbs. pressure, will make 4,824 cubic inches. The total heat required to generate 3,376.8 cubic inches of steam of 100 lbs. absolute pressure from water of 60 degrees is 519.9 units, so that to do the same work by using steam of *high pressure cut off at one-third of the stroke,* using steam of *low boiler*

* Rankine.

pressure full stroke, and using *wire-drawn steam full stroke,* would, in the example we have selected, require 247.5, 527 and 519.9 units of heat respectively.

QUESTION 62. *To what extent can we work steam expansively, with advantage and economy?*

Answer. The theoretical economy of using steam increases with the degree of expansion and the pressure. This is shown very clearly in the following table, in the first column of which the number of inches of the piston stroke is given during which steam is admitted to a cylinder 16 in. in diameter and 24 in. stroke. In the second column is given the pressure of the steam, or *initial pressure,* as it is called, which must be admitted into the cylinder in order to produce a mean pressure of 70 lbs. per square inch when it is cut off at the point indicated in the first column. In the third column is given the total heat which is required to generate the steam required in each case, and in the last column the percentage of saving is given which results from the different degrees of expansion and a mean pressure of 70 lbs. per square inch in each case.

RESULTS OF USING STEAM EXPANSIVELY.

Period of admission or point of cut-off.	Initial pressure of steam in pounds per square inch.	Total heat of steam used, in units.	Percentage of saving compared with full stroke.
Full stroke........................	70.	527.	
18 in. = Three-quarters of the stroke,	72.5	408.7	22½
12 in. = One-half " "	82.7	309.5	41¼
8 in. = One-third " "	100.	247.5	53
6 in. = One-quarter " "	117.4	215.9	58
4 in. = One-sixth " "	150 5	186.5	64½
3 in. = One-eighth " "	181.8	165.8	68½
2 in. = One-twelfth " "	241.4	144.8	72½

From this table it will be seen that theoretically 22½ per cent. of heat is saved by cutting off at ¾ of the stroke and using steam of 72.5 lbs. pressure instead of steam of 70 lbs. worked full stroke. Cutting off at half stroke and using steam of 82.7 lbs., $41\frac{1}{4}$ per cent. of heat is saved, and cutting off at quarter stroke with steam of 117.4 lbs. saves 58 per cent. of heat; and at one-twelfth of the stroke, or expanding steam of 241.4 lbs. pressure to twelve times its volume, saves $72\frac{1}{2}$ per cent. of heat.

As stated before, the above is the *theoretical* advantage of using steam expansively. There are, however, practical difficulties in the way of using some of these high degrees of expansion. It has already been explained that if steam is cut off early in the stroke and the degree of expansion increased, the pressure and consequently the temperature of the steam must also be increased. The danger of explosion is greater with the higher pressures, and stronger and more expensive boilers and machinery are therefore needed. With steam of very high temperature the metal of the cylinders, pistons and valves becomes so much heated that they soften, and then the friction of the one on the other causes them to cut or scratch each other. The high temperature at the same time destroys the oil or other lubricant used in contact with the steam. It is also impossible to admit and cut off steam very early in the stroke with the ordinary mechanical appliances used for moving slide-valves of locomotives. This latter difficulty will be more fully explained hereafter.

PART VI.

GENERAL DESCRIPTION OF A LOCOMOTIVE ENGINE.

QUESTION 63. *What are the principal parts of an ordinary locomotive engine?*

Answer. A boiler for generating steam and a pair of high-pressure steam engines, which are all mounted on a suitable frame and wheels adapted for running on a track consisting of two iron or steel rails.

QUESTION 64. *How is the power of high-pressure engines applied to locomotives?*

Answer. By connecting the engines with the wheels so as to give the latter a rotary motion.

QUESTION 65. *When they revolve what will occur?*

Answer. Either they will slip on the track, or the locomotive will move either backward or forward, according to the direction the wheels are turning.

QUESTION 66. *What will determine whether the wheels will slip or the locomotive move?*

Answer. The friction or *adhesion*, as it is called, between the wheels and the track. If this adhesion is greater than the resistance opposed to the movement of the locomotive, the latter will overcome the resistance; but if the latter is greater than the friction, the wheels will slip.

QUESTION 67. *Upon what does the amount of friction or adhesion of the wheels depend?*

Answer. Chiefly on the weight which they bear, but to some extent upon the condition of the rails. Under ordinary circumstances, the adhesion of the wheels of a locomotive is in direct proportion to the weight they carry.

QUESTION 68. *Why are two cylinders employed on locomotives?*

Answer. Because if only one was used, it would be impossible or very difficult to start the engine, if it should stop on one of the dead points.

QUESTION 69. *How is this difficulty overcome by the use of two cylinders?*

Answer. By attaching the two cranks to the same shaft or axle, and placing them at right angles to each other, so that when the one is at a dead point the other is in the position where the steam can exert the maximum power on the crank.

QUESTION 70. *How are the cranks of an ordinary locomotive made?*

Answer. They are cast in one piece with the wheels that drive the locomotive, which are therefore called *driving-wheels.* In this country the centre portion of such wheels, or *wheel-centres* as they are called, is always made of cast iron, with tires of wrought iron or steel around the outside, and is fastened to the axles of the locomotive. The shaft of a locomotive engine is called the *main driving-axle,* and the wheels attached to it the *main driving-wheels.*

QUESTION 71. *How are the cylinders and driving-wheels of a locomotive usually placed?*

Answer. The cylinders *A*, plates I, II and III, are placed at the front end of the locomotive, and the main driving-axle, *B*, far enough behind them to permit the connecting rods, *C*, to be attached to pins, *D*, in the cranks, called *crank-pins*. In this country these cranks are now universally placed on the outside of the wheels, and therefore the cylinders must be placed far enough apart (as shown in fig. 40 and Plate III) to permit the connecting-rods to be attached to the

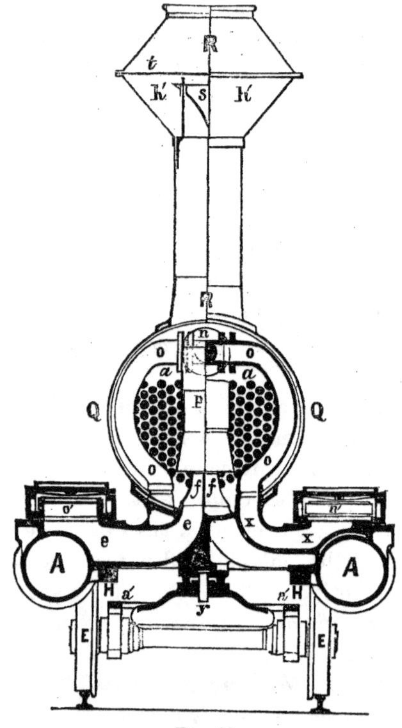

Fig. 40.
Scale ¼ in.=1 foot.

crank-pins. The cylinders are therefore placed outside the frames, *H, H,* Plate III, (the latter are inside of the wheels,) and are now nearly always horizontal, although in old engines they are often inclined. Plate I is a side view of an ordinary eight-wheeled American locomotive, Plate II a longitudinal section, Plate III a plan, and fig. 40, a transverse section through the cylinder and smoke-box.

QUESTION 72. *What are the smaller wheels, E E, called, and what are they for?*

Answer. They are called *truck-wheels* and carry the weight of the cylinders and other parts of the front end of the locomotive, and serve to guide and steady the machine in a manner which will be more fully explained hereafter.

QUESTION 73. *Why are more than one pair of driving wheels necessary for locomotives?*

Answer. Because if all the weight which is needed to create the requisite adhesion of the wheels of locomotives to pull heavy loads was placed on one pair of wheels, it would be so excessive as to partly crush and injure the rails. It is therefore distributed, usually on two pairs, but sometimes on three or four or even more pairs.

QUESTION 74. *Where is the second pair of driving-wheels usually placed?*

Answer. These wheels, *F*—called the *back* or *trailing driving-wheels*—are, in the ordinary type of locomotives used in this country, situated behind the main driving-wheels, far enough back to give the room necessary for the boiler, *G*, between the two axles, as shown in plates I, II and III.

QUESTION 75. *How are the axles, cylinders, etc., held in the right position in relation to each other?*

Answer. By longitudinal frames, *H, H, H, H,* which

hold the axles in the proper position, and are bolted to the cylinders, and also fastened to the boiler at *I, I,* Plate I.

Question 76. *How is a locomotive engine made to run either backward or forward?*

Answer. By having two eccentrics, *J, J,* Plate III (also shown in Plate II,) for each cylinder. One of these is fixed or *set* on the shaft in such a position as to move the valve so that the engine will run in one direction; the other eccentric is set so that the engine will run the reverse way. The ends of the two eccentric rods are attached to what is called a *link, L,* (Plates II and III,) the object of which is to furnish the means of quickly engaging and disengaging either eccentric rod to or from the rocker, *K.* The link is operated by a system of levers, consisting of the lifting shaft, *M,* and arms, *N, N,* and the reverse lever, *O, O,* (Plate II). The principles and working of these will be more fully explained hereafter.

Question 77. *What are the principal parts or "organs" of a locomotive boiler?*

Answer. 1. A fire-place, or, as it is called a *fire-box, G,* (Plate II,) which is surrounded with water.

2. A cylindrical part, *P P,* (Plates I and II,) attached to the fire-box at one end and to a chamber, *Q,* called the *smoke-box,* at the other

3. The tubes or flues *a a′*, (Plate II and fig. 40,) which connect the fire-box with the smoke-box and pass through the cylindrical part of the boiler and are surrounded with water.

4. The smoke-stack or chimney *R R.*

Question 78. *What is each of these parts or organs for, and of what do they consist?*

Answer. The fire-box *G* furnishes the room for burning the fuel, and consists of an inner and outer shell made of boiler plate, with the space between the two filled with water; a grate, *b b*, (Plate II,) formed of cast-iron bars, with spaces between them for admitting air for the combustion of the fuel, which is placed on the top of them; a door, *C*, called the *furnace-door*, for supplying the grate with fuel; a receptacle, *d d*, below the grate, to collect ashes, and therefore called the *ash-pan*, which is supplied with suitable dampers, *n'*, *n'*, for admitting or excluding the air from the fire.

The cylindrical part *P P*, or *waist* of the boiler as it is sometimes called, contains the greater part of the water to be heated.

The flues or tubes, as they are generally called, of which a locomotive has from one to two hundred, are usually two inches in diameter, and about eleven feet long. They conduct the smoke and products of combustion from the fire-box to the smoke-box. These tubes are made of small diameter so as to sub-divide the smoke into many small streams and thus expose it to a large radiating surface through which the heat is conducted to the water.

The smoke-stack serves partly for removing into the open air the smoke which passes through the flues, and partly for producing a strong draft of air, which is indispensably necessary for the rapid combustion of the fuel, and also for collecting and extinguishing the sparks from the fire.

QUESTION 79. *How is the draft produced in locomotive boilers?*

Answer. By conducting the exhaust steam through

pipes (*e, e*, fig. 40) from the cylinders to the smoke-box and allowing it to escape up the smoke-stack from apertures, *f, f*, (Plate II, fig. 40.) called ***exhaust nozzles.*** The strong current of steam thus produced in the smoke-stack produces a vacuum, by which the smoke is sucked into the smoke-box with great power and forced out of the smoke-stack into the open air.

QUESTION 80. *How are the water and fuel carried which must be supplied to a locomotive while it is running?*

Answer. The water is carried in a tank, which is constructed in the form of the letter U, so as to give room for the stowage of fuel between its two branches or sides. This tank is carried on a set of wheels, and forms a separate vehicle, independent of the locomotive, called a *tender,* the construction of which will be explained in a future chapter.

QUESTION 81. *What are the dimensions of the principal parts of a locomotive?*

Answer. There is a great variety in the plan, size and capacity of locomotives, but the type which is more generally used in this country than any other, and which has been selected for the preceding illustrations, and will be described in the succeeding chapters of the Catechism, has four driving and four truck wheels, and weighs in working condition about 60,000 lbs. The following are the dimensions of its principal parts: The driving-wheels are about 5 feet and the truck-wheels from 26 to 30 inches in diameter. The longitudinal distance between the centres of the driving-wheels is usually about 7 feet, and between the centres of the truck-wheels 5 ft. 9 in., and the total distance from the centre of the back driving-wheels to the centre of the front truck-wheels, which is called the *wheel-base*, is 21 ft. 8 in. The weight on each driving-wheel is usually about 10,000 lbs., and on each truck-wheel about 5,000 lbs. The cylinders are 16 in. in diameter and the piston has 24 in. stroke, and the connecting-rod is 7 ft. long measured between the centres of the pins to which it is attached. The centres of the cylinders are about 6 feet apart, measured across the track. The fire-box inside is 5 feet long and 2 ft. 11 in. wide, and the cylindrical part of the boiler is 4 feet in diameter measured on the outside of the smallest portion. The water spaces around the fire-box are about 3 inches wide. There are 140 tubes, which are 2 in. in diameter measured on their outside, and 11 ft. long. The inside of the smoke-stack is 16 in. in diameter, and it is 14 ft. 3 in. high measured from the top of the rails. The tender carries about 1,800 gallons of water and about 8,000 lbs. of coal. When loaded it weighs about 40,000 lbs., making the total weight of the engine and tender 100,000 lbs.

The following is a list of parts designated by the letters of reference on plates I, II, III and fig. 40.

A, *A*, Cylinders.
B, Main driving-axles.
C, Main connecting-rods.
D, Main crank-pins.
E, *E*, Truck-wheels.
F, Axle of trailing-wheels.
G, Fire-box.
H, *H*. *H*, Frames.
I, *I*, Frame-clamps.
J, *J*, Eccentrics.
K, Rockers.
L, Link.
M. Lifting-shaft.
N, *N*, Lifting arms,
O *O*, Reverse-lever.
P *P*, Cylinder part of boiler.
Q, Smoke-box.
R *R*, Smoke stack.
S. Pilot or cow-catcher.
T, Head-light.
U, Bell.
V, Sand-box.
W, Whistle.
X, Dome.
Y *Y*, Cab or house.
Z, Back or trailing-wheel crank-pin.
A′ Pump air-chamber.
B′, *B′*. Main driving-wheels.
C′ *C′* *C′*, Supply pipe.
D′ Front platform.
E′ Bumper timber.
F′ *F′*, Back driving-wheels.
G′ Coupling-pin.
H′ Friction-plate.
I′ Check valve.

K′ K′, Foot-board.
L′ Lazy cock.
M′ Mud drum.
N′ N′, Springs.
P′ Pump.
R′ Drop-door of grate.
S′ Steam gauge.
T′ T′ Feed pipes.
a a′ Tubes.
b b, Grates.
c, Fire-box door.
d d, Ash pan.
f f, Exhaust-nozzles or blast-pipes.
g, Safety-valve lever.
h h, Cross-heads.
i i, Running-board.
j, Throttle-stem.
l. Throttle-pipe.
m m, Dry pipe.
n, T-pipe.
o o, Steam-pipes.
p. Petticoat pipe.
q, Smoke-box door.
r, Piston.
s, Spark-deflector or cone.
t, Wire-netting in stack.
u u u, Boiler-lagging.
v, Safety-valve.
w w, Sector or quadrant.
x, Blow-off cock.
y, Truck centre-pin.
z, Throttle-lever.
a′ a, Tubes.
b′ b′, Truck frame.
c′ c′, Bed-plate.
d′, Boiler brace.
e′ e′, Sand pipe.
f′ f′, Equalizing lever for driving-wheels.
g′ g′, Guide-bars or rods.
h′ h′. Receptacle for sparks.
i′ i′, Bell rope.
j′ j′, Guide yoke.
k′. Valve-stem.
l′ l′, Truck equalizing lever.
m′ m′ m′, Hand rail.
n′, Blow-off cock in mud-drum.
o′, Spring balance.
p′, Pump plunger.
q′ q′, Foot steps.
r′. Brace to smoke-box and frame.
s′ s′, Steam-chest.
t′ t′ t′, Crown-bars.
u′, Head-light lamp.
v′, Main valve.
w′, Blow-off cock handle.
x′, Bell-crank for throttle-valve.
y′, Piston-rod.
z′, Draw-bar.

PART VII.

THE LOCOMOTIVE BOILER.

QUESTION 82. *How does the quantity of steam generated in locomotive boilers in a given time compare with that generated in the boilers of stationary and marine engines?*

Answer. Locomotive engine boilers must produce much more steam in a given time, in proportion to their size, than is required of the boilers of any other class of engines, (excepting perhaps those of steam fire-engines,) because the space which locomotive boilers can occupy and also their weight is limited.

QUESTION 83. *How is their steam-generating capacity increased above that of marine and stationary boilers?*

Answer. By creating a very strong draft of air through the fire and then passing the smoke and heated air through a great many small tubes, which are surrounded by water. By this means the smoke and hot air are divided into many small streams or currents which are exposed to the inside surface of the tubes to which and to the surrounding water their heat is imparted.

QUESTION 84. *How is the action of the exhaust steam in producing a draft in the chimney explained?*

Answer. The exhaust steam escapes from the cylinders through one or two contracted openings or exhaust-nozzles (*f*, Plate II, also shown in fig. 40*),

* The term *blast-orifice* is also often used to designate these parts of locomotives.

which point directly up the centre of the chimney or smoke-stack. The exhaust steam escapes from this orifice with great velocity, and expands as it rises, so that it fills the pipe *p* and the smoke-stack *R R*. It thus acts somewhat like a plunger or piston forced violently up the chimney, and pushes up the air above it, and, owing to the friction of the particles of air, carries that which surrounds it along up the stack, from which it all escapes finally into the open air, thus leaving a partial vacuum behind in the smoke-box. The external pressure of the atmosphere then forces in air through any and every opening in the smoke-box, to take the place of that already drawn out or exhausted from it. As the only inlet is through the tubes, to which the gases of combustion have free access from the fire-box, and as the external air can only pass through the fire-grate, and through the burning fuel, to reach the fire-box, there is a constant draft of air through the grate as long as the waste steam escapes from the blast-pipe and up the chimney. It is thus that, within certain limits, the more the steam that is required, the more the steam that is produced; for all the steam used in the engine draws in the air in its final escape, to excite the fire to generate more steam.* Sometimes one blast-orifice is used for each cylinder, as shown in plates II and III and fig. 40; in other cases the exhaust steam from each cylinder escapes through the same orifice.

QUESTION 85. *How much water is it necessary to evaporate in order to furnish the steam required to run an ordinary train at its usual speed?*

---

* Colburn's Locomotive Engineering.

Answer. For an ordinary "American" locomotive,* weighing 60,000 lbs. and with cylinders of 16 inches diameter and 24 inches stroke, from 6,000 to 12,000 lbs. of water must be evaporated per hour.

QUESTION 86. *How much water will a pound of coal evaporate in ordinary practice?*

Answer. The quantity of water which is converted into steam by a pound of coal varies very materially with the quality of the coal, and the construction and condition of the boiler; but from 6 to 8 lbs. of water per pound of coal is about the average performance of ordinary locomotives. It is, therefore, necessary to burn from 500 to 2,000 lbs. of coal per hour in order to generate the quantity of steam required by ordinary engines.

QUESTION 87. *How large a grate is needed to burn this quantity of coal?*

Answer. The maximum rate of combustion may be taken at about 125 lbs. of coal on each square foot of grate surface per hour, so that to burn 2,000 lbs. we need a grate with about 16 square feet of surface.

QUESTION 88. *How much heating surface is needed for a given size of grate?*

Answer. In common practice about 50 square feet of heating surface are given for each square foot of grate. There are, however, no reasons for the proportions of either grate or heating surface which are given, excepting that it has been found that they work well in practice. It is, however, quite certain that the larger a boiler is, and the greater its heating surface in proportion to the steam it must generate, other

* In speaking of "American" locomotives, we mean locomotives like that shown in Plate I, with four driving-wheels and a four-wheeled truck, and shall so use the term hereafter.

things being equal, the more economical will it be in its consumption of fuel, or, in other words, the more water will it evaporate per pound of coal.

QUESTION 89. *Why is it necessary to use small tubes or flues in order to have the required amount of heating surface?*

Answer. Because there is a great deal more surface in a small tube of a given length, in proportion to the space it occupies, than in a large one. Thus a tube *two* inches in diameter and eleven feet long has 829 square inches of surface, and one *four* inches in diameter has 1,658 square inches, or just double the quantity. But the four-inch tube occupies *four times* as much space as the other, as it is twice as high and twice as wide. Therefore, in proportion to the space it occupies, the tube which is two inches in diameter has twice as much surface as the larger one. If we compare a two-inch with an eight-inch tube, we will find that the former has *four* times as much surface, in proportion to its size, as the eight-inch tube. As the size and weight of locomotive boilers are limited, it is therefore necessary, in order to get the requisite heating surface in the space to which we are confined, to use tubes of small diameter.

Small tubes also have the advantage that they may be made of thinner material, and yet have the same strength to resist a bursting pressure from within, or a collapsing pressure from without, as larger tubes made of thicker metal. The advantage of thin tubes is, that the heat inside of them is conducted to the water outside more rapidly than it would be through thicker metal, which is important when combustion is as rapid as it is in locomotive boilers.

The reason tubes of smaller diameter than two inches are not ordinarily used is because they are then liable to become stopped up with cinders and pieces of unconsumed fuel.

QUESTION 90. *How is the fire-box of a locomotive constructed?*

Answer. It usually consists of a rectangular box (*G*, figs. 41 and 42) about three feet wide* and, for the size of engine we have selected as an example, about five or five and a half feet long inside. This box is composed of metal plates, either iron, steel or copper, which, excepting on the front side, are from $\frac{5}{16}$ to $\frac{3}{8}$ of an inch thick. This box is called the ***inside shell*** of the fire-box, and is surrounded by another shell, *A B C D E F*, fig. 42, of either iron or steel plates, of about the same thickness as those composing the inside. This is called the *outside shell* of the fire-box and, as already explained, is so much larger than the inside that there is a space, called the *water-space*, from $2\frac{1}{2}$ to $4\frac{1}{2}$ inches wide, on all the sides of the fire-box between the inner and outer plates.

The top *g*, *g*, of the inside shell, which is called the *crown-sheet* or *crown-plate*, is flat, whereas the outside shell is arched, as shown in fig. 42. To the front plate of the inside shell the tubes *a a'*, *a a'* are attached. For this reason its thickness is usually made greater than that of the other plates, and is usually from $\frac{3}{8}$ to $\frac{3}{4}$ of an inch. The edges of one of the plates at each corner of the fire-box, where they are united together, as shown in figs. 41 and 42, are bent at right angles, and

* The width is dependent upon the distance between the rails, or *gauge* of the road, as it is called. The above size is for a 4 feet $8\frac{1}{2}$ in. gauge.

the other is fastened to it with rivets from $\frac{5}{8}$ to $\frac{3}{4}$ of an inch in diameter.

The inside and the outside shells of the fire-box are united to each other by a wrought-iron bar or *ring* (*A F*, figs. 41 and 42) which completely surrounds the inner shell and closes the water-space between the two shells. This bar is bent and welded to the proper form to extend around the bottom of the inside fire-box, and it is riveted to both shells. The water in the water-space is in free communication with the rest of the water in the boiler; and thus the flat sides of the respective shells of the fire-box are exposed to the full pressure of the steam, which tends to burst the outside shell and collapse the inside one. These flat sides, by themselves, would be unable to resist the strain upon them, but as the strain upon the respective fire-boxes is in opposite directions, and necessarily equal for equal areas of surface, tie-bolts, *n, n, n, n,* (figs. 41 and 42,) or, as they are called *stay-bolts*, which are from $\frac{3}{4}$ to 1 inch in diameter, are screwed through the plates at frequent intervals, usually from $3\frac{1}{2}$ to $4\frac{1}{2}$ in. apart, so as to connect the two fire-boxes securely together, the ends of the stay-bolts being also riveted or spread out by hammering so as still further to increase their holding power. These bolts, owing to the expansion and contraction of the boiler and other strains to which they are subjected, very frequently break, and if they are made of solid bars of metal there is no way of discovering with certainty whether they are in good condition or not without taking the boiler to pieces. They should therefore be made of the best quality of wrought iron, brass or copper and should also be made tubular, that is they

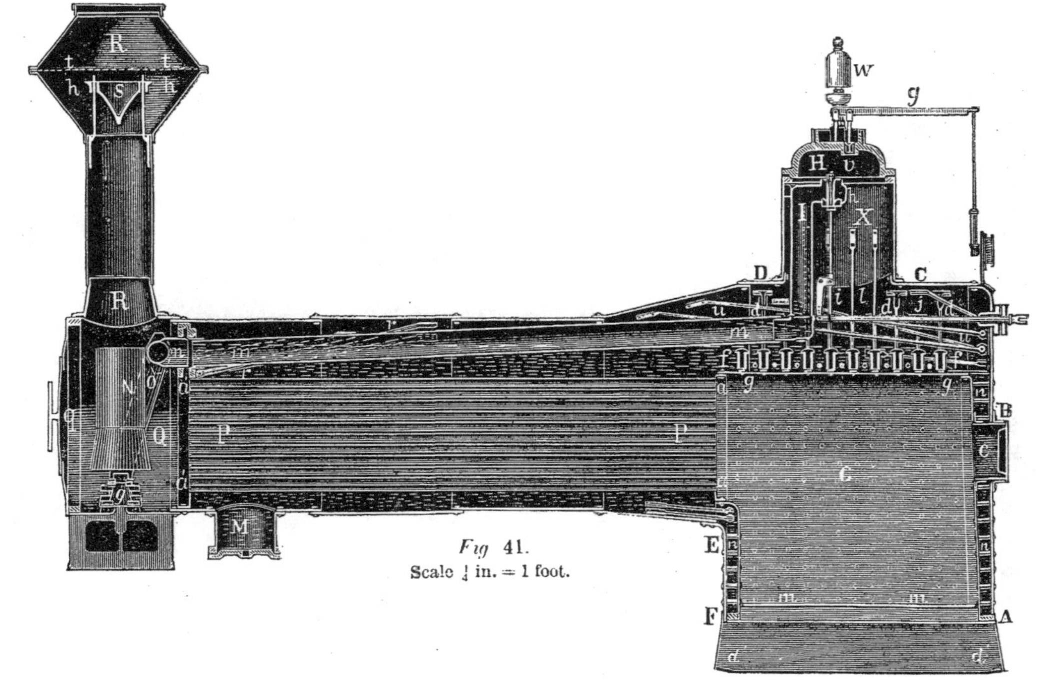

Fig 41.
Scale ¼ in. = 1 foot.

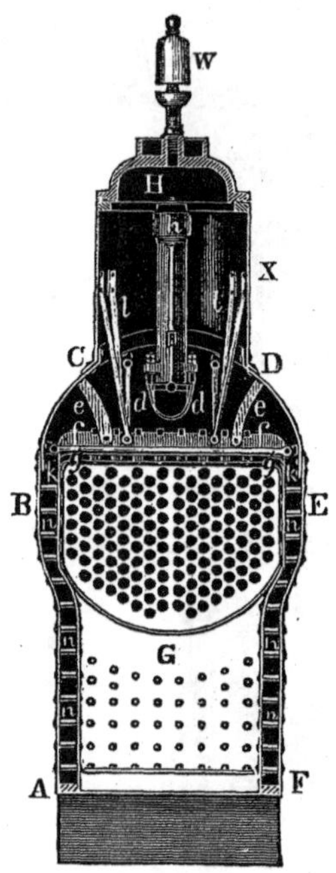

Fig. 42.
Scale ¼ in. = 1 foot.

should have a hole through the centre, so that when they break the water will escape at the fracture into the hole and the leak will thus indicate the defect and danger. The latter is much greater from this cause than is usually supposed, and it is not unusual to find on taking a boiler to pieces that a large number of the stay-bolts are broken.

QUESTION 91. *How can the strain on the flat surface of a boiler between the stay-bolts be calculated?*

Answer. By MULTIPLYING THE AREA IN INCHES

BETWEEN ADJACENT STAY-BOLTS BY THE PRESSURE. The reason for this is, that each stay-bolt must sustain the pressure on a part of the plate to which it is attached. Thus in fig. 43 it is plain that the bolt *S*

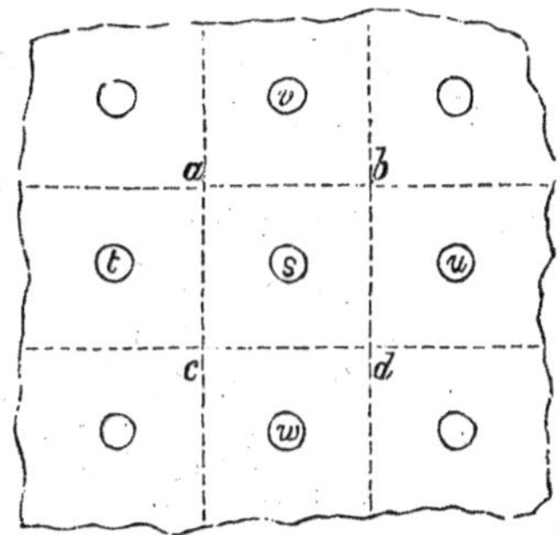

Fig. 43. Scale 1¼ in.=1 foot.

must sustain the pressure on one-half of that part of the plate between it and the bolts *v, t, w, u,* around it, or the pressure on the square *a b d c,* whose sides are equal to the distance (4 inches) between the centres of the bolts. With a pressure of 100 pounds per square inch, the calculation would therefore be: $4 \times 4 \times 100 =$ 1,600 lbs. on each bolt.

Stay-bolts should never be subjected to a strain of more than one-eighth or one-tenth of their breaking strength.

QUESTION 92. *How do stay-bolts often fail without breaking?*

Answer. By tearing or *stripping* the thread of the bolt, or that in the plate, but oftener perhaps by the stretching of the plates between the holes. With a heavy pressure, the tendency of the plates between the holes, especially if they are heated very hot, is to "bulge" outward and thus stretch the hole in every direction until it is so large that the bolt is drawn out without much injury to the screw-thread.

QUESTION 93. *How is the flat-top or crown-sheet strengthened?*

Answer. It is sometimes strengthened with stay-bolts similar to those used for the sides, which pass through the inner and outer shells;* but usually the crown-sheet is strengthened by a series of iron bars, (*f, f,* fig. 41 and 42) called *crown-bars,* placed on edge, and of considerable depth, which are firmly fastened to it by T-head rivets or bolts. The crown-sheet can therefore only be crushed downwards by bending these bars, which are of great strength. They usually extend crosswise of the length of the fire-box, but are sometimes placed lengthwise. These bars bear on the fire-box only at each end, as shown in fig. 42, and are usually made with a projection, *k, k,* which rests on the edge of the side plates. Iron rings or washers from $\frac{3}{4}$ to $1\frac{1}{2}$ inches thick are interposed between the plate and the bars at the points where the bolts or rivets which secure the rivets pass through. This permits the water to circulate under the bars, and prevents the crown-sheet from being burnt or overheated, as it would be if the water were excluded from the whole under surface of the crown-bars. †The crown-bars are also attached to the outer shell and the dome by *braces, e, e, l, l.*

The opening *c,* fig. 41, at the back end is for the door through which fuel is supplied to the grate.

* This method of staying crown-sheets has been extensively used on the Baltimore & Ohio and Reading railroads, and is now very generally used in Europe.

† Colburn's Locomotive Engineering.

Question 94. *How are the grates constructed?*

Answer. They are generally made of cast-iron bars, and for burning coal are usually arranged so that the fire can be shaken by moving the bars. For burning anthracite coal, the grates are sometimes made of wrought-iron tubes, through which a current of water circulates to prevent them from being overheated.

Question 95. *How are cinders and burning coals prevented from falling through the grate upon the road?*

Answer. By attaching a sheet-iron receptacle or ash-pan (*d′ d′*, fig. 41) as it is called, under the grate, which it completely encloses from the outside air. This then serves two purposes, as it is often important when the engine is standing still to prevent any access of air to the fire-box, and therefore the ash-pan is made to fit tighly to the fire-box. Suitable doors, or *dampers* as they are called, are placed in front and behind, and sometimes on the sides, which can be opened or closed to admit or exclude air as may be needed.

Question 96. *How are the tubes or flues of a locomotive arranged?*

Answer. They are fastened into accurately drilled holes in the tube sheet (*a, a,* figs. 41 and 42) which forms the front of the fire-box and in similar holes in a plate (*a′, a′,* fig. 41,) which forms the front end of the cylindrical part of the boiler. They thus connect the fire-box with the smoke-box. The tubes are arranged so that each tube will have a space of from $\frac{5}{8}$ to $\frac{7}{8}$ of an inch between it and those adjoining. The position of the holes for the tubes in relation to each other is determined by describing from the centre of one tube (*o,* fig. 44) a circle with a radius, *o k,* equal to the sum of the diameter of a tube and the distance which they are intended to be apart, and then subdividing this circle with the radius into six parts, *k, r, s, l, g* and *p*. Each point of subdivision and also

Fig. 44. Scale ¼.

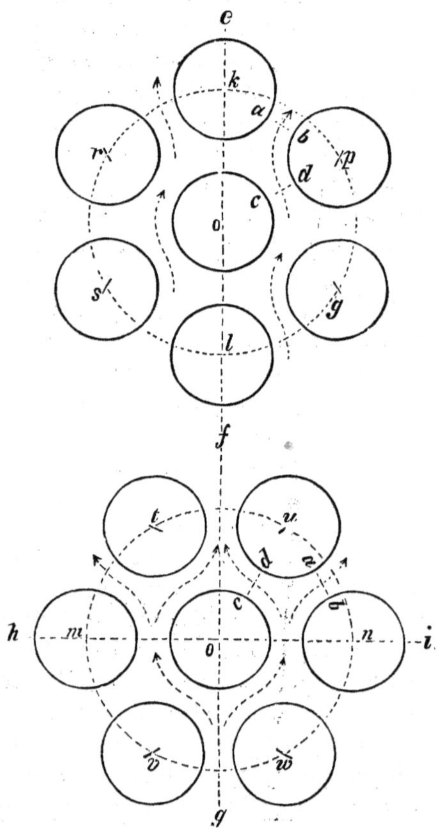

Fig. 45. Scale ¼.

the centre, *o*, of the circle will be the centre of a tube. By drawing them from these centres it will be found that the distances *a b*, *c d* between adjoining tubes will be the same between all of them. By describing circles from the centres of the outside tubes and subdividing the circles as before the position of other tubes will be determined around those first laid down. This can, of course, be carried out indefinitely. A difference in the arrangement of the tubes will be observed if, when we subdivide the first circle shown in fig. 44, instead of commencing from the intersection of a vertical line we begin from a horizontal line, *h i*, as shown in fig. 45. In the former case the tubes are said to be in *vertical rows*, and in the latter in *horizontal rows*. It is apparent from the figures and as shown by the arrows that the water can circulate in ascending currents more freely when tubes are arranged in vertical rows than when they are arranged horizontally.

QUESTION 97. *How are the tubes fastened and made water-tight in the tube-sheets?*

Answer. They are inserted into the holes drilled to receive them, and the ends are allowed to project about

Fig. 46. Scale ½.

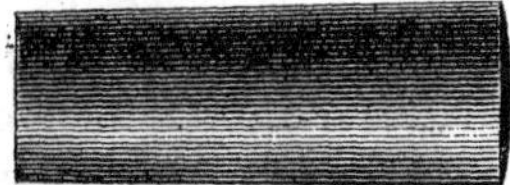

Fig. 47.

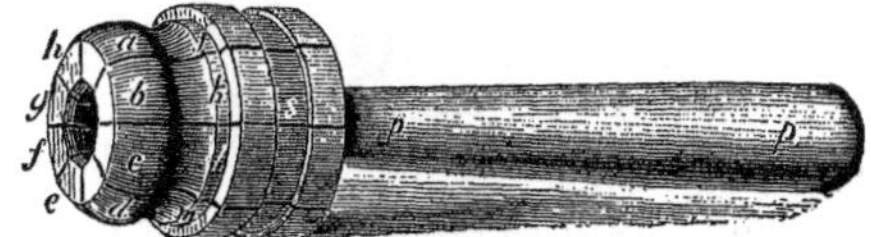

a quarter of an inch beyond the tube-sheets. A tapered plug, fig. 46, is then driven into the tube, to expand it so that it will fit the hole. A tool is used called a *tube-expander*, fig. 47, which is what might be called an expanding plug, consisting of a number of sections, *a*, *b*, *c*, *d* , *e*, *f*, *g*, *h*, held together by a spring clasp *s*, which embraces them, as shown in the engraving. This plug when the sections are drawn together is inserted into the mouth of the tube, and the tapered plug *p p*, is then driven into the opening left in the centre of the cluster of sections, which are thus expanded. By this means, the ridge *a b c d* expands the tube at the inner edge of the tube-sheet, forming a ridge or corrugation, as shown at *c c*, fig. 48. At the same time the shoulder *j k l* on the tool expands the outer edge of the tube somewhat as is

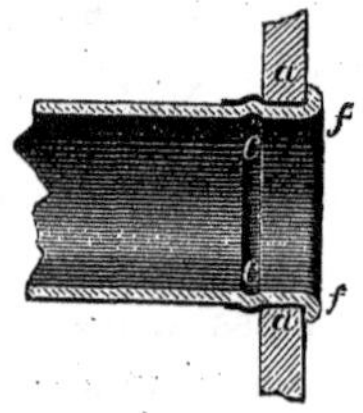

Fig. 48. Scale ½.

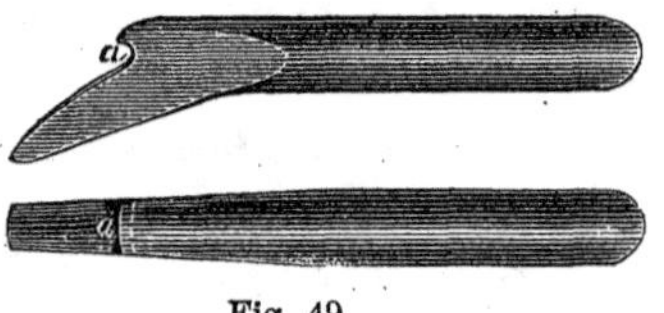

Fig. 49.

shown at *f f*, fig. 48. By repeating this process, and slightly turning the expander each time, the tubes can be made perfectly water-tight. There are other forms of tube-expanders, but the one described, known as Prosser's expander, is more generally used than any other. In many cases, after the tubes are expanded with the tool described, the outer edge is turned over still more with what is called a *thumb-tool*, fig. 49, probably from its resemblance in form to a man's thumb. By placing the curved shoulder *a* on the end *f*, fig. 48, of the tube it is turned over, somewhat in the form shown in the engraving, by repeated blows of a hammer on the end of the tool. Copper ferrules, represented by the black shading, *a a*, are also much used now on the outside of locomotive tubes, and it is said that with them the joints can be kept tight much easier than without. By turning over the outside edge of the tube as shown in fig. 48, it not only protects the copper ferrule, but, as the tubes must act as braces to sustain the pressure of steam in the flat tube-sheets, it gives the joints the requisite strength for resisting such strains.

QUESTION 98. *How can the strain on the cylindrical part of a boiler be calculated?*

Answer. BY MULTIPLYING THE DIAMETER IN INCHES BY THE LENGTH IN INCHES AND THE PRODUCT BY THE STEAM-PRESSURE PER SQUARE INCH. Thus for a boiler 48 inches in diameter and 10 feet long with 100 pounds pressure the calculation would be $48 \times 120 \times 100 = 576{,}000$ lbs.

QUESTION 99. *Why do we multiply the diameter, instead of the circumference, by the length, to get the strain on the cylindrical part?*

Answer. The reason for multiplying by the diameter instead of by the circumference is because only a portion of the pressure on the inside surface of the boiler exerts a force to burst the shell at any one point. Thus, supposing the following diagram, fig. 50, to represent a section of a boiler, if we have a force acting on the shell in the direction of the line *a b*, at the point *b*, where it is exerted against the shell of the boiler, it would be composed of two forces, one acting in the direction *b e*, and tending to tear the boiler apart on the line *c d*, and the other acting in the di-

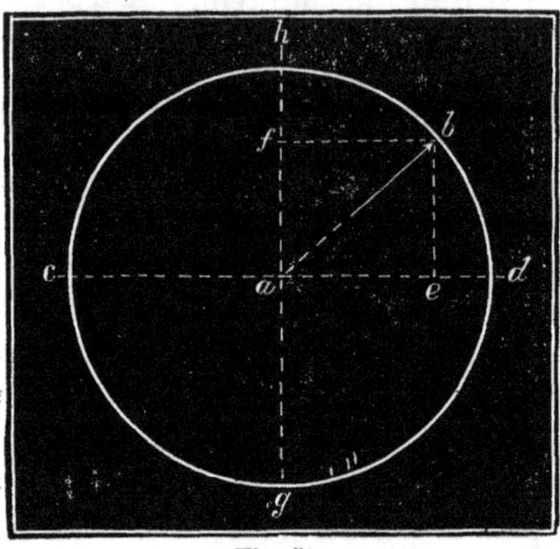

Fig. 50.

rection *f b*, to tear it apart on the line *h g*. It is so with all pressure inside the boiler, excepting that, say *a h*, which acts exactly at right angles to the line of rupture *c d*, it is all composed of two forces, only one of which tends to tear the boiler apart at one point. It is therefore only a part of the pressure on the circumference which tends to burst the boiler at a given place, and that part is equivalent to the pressure on a surface whose width is equal to the diameter and not the circumference.

This we know is a little difficult for those to understand who are not familiar with the principles of what is called the "resolution of forces," and we will therefore try to make it clear in another way.

To do this we will suppose that we have a boiler, *a b*, fig. 51, made in two halves and bolted together at *a* and *b* by flanges. It is evident that if we brought a pressure against the inside of the flanges in the direction of the darts *c* and *d*, such a pressure would

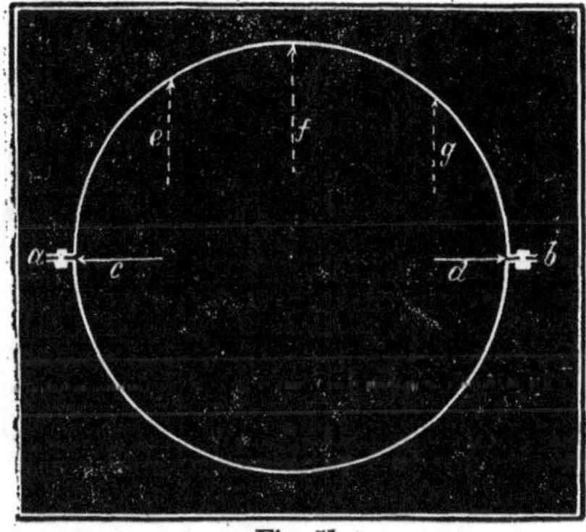

Fig. 51.

not have a tendency to tear apart the bolts *a* and *b*. Some distortion of the boiler might in fact take place, if, for example, we put a jack-screw inside and forced out the flanges as indicated, without subjecting the bolts to a tensile strain. We see therefore that the forces acting in the direction *c* and *d* have no tendency to tear apart the bolts at *a* and *b*, but it is only the forces such as *e*, *f* and *g*, which act at right angles to *a b*, that exert a strain on the flanges.

That this force is equivalent to a pressure on a surface with a width equal to the diameter of the boiler is apparent if we suppose that we have a boiler, *a b*, fig. 52, and that each half, *c* and *d*, is nearly filled with some substance, say wood or cement, which is fitted so tight that no steam can get between it and the shell of the boiler. It is apparent now that if we admit steam into the space *f*, the force exerted on the bolts *a* and *b* is that due to the pressure on the surface of the wood or cement exposed to the steam whose width is equal to the diameter of the boiler. It might

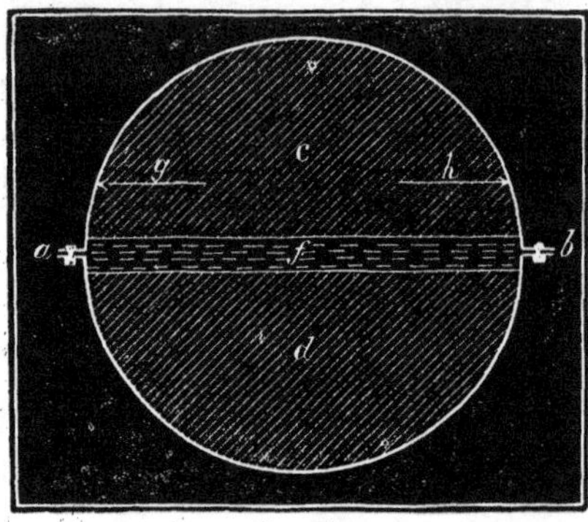

Fig 52.

be said though that if this substance were elastic, like india-rubber, the effect of the steam would be different. If it were elastic, and a pressure on the surfaces *f* caused it to spread in the direction *g* and *h* so as to produce a pressure in those directions, it would, as has already been shown, not exert a force on the bolts *a* and *b* to tear them apart, but have a tendency to rupture the boiler at right angles to *a b*. The sides of the boiler must therefore have a strength sufficient to resist this force which tends to tear them asunder. If the boiler is made of iron $\frac{3}{8}$ inch thick there would be a sectional area of 45 square inches on each side, or a total of 90 square inches, to resist this strain, so that each square inch must bear 6,400 lbs. of strain. The correctness of this rule can be demonstrated by the use of mathematics, which would be out of place here. Its practical truth has however been proved by experiment.

QUESTION 100. *How much strain per square inch is good boiler plate capable of resisting, and how much is it safe to subject it to?*

Answer. There is great variation in the tensile strength* of rolled iron boiler plate, but that of good plate will average about 50,000 pounds per square inch, if the strain is applied in the direction of the "grain" or the fibres of the iron †, and about ten per cent. less if the strain is applied crosswise of the grain. It has, however, been found by experiment that when a tensile strain is applied to a bar of iron or other material, it is stretched a certain amount in proportion to the length of the bar and to the degree of strain to which it is subjected. It is found that if this strain does not exceed about one-fifth of that which would break the bar, it will recover its original length, or will contract after being stretched, when the strain is removed. The greatest strain which any material will bear without being permanently stretched is called its *limit of elasticity,* and so long as this is not exceeded no appreciable permanent elongation or "set" will be given to iron by any number of applications of such strains or loads. If, however, the limit of elasticity is exceeded, the metal will be permanently elongated, and this elongation will be increased by repeated applications of the strain until finally the bar will break. At the same time the character of the metal will be altered by the repeated application of strains greater than its elastic limit, and it will become brittle and less able to resist a sudden strain, and will ultimately break

*A force exerted to pull any material apart is called a *tensile strain,* and if exerted to compress it is called a *compressive strain.*

† It should be explained that in the process of manufacturing iron by rolling, the iron is stretched out into fibres in the direction in which it passes between the rolls.

short off. It is therefore unsafe to subject iron, or in fact any other material, to strains greater than its elastic limit. This limit for iron boiler plates may be taken at about one-fifth its breaking, or, as it is called, *ultimate* strength. It should be remembered, however, in this connection, that it often happens that the steam pressure is not the greatest force the boiler must withstand, as sudden or unequal expansion and contraction are probably more destructive, to locomotive boilers especially, than the pressure of the steam.

QUESTION 101. *How are the plates of boilers fastened together?*

Answer. With rivets, which are made with a head at one end, and are inserted while they are red-hot into holes drilled or punched in the edges of the plates. After they are in the holes a head is formed on the other end, either with blows from hand hammers, or by a machine constructed for the purpose. In these machines the rivet after it is in the holes is brought between a fixed and a movable die, the head which is made with the rivet being placed against the fixed die, and the movable die is then pressed, either by steam or hydraulic pressure with great force against the other end of the rivet, thus forcing the end of the rivet into the form of the die, which is made of the proper shape and size for the rivet head. The powerful pressure which is thus brought on the rivet causes it to be pressed into all parts of the two holes, thus completely filling them both; whereas with hand riveting, the holes are not nearly so completely filled, as it is impossible with blows of a hammer to subject the rivets to so powerful or uniform a pressure as the machine brings upon them.

QUESTION 102. *What is the strength of riveted seams compared with that of the solid plate?*

Answer. The strength of a riveted seam depends very much upon the arrangement and proportion of the rivets, but with the best design and construction, the seams are always weaker than the solid plates, as it is always necessary to cut away a part of the plate for the rivet holes, which weakens the plate in three ways: 1. By lessening the amount of material to resist the strains. 2. By weakening that left between the holes. 3. By disturbing the uniformity of the distribution of the strains. The first cause of weakness is obvious from an inspection of an ordinary seam, riveted with a single row of rivets, fig. 53. In this we have two plates $7\frac{1}{2}$ inches wide and $\frac{3}{8}$ thick fastened with four rivets $\frac{11}{16}$ inches in diameter and $1\frac{7}{8}$

Fig. 53

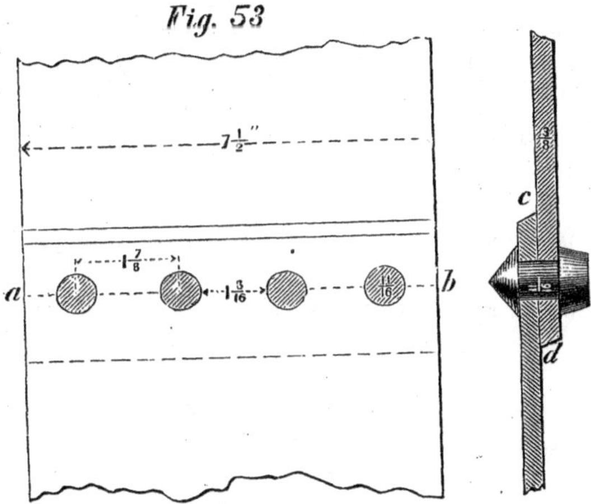

inches from centre to centre. The section of the

plate calculated with decimals* would therefore be $.375 \times 7.5 = 2.81$ square inches. A piece $\frac{11}{16}$ inch wide and $\frac{3}{8}$ inch thick would be removed to form each hole, or a sectional area for the whole plate of $.375 \times .6875 \times 4 = 1.03$ square inches, so that the section of the plate would be reduced through the holes $2.81 - 1.03 = 1.78$ square inches. In other words, on the dotted line *a b* it will have only about 63 per cent. of the sectional area of the solid plate.

The second cause of the reduction of strength is owing to the injury sustained by the plates during the process of drilling and punching. The knowledge existing regarding this subject is not very accurate, although numerous experiments have been made to determine the exact amount of weakening caused by punching plates. It is, however, certain that in many cases the strength of the metal *left* between the holes of boiler plates is reduced from 10 to 30 per cent. by the process of punching. It is probable, however, that soft ductile metal is injured less than that which is harder and more brittle. Some kinds of steel plates are especially liable to injury from punching. It is also probable that the condition of the punch, and the proportions of the die used with it, have much to do with its effect upon the metal.

The third cause of weakness is owing to the fact that if one or more holes are made in a plate of any material, and it is then subjected to a tensile strain, the strain, instead of being equally distributed through the section left between the holes, will be greatest in that part of the metal nearest them. This can be illus-

---

* In the following calculations all the dimensions have for convenience been reduced to decimals.

trated by taking a band of india-rubber, fig. 54, and cutting a round hole in it to represent a rivet hole. If we

Fig. 54

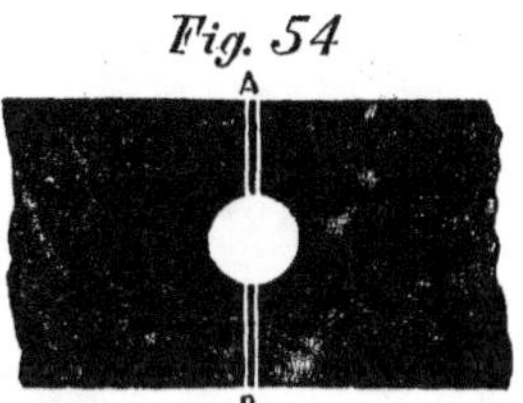

Fig. 55

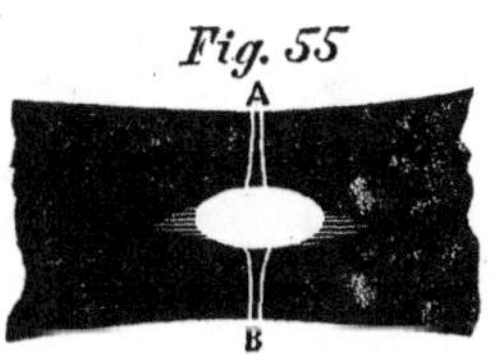

draw two parallel lines, *A B*, across the band and then stretch it, the lines, instead of remaining parallel when the band is stretched, will separate most next to the hole, as shown in fig. 55, indicating that the fibres of the rubber nearest the hole are strained most. A similar effect takes place when a plate of iron is stretched, so that a fracture is liable to begin next to the hole, after which the plate will be broken as it were in detail.

QUESTION 103. ***How may a boiler seam like that shown in fig.* 53 *break?***

Answer. It may break in three different ways:

1. By the plate tearing between the rivet holes on the line ***a b.***

2. By the rivets shearing off.

3. By the plate in front of the rivets crushing, as shown in fig. 56.

QUESTION 104. ***How can the strength of a boiler seam be calculated at each of these three points?***

Answer. The strength through the rivet holes is calculated by TAKING THE AREA IN SQUARE INCHES OF THE METAL WHICH IS LEFT BETWEEN THE RIVET HOLES, AND MULTIPLYING IT BY THE ULTIMATE STRENGTH OF THE METAL AFTER THE HOLES ARE

MADE. Thus, in fig. 53, the area of each of the plates between the rivet holes is 1.78 square inches. As al-

Fig. 56

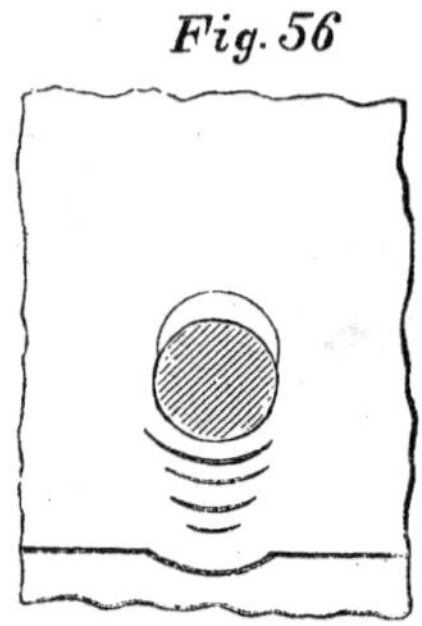

ready stated, good boiler plate will break at a strain of about 50,000 pounds in the direction of its fibres,* but the strength of the metal left between punched holes is probably 20 per cent. and that between drilled holes 10 per cent. less than that of the solid plate. We must, therefore, in calculating the strength of a punched seam, take the ultimate strength of the metal between the holes at only 40,000 pounds per square inch. The calculation for the strength through the holes would therefore be: $1.78 \times 40{,}000 = 71{,}200$ pounds.

It has also been found by experiment that the strength of rivets to resist shearing is about the same as that of good boiler plate to resist tearing apart, or 50,000 lbs. per square inch. The strength of the rivets, therefore, is calculated by MULTIPLYING THE AREA IN SQUARE INCHES OF ONE RIVET BY THE NUMBER OF RIVETS, AND THE PRODUCT BY THE STRENGTH

* Boiler plates should always be so arranged that the greatest strain will come on them in the direction of their greatest strength, which is parallel with the fibres of the metal.

OF THE METAL TO RESIST SHEARING. The calculation for fig. 53 would therefore be:

Area of $\frac{11}{16}$ rivet=.3712×4×50,000=74,240.

or a little more than the strength of the plates through the holes.

The resistance offered by a plate to the crushing strain of a rivet has been found also by experiment to be about 90,000 pounds per square inch. It can be proved that the area which resists the crushing strain of a rivet in a plate, fig. 53, IS MEASURED BY MULTIPLYING THE DIAMETER OF THE RIVET BY THE THICKNESS OF THE PLATE. The calculation for the strength of this part of the seam will therefore be: diameter of hole = .6875×.375×4×90,000=92,812.

The strength of the solid plate would be EQUAL TO ITS SECTIONAL AREA MULTIPLIED BY 50,000 POUNDS, or 7.5×.375×50,000=140,625 pounds. The ultimate strength of our seam would then be as follows:

Plates through rivet holes	(tearing)	= 71.200 lbs.
Rivets	(shearing)	= 72,240 lbs.
Plates in front of rivets	(crushing)	= 92,812 lbs.
Solid plate	(tearing)	=140,625 lbs.

It will thus be seen that the strength of the weakest part of the above seam, fastened with a single row of rivets in punched holes, is very little more than half (50.6 per cent.) of that of the plates. It will be noticed that the weakest part of the seam is the plates between the holes.

QUESTION 105. *How can the strength of such a single-riveted boiler seam be increased?*

Answer. The most obvious way of increasing the strength of such a seam is to place, or, as it is called, *space,* the rivets further apart, which would leave more metal between the holes, and thus strengthen the seam at its weakest part. But if this is done, it is said that there is difficulty in keeping the seam water-tight, as the plates are then liable to spring apart between the rivets. Another way of increasing its strength is to drill the rivet holes. As already stated, the difference in the strength of the metal left between drilled and punched holes has been shown to be from 10 to 20 per cent. There is also another advantage in drilling the holes for rivets. In punching them, it is necessary to punch each plate separately, and even with the utmost care and skill it is impossible to get the holes to match perfectly. Some of them will overlap each other, as

Fig. 57

Fig. 58

Fig. 59

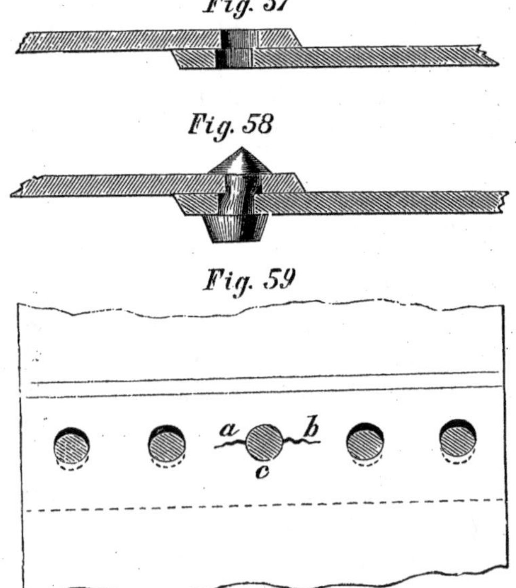

shown in fig. 57, so that when the rivet is set, it will assume somewhat the form shown in fig. 58. There is then danger that those rivets which fill the holes that match each other will be subjected to an undue strain. If, for example, we have five rivet holes, as shown in fig. 59, and only the centre ones correspond with each other, then the rivets in all the other holes will assume somewhat the form shown in fig. 58, and therefore the centre rivet *c*, in fig. 59, which fits the holes accurately, must take the strain of the other four until they draw up "to a bearing." Under such circumstances, which are not unusual, there will be great danger either of shearing off the rivet *c*, or of starting a fracture in the plates, as indicated by the irregular line *a b*, between the adjoining rivets. It is also obvious that a rivet like the one in fig. 58 will not hold the plates together so well as one which fits more perfectly, as shown in section in fig. 53, and therefore there is more danger of leakage between the plates from badly fitted rivets than from those which fill the holes more perfectly; consequently rivets which fit imperfectly must be placed nearer together than those which are well fitted. It is true that rivets which are set with a riveting machine fill any inaccuracies of the holes more perfectly than those which are set by hand. But even if they are made to fill the holes as shown in fig. 60 they are still not so strong

Fig. 60

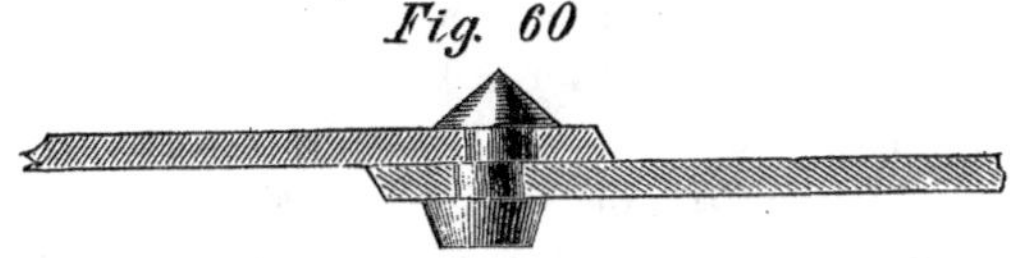

to resist shearing nor so efficient in holding the

plates together as they would be if the holes conformed more perfectly to each other. In drilling the holes, the second plate can be drilled from the holes in the first, so that the holes in each will correspond with each other perfectly. The rivets will therefore fit more accurately, and consequently can be spaced further apart, and still keep the plates tight, and thus have more material between the holes, which is the weakest part of the seam. It has been shown that a rivet $\frac{11}{16}$ inch in diameter has a resistance to shearing of 18,560 pounds. There is therefore no advantage in spacing such rivets further apart than $1\frac{13}{16}$ from centre to centre, because the metal left between drilled holes that distance apart would be slightly stronger than the rivets. If therefore the rivets are placed further apart, their diameter must be increased. There is, however, a limit beyond which the diameters of rivets cannot be increased with advantage, because if we increase their diameters, their sectional area to resist shearing is increased in proportion *to the square of the diameter*, whereas the section of metal in the plate to resist crushing is increased only *in proportion to the diameter.* This will be apparent if we compare a rivet $\frac{1}{2}$ inch with one 1 inch in diameter. The first has a sectional area of .1963 inch, the other .7854 inch, or *four* times that of the first one. Now the area which resists the crushing strain of the rivets is increased only in proportion to their diameters, or is *twice* as much for the one as for the other. If, therefore, we increase the diameters of the rivets, we very soon reach a point at which the plate has less strength to resist crushing than the rivet has to resist shearing. The diameter of rivet which will give just the same resistance to both strains varies with the thickness of the plates; with $\frac{3}{8}$ inch plates a $\frac{7}{8}$ rivet will have a resistance to shearing of 30,065 pounds and the plate in front of it a resistance to crushing of 29,530 pounds. A $\frac{7}{8}$ rivet is, therefore, the largest size which can be used to advantage in $\frac{3}{8}$ plates. If now we were to space such rivets so far apart that the metal left between the holes would have a strength just equal to that of the rivets, we would have the strongest possible seam that can be made with a single row of rivets. This distance would be $1\frac{3}{4}$ inches between the edges of the rivets, or $2\frac{5}{8}$ from center to center, as shown in

Fig. 61

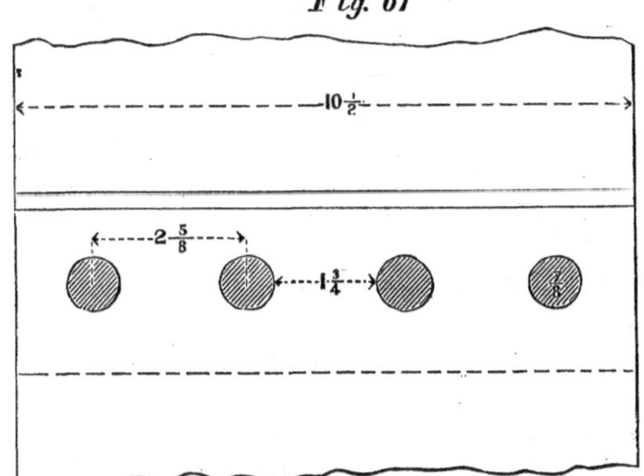

fig. 61. The following table will show the strength of such a seam composed of four rivets, and two plates $10\frac{1}{2}$ inches wide,* with drilled holes:

Plates through rivet holes	(tearing)	118,125 lbs.
Rivets	(shearing)	120,260 lbs.
Plates in front of rivets	(crushing)	118,125 lbs.
Solid plates	(tearing)	196,875 lbs.

* It has been necessary to take for an illustration, plates of a different width from the preceding example, in order to get an even number of spaces between the rivets in each case.

From this it is seen that the strength of the seam with drilled plates is 60 per cent. of that of the solid plates, or it is about $18\frac{1}{2}$ per cent. stronger than that made with plates having punched holes and the rivets nearer together. It should be noted that a great part of the superiority of the seams made with drilled holes is due to the superior accuracy of the work done in that way, which makes it possible to use larger rivets spaced further apart. It is probable that with the use of some recently designed machines, intended to produce greater accuracy in punching rivet holes, part of the above advantage may be realized with that kind of work. The greatest distance that rivets may be spaced apart without incurring danger of leakage between the plates must, however, be determined more by practical than theoretical considerations. It is certain, however, that rivets may be spaced much further apart than they are in ordinary practice, and the seams still be kept tight, if the work is done with sufficient accuracy and care.

QUESTION 106. *What other methods are there of making boiler seams which are stronger than those which have been described?*

Answer. In this country two rows of rivets are used and also what is called a *"welt,"* or *covering-strip,* the latter with both single and double-riveted seams.

QUESTION 107. *How are the rivets arranged when two rows are used?*

Answer. They are often placed just behind each other as shown in fig. 62, which is called *chain-riveting.* Such an arrangement of rivets obviously adds nothing to the strength of the seam, because its weakest part, as has already been shown, is the section of the plates through the rivet-holes, and this is not at all strengthened by adding another row of rivets, because the

Fig. 62

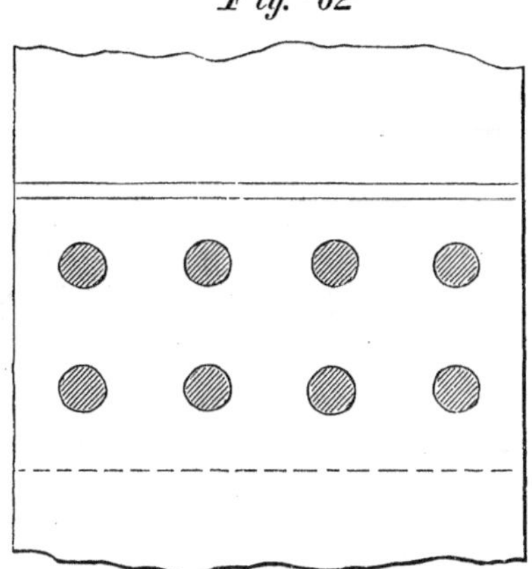

plates are just as liable to break through the rivet-holes with two rows of rivets as they would be with one.

A much better arrangement is to place them alternately in the two rows, as shown in fig. 63. Rivets arranged in that way are said to be ***staggered***, or placed *zigzag*. The method of laying off the holes and proportioning such a seam in order to get the most strength is, first, to determine the greatest distance which can be allowed between the rivet-holes, and yet keep the seams water-tight. Supposing this is $1\frac{5}{16}$ inches,* with plates $\frac{3}{8}$ inch thick, the diameter of rivet whose sectional area will give an equal amount of strength must then be calculated. From the preceding data it will be found that for drilled plates the

* That and even greater distances between the edges of the holes are now used successfully with $\frac{3}{8}$-inch plates.

resistance of the portion left between such holes will be 22,148 pounds, and a rivet $\frac{3}{4}$ inch in diameter will

Fig. 63.

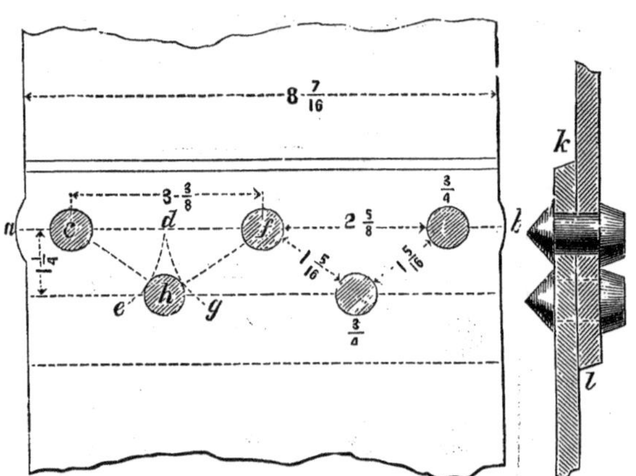

have a resistance of 22,085 pounds. On the line *a b*, fig. 63, which is to be the first row of rivets, we will draw one hole, *c*. From the center of this hole we will describe the arc of a circle, *d e*, with a radius, *c d*, equal to the sum of the distance between the holes, $1\frac{3}{8}$ inches, and one-half the diameter of the hole, or $\frac{3}{8}$ inch, making the radius $1\frac{3}{4}$ inches. From *d*, the intersection of this arc with the line of rivets, *a b*, with the same radius, we will step off the distance *d f f* will then be the centre of the second rivet-hole on the line *a, b*. The rivet can therefore be drawn, and from its centre, with the same radius employed before, another arc, *d g*, should be drawn. If now we draw a rivet-hole (*h*) between the two arcs and touching each of them, we will have all three of the holes so arranged that the metal between the holes *c, f*, will be just equal to that between them and the hole *h*. In other words, the strength of the plates on the line *c f* is just the same as on the line *c h f*. Therefore the strength of the plates on the straight line *a b* is just the same as on the zigzag line *c h f*, etc. The strength of this seam would therefore be as follows:

Plates through rivet-holes	(tearing)	110,742 lbs.
Rivets	(shearing)	110,425 lbs.
Plates in front of rivets	(crushing)	126.562 lbs.
Solid plates	(tearing)	158,205 lbs.

The weakest portion of this seam, it will be seen, has a strength of 70 per cent. of the plate, or is 38 per cent. stronger than a single-riveted seam with punched holes. If we were to use $\frac{7}{8}$ inch rivets and make the spaces between them $1\frac{3}{4}$ inches, the strength of a similar seam would be as follows:

Plates through rivet-holes	(tearing)	147,656 lbs.
Rivets	(shearing)	150,325 lbs.
Plates in front of rivets	(crushing)	147,050 lbs.
Solid plates	(tearing)	205,078 lbs.

This seam would then have a strength of 72 per cent. of the solid plates, or be $42\frac{1}{4}$ per cent. stronger than the ordinary riveted seam with punched holes. It is important to observe that an increase of strength results from the use of larger rivets spaced farther apart than is usual in ordinary practice, and that this is possible only with the best and most accurate workmanship.

QUESTION 108. *What is the form of construction of boiler seams made with a welt or covering-strip?*

Answer. The plates (*a*, *b*, fig. 64) are lapped over each other as for an ordinary seam. Another plate, *c*, about nine inches wide, is then placed on the inside of the seam and bent so as to conform to the lap of the two plates. The rivets *r*, whether a double or single row, pass through all three plates, and two more rows

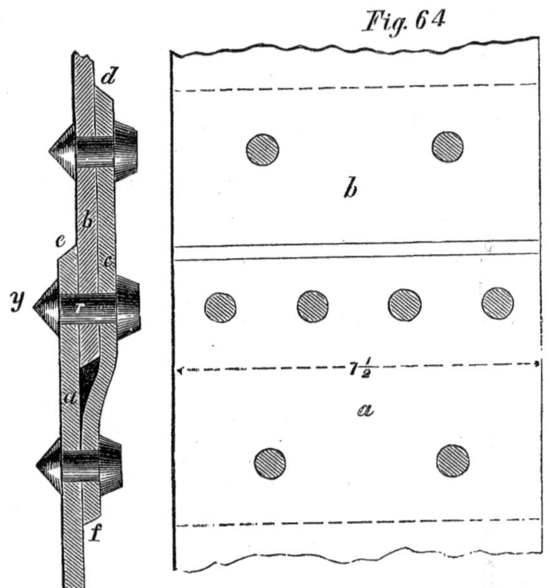

of rivets are put next to the edges of the covering plate, *c*. It is plain that the strength of the seam, *r*, is increased up to a certain point by an amount just equal to that of the rivets in the edges of the covering plate. If, however, these are placed too close together, the plates *a* and *b* will be weaker through the outside rows of rivets than the seam is through either of the outside ones and the middle one taken together. If, for example, we take a single-riveted seam, like that shown in fig. 53, whose strength is only a little more than half that of the solid plate, and should add to it a covering plate, as shown in fig. 64, and then space the rivets in the edges of the covering plate the same distance apart as in the middle seam, then obviously the plates would be just as liable to break through the outer rows of holes as through the center row before the covering plate was added. If, however, the holes in the two outside plates are spaced at say twice the distance apart, or 3¾ inches, then the only way the seam can break through the outer rows of holes is by shearing the rivets, because the plates between the holes are then stronger than the rivets. But before these rivets can be sheared, the centre seam must give way. Thus the strength of such a seam is equal to THE SUM OF THE STRENGTH AT THE WEAKEST POINTS OF THE MIDDLE AND THE OUTSIDE SEAMS. The strength of the plates between the holes of the outside rows of rivets must, however, be as great as the sum referred to, otherwise the seam will be the weakest at that point, and the failure will occur there. The rivets in the outside rows should be spaced at least twice as far apart as those in the middle seam. The number of rivets to resist shearing will then be 50 per cent. greater, so that the strength of a seam like that shown in fig. 53, with a covering plate added, will be as follows:

Plates through outside rows of rivet-holes (tearing)..........	91,880 lbs.
Rivets in one outside and middle row (shearing)............	111,360 lbs.
Plates in front of rivets (crushing)...........................	139,218 lbs.
Solid plates (tearing)..	140,625 lbs.

An ordinary single-riveted seam with punched holes, with a welt or covering plate added, would thus have a strength equal to 65.3 per cent. of the solid plate, or be 29 per cent. stronger than the seam without the covering plate. It is probable, however, that the injury to the plate from punching the outside rows of holes which are further apart is not so great as it is when they are punched nearer together and to the edge, so that the strength is somewhat greater than our estimate.

The relative strength of the different forms of seams described in percentage of the strength of the solid plate is then as follows:

	Percentage of strength compared with solid plate.
Single-riveted seam, punched holes........$\frac{11}{16}$ rivets	50.6
" " drilled " ....$\frac{7}{8}$ "	60.
Double-riveted seam, drilled zigzag holes..$\frac{3}{4}$ rivets	70.
" " " " " $\frac{7}{8}$ "	72.
Single riveted seam, punched holes with covering plate.......	65.3

QUESTION 109. *Are there any other forms of boiler seams used?*

Answer. In Europe what are called *butt-joints* are used to some extent. In these the ends of the two plates abut against each other, with a covering strip on one or both sides. This form of joint is, however, not used in this country, and therefore its peculiarities will not be described.

QUESTION 110. *How are the seams of boilers made water-tight?*

Answer. By what is called *caulking.* That is, by the use of a blunt instrument somewhat resembling a chisel, the end of which is placed against one or both of the edges of the plates *c, d,* fig. 53, which are then riveted down by blows of a hammer, somewhat as the joints of a ship are made tight. Before the edges, which are called the *caulking edges,* of the plates are made tight in this way, they are cut or trimmed off with a chisel. In this process the plate under the edge is often injured seriously by the carelessness of workmen, who sometimes allow the chisel to cut a groove in the plate under the edge, thus weakening it at a point where the greatest strength is needed. There is also danger of forcing the plates apart in the manner shown in fig. 65, if it is done carelessly and with a heavy hammer.

Fig. 65

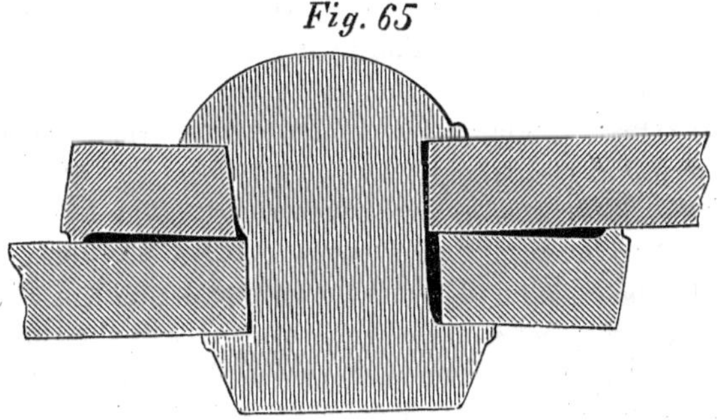

QUESTION 111. *How are the flat ends of the boiler strengthened?*

Answer. By braces, *u, u, r, r,* fig. 41, which are fastened to the end plates and to the outer shell of the boiler. They are fastened at one end to ⊥ shaped pieces called *crow-feet,* which are riveted to the end plates of the boiler. At the other end they are made with a broad foot, which is riveted to the outer shell of the boiler. Especial attention should be given to the form, proportion and arrangement of these braces when a boiler is constructed, and they should be frequently examined while the engine is in use, as they are liable to be neglected or carelessly constructed and to become weakened or broken by corrosion, or the constant strain to which they are subjected. Great ignorance is often displayed in the design and proportions of these braces, especially in their attachments to the shell of the boiler.

QUESTION 112. *How should the braces for strengthening the ends of a boiler be proportioned?*

Answer. Every part should be made equally strong. If, for example, the brace itself is made of a bar of round iron one inch in diameter, its sectional area would be .7854 square inch. The iron used for these braces should be of such strength that a force of not less than 50,000 lbs. per square inch of transverse section should be required to tear it apart lengthwise. A bar of the size referred to would therefore require not less than 39,270 pounds to pull it apart. All the other parts should be capable of resisting an equal strain. It is, for example, not unusual to find a brace of the size we have described, and even of larger diameter, fastened to a crow-foot which is attached to the boiler plate with two rivets $\frac{5}{8}$ inches in diameter. A similar fastening for the other end of the brace is also often used. The sectional area of these two rivets is considerably less than that of the brace, and at the same time the strain is brought upon them at such an angle as to have a tendency to "snap" them off. For this reason, and also because a rivet is apt to be deteriorated in strength by the hammering, the rivets should always have a sectional area very nearly or quite double that of the bar which forms the brace. The metal around the eyes through which the pins are inserted should also be carefully proportioned, and the transverse section at any one point should always be at least $1\frac{1}{2}$ times greater than that of the bar. The area of the pins used for attaching the bars to the crow-feet should always be a little more than half that of the bar. That is, an inch bar should have a pin not less than $\frac{3}{4}$ inch in diameter. When flat braces are used, it is not unusual to find a bar 3 inches wide with a hole an inch in diameter punched or drilled so near the end that a pin is sure either to pull out the end of the bar or else to break it crosswise at the hole with a much less strain than the brace itself would resist. The ends of braces should always be enlarged enough to give them sufficient strength to resist as much strain as the bar itself. Although these precautions may appear unimportant, and unfortunately are often so regarded, yet it is upon just such details as these that the lives and the safety of every locomotive runner, fireman and others near them are constantly dependent.

QUESTION 113. *How much water is usually carried in a locomotive boiler?*

Answer. There must always be enough water in the boiler to cover completely all the parts which are exposed to the fire, otherwise they will be heated to so high a temperature as to be very much weakened or permanently injured. In order to be sure that all the heating-surface will at all times be covered with water, it is usually carried so that its surface will be from 4 to 8 inches above the crown-sheet.

QUESTION 114. *How much space should there be over the water for steam?*

Answer. No exact rule can be given to determine this. It may, however, generally be assumed that the more steam space the better. In order to increase the steam room, locomotive boilers are very generally made in this country with what is called a *wagon-top,*

10

D C, fig. 41, that is, the outside shell of the boiler over the fire-box is elevated from 4 to 12 or even 18 inches above the cylindrical part.

QUESTION 115. *What is a steam-dome and for what purpose is it intended?*

Answer. A *steam-dome, X*, fig. 41, is a cylindrical chamber made of boiler-plate and attached to the top of the boiler. Its object is to increase the steam room and to furnish a reservoir which is elevated considerably above the surface of the water, from which the supply of steam to be used in the cylinders can be drawn. The reason for drawing the steam from a point considerably above the water is that during ebullition more or less spray or particles of water are thrown up and mixed with the steam. When this is the case, steam is said to be *wet*, and when there is little or no unevaporated water mixed with it it is said to be *dry*. It is found by experience that wet steam is much less efficient than that which is dry. There is also danger that the cylinders, pistons or other parts of the machinery may be injured if much water is carried over from the boiler with the steam, because water will be discharged so slowly from the cylinders that there is not time for it to escape before the piston must complete its stroke, so that the cylinder-heads will be "*knocked out*," or the cylinder itself or the piston will be broken. The reason for drawing or "*taking*" steam from a point considerably above the water is because there is less spray there than there is near the surface, and the hottest steam, which is also the dryest, ascends to the highest part of the steam space.

QUESTION 116. *Where is the dome usually placed?*

Answer. In this country it is usually placed over the fire-box, but in Europe it is placed further forward, either about the centre of the boiler or near the front end of the tubes. Sometimes two domes are used on engines, in this country, one over the fire-box and another near the front end.

QUESTION 117. *How is the steam conducted from the dome to the cylinders?*

Answer. By a pipe *I m m*, fig. 41, called the *dry-pipe*, which extends from the top of the dome to the front tube-plate. On the front side of the tube-plate and inside the smoke-box two curved pipes, *O*, fig. 41, (shown also in fig. 43,) called *steam-pipes*, are attached to the dry-pipe at one end, and to the cylinders at the other. The vertical portion of the dry-pipe in the dome, sometimes called the *throttle-pipe*, is usually made of cast iron, the horizontal part of wrought iron, and the steam pipes of cast iron.

QUESTION 118. *How is the loss of heat from locomotive boilers by radiation and convection prevented?*

Answer. By covering the boiler and dome with wood, called *lagging*, about $\frac{7}{8}$ inch thick, which is a poor conductor of heat, and then covering the outside of the wood with Russia iron, the smooth, polished surface of which is a poor radiator of heat.

QUESTION 119. *What is the smoke-box for?*

Answer. The smoke-box *Q* is simply a convenient receptacle for the smoke before it escapes into the chimney or smoke-stack, which is attached to the top of the smoke-box. It also affords a convenient place for the steam and exhaust pipes, where they are surrounded with hot air and smoke, and not exposed to loss of heat by radiation. The front end of the smoke-box is usually made of cast iron, with a large door in the centre which affords access to the inside.

QUESTION 120. *How are the chimneys or smoke-stacks of locomotives constructed?*

Answer. The forms of smoke-stacks which have been used are almost numberless. For burning bituminous coal and wood they are generally made with a central pipe, *R,* fig. 41, and a conical-shaped cast-iron plate, *S,* called the *cone* or *spark deflector,* which, as the latter name implies, is intended to deflect the motion of the sparks and cinders which are carried up with the ascending current of smoke and air in the pipe *R,* so as to prevent them from escaping into the open air while they are incandescent, or "alive." A wire netting, *t t,* is also provided, which is intended as a sort of sieve to enclose the sparks and cinders, and at the same time allow the smoke to escape. The receptacle *h h* is intended as a chamber in which the burning cinders will be extinguished before they escape. For burning anthracite coal, a simple straight pipe, without a deflector or wire netting, is ordinarily used.

QUESTION 121. *What are the proportions and materials usually employed in the construction of smoke-stacks?*

Answer. The inside pipe *R,* fig. 41, is usually made of the same diameter as the cylinders, or an inch or two smaller. For the other dimensions there are no established rules, excepting for the height of the top of the chimney above the rail, which is usually from 14 to 15 feet. The outsides of smoke-stacks are made of sheet iron, but the upper part is now sometimes made of cast iron, so as to withstand the abrasion of the sparks and cinders longer than sheet iron will.

For very warm and damp climates, the outsides of smoke-stacks are sometimes made of copper to resist corrosion, which is very destructive to all iron structures in those countries. The wire netting is made of iron or steel wire from $\frac{1}{10}$ to $\frac{1}{30}$ of an inch in diameter, and with from 3 to 4 meshes to the inch.

QUESTION 122. *What is the pipe N, fig. 41, intended for?*

Answer. It is intended to conduct the exhaust steam and a portion of the smoke from the bottom of the smoke-box, where the steam escapes, to the base of the smoke-stack. In nearly all European engines, the exhaust steam escapes at the top of the smoke-box just below the aperture of the smoke-stack. There is, however, often difficulty in equalizing the draft in the tubes, that is, to get an equal amount of smoke to pass through all of them. By the use of the pipe *P*, called the *inside pipe* or *petticoat pipe*, it is thought that the draft in the tubes can be equalized much better, as a part of the smoke is drawn out of the smoke-box at the top and part at the bottom of the smoke-box. The pipe is usually made in two parts, which slide into each other like a telescope. The distance of the upper end from the top of the smoke-box and that of the lower end from the bottom can thus be increased or diminished, and if the draft is greater through the upper tubes than through the lower ones, or *vice versa*, it can be regulated or equalized by simply raising or lowering the top or bottom of the petticoat pipe. Sometimes this pipe is made with openings and a kind of deflectors over them between the two ends. It is then called a *flounced petticoat pipe*, for obvious reasons.

No exact theory can be stated regarding the proportions of these pipes, or the results effected by them, which can be determined only by practical experience. Some more accurate knowledge concerning them is, however, much needed.

PART VIII.

THE BOILER ATTACHMENTS.

QUESTION 123. *How is water supplied to the boiler to replace that which is converted into steam?*

Answer. It is usually forced into the boiler against the steam pressure by force pumps, but another instrument called an *injector* is now much used.

QUESTION 124. *What is the form of construction and principle of the operation of such force pumps?*

Answer. The ordinary single-acting force pump, fig. 66, used on locomotive and other steam engines consists of a *pump barrel, A A,* which is a cast-iron or brass cylinder in which a tight-fitting piston, *B B,* called the *pump-plunger,* works. This piston or plunger is simply a round rod which works air-tight through what is called a *stuffing box, C,* whose construction will be fully explained hereafter. The plunger receives a reciprocating motion, usually from the piston-rod of the engine, but is sometimes worked by a small crank attached to one of the crank-pins, or by an eccentric on one of the axles. The pump-barrel is connected with the water-tank of the tender by the *suction-pipe, D,* and with the water-space of the boiler by the feed-pipe, *E E.* Over the suction-pipe *D* is a valve, *F,* called the *suction-valve,* which opens upward, and below the feed-pipe, *E,* is another valve, *G,* called the *pressure-valve.* These valves are cylindrical and made of brass, and rest on brass seats, *g*, *g*, to which they are fitted so as to be water-tight. They work in guides, *k*, *k*, called *cages*, the form of which is more clearly shown in the section, fig. 67, and the plan, fig. 68. When the plunger is drawn out of the pump-cylinder it creates a vacuum behind it, and the pres-

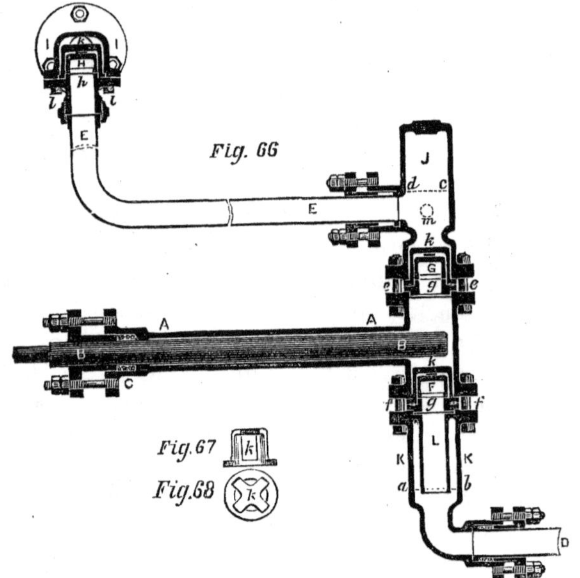

Fig. 67
Fig. 68

sure above the valve *G* closes it, while the atmospheric pressure on the water in the tank forces it into the suction-pipe, opens the valve *F*, and fills the pump-cylinder. When the plunger is forced back again the force with which it presses against the water in the pump-barrel, *A*, closes the valve *F*, and opens the pressure-valve *G*, and the water is then forced through the feed-pipe into the boiler. In order to be certain that the water in the boiler will not flow back into the pump, and also to prevent all the water and steam in the boiler from escaping in case of accident to either the feed-pipe or pump, another valve, *H*, fig. 66, called a *check-valve,* is placed between the feed-pipe and the boiler. The construction of this valve is similar to that of the pressure and suction valves. It is inclosed in a cast-iron or brass case, *I I.* All of these valves have cages in which they work and which also act as stops, which prevent them from rising from their seats further than a certain distance. This distance is called their *lift*, and the successful working of the pumps depends very much on the amount of lift which the valves have. This is usually from $\frac{3}{16}$ to $\frac{1}{2}$ inch.

Over the pressure-valve *G* is a chamber, *J*, called an air chamber. When water is forced into this chamber, it is obvious that as soon as it rises above the mouth of the pipe *E*, the air above the surface, *c d*, of the water will be confined in this chamber. This confined air, being elastic, will be compressed and expanded by the pressure of the water, so that it forms a sort of cushion, which relieves the pump and the pipes from the sudden shocks to which they are subject, owing to the rapid motion of the pump-plunger.

Another air-chamber, *K K*, is sometimes placed below the suction-valve *F.* The object of this is to supply a cushion to relieve the suction-pipe from the shock which is caused by the sudden arrest of the motion of the water in the pipe when the valve *F* is closed. When the pump-plunger is drawn out, the water flows through the valve *F* to fill the vacuum in the pump-barrel, *A A*, and consequently all the water in the suction-pipe is put in motion. As soon as the plunger returns, the valve *F* is closed and the motion of the water is suddenly arrested, thus producing more or less of a shock in the pipe *D*. When the water in the air chamber *K K* rises above the line *a b*, it is evident that the air above that line will be confined in the space surrounding the pipe *L*. This air then forms a cushion in the same way as that in the upper air chamber *J* does, which has already been explained. The advantages of the lower air chamber are, it is thought, more imaginary than real.

QUESTION 125. *How can the pump be taken apart and the valves examined?*

Answer. By removing the bolts *e*, *e*, the upper air chamber can be taken off, and by taking out the bolts *f*, *f*, the lower one can be taken down, and the valves and cages removed. The check-valve *H* can be taken out by removing the bolts *l*, *l*, which hold up the valve-seat *h* and the valve and cage.

QUESTION 126. *How can it be known whether the pump is forcing water into the boiler?*

Answer. To show this a cock, called a *pet-cock*, is attached to the upper air chamber in the position shown by the dotted circle *m*.* By opening this cock, if the pump is working, a strong jet of water will be discharged from it during the backward stroke of the pump-plunger. If the pump is not forcing water into the boiler, or is working imperfectly, the stream discharged from the pet-cock will be weak, and the backward and forward strokes of the plunger will thus not be very definitely indicated by the discharge from the pet-cock.

---

* The pet-cock is sometimes attached to the feed-pipe.

Another small cock is often attached to the lower air chamber, or to the feed-pipe, to allow the water to escape from the pump in cold weather, when the engine is not working, so as to prevent it from freezing.

QUESTION 127. *Why is it necessary to be able to regulate the quantity of water which is forced into the boiler by the pumps?*

Answer. Because when the engine is working hard, that is, pulling a heavy load up a grade, more steam and consequently more water are consumed than when it is not working so hard, and therefore more water must be forced in to supply the place of that which is used in the form of steam. If more water is forced in than is consumed, the water will rise and fill the steam-space and a part of it will then be carried into the cylinders without being evaporated. If too little water is forced into the boiler, the heating surface will not be covered, and there will consequently be danger that those portions which are exposed to the fire will be overheated and injured.

QUESTION 128. *How is the supply of water which is fed into the boiler by the pump regulated?*

Answer. By a cock in the suction-pipe called a *feed-cock,* which can be regulated by the locomotive runner, so that more or less water is supplied to the pump. There is also a valve in the water tank by which the supply of water can be regulated.

QUESTION 129. *On what part of the locomotive are the pumps usually placed?*

Answer. They are usually attached to the frames behind the cylinders, and are worked by the piston-rod, as will be more fully explained hereafter; but they are sometimes placed inside of the frames, that is, between the wheels, and worked from an eccentric on one of the axles, and sometimes they are placed outside of the wheels near the back part of the locomotive, and worked from short cranks attached to the crank-pins.

QUESTION 130. *What provision is made for preventing the water in the pumps from freezing in cold weather?*

Answer. Pipes which communicate with the steam-space of the boiler are attached to each of the suction-pipes, so that, by opening valves in the former, steam is admitted into the suction-pipes to heat the water in them. By admitting this hot water into the pump, it is kept warm, and the water is thus prevented from freezing.

QUESTION 131. *What is an "injector"?*

Answer. It is an instrument in which a jet of steam from the boiler mingles with and forces a continuous jet of water into the same boiler against its own pressure.

QUESTION 132. *What is the action of the injector and what are the names of its essential parts?*

Answer. All injectors have certain parts in common. These may be shown in the simplest form of instrument, as in the fixed-nozzle injector, a section of which (omitting all detail of construction) is shown in fig. 69.

The steam from the boiler, passing through the pipe *A*, enters the *receiving-tube C.* Here it is joined by the water which enters the pipe *B.* The water condenses the steam in the *combining-tube D*, and a water jet is formed which is driven across the *overflow* space *F F*, and enters the *delivery-tube H*, thence past the *check-valve I* into the boiler. During the passage of the water from *D* to *H*, as it passes across the *overflow* space *F*, if too much water has been supplied to the steam, some will escape at this point and flow out through the *overflow nozzle G*, while if too little water has been supplied, air will be drawn in at *G*, and carried into the boiler with the water. The names of the essential parts seem very applicable when we notice that steam is *received* from the boiler at *C*, *combines* with the water at *D*, and both are *delivered* to boiler through *H*.

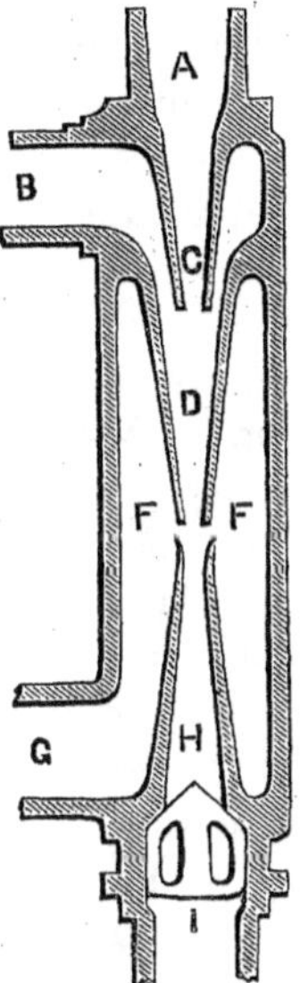

Fig. 69.

QUESTION 133. *How is the operation of the injector explained?*

Answer. Steam escaping from under pressure has a much higher velocity than water would have under the same pressure and condition. The escaping steam from the *receiving-tube* unites with the feed-water in the combining-tube, and gives to this water a velocity greater than it would have if escaping directly from the water-space in the boiler. The power of this water to enter the boiler comes from *its weight* moving at the *velocity* acquired from the steam, and it is thus enabled to overcome the boiler pressure.

This can be illustrated with a wooden croquet ball, which will float on the surface of water and will require considerable force to make it sink. If, however, it is thrown violently into the water, it will sink to a considerable depth before its buoyancy will overcome its momentum, or *actual energy*. If, however, we were to take a very light, hollow wooden or india-rubber ball, no matter how violently we throw it into the water, it will not sink, because the total *actual energy* of any body IS PROPORTIONAL TO ITS WEIGHT MULTIPLIED BY THE SQUARE OF ITS VELOCITY, and therefore if we throw the hollow ball at the same velocity as the solid one, the former will still have much less energy than the latter. Now, as already stated, steam under a given pressure escapes from an orifice with a very much greater velocity than water. But steam being very light, if its weight is multiplied by its velocity its total energy will be comparatively small. Now in the injector, a portion of the high velocity of steam is imparted to the heavy water, because this water is presented to the action of the steam, not in a mass, as in the boiler, but in small quantity and in such a position that it can easily escape, so that it gradually acquires as high a velocity as the escaping steam can impart, and at the same time the steam is condensed, and therefore there is a heavy substance with a high velocity, whose actual energy is sufficient to overcome the pressure in the boiler. If the steam were not condensed we would have a comparatively light substance moving at a high velocity, which, as has already been explained, would have little actual energy, and would therefore not overcome the boiler pressure.

QUESTION 134. *Does this involve any principle like a perpetual motion, or of work done without consumption of power?*

Answer. No, the steam escapes *as steam,* and is returned to the boiler *as water* with its bulk reduced, say 1,000 times, and if it carries with it twenty times its weight of fresh feed-water, there would still be a loss of pressure or effective force in the boiler sufficient to do the work required in introducing the water.

QUESTION 135. *Will the injector feed hot water?*

Answer. The instrument will not work when the feed-water is too hot to condense the steam, for the reasons given above, and the amount of water thrown is always the greatest when the feed-water is the coldest. Steam at a low pressure can be condensed more readily than steam of higher pressure, because it contains less heat. The feed-water may be used hotter to condense low steam than to condense high steam. In using the injector, the lower the boiler pressure the hotter may be the water within certain limits, the limit being the possible condensation of the steam.

QUESTION 136. *Will a "fixed-nozzle" injector, such as has been described, answer as a boiler feeder on locomotives?*

Answer. It will answer at some one pressure of steam, to which pressure it may have been adapted in making the instrument, and at that pressure it will work admirably; but it will not work satisfactorily at any other pressure, either higher or lower, and has not much range in quantity of water delivered.

QUESTION 137. *What is required to make an injector work at different pressures?*

Answer. The instrument must be so made that the water passage between the receiving tube and the combining tube can be varied in size. This is usually done by making the combining and receiving tubes conical and moving the former to or from the latter, thus contracting or enlarging the water space. Such adjustment must be made at each change of steam pressure in the boiler. If this adjustment is made *by hand*, as in some kinds of injectors, it requires constant attention, if the steam pressure varies frequently.

QUESTION 138. *How has this regulation been accomplished without such attention?*

Answer. In the SELF-REGULATING INJECTOR, fig. 70, by using the escape water at overflow to push the combining tube towards the receiving tube and the in draught of water at the same place to pull the combining tube away from the receiving tube. This can be explained as follows:

The case, *G*, of the instrument has two inlets, one for steam, the other for water, the two being separated by the plate *F F.* Steam passes into the *receiving tube*, *A*, and its escape is regulated by a taper-plug, *B*, worked by a screw, *B*, and handle, *H.* At the upper end of the *combining tube*, *C*, where it swells out into a bell mouth, is a piston, *N N*, sliding in the case; the lower end at *C* is guided by the upper end of the *delivery tube D.* The delivery tube *D* is stationary. The *overflow* opening is at *O.* The action of this instrument may be thus described: Steam entering the receiving tube *A* escapes through its lower end when the plug *B* has been drawn back. It unites with the water surrounding it in the space *N N*, is condensed and passes with the feed-water into the delivery tube, *D*, and thence into the boiler. If too much water enters the combining tube, some will escape at the overflow, *O*, and filling the space below the piston, *N N*, will force the combining tube up towards the receiving tube, and, thus contracting the space between them, will diminish the water supply; while,

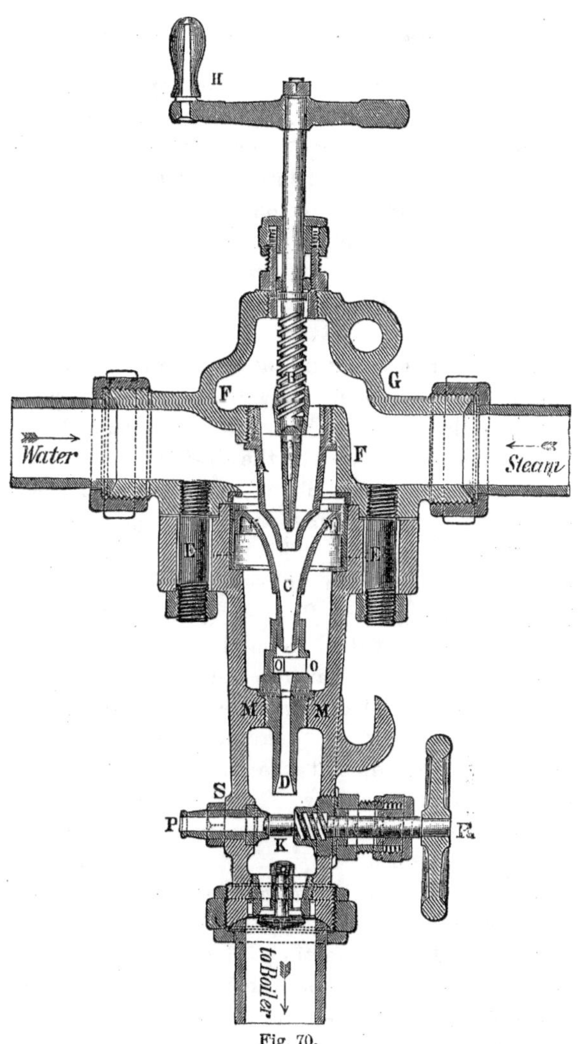

Fig. 70.

11*

if it gets too little water in this space, it will take some in at the overflow *O*, and thus draw down the piston *N N*, and enlarge the space, giving more water to the instrument. This self-regulating principle enables the instrument to continue working efficiently, no matter how much the steam pressure in the boiler varies.

QUESTION 139. *How do you start this kind of injector to working?*

Answer. You screw in the plug *B* by means of the handle *H*, and open wide the starting-valve *K* by the handle *R*. This valve being open allows the water pouring through the instrument to escape through the pipe *P*. Steam being admitted from the boiler, some of it will pass through a small hole in the centre of the plug *B*. This will give sufficient steam to draw some water in and establish a current through the tubes and out at *P*, when, if the plug be drawn back by means of the handle H, more steam will enter and more water be drawn in until an escaping stream of considerable velocity is driven out at *P*. Then the plug *B* may be drawn back all the way. The valve *K* may be closed, and the jet will force open the check-valve (just below *K*) and flow into the boiler, after which the instrument can be regulated by means of the handle *H*.

QUESTION 140. *What attachments are needed besides the instrument to render it effective?*

Answer. First, a starting-valve in a convenient position to admit steam from the boiler; a water-check in the feed-pipe in connection with an alarm-check; these last are to notify the engine-runner whenever the injector ceases to work, as would be the case when too small an amount of steam had been admitted, in which case the steam is driven back into the feed-water pipe and, being partly stopped by means of the water-check, lifts the valve of the alarm-check and escapes into the waste-pipe.

QUESTION 141. *In what position and in what location on the engine should the injector be placed?*

Answer. The injector may be placed vertically, on its side, that is horizontally or inclined, or even be placed upside down, as it will work in either position, but it must be accessible. If it can be placed below the water level in the tank, as conveniently as not, so that the water will flow to it and yet so that the instrument can be operated, it will start more readily than if it has to lift the water. It should be on the right-hand side of the engine if it is to be used as the regular feed in running. If it is to be used only as a feeder when the engine is standing, it may be placed on the left-hand side.

QUESTION 142. *What is required to keep the instrument in working order?*

Answer. Constant use is better than occasional use. The piston that moves the combining-tube must slide freely in the case. The starting-valve must be in good order and capable of being closed tight. Steam leaking into the instrument when it is not working heats it up and causes delay in starting. All the pipe connections must be tight, so as to prevent the leaking in of air. The pipe carrying steam to the instrument should be from such part of the boiler as will insure the use of dry steam, and the waste-pipe must not be contracted. The instrument represented by the engraving is the kind manufactured by Messrs.

Fig. 71.
Scale $\frac{1}{4}$ in.=1 foot.

LIST OF PARTS DESIGNATED BY LETTERS OF REFERENCE IN FIG. 71.

A, Furnace Door.
B, *B*, Driving Wheels.
C, Driving Axle.
D, *D*, Suction Pipes.
E, Ash Pan Damper.
F, *F*, Foot Steps for getting on and off the Locomotive.
G, *G*, Hand Holds for getting on and off the Locomotive.
H, *I*, Cab.
J, *J*, Doors in front of Cab.
K, *K*, Windows in front of Cab.
L, Steam Gauge.
M, Spring Balance.
N, Steam Gauge Lever,
O′ O, Throttle Lever.
P, Water Gauge.
Q, Tallow Can.
R, Drip Pipe for Gauge Cock.
T′ T, Rod for operating Feed Cock.
T′, Regulator for Feed Cock.
U V, Reverse Lever.
W, Whistle.
X, Blow-Off Cock.
Z, *Z*, Frames.
a, *a*, Heater Cocks.
a, *a′*, Heater Pipe.
b, Blower Cock.
c, *c*, Oil Cups for oiling Main Valves.
d, Handle for opening Valves in Sand Box.
e, *e*, Handles for opening Pet Cocks.
f, Handle for opening Cylinder Cocks.
g, Whistle Lever.
h,′ Whistle Handle.
h, Rod connecting Whistle Handle to Whistle Lever.
j, Handle for left hand Feed Cock.
k, *k*, Fastenings for Cab Doors.
l, *l*, Handles for opening Ash Pan Dampers.
m m, Lever for shaking Grate Bars.
n, Bell Crank for opening front Ash Pan Damper.
o, *o*, Check Chains.
p, Pipe for carrying off water from Gauge Cocks.
s, *s*, *s*, *s*, Gauge Cocks.
w, Handle for opening Blow-Off Cock.

William Sellers & Co. of Philadelphia. Beside this, Mack's and several other kinds of injectors are now used.

QUESTION 143. *How can the height of the water in the boiler be known?*

Answer. Two appliances are used by which the height of the water in the boiler can be observed. These are: 1. *Gauge* or *try cocks.* 2. The *glass water gauge.*

Every locomotive is provided with four or more gauge-cocks, which are usually placed at the back end of the boiler, where they can easily be seen and

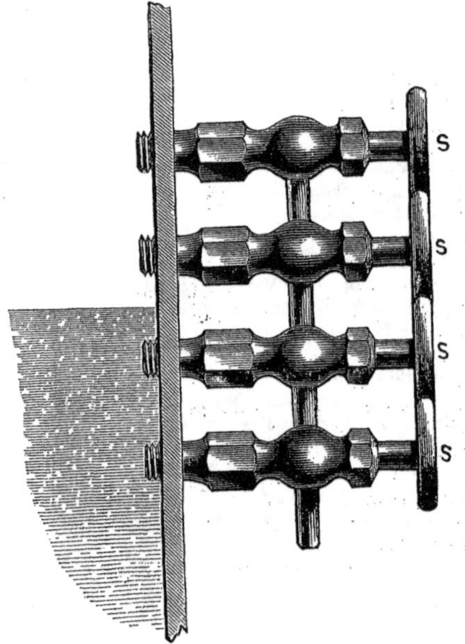

Fig. 72. Scale ¼.

reached. These cocks, *s*, *s*, *s*, *s*, are shown in fig. 71, which represents the back end of a locomotive, and to which frequent reference will be made. They are also shown on a larger scale in fig. 72, which represents the end plate of the boiler in section. They communicate with the inside of the boiler and are so placed that one is three or four inches above the other. The two upper cocks are placed above the point where the surface of the water should be when the engine is working, and the two lower ones below it, so that the upper ones communicate with the steam space and the lower ones with the water. When these cocks are opened, if the water is at its proper height, steam is discharged from the two upper ones, and water from the two lower ones.

When a gauge-cock which communicates with the steam space is first opened, it is usually filled with condensed water, so that it should usually be kept open for a little while until this water is discharged. If the upper cocks are opened and continue to discharge *water*, they indicate that there is *too much* water in the boiler; on the other hand, if steam is discharged when the lower cocks are opened, then there is too little water in the boiler, and the heating surface is in danger of being exposed to the fire without being covered with water, and consequently overheated, or as it is called "burned," and so injured as to become too weak to bear the strain to which it is subjected by the pressure of the steam. There is then great danger that the crown sheet may be crushed down by the pressure of the steam above it, or that the boiler may be exploded. Even if no accident occur, the boiler is in great danger of permanent injury from overheating when the water is allowed to get too low.

Below the gauge-cocks *s, s, s, s,* fig. 71, an inclined cylinder, *R,* called a *drip-pipe,* is placed with openings to receive the water and steam which are discharged from the cocks. This water is conducted away by the pipe *p.*

The *water-gauge, P,* fig. 71, which is shown in section in fig. 73, consists of an upright* glass tube, *a a,* which is from one-half to three-quarters of an inch in diameter, and from 12 to 15 inches long. The glass is about one-eighth of an inch thick. At its ends it communicates with the steam and water of the boiler through brass elbows, *b, c.* The openings in these elbows, which communicate with the boiler, are closed by the valves or plugs, *d, e,* which are worked by screws and handles, *f, g.* The glass tube, when it is attached to the elbows, is made steam-tight by rubber rings, which are pressed tight around the tube by *packing-nuts, h, i.* The elbows are provided with the valves, *d, e,* so that in case the glass tube breaks the steam and water can be shut off, so as not to escape through the elbows. The lower elbow is provided with a blow-off cock, *k,* through which any sediment or dirt which collects in the glass tube or elbows can be blown out. When the valves in the upper and lower elbows are opened the steam flows into the glass tube through the upper one, and water through the lower one, and the water assumes a position in the glass tube on a level with the surface of that in the inside of the boiler; that is, the position of the water

*Sometimes these tubes are, for convenience, inclined, as shown in fig. 71.

in the boiler becomes visible in the glass tube. On account of the constant variations of the water in the boiler, the column of water in the glass never remains

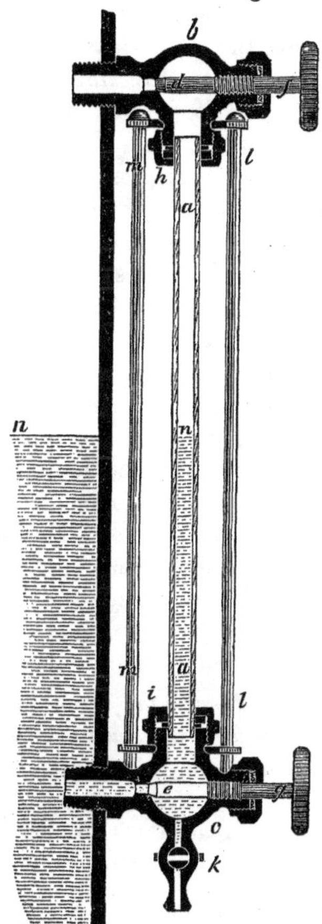

Fig. 73.
Scale 3 in.=1 foot.

stationary, but plays up and down as long as the boiler is working. But if the communication between the glass tube and the boiler is closed, then the water in the tube becomes stationary and the water gauge is useless. In order that there may be no obstruction of the glass tube by mud or dirt from the water, it must be *blown out* often. To do this the lower valve, *e*, is closed, and the blow-off cock, *k*, and the steam valve, *d*, are opened. The steam pressure in the tube on top of the column of water will force it out of the blow-off cock, and the mud and dirt will be carried with it.

If from any cause the glass tube is broken, first of all the water-valve *e* should be closed and then the steam-valve *d*, so as to prevent the hot water and steam which will escape from the broken glass from scalding those who are working the engine. By unscrewing the nuts *h* and *i* the old glass can easily be removed and a new one substituted in its place.* Care should be taken in putting in new glasses not to screw the packing nuts down any more than just sufficiently to make the rubber rings steam-tight around the glass tubes. If they are screwed too tight they are apt to produce a strain on the tube, so that the slightest expansion by heat or contraction from cold will break it.

QUESTION 144. *How is the steam pressure in boilers prevented from exceeding a certain limit?*

Answer. By what are called *safety valves.* These consist of circular openings, *a*, fig. 74, about three inches in diameter placed usually on the top of the dome,† and covered by a valve, *b*, which is pressed

*Extra glasses should always be carried with an engine so as to be substituted in case of accident to the one in use.

† One of these, *v*, is shown in fig. 41.

down either by a lever, *c c,′* and spring, *d,* as shown in fig. 74, or by a spring alone, as in fig. 76. Two of these valves are usually placed on the top of the dome, so that if one gets out of order the other one will allow

Fig. 74.
Scale 1½ in.=1 foot.

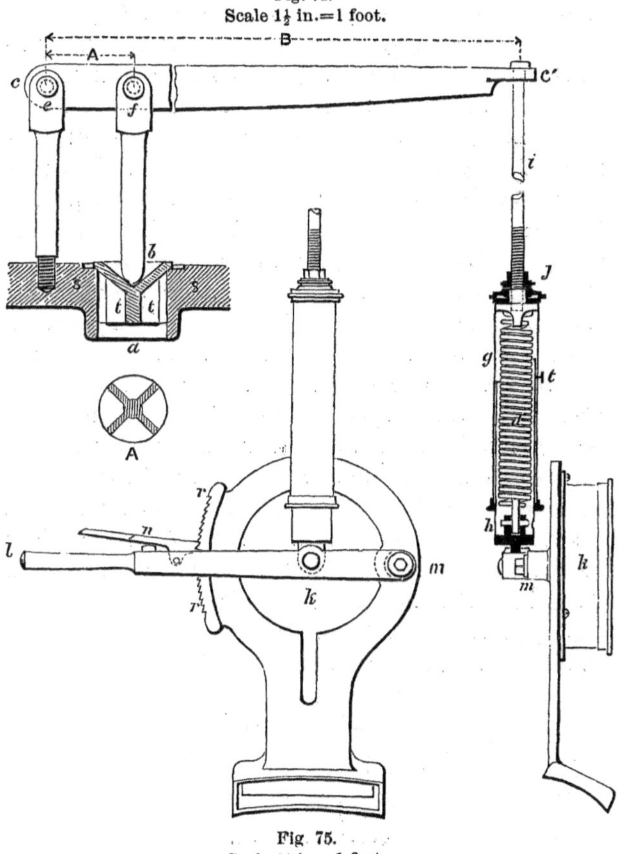

Fig. 75.
Scale 1½ in.=1 foot.

the steam to escape as soon as its pressure exceeds that which, it has been decided, the boiler can safely bear. This pressure, in locomotive boilers, is usually from 100 to 130 pounds per square inch.

QUESTION 145. *How is the amount of pressure which must bear on top of a safety-valve determined?*

Answer. This pressure is determined BY MULTIPLYING THE AREA OF THE OPENING FOR THE VALVE IN SQUARE INCHES BY THE GREATEST STEAM PRESSURE, IN POUNDS PER SQUARE INCH, WHICH THE BOILER IS INTENDED TO BEAR. Thus, if the opening for a safety-valve is three inches in diameter, its area will be seven square inches, and, therefore, if the greatest steam pressure which it is intended that the boiler shall bear is 100 lbs. per square inch, the valve must be pressed down with a pressure equivalent to $7 \times 100 = 700$ pounds. If the pressure on the valve is produced by a lever, as in fig. 74,* then the total weight of the safety-valve must be MULTIPLIED BY THE SHORT ARM OF THE LEVER, (or the distance *A* between the centre of the fulcrum *e* and that of the load *f*,) AND DIVIDED BY *B*, THE TOTAL LENGTH OF THE LEVER. In fig. 74 the short arm of the lever is $3\frac{1}{2}$ inches, and the whole length 35 inches; therefore if the valve is to be pressed down with a pressure of 700 pounds, the pressure on the end of the lever would be calculated as follows:

$$\frac{700 \times 3\frac{1}{2}}{35} = 70 \text{ lbs}$$

The spring *d* must therefore pull down on the end of the lever with a tension equal to 70 pounds. When

* The lever is represented in the engraving with a piece broken out, in order to save room.

the pressure of the spring bears directly on the valve, as shown in fig. 76, then the tension of the spring must be just equal to the pressure on the valve. This tension is produced by screwing down the nuts, *c, c.* The spring *d,* which produces the requisite pressure on the end of the safety-valve lever, fig. 74, is arranged inside of two cylinders, *g* and *h,* which slide over or into each other like the sections of a telescope. This arrangement is called a *spring-balance.* The spring, *d,* is attached to the covered ends and draws them towards each other. The upper cylinder *g* is connected by a rod, *i,* to the flattened end of the lever *c′*, which has a hole drilled through it to receive the rod. The other end of the rod is screwed into the upper cylinder *g.* This rod is sometimes arranged so that it can be either lengthened or shortened by the nut *j.* By lengthening or shortening the distance, the tension of the spring is either diminished or increased. The lower cylinder of the spring-balance, represented in fig. 74, is attached to a lever, *m,* which is fastened to the back of the *steam-gauge k.* This is shown more clearly by fig. 75, which represents the back of the gauge, and also the lever, *l m,* whose fulcrum is at *m.* The spring-balance is attached to the lever at *k.* By drawing down the lever the tension of the spring is increased, and by raising it up it is diminished. The lever is held in any desired position by the latch, *n,* and the ratchet *r r.* By this contrivance, which is employed on the engines built at the Grant and also at the Baldwin Locomotive Works, the pressure on the valve can at once be either increased or diminished, which it is often desirable to do, especially when an engine is not at work. The spring-balance is shown in fig. 71, and is indicated by the letter ***M*** and the lever by *N.* Unless the pressure of the steam exceeds that on top of the valve, it will of course not be opened. As there is always danger that a safety-valve or some of its attachments may become corroded or otherwise disordered, so that it will not act promptly or with certainty, it is desirable to open it frequently, so as to be sure that it is in good working order. To do this the pressure on the valve must be reduced below that in the boiler, which can very conveniently be done with the *spring-balance* lever which has been described.

The lower cylinder of the spring-balance sometimes carries an index or pointer, *t*, fig. 74, which protrudes through a slot in the cylinder *g*, and indicates the amount of pressure of the spring on a scale marked along the slot on the outside of the cylinder. If it is desired that the safety-valve should open when the steam pressure reaches 100 or any other number of pounds per square inch, the spring-balance is subjected to a tension which will bring an amount of pressure on the top of the safety-valve equal in pounds per square inch of its surface to that of the steam pressure desired.*

There should always be some provision made which will render it impossible to increase the steam pressure beyond that which it has been determined that the boiler will safely bear. This is usually done by arranging one of the safety-valves with a lever, as shown in fig. 74, and the other without, like that in fig. 76. The latter is often covered and sealed or locked

* In loading a safety-valve allowance must always be made for the weight of the lever and the valve.

up, so as to be beyond the control of the locomotive runner.

The safety-valves are usually fitted into conical seats, *S S*, figs. 74 and 76, so as to be perfectly steam-tight, and are made with wings or guides, *t*, *t*, the form of which is shown in the sectional plan *A*, figs. 74 and 76, under the valve. These guides are intended to keep the valves in the proper positions in relation to their seats.

As soon as the steam pressure under the valves becomes greater than the pressure of the springs on top of them, the valves will be lifted up and the steam will escape until the pressure in the boiler is relieved. It will be seen, however, that although the surface of the valve which is exposed to the pressure of the steam is equal to the area of the opening for the valve, after it is lifted from its seat and the steam escapes all around the edge, a larger surface will be exposed to the pressure of the escaping steam. For this rea-

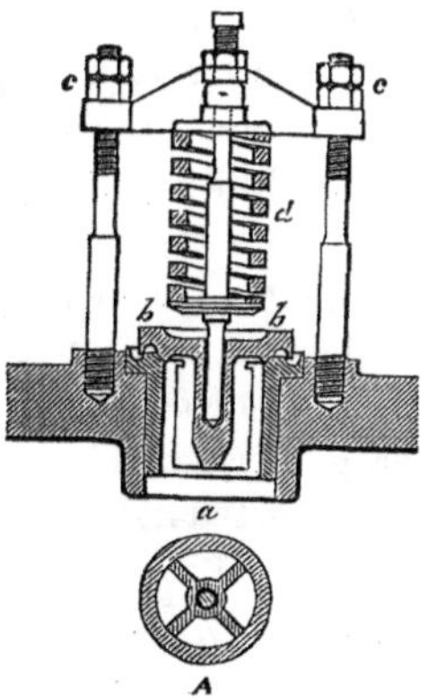

Fig. 76. Scale ⅛.

son, it will be found that after a valve is opened steam will escape, or "*blow off*," as it is termed, until the pressure is several pounds lower than it was when the valve first opened. Advantage has been taken of this fact in the valve shown in fig. 76, which is called the "Richardson" valve, which is now much used. The top of this valve is made larger in diameter, so as to expose more area to the escaping steam. Grooves are also made around the edge of the valve and the seat. These, it is claimed, produce some sort of reflex action of the steam, which keeps the valve open longer than it otherwise would be.

QUESTION 146. *How is the steam pressure in the boiler indicated?*

Answer. By an instrument called a *steam-gauge.* There are a great variety of such instruments made, but they may all be divided into two classes, and they all operate upon one of two principles. In the one class the pressure of the steam acts upon a diaphragm or plate of some kind, as shown in fig 77, which represents a section of a gauge of this kind; *a b* is a metal plate made with circular corrugations, as shown in section and also by the shading in fig. 78, which represents a front view of the gauge with a part of the dial-plate removed. The steam enters by the pipe *c* and the small opening *d,* and fills the chamber *e* behind the metal plate or diaphragm. The corrugations of the latter give it sufficient elasticity, so that when the pressure is exerted behind it, it will be pressed outward by the steam. If it were flat, it is plain that it would not yield, or only to a very slight degree, to the pressure of the steam. In the centre of the diaphragm on the outside is a pin or stud, *f,* which bears against the plate. This stud is attached to a bent lever or "*bell-crank*,"* *g h k*, whose fulcrum is at *h*. To the outer end, *k*, a rod, *l*, figs. 77 and 78, is attached, the lower end of which is connected to the short arm *m* of a toothed segment, *n*, whose fulcrum is at *o*. This segment gears into a small pinion, *p*, which is attached to a spindle or shaft, which carries a poin-

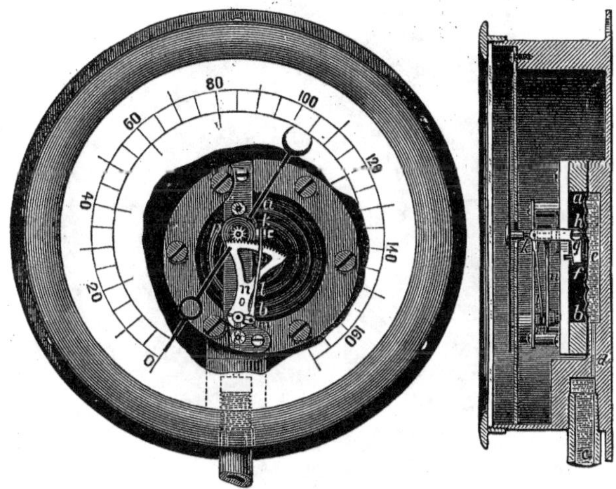

Fig. 78. Fig. 77.

ter, fig. 78. It is obvious now that if the diaphragm, *a b*, is pressed outward, it will move the bent lever *k h g*, the motion of which will be communicated by the rod *l* to the toothed segment *n*, which will in turn revolve the pinion *p*, and thus move the hand or index. We have selected for this illustration one of many forms of this kind of gauge. The mechanical appliances for communicating the motion of the diaphragm

* A *bell-crank* is a lever with an elbow in it.

to the index or pointer are different in the gauges made by different manufacturers. The form of the diaphragm also differs. In some cases it is made of a metal plate; in others a spiral spring is used, covered with india-rubber to make it steam-tight. The steam-gauge represented by figs. 77 and 78 is the form manufactured by M. B. Edson, of New York.

Fig. 79.

In the other class of gauges, shown in fig. 79, the steam acts upon a bent metal tube, *a b c*, usually of a flattened or elliptical section. It may not be known to all readers that if a tube bent, say in the form of the letter U or C, is subjected to the pressure of a liquid or gas on the inside, the force exerted by the pressure has a tendency to straighten out the tube.

This is due to the tendency which a tube of an elliptical or flat section has to change the shape of the latter and approximate to a circular form when the inside is subjected to a pressure. Thus let *A B*, fig. 80, represent a cross section, and *a b d c*, a longitudinal section of a part of such a tube contained between two radii, *O a* and *O b*, drawn from the centre *O* of the curve in which the tube is bent. If now we subject the inside of *A B* to a pressure it will have a ten-

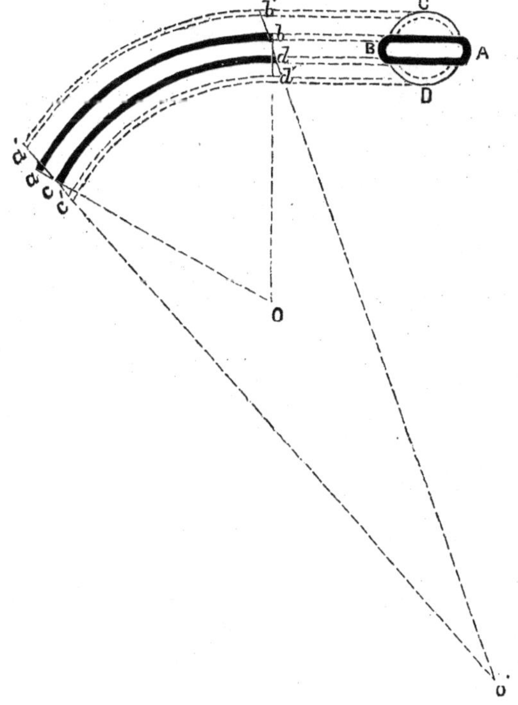

Fig. 80.

dency to assume the form of the circle *C D*, and would then be represented in the longitudinal section by the dotted lines *a′ b′ d′ c′*. If now we draw radial lines through *a′ c′* and *b′ d′*, it will be found that they intersect at *O′*, instead of *O*, which was the original centre of the curve of the tube. It will be seen that as the section of the tube approximates to the form of a circle, the portion *a b* which is outside the curve will be moved farther from the centre, while the other side, *c d*, is moved nearer to it. As indicated by the radial lines, when this occurs either the outside must be lengthened and the inside shortened, to conform to the radial lines *a O* and *b O*, or else the tube will be straightened so that the radial lines will assume the position *a′ O′* and *b′ O′*.

The phenomenon of the straightening of the bent tubes of steam gauges is frequently attributed to the difference between the area of the inside and outside of the curve. This error was shared by the writer, until the fallacy of the reasoning which supported it was pointed out to him.

In the gauge represented in fig. 79, (in which the dial-plate is removed), one end, *c*, of the tube is attached at *d* to a lever which has a toothed segment, *e*, at the other end. The end *a* of the tube is connected with the lever at *f*. The connection at *d*, therefore, forms the fulcrum of the lever. It is obvious that as the two ends of the bent tube are forced apart by the steam pressure, the lever and the segment have motion imparted to them. The latter gears into a pinion on the spindle of the index or pointer, *r r*, which thus indicates on the dial the degree of pressure in the tube. The latter is connected with the boiler by a tube attached at *g*. Various forms of this kind of steam-gauge are also made, but all act on essentially the same principle.

The position of the steam-gauge on the engine is shown at *M*, in fig. 71.

Question 147. ***Why is the pipe which connects the steam-gauge with the boiler bent as shown in fig.* 71?**

Answer. To prevent the hot steam from coming in contact with the metal plate or tube, as it is found that the heat of the steam affects their elasticity. When a bent tube is used, the steam from the boiler is condensed and fills the bent portion so that when the steam pressure comes on the surface of the water it forces it up the other leg of the tube into the gauge. A cock is attached to this pipe so that the steam can be shut off in case the gauge should get out of order or require to be removed while there is steam in the boiler.

Question 148. ***How can the accuracy of a steam-gauge be tested?***

Answer. When the gauge is in good working order, the index or pointer moves easily with every change of pressure in the boiler, and if the steam is shut off from the gauge, the index should always go back to 0. In order to determine the accuracy of its indications, however, they should be tested with a column of mercury. This consists of a long, vertical tube, terminating at its base in a closed vessel filled with mercury. The gauge is then attached to the top of this vessel and water or oil is forced into the vessel on top of the mercury and into the gauge. A pressure of one pound per square inch will force up the column of the mercury 2.04 inches, so that by graduating the tube

13

into spaces that distance apart, the divisions will indicate the pressure in pounds per square inch. Thus, a pressure of 50 pounds would force up the column of mercury 102 inches, and with 100 pounds pressure the column would rise 204 inches, and therefore, when the mercury reaches these or any other points, the steam-gauge, if it is accurate, should indicate equivalent pressures.

The ordinary steam-gauges are very liable to get out of order, and therefore they should be frequently tested to ascertain whether their indications are correct.

QUESTION 149. *What is the steam whistle, and for what purpose is it used?*

Answer. The *steam-whistle, W*, fig. 71, and shown in section on a larger scale in fig. 81, consists of an inverted metal cup or bell, *A*, made usually of brass. The lower edge of this cup is placed immediately over an annular opening, *a a*, from which the steam escapes and strikes the edge of the cup or bell, which produces a deep or shrill sound, according to the size or proportions of the whistle. The annular opening *a a* is formed by the plate or cover, *a a*, which nearly fills the mouth of the cup *B*, which is attached to the stem *c*. The latter is screwed into the top, *D*, of the dome. Communication with the steam-space of the boiler is either opened or closed by a valve, *b*, which is attached to a sort of spindle, *d*, which extends upward inside of the stem *c*. This spindle does not entirely fill the opening in the stem *c*, so that the steam which enters when the valve *b* is opened rises and escapes through the holes *e, e, e*, into the cup *B* and out through the annular opening *a a*. The valve is opened by the lever *E*, whose fulcrum is at *f*. The end *g* of this lever is connected by a rod, *h*, figs. 81 and 71, with the cab, and by a suitable handle or lever, *h' h'*, fig. 71, it can be opened and the whistle be blown

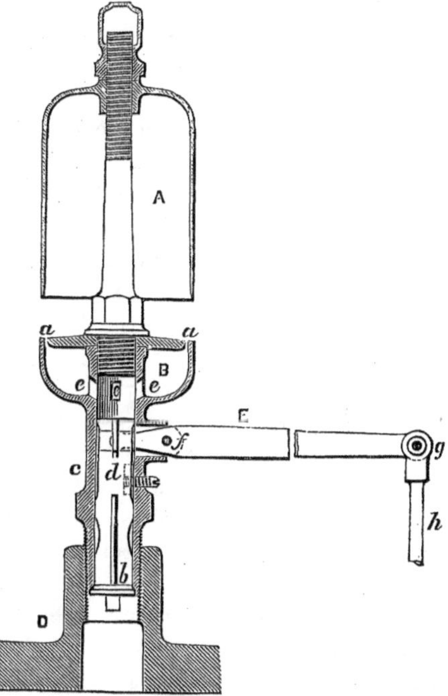

Fig. 81. Scale 1½ in.=1 foot.

at any time by the locomotive runner or fireman to give signals to the trainmen or of the approach of a train to a station, or to warn persons to get off of the track.

QUESTION 150. *How is a locomotive boiler emptied and cleaned?*

Answer. One or two large cocks, called *blow-off* cocks, *X*, fig. 71, are placed near the bottom of the fire-box, either in front or behind, and sometimes on the side. By opening either of these the water in the boiler is blown out, and much of the loose mud and dirt is carried out with the water. The cock *X*, fig. 71, is opened by a handle, *w*, which is connected with the cock by a rod.

In order to clean out the mud and scale which are not entirely loose, what are called *mud-holes* or *hand-holes* are placed in the corners of the fire-box near the bottom. These are oval-shaped holes, about 4½ inches long and 2½ inches wide, and covered with two metal plates, one of which is put inside the boiler and the other outside, and fastened with a bolt through both. Another hand-hole is sometimes placed in the bottom of the front tube-sheet. When the boiler is emptied of water these hand-holes are uncovered, and as much dirt is removed as can be scraped out of these holes. A hose pipe is then inserted and a strong stream of water is forced in, which washes out nearly all the loose dirt, so as to leave the boiler comparatively clean.

When the water is very impure, what is called a *mud-drum*, *M*, fig. 41, is used. Much of the mud and dirt is deposited in this receptacle, from which it can easily be removed by taking off the cast-iron cover on the bottom of the drum. The cover is also provided with a blow-off cock, which is shown in the figure referred to.

QUESTION 151. *What other attachments are there to the boiler of a locomotive?*

Answer. There are two cocks, *a, a*, fig. 71, called

heater-cocks, which are connected with pipes to the feed-pipes *D D*, to admit steam to the latter to prevent the water in them from freezing. There is also another cock, *b*, called a *blower-cock*, which is connected to the smoke-stack by a pipe *b*, *b*. Steam is conducted through this pipe and escapes up the chimney in a jet, thus producing a draft when the engine is not working. This arrangement is called a ***blower*** and is used to blow the fire when the engine is standing still. The action of the jet is similar to that of the exhaust steam which escapes up the chimney, excepting that the steam from the jet escapes in a continuous stream instead of distinct "puffs," as it does when it is liberated alternately from one end of the cylinders and then from the other.

T' is a handle which is connected by a rod, *T' T*, with the feed-cock (not shown in the engraving) in the pipe *D*. This cock can be opened or closed by the handle, and the supply of water fed into the boiler by the pump can thus be regulated. *J* is a handle on the other side of the engine, for regulating the working of the pump on that side.

e, *e* are handles, also connected by rods with the pet-cocks on the pumps. These cocks can thus be opened or closed, and it can then be known whether the pumps are working.

A is the furnace door, which is fastened by a latch. The latter has a chain, *Q*, attached to it by which it can be conveniently opened or closed. The door also has a circular register with six holes to admit air into the furnace. These holes can be opened or closed by the revolving circular disc shown in the engraving.

QUESTION 152. *How are the grates constructed?*

Answer. As has already been explained, they are made usually of cast-iron bars,* *A, A, A,* figs. 82 and 83, called *grate-bars.* Fig. 82 is a plan, and fig. 83 a horizontal section of one form of grate. The bars in this kind of grate are usually cast in pairs, or some-

Fig. 82. Scale ¾ in. = 1 foot.

* In Europe and in some few cases in this country they are made of wrought iron.

Fig. 83. Scale ¾ in. = 1 foot.

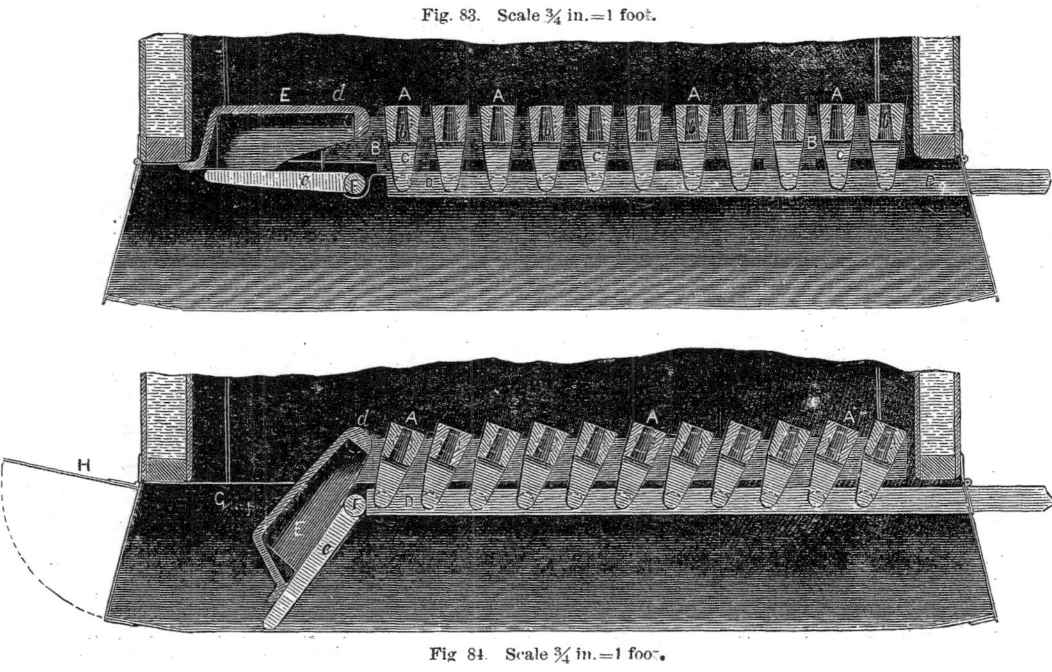

Fig 84. Scale ¾ in. = 1 foot.

times three or more are cast together. They are made wider on the top than on the bottom edges, as shown in the section, fig. 83, so that cinders and ashes will fall through easily, and also to give free access to the air from below. They are usually from $\frac{3}{4}$ to $1\frac{1}{2}$ inches wide on the top, and about $\frac{3}{4}$ inch on the lower edges. The spaces between the bars are made from $\frac{1}{2}$ to $1\frac{1}{4}$ inches wide. For burning wood the bars are placed comparatively close together and are stationary, but for burning bituminous coal they are usually made so that they can be moved, in order to shake or stir up the fire, just as is necessary in an ordinary stove or grate fire. In the grate we have illustrated the bars, *A, A* are cast in pairs, and run crosswise of the fire-box. The ends are made with a sort of journals, *b, b,* which rest on two supports, *B, B,* called *bearing bars,* which have suitable indentations to receive the ends of the grate-bars. The latter have arms, *C, C,* fig. 83, cast on the under side, to which a bar, *D D,* is attached. By moving this bar back and forth, the grate-bars have a rocking motion imparted to them, as shown in fig. 84. It is evident that in this way the fire over the whole surface of the grates will be disturbed or shaken. The bar, *D D,* is moved by a lever, *m m,* shown in fig 71. An extension piece, not shown in fig 71, is used with the lever *m m,* so as to increase its length; but it is removed after it has been used, so as not to be in the way of the fireman. Grates which have movable bars are called *shaking* or *rocking grates.* A great variety of such grates are made and in use, to describe which would require more room than is available here.

For burning anthracite coal what are called *water-*

grates are used. These consist of wrought-iron tubes, 2 inches in diameter outside, which are fastened in the front and back plates of the fire-box and are inclined upward from the front end, so that there will be a continued circulation of water through them to keep them cool and thus prevent them from being burned out by the intense heat of the fire.

QUESTION 153. *How is the fire removed from the fire-box when it is necessary to do so?*

Answer. In bituminous coal burning engines, what is called a *drop-door, E E,* figs. 82, 83 and 84, is provided for that purpose. This door is supported partly on journals, *d, d,* similar to those in the grate-bars, on which it can turn, and is held up or prevented from dropping by arms, *e, e,* attached to a shaft, *F F.* This shaft is operated by a lever, *f f,* fig. 82, outside the fire-box.

When the arms are in the position represented in fig. 83, the drop-door is held up in the place in which it is shown; but when they are turned as in fig. 84, the door falls down so that the burning coal can be taken out of the opening at *G,* and, by raising up the ash-pan damper, *H,* fig. 84, can be raked out on the track or into suitable pits usually provided for this purpose. The drop-doors are sometimes perforated so as to admit air to the fuel on top of them.

The grates for burning anthracite coal usually have about four solid wrought-iron bars between that number of tubes. These bars can be withdrawn, and the fire then falls into the ash-pan through the opening left by the withdrawal of the tubes.

QUESTION 154. *How are the dampers of the ash-pan operated?*

Answer. They are connected by suitable rods and levers with two handles, *l*, *l*, fig. 71, which are raised or lowered, thus opening or closing the dampers.

PART IX.

THE THROTTLE-VALVE AND STEAM PIPES.

QUESTION 155. *How is the steam admitted to and the supply regulated or shut off from the cylinders?*

Answer. By a valve, *h*, fig. 41, called a *throttle-valve*, which is usually placed at the end of the pipe *I*, near the top of the dome. Throttle-valves are sometimes placed in the smoke-box at the front end, *n*, fig. 41, of the dry-pipe. Until within a few years they consisted of plain slide-valves which covered openings similar in form to the steam-ports, but smaller in size. The pressure on such valves is of course greatest when there is no steam underneath, which is the case when the valves are closed. It is then very difficult to open them, and as it is important that the supply of steam admitted to the cylinders when the locomotive is started should be easily regulated, such valves are objectionable, and therefore the form has been introduced which is illustrated in fig. 41, and also on a larger scale in fig. 85, which represents a longitudinal section of the throttle-pipe and valve. This is what is called a *double-poppet valve,* and consists of two circular discs, *a* and *b*, which cover two corresponding openings in the end of the pipe *I*. When these discs are raised up, as shown in fig. 85, steam flows in around their edges, as represented by the darts. It will be observed that the steam pressure in the boiler comes on top of the disc *a* and against the under side of *b*. The pressure on the one thus neutralizes or balances that on the other. If the two discs were of the same size, the pressure of the one would be exactly the same as on the other; but as they are joined together and are made to fit steam-tight on their seats by what are called ***countersunk joints,*** their diameters must be some-

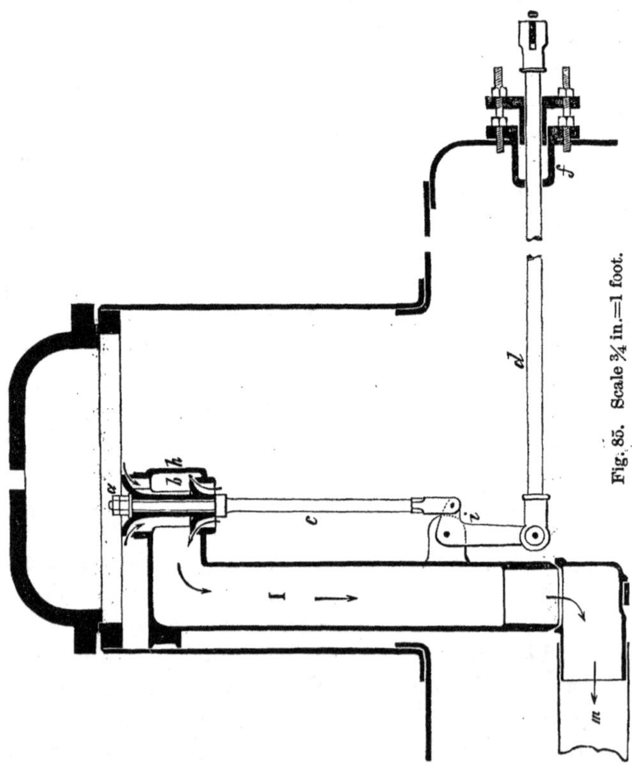

Fig. 85. Scale ¾ in.=1 foot.

what larger than the openings they cover. The only practicable way, therefore, by which the lower disc *b* can be introduced into the end *h* of the pipe *I* so as to cover the lower opening is through the upper opening *a*. For this reason the lower disc must be made smaller than the upper one, and therefore the pressure on the upper one, being in proportion to its size, has a constant tendency to close the valve. As it is of the greatest importance that a throttle-valve

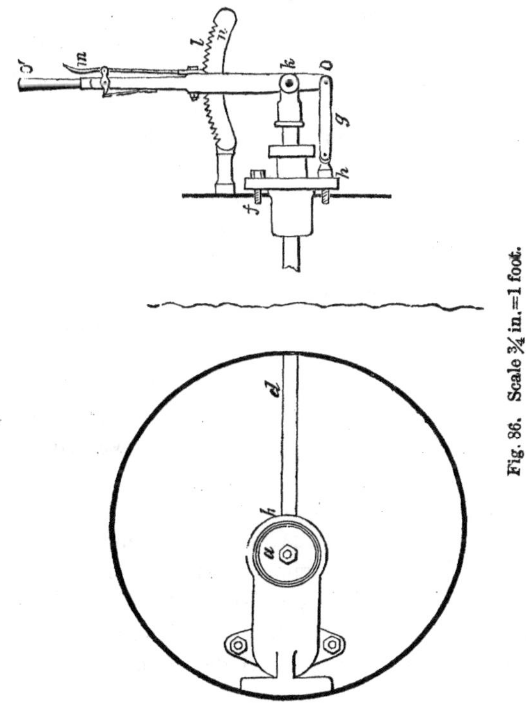

Fig. 86. Scale ¾ in.=1 foot.

should remain closed after steam is shut off, and never be opened at any time accidentally, the arrangement described accomplishes just what is needed—that is, makes the valve work comparatively easily, and at the same time keeps it closed after the steam has been shut off.

QUESTION 156. *How is the valve opened and closed?*

Answer. By a lever, *O′ O*, called a *throttle-lever*, figs. 85, 86* and 71. This lever is connected by a rod, *d*, called the *throttle-stem*, with a bell crank, *i*, the other arm of which works the rod *c*, to which the throttle-valve is attached. The rod *d* works through a steam-tight stuffing-box, *f*, in the back end of the boiler. The end of the throttle-lever is attached to two links, *g*, fig. 86, which are fastened by a pin to the stud *h*. These links have a slight vibratory motion, which enables the pin *k*, by which the lever *O′ O*, is fastened to the rod *d*, to move in a straight line, which is necessary in order that the rod *d* may work steam-tight in the stuffing-box, *f*. The throttle-lever has a latch, *l*, which gears into a curved rack, *n*, so as to hold the lever and valve in any required position. This latch is operated by a trigger, *m*. Various other devices are used to fasten the throttle-lever and thus hold it in any position required.

QUESTION 157. *How are the steam pipes constructed?*

Answer. The steam, after it is admitted by the throttle-valve, as was explained in answer to Question 155, passes into the throttle-pipe *I* and the dry-pipe *m m*, fig. 41. At the front end of the dry-pipe a pipe, *n*, figs. 40 and 41, which divides into two branches like the top of the letter T and is therefore called a

* Fig. 86 is a plan, showing the *top* of the valve and lever.

T-pipe, is attached. The steam-pipes *o*, *o*, fig. 40, are connected to each of the two branches of the T-pipe at one end and to the cylinders at the other.*

These pipes, being in the smoke-box, are exposed to great changes of temperature, and are therefore subjected to expansion by heat and contraction by cold. The joints are therefore constantly subject to disturbance by the contraction and expansion of the pipes and so are difficult to keep tight. It is also practically impossible to construct the boiler, the cylinders and the pipes with perfect accuracy, and therefore a small amount of adjustability and flexibility is necessary in the joints of the pipes. If, for example, the opening *x* in the cylinder, fig. 40, were either too near or too far from the cylinder of the engine, it would be necessary to move the end of the pipe *o* either to the right or to the left in order to connect it with *x*. If the joint of the upper end of the steam-pipe were attached to the T-pipe with a flat joint like that shown at *a b*,

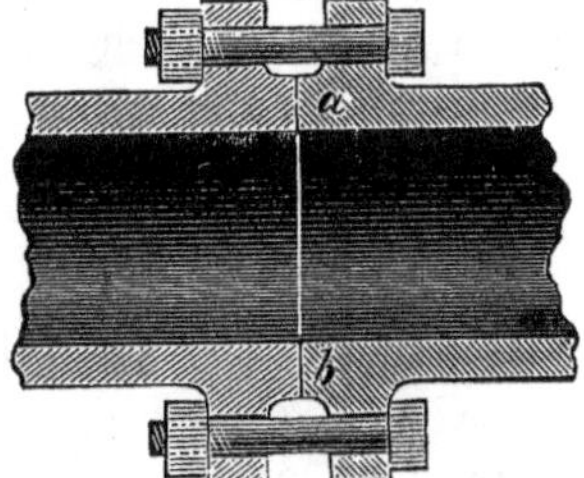

Fig. 87. Scale 1½ in.=1 foot.

fig. 87, it would be impossible to move the lower end of the steam-pipe either to the right or to the left without disturbing the joint and causing it to leak.

* In fig. 40 the right-hand side represents a section through the steam-pipe *o o*, and the left a section through the exhaust pipe *e e*.

For this reason these pipes are connected with what are called *ball joints*, fig. 88, that is, the end *a b* of one

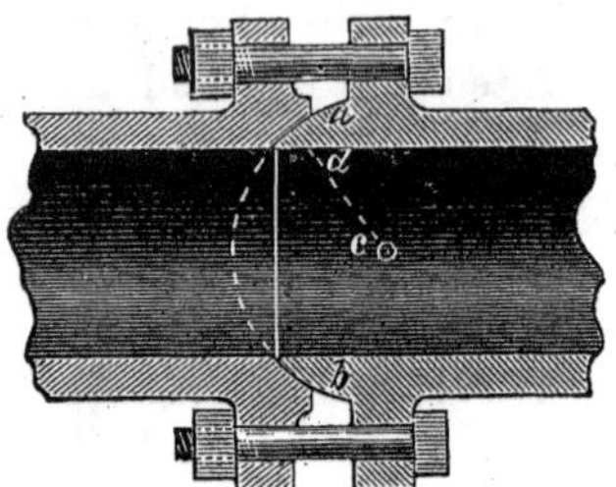

Fig. 88. Scale $1\frac{1}{2}$ in.=1 foot.

of the pipes is turned into the form of a part of a sphere,* and the other end into a corresponding concave form. It is known that a sphere will fit into a corresponding socket in any position; for example, an acorn in its cup or the bones at the hip or shoulder joints. If, therefore, the pipes are joined with such spherical or *ball-joints* as they are called, the lower end can be moved sideways several inches either way, and the joint will still be steam-tight if it is then firmly bolted together. Even after it is bolted together it will have so much flexibility that the expansion and contraction of the pipes will not cause it to leak.

There is, however, still another difficulty. Although the lower end of the pipe, *o o*, fig 40, can, with a ball-joint above, be moved in any direction horizontally, yet if the pipe is too long or too short it is obvious such a joint will not permit it to be moved up or down. A joint with a flat surface, like that shown in fig. 87,

* The dotted lines indicate what would be the form of the sphere if the pipe was solid instead of hollow.

would, however, permit such motion in the pipe without leaking. If, for example, the steam-pipe were $\frac{1}{8}$ of an inch too short, it might be drawn down that distance, and if the upper joint were then screwed up it would still be steam-tight. In order, then, to get both vertical and lateral flexibility in the joints of the steam-pipes, a ring, *a b*, fig. 89, is interposed between

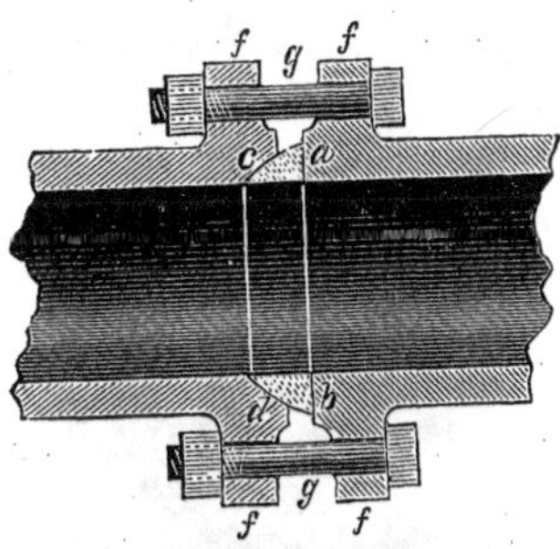

Fig. 89. Scale $1\frac{1}{2}$ in.=1 foot.

the pipes. One side of this ring is spherical and the other flat, so that the pipes can move either around the spherical part or slip up or down or sideways on the flat surface of the ring. In this way the pipes are flexible and adjustable in every direction, and for all kinds of motion caused by expansion, or which may be needed when the parts are put together. Sometimes the joints at one end only of the steam-pipes are made in this way, and the other is connected with a simple ball-joint.

In designing these joints their form should be drawn with a radius, *c d*, fig. 88, from one centre, *c*, so that the surface of the joint will form a part of a sphere. If they are drawn from two centres, as is sometimes done, it is obvious that the surface of the joint will not be a part of a sphere, and therefore will not have the requisite flexibility. The surfaces of the joints are carefully turned to the proper form, and then made steam-tight by scraping or grinding them with emery and oil, and the pipes are then fastened together with bolts, *g*, *g*, fig. 89, and flanges, *f f*, cast on the pipes.

QUESTION 158. *How are the exhaust pipes constructed?*

Answer. They are made of cast iron. When two nozzles are used they are generally cast together, as

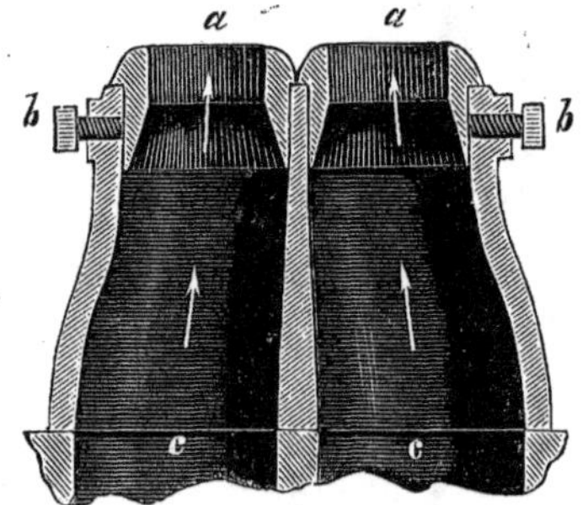

Fig 90. Scale 1½ in. = 1 foot.

shown in fig. 90. When only one is used, the form of the pipes resembles somewhat that of an inverted letter λ, as shown in fig. 91, so as to cover the two openings which connect with the cylinders. The tops of these pipes have rings or bushings, *a a*, fitted into them, which are held by set screws, *b*, so that they can easily be removed and others with larger or smaller openings be substituted. If the openings in the exhaust-nozzles are small, the steam must be discharged at a higher rate of speed, in order to exhaust all that is in the cylinders, than if the blast orifices are larger. Therefore, if the latter are reduced in size, the draft becomes more violent, but at the same time the ***back-pressure*** in the cylinder (which will be explained hereafter) is increased. It therefore becomes necessary to adjust the size of the blast orifices

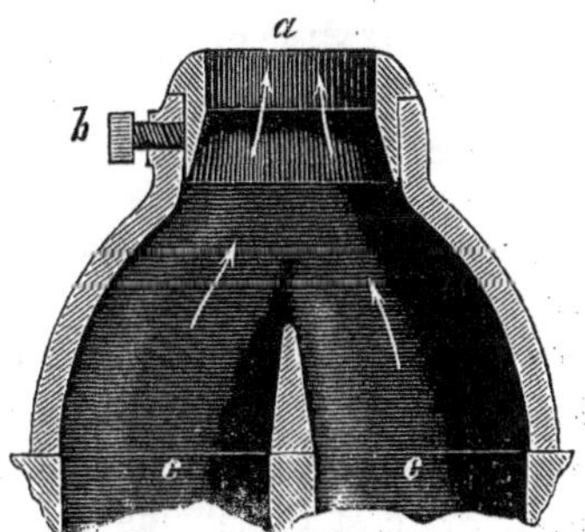

Fig 91. Scale 1½ in.=1 foot.

with the greatest care, so as to have them just small enough to produce the required draft and yet leave them as large as possible, so as to reduce the back-pressure. For these reasons what are called *variable exhausts* are sometimes used. In these the blast orifice can be increased or diminished at pleasure, and thus regulated to suit the conditions under which an engine is working. A great variety of such devices has been used, but now nearly all have been abandoned for the simpler arrangement described, which is not variable when the engine is working.

PART X.

THE CYLINDERS, PISTONS, GUIDE-RODS AND CONNECTING-RODS.

QUESTION 159. *How are the steam cylinders constructed?*

Answer. They are made of hard cast iron, and have the steam and exhaust ports and valve-seats cast with them. The harder the iron the better will the cylinders withstand the wear of the pistons and valves, but they must at the same time be made soft enough, so that after they are cast the inside can be bored out perfectly cylindrical, the ends turned off, the bolt-holes drilled, and the valve-seats planed smooth.

Fig. 92 represents a longitudinal section through the centre of the cylinder and steam-chest. Fig. 94 is a plan of the same parts with the cover of the steam-chest and the valve removed. The left-hand side of fig. 95 shows a transverse section through the centre *c d*, fig. 92, of the cylinders, and the right side is a section through the steam-pipe *G h*, *fig.* 94. The same letters indicate like parts in the three different views.

The cylinders of locomotives in this country are now universally placed on the outside of the wheels, as has already been described. In order to fasten them securely together and to the boiler, they are attached to what is called a *bed-plate* or *bed-casting*, *D D*, figs. 94 and 95, which is placed between them. Some builders make this bed-casting in a separate piece, and the cylinders are then bolted to it on the outside, about at the dotted lines, *l*, *m*, fig. 95. Others cast one-half of it with each cylinder, as shown in our engravings, and then bolt them together at the line *i*, *j*, which is the centre of the engine. The bed-casting is also bolted to the smoke-box by the flanges *E*, *E*. The cylinders are bolted to the frame *F* with bolts, *m* and *k*, fig. 95

After the cylinders are bored out, and the ends turned off, ***heads***, A and *B*, figs. 92 and 94, are fitted with steam-tight joints to each end. These heads are fastened with bolts and nuts, *a*, *a*, *a*, to flanges, *C*, *C*.

QUESTION 160. *How is the steam conducted to and from the cylinders?*

Answer. Two pipes or passages are cast in each cylinder, the one, *G G′*, fig. 95, for admitting steam into the steam-chest, and the other, *H H′*, for exhausting it from the cylinders. The one *G G′* is called the ***steam-passage***, and the other, *H H′*, the ***exhaust-passage***. The steam-passage terminates at one end with a round opening, *G*, figs. 94 and 95, to which the steam-pipe *o*, figs. 40 and 95 is attached inside of the smoke-box. At the other end it divides into two branches, *G′*, *G′*, fig. 94, each of which terminates in an opening, *g*, *g′*, inside of the steam-chest. The steam is thus delivered at both ends of the chest, and can pass freely into each of the steam-ports. By making the cylinders in this way, they are exactly alike for each side of the engine, or, to use a shop phrase, there are "*no rights and lefts*," so that a cylinder casting can be

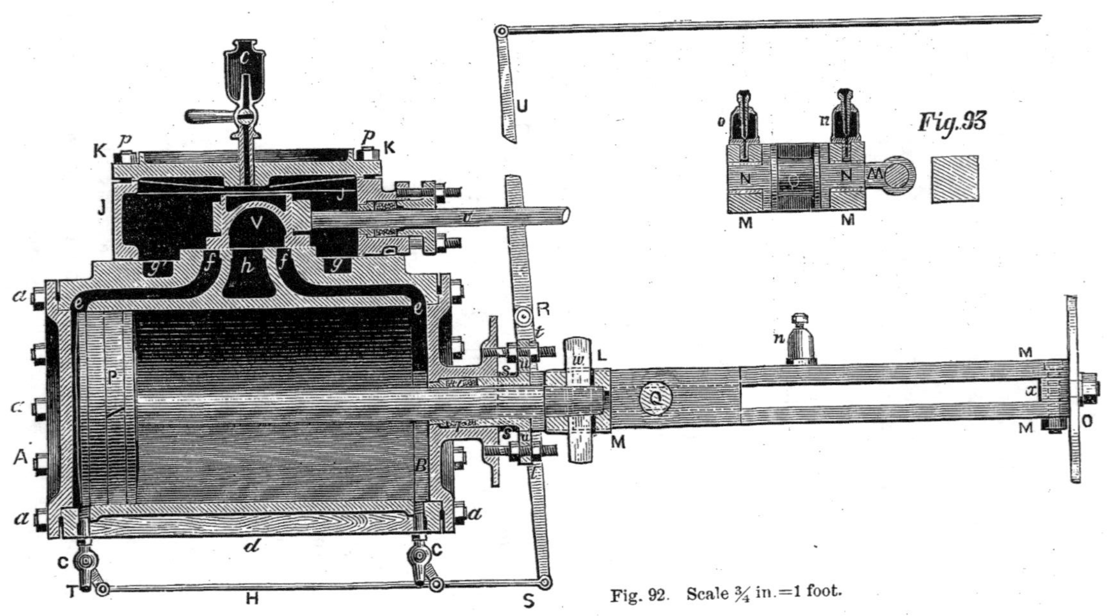

Fig. 92. Scale ¾ in. = 1 foot.

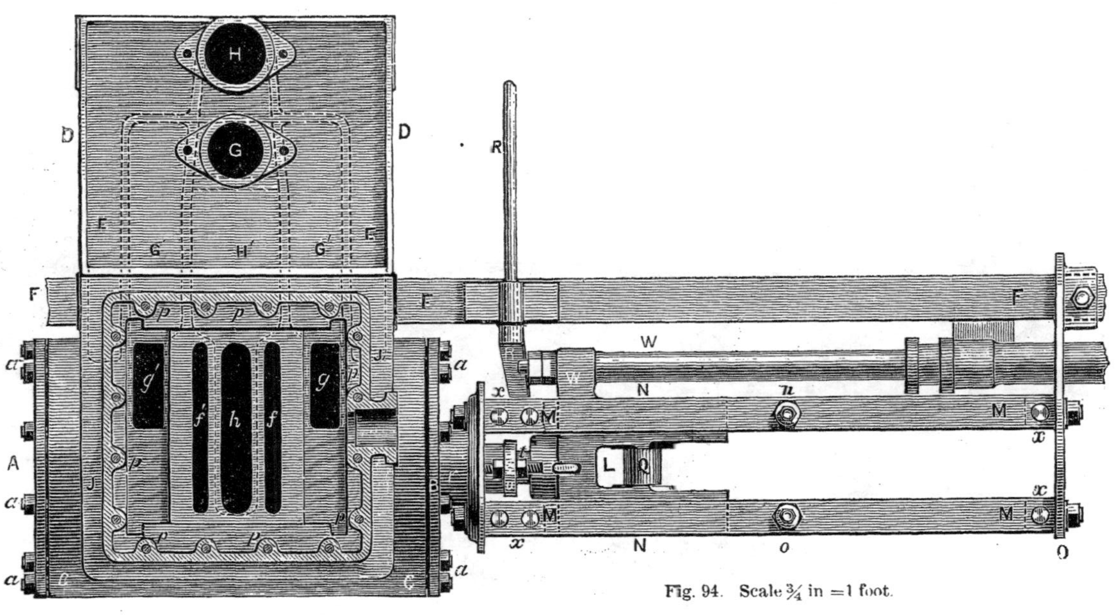

Fig. 94. Scale 3/4 in = 1 foot.

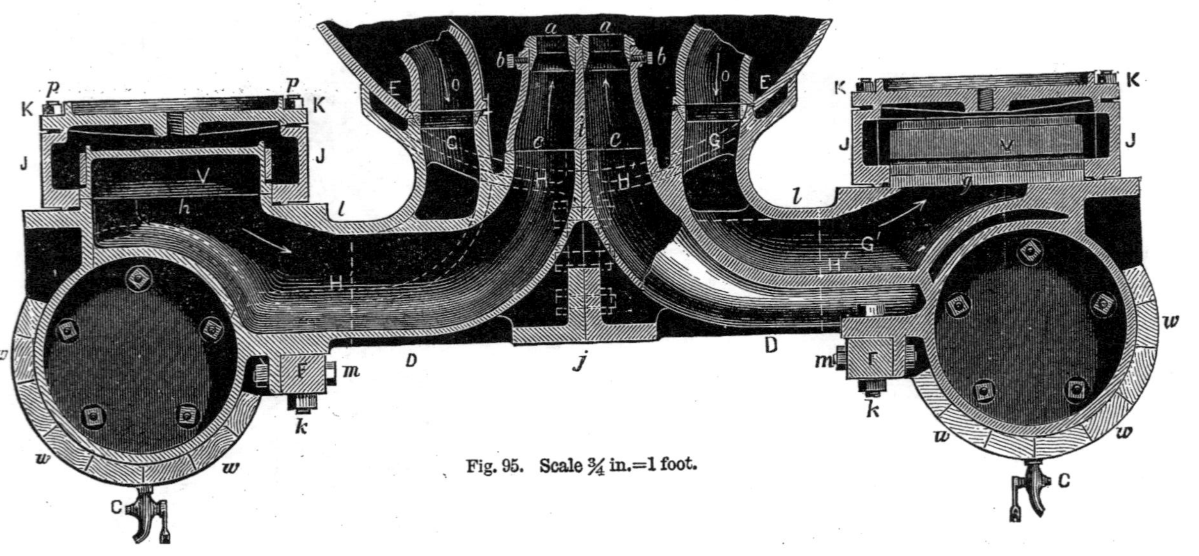

Fig. 95. Scale 3/4 in.=1 foot.

used for either side of the engine. This method of making cylinders has been adopted by a number of the principal builders in this country, but is by no means universal.

QUESTION 161. *How is the steam-chest constructed?*

Answer. It usually consists of two castings, one of which, *J*, figs. 92 and 94, is a square cast-iron box made open at the top and bottom. This rests on the top of the cylinder casting and is joined to the latter with a steam-tight joint. On top of it is a cast-iron cover, *K K*. The steam-chest and cover are held down by bolts, *p, p*, which are screwed into the cylinder casting and have nuts on top.

QUESTION 162. *How are the slide-valves made to work steam-tight on the valve-seats?*

Answer. They are first planed off smooth, and then filed and scraped until the two touch each other over the whole of their surfaces in contact. The valve-stem *v*, fig. 92, works steam-tight through a stuffing-box on the steam-chest.

QUESTION 163. *How are the valves and pistons oiled?*

Answer. The oil is usually introduced into the steam-chest through a cock, *c*, fig. 92, called an *oil-cock.* From this cock it flows down upon the valve and is conducted by suitable holes and channels to the valve-face and from there through the steam-ports to the cylinder and piston. Sometimes, for greater convenience, oil-cocks *c, c*, fig. 71, are placed inside of the cab and communicate by pipes with the steam-chests.

The valves are oiled by pouring oil or melted tallow into the oil-cocks when the steam is shut off from the steam-chests and cylinders. When the pistons are working in the cylinders without steam, they create a partial vacuum, so that if oil is then poured into the oil-cocks it will be sucked into the steam-chests, or, in other words, it will be forced in by the pressure of the air above it. *Q*, fig. 71, is a shelf attached to the boiler to receive an oil-can filled with oil or tallow, which is thus melted or kept in a fluid condition by the heat of the boiler.

QUESTION 164. *How are the cylinders and steam-chests protected so as to prevent, as far as possible, the heat in the steam from being lost?*

Answer. The sides of the cylinders are covered with wood, *w, w, w*, fig. 95, called the *cylinder lagging*, and the wood is covered outside with Russia iron or brass, which is called the *cylinder-casing.* The ends of the cylinders have light metal covers, called *cylinder-head covers*, made of cast iron, brass or sheet metal. The steam-chest is covered in a similar way so as to be surrounded either with a covering of wood or of confined air. Sometimes coarse felt is used for the purpose. The covering, excepting the cylinder lagging, is not shown in the engravings.

QUESTION 165. *For what purpose are the cocks C, C, figs.* 92 *and* 95, *at each end of the cylinder, used?*

Answer. They are used to exhaust the water which collects in the cylinders. When the engine is not working the cylinders and steam-pipes are all cooled off, so that when steam is first introduced into them a great deal of it is condensed until they become warmed. Water is also frequently carried over from the boiler with the steam. When this occurs the boiler is said to *prime*, or to "*work water*." This water and that produced by the condensation of steam collect in the bottom of the cylinder and will not escape through the exhaust-pipes until the piston moves up so near to the end of the cylinder that the water will fill the whole space between it and the cylinder-head. As has already been stated, it will then escape so slowly that the momentum of the piston and other machinery is liable to "knock out" the cylinder-heads or even break the cylinder itself. The cocks *C*, *C*, called *cylinder-cocks*, are therefore placed in the under side of the cylinder, so that when they are open if there is any water in the cylinder it will escape through the cocks. They are therefore always opened when the engine is starting, or at any other time when there is any indication that there is water in the cylinders.

QUESTION 166. *How are these cocks opened and closed?*

Answer. A shaft, *R R*, figs. 92 and 94, which extends across the frames, has an arm, *R S*, fig. 92, at each end. These arms are connected by rods, *S T*, with the handles of the cylinder-cocks. The shaft also has a vertical arm, *R U*, the upper end of which is connected by a rod with the cab. At the end of the rod is a suitable handle, *f*, fig. 71, by which the cocks can be either opened or closed at pleasure by the locomotive runner.

QUESTION 167. *How is the piston-rod fastened to the piston?*

Answer. It fits into a straight or tapered hole in the piston-head, in which it is fastened either with a key, *k k* as shown in figs. 96 and 97,* or by a nut on the front side of the piston.

* Fig. 96 is an end view of the piston with the follower-plate removed. Fig. 97 is a section through the centre.

QUESTION 168. *How is the piston constructed?*

Answer. It is made of two cast-iron pieces, *B* and *C*, fig. 97, the one, *B*, called the *piston-head* or *spider*, to which the piston-rod *D* is attached. The other part, *C*, called the *follower-plate*, is bolted to the piston-head by the bolts *c, c*, called *follower-bolts*. The piston-head has lugs or projections, *d, d, d*, fig 96, cast on the inside, to which the follower plate is bolted. Hollow spaces are thus left between these lugs.

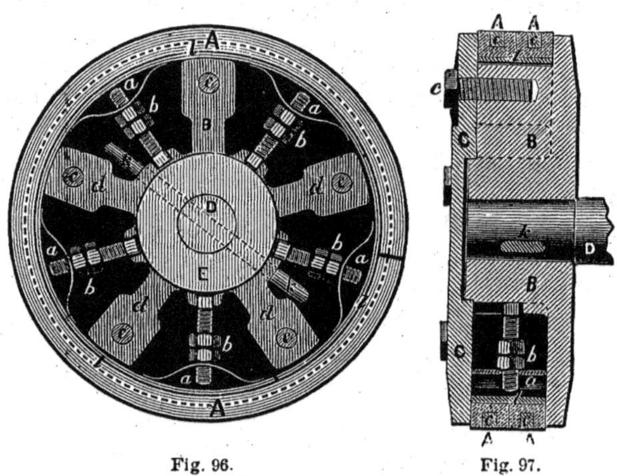

Fig. 96. Fig. 97.

Scale 1½ in.=1 foot.

QUESTION 169. *How is the piston made to work steam-tight in the cylinder?*

Answer. By means of two rings, *A, A*, figs. 96 and 97, called *packing-rings*. These rings are turned of the same size or a little larger in diameter than the cylinder. They are then cut open at one point in their circumference so that they can be pressed apart or expanded by the springs *a, a*, called *packing springs*, on the inside of the rings. These springs are pressed out by the nuts and bolts *b, b,* called *packing-bolts* and *packing-nuts,* so that when the rings wear they can be expanded so as to fill the cylinder completely. The place where the one ring is cut is placed opposite that of the opening in the other ring, or they are made to *break joints,* as it is called. This is done to prevent the steam which leaks through the opening where the one ring is cut from passing through to the other side of the piston. These rings are usually made of brass and have grooves, *c, c,* fig. 97, turned in them, which are filled with what is called Babbitt's metal. This metal is used because it is less liable to scratch the cylinders than brass alone. Another ring, *l l,* made of cast iron and as wide as the two brass rings, is placed inside of the latter and is intended to furnish a bearing for the springs, and thus distribute the pressure of the springs equally on the packing rings. This iron ring is also cut open at one point.

QUESTION 170. *How is the piston-rod made to work steam-tight through the cylinder-head?*

Answer. By what is called a *stuffing-box.* This consists of a cylindrical chamber, *r r,* fig. 92, which is made about 1½ inches larger in diameter than the piston-rod. This leaves a space ¾ of an inch wide all around the rod. This space is filled with hemp or some other fibrous material, called *packing,* saturated with oil or melted tallow. This packing is compressed by a hollow cylinder, *s s,* called a *gland,* the inside of which fits the piston-rod and the outside the stuffing-box. This gland is forced into the stuffing-box by nuts, *t, t,* which are screwed down on a flange, *u,* attached to the gland. The packing is thus compressed in the stuffing-box and forced against the piston-rod, which is made smooth and perfectly round and straight, and against the side of the stuffing-box, so that no steam can escape around the piston-rod. A brass ring or "*bushing*" is often put into the cylinder-head and in the gland where it touches the piston-rod,* because brass will bear the friction of the rod better than cast iron, and when it is worn out it can be removed and a new one substituted in its place.

QUESTION 171. *Why is the end of the piston-rod made to work in guides?*

Answer. Because it must move in a straight line if it and the piston work steam-tight in the cylinder. By referring back to fig. 2, it is obvious that if a pressure be exerted against the piston *B* and communicated to the crank-pin *N* by the connecting-rod *E*, the latter, excepting at the dead-points, will exert a pressure either upward or downward, according to the direction the piston is moving. This pressure would bend the piston-rod if no provision were made to prevent it. For this reason, therefore, the end of the piston-rod is attached to what is called a *cross-head*, *L*, figs. 92 and 94, which works in guides, *M, M.* The cross-head is made of cast iron and has slides, *N, N*, figs. 93 and 94, one on each side, each of which works between a pair of guide-bars or rods, *M, M*, shown in section in fig. 93.† These guide-rods, or *guides* as they are called, are planed and finished with great accuracy so as to be straight and smooth, and are attached to the cylinder-head at one end, and to a sup-

* Locomotive piston-rods are now usually made of steel.

† Fig. 93 is a transverse section through the guides at *n*, fig 92.

port, *O*, called the *guide-yoke*, which is fastened to the frame at *F*, fig. 94, and also usually attached to the boiler. The guides are set with great care, so as to be exactly parallel with the axis or centre line of the cylinder, so that the cross-head will slide in exactly the same path that the piston-rod will if it moves in a straight line. If then the piston-rod and the connecting-rod are attached to the cross-head, all the strain produced by the obliquity of the connecting-rod will be borne by the guides, thus relieving the piston-rod, and making it certain that it will move in a straight line.

QUESTION 172. *How are the piston and connecting-rods attached to the cross-head?*

Answer. The end of the piston-rod fits into a tapered hole in the cross-head and is held by a key, *w*, figs. 92 and 94. The connecting-rod is attached to a pin, *Q*, called a ***wrist-pin***, which is cast with the cross-head.

QUESTION 173. *How is the wear of the slides lessened and compensated?*

Answer. Sometimes they are made with brass wearing pieces called *gibs*, shown at *N*, *N*, fig. 93, which are placed between the slides and the guides. These gibs can either be removed and new ones substituted when they become very much worn, or by inserting thin pieces of metal, called liners, between them and the cross-head, they will be spread apart so as to fill the space between the slides. The slides are now, however, oftener made without gibs, and have recesses either cast or drilled in them, which are filled with either Babbitt's metal or glass bearings, which latter are said to wear very well. The guides are bolted at each end to blocks, *x*, *x*, called ***guide-blocks***, which can be planed off so as to bring the guides nearer together when they and the slides are worn. Sometimes liners are placed between the blocks and the guides, which can be removed when it is necessary to bring the guides nearer together.

QUESTION 174. ***Are the top and bottom guides worn alike?***

Answer. No: the top guide in ordinary engines is worn the most, because the pressure of the slides is always on the top guide when the engine is running forward, and on the bottom guide when it is running backward. This will be understood by referring back to the series of figures from 11 to 24. It will be noticed that in the backward stroke of the piston, represented by figs. 11 to 17, the strain on the connecting-rod tends to *push* the cross-head upward, and in the forward part of the stroke, figs. 18 to 24, the connecting rod *pulls* the cross-head in the same direction. If the crank turned the opposite way, this action would be reversed and the cross-head would then be alternately pushed and pulled downward, and the bottom guides would then be worn the most. As nearly all locomotives run forward more than backward, the tops guides are usually worn the most.

QUESTION 175. ***How are the slides oiled?***

Answer. Oil cups, ***n***, ***o***, figs. 92, 93 and 94, are placed about the middle of the top guide. These cups usually have a reservoir to hold a supply of oil, and are so constructed that it will be gradually fed on the slides, which are thus constantly and regularly lubricated.

QUESTION 176. ***How are the pumps worked from the piston-rods?***

Answer. The pump-plunger is attached to a projection, *W*, figs. 92 and 93, called the *pump lug*, cast on one of the slides of the cross-head. The plunger thus receives a reciprocating motion from the piston.

QUESTION 177. *How are the connecting-rods made?*

Answer. They are made of flat bars of wrought iron. The rods which connect the cross-heads with the driving-wheels are called *main connecting-rods*, and the rods which connect or couple the driving-wheels together are called *coupling-rods.** Fig. 98 represents a side view and a plan of a main connecting-rod. In the side view the end *B*, and in the plan both ends of the rod are shown in section. It is attached to the wrist-pin at *A* and to the crank-pin at *B*. Fig. 99 represents similar views of a coupling-rod. To save room in the engraving each of these rods is represented with a part of the middle broken away. The main rods are usually made wider at *G*, next the crank-pin, than at the other end, as it has been found that they are most liable to break at that end. The coupling-rods are now made either straight or somewhat wider in the centre.

QUESTION 178. *How are these rods prevented from getting loose on the pins from the wear of the latter in the inside of the holes of the rods?*

Answer. The ends of the rods are provided with what are called *brass-bearings*,† or "*brasses*," *c*, *d*, and *e*, *f*. These brasses are made in pairs, so as to embrace the pins, from each side. They are held by ⊃-shaped clamps, *s s s*, called *straps*, which are bolted

* They are also often called *side* or *parallel-rods*, but the term *coupling rods* is considered the best.

† The portion of a shaft pin or spindle subjected to friction is called a *journal*, and the surface which presses or "bears" against it is called a *bearing*

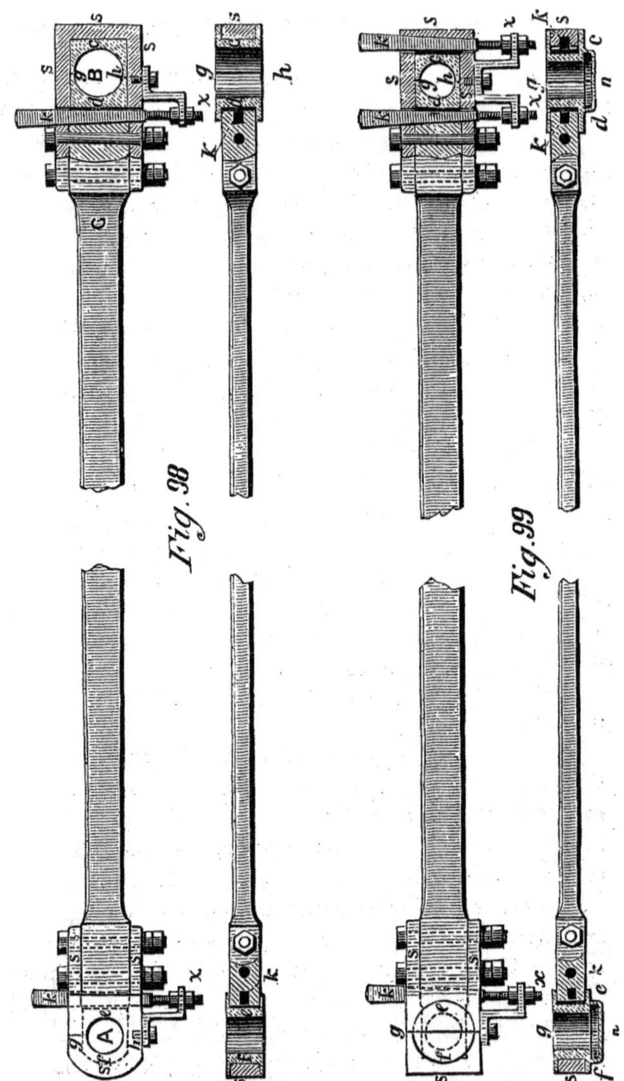

Scale ¾ in.=1 foot.

to the rods. When the brass-bearings become worn, they are taken out of the straps, and a portion of their surfaces of contact with each other is filed away, thus allowing them to come nearer together, and thereby reducing the size of the hole which receives the pin or journal. In order to prevent their being loose in the straps, tapered or wedge-shaped *keys*, *k*, *k*, which bear against the brasses, are fitted in the straps and rods. By driving down these keys the brass bearings are forced together, thus reducing the size of the hole for the journal, and making the rods fit tightly on the pins. A hard steel plate, shown by dark shading in the engraving, is sometimes interposed between the keys and the brasses to prevent the key from indenting the surface of the soft brass. As the keys are very liable to get loose and fall out, they are held either by screws and nuts, *x*, *x*, as shown in the engraving, or by *set-screws* on the side of the rods. The whole arrangement of straps, keys and brasses is called a *stub-end.*

QUESTION 179. *How are the journals of the crank-pins oiled?*

Answer. By oil-cups attached to the straps, above the journals, similar to the cups used on the *guide-rods*, but which are not shown in the engravings of the connecting-rods. Sometimes *oil-cellars*, as they are called, are attached to the under side of the straps. These are metal boxes, which are filled with oil, which is agitated violently by the rapid motion of the rods, and is thus applied to the journals through holes drilled in the straps. In order to confine the oil and prevent its leaking out around the journals of the coupling-rods, the brasses at *m*, *m*, fig. 99, are usually made so as to enclose the outside end of the crank-pin, which thus not only keeps the oil in, but excludes the dust. The brasses are usually lined with Babbitt's or some other kind of soft metal, which is thought to be less liable to heat from the friction of the journals.

QUESTION 180. ***Are the coupling-rods always made with stub-ends?***

Answer. No; their ends are sometimes made in one piece—that is, without straps or keys. The holes which receive the crank-pins then have brass rings or ***bushings***, as they are called, which fit tightly and are driven into the holes, and form the bearings on the pins. When these rings become worn they are driven out and new ones put in.

QUESTION 181. ***What is meant by the term lost motion?***

Answer. It is used to designate the wear of machinery, which causes a loss of motion in some of the parts. Thus if the bearings of the main connecting-rods are worn, the piston must move a distance equal to the wear at each end of the stroke before it moves the crank-pin. Lost motion might therefore be called the looseness of the parts. When we speak of *taking up* the lost motion, we mean making parts which were loose fit tightly.

PART XI.

THE VALVE-GEAR.

QUESTION 182. *What is meant by the valve-gear of a locomotive?*

Answer. By the valve-gear is meant the arrangement of eccentrics, rods, links, rockers, etc., by which the valves are moved and their motion regulated.

QUESTION 183. *What is required of the valve-gear in working a locomotive?*

Answer. It must be so arranged that the locomotive can be run either backward or forward, and so that the motion of the wheels can be reversed quickly and with certainty. It should enable the runner to employ the greatest power of the engine by admitting steam into the cylinders during the whole or nearly the whole of the stroke of the pistons, or when less power is required, to use the steam more economically by working it expansively, which latter is accomplished with the present appliances by changing the travel of the valve.

QUESTION 184. *How is the valve gear constructed so as to run the engine either backward or forward?*

Answer. As already explained, in answer to question 76, two eccentrics are provided for each cylinder. These are set so that one of each pair will run the locomotive in one direction, and the other two the reverse way.

QUESTION 185. *How must the eccentrics for each cylinder be set in order that the one may run the engine forward and the other backward?*

Answer. This can be best explained by reference to fig. 100, in which the piston, *P*, is represented at the beginning of the backward stroke, and the valve *V* has the requisite lead and is just about to open the front steam-port. It is obvious that, in order to complete the backward stroke of the piston, the front port must be opened to admit steam into the front end of the cylinder, and therefore the valve must be moved in the direction indicated by the dart *a*. To do this, the upper arm of the rocker *r* must move in the same direction, and the lower arm must be moved the reverse way, as indicated by the dart *e*. If the crank is intended to move in the direction indicated by the dart *N*, then the centre of the eccentric must be above the centre of the shaft or axle, in order to move the rocker in the direction indicated by the dart *e*. Supposing, however, it was intended to move the crank the reverse direction, as shown by the dart *N* in fig. 101; it is evident in that case that the valve must be moved in the same direction as before, in order to open the front steam-port and thus admit steam to force the piston back. But if the crank turns in the direction shown by the dart *N*, fig. 101, then the centre of the eccentric must be placed *below* the centre of the axle in order to move the lower rocker arm in the direction of the dart *e* and the valve in that indicated by *a*. It will thus be seen that the centres of the eccentric for running forward and that of the one for running backward must be placed, the one above and the other below the centre of the axle

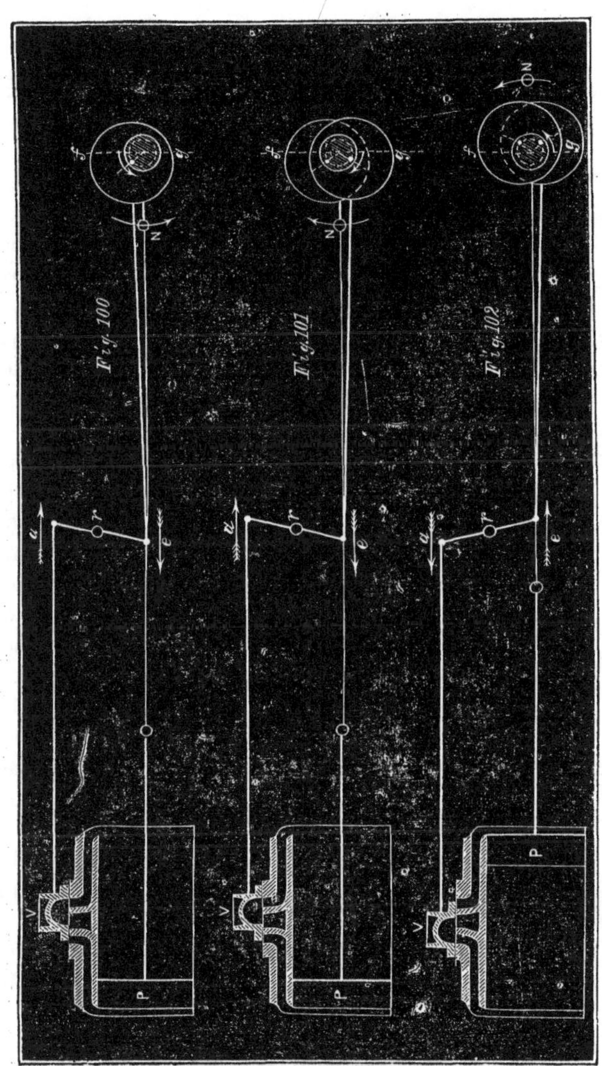

Scale $\frac{3}{8}$ in. = 1 foot.

at the beginning of the stroke of the piston, as shown in figure 101.

QUESTION 186. *Why is it that the centres of the eccentrics are not placed opposite to each other on the axle?*

Answer. Because before the beginning of the stroke of the piston it is necessary to move the valve from its middle position a distance equal to the lap before the steam-port begins to open. If we have a valve like that shown in fig. 10—that is, without any lap—the centres of the eccentrics could be placed at right angles, or, as mechanics say, "square" with the crank, as was shown in fig. 11, and exactly opposite to each other, because such a valve begins to take steam as soon as it moves from the middle of the valve-face. If, however, we have a valve like that shown in fig. 27, it is plain that before it will admit or *take* steam, as it is called, in either of the steam-ports, it must be moved from the centre of the valve-face, or its *middle position,* a distance equal to the lap, *L.* For this reason, therefore, the eccentric, instead of being placed at *half-throw,** as it is called, must be so far ahead of the middle position as to have moved the valve a distance equal to the lap, and if any lead is given to the valve, equal to the lap and lead together. In figs. 100 and 101, *f g* is a vertical line at right angles to the crank at the beginning of the stroke. It will be seen that the centre of each of the eccentrics is set far enough ahead of this line to give the valve the required lead. When the piston reaches the back end of the cylinder, the two eccentrics will occupy the position shown in fig. 102, in which posi-

*This would be at right angles to the crank when the piston is at the end of the stroke.

tion the lower one would move the valve so as to turn the crank in the direction of the dart *N*, and the upper one in the reverse direction. It will be seen that in this position both of the eccentrics are again ahead of half-throw, when the piston is at that end of its stroke.

QUESTION 187. *How is the motion of either eccentric communicated to the valve?*

Answer. The ends of each pair of eccentric-rods are connected together by a link, *a b*, fig. 103. This link has a curved groove or slot, *a b*, in it, in which a block, *B*, fits accurately, so that it can slide freely from one end to the other. This block is attached to the lower rocker-arm by a pin, *c*, which works freely in the block. The two eccentric-rods *C* and *D* are attached to the ends of the link at *e* and *f* by pins and knuckle-joints. It is apparent that if the link is down, or in the position shown in fig. 103 and also on a smaller scale in fig. 104, the motion of the upper eccentric-rod, which is usually used for the forward motion, will be imparted to the rocker, and thus to the valve, and when the link is in the position shown in fig. 105, that the valve will be moved by the lower or backward eccentric-rod *B*. In order to reverse the engine, it is then only necessary to provide the means of raising and lowering the links. This is done by a shaft, *A*, fig. 103, called a *lifting-shaft*, which has two horizontal arms, *E*,* one for each link, and a vertical arm, *F*. The links are suspended from the ends of the horizontal arms by rods or bars, *g h*, called *link-hangers*, which are connected to the links and to the arms above by pins, which enable the hangers to vi-

* Only one of these is shown in the engraving.

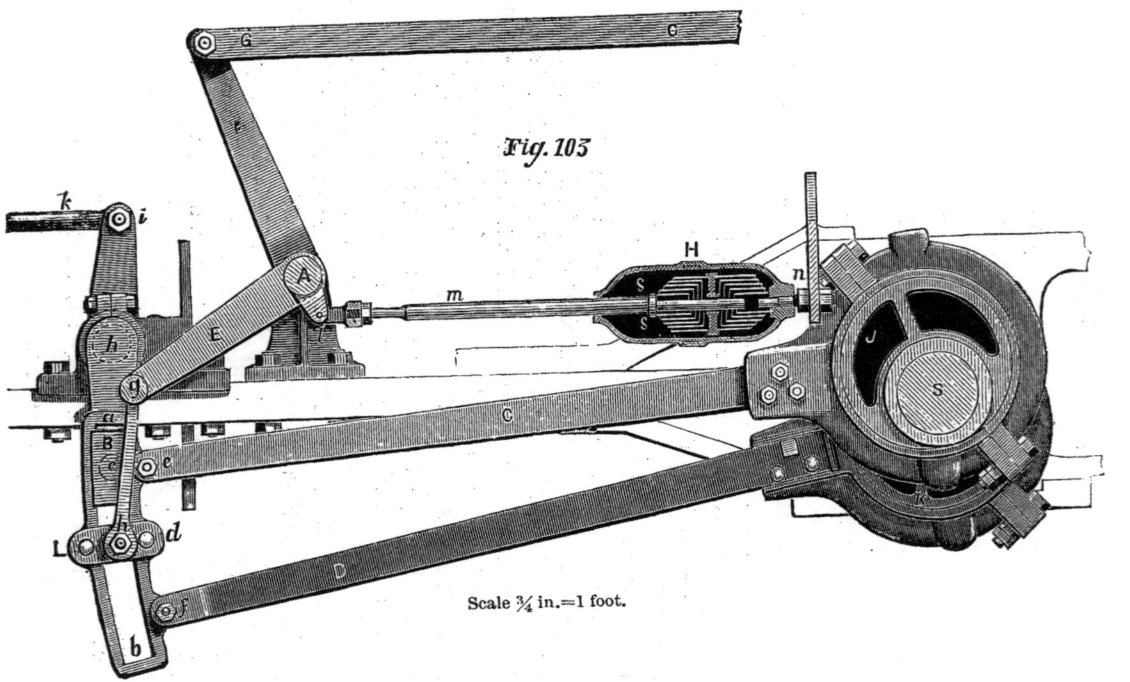

Fig. 103

Scale ¾ in.=1 foot.

brate freely. The lower pin is attached to a plate, *L d*, called a *link-saddle,* which is bolted to the link. The vertical arm of the lifting-shaft is connected by a rod, *G G,* called the *reverse-rod,* to a lever *O, O,* Plate II. in the cab called a *reverse-lever,* the construction of which will be explained hereafter. This lever is worked by the locomotive runner, and by moving the upper end of it forward, the link will be lowered, and the rocker and valve will be moved by the forward

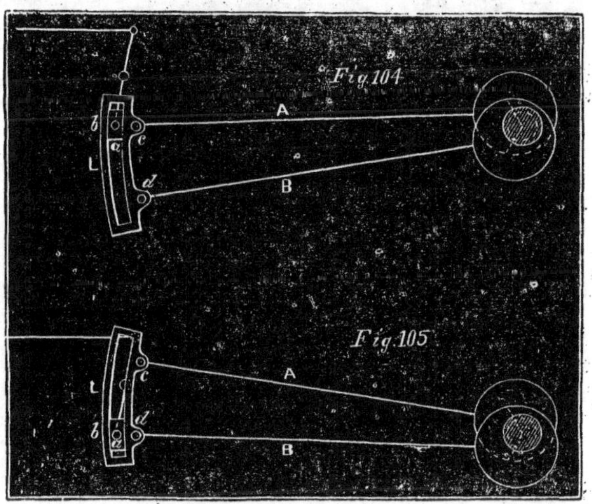

Scale, ⅜ inch = 1 foot.

eccentric; and if the reverse-lever is moved back, the link will be raised, and the backward eccentric will move the valve. When this is done, the valve-gear is said to be thrown into the *forward* or *backward motion,* or *forward* or *back gear.*

QUESTION 188. *How is the travel of the valve changed by the motion of the link?*

Answer. By either raising or lowering the link, so that the link-block and rocker-pin will be some distance above or below the eccentric-rods. Thus in fig. 104, the motion of the upper eccentric-rod, and in fig. 105 that of the lower or *back* eccentric-rod is communicated to the rocker-pin and the valve. If, however, the link should be raised so that the link-block and rocker-pin are somewhat below the upper or forward

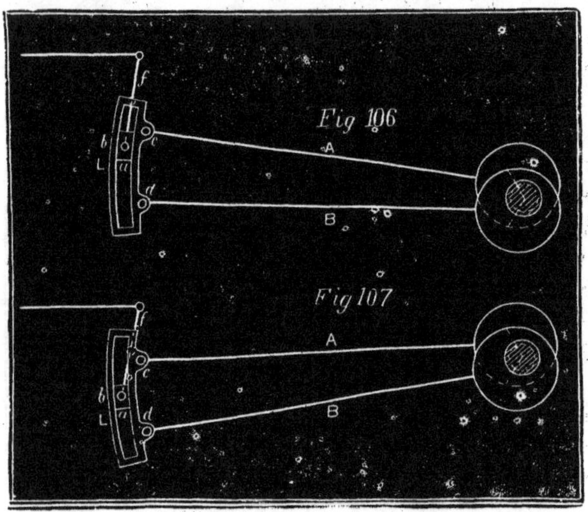

Scale, ⅜ inch = 1 foot.

eccentric-rod, as shown in fig. 106, then the motion imparted to the rocker and valve will partake somewhat of that of the upper and also of the lower eccentric-rod. So long as the rocker-pin is above the centre of the link, the motion of the valve will partake most of that of the upper or forward rod, and the engine will then run forward, but when the rocker-pin is below the centre of the link, its motion will be influenced more by the back eccentric-rod, and the engine will then run backward.

The motion of the link, which is somewhat complex and difficult to understand clearly, will perhaps be understood better if we represent it in a number of successive positions of the whole stroke of the piston, as was done to show the motion of the eccentric in figs. 11 to 24. We will therefore suppose that the link is in what is called *full gear forward,* as shown in figs. 103 and 104. In fig. 108 the link is in the position it would occupy at the beginning of the stroke of the piston; in fig. 109 it is in that which it will be in when the piston has moved four inches; in fig. 110, when it has moved eight inches; in fig. 111, twelve; and in figs. 112, 113 and 114, sixteen, twenty and twenty-four inches. Figs. 114 to 119 represent the successive positions of the link during the return stroke. In order to show the different positions of the link we have represented on a larger scale, in fig. 120, the successive positions of the centre line of the link, which will indicate the motion imparted by it to the rocker. In order to designate each of these positions, the centre lines in fig. 120 are numbered + and — 0, 4, 8, etc., etc., to correspond with similar numbers in figs. 108 to 119.

Thus the line *-o -o,* represents the position of the centre of the link which it occupies at the beginning of the stroke as shown in fig. 108. The line -4 -4, that represented by fig. 109, when the piston has moved 4 in. The lines -8 -8, -12 -12, -16 -16, -20 -20, 24 24, +4 +4, etc., the successive positions of the centre of the link represented in figs. 108 to 119. The dot-

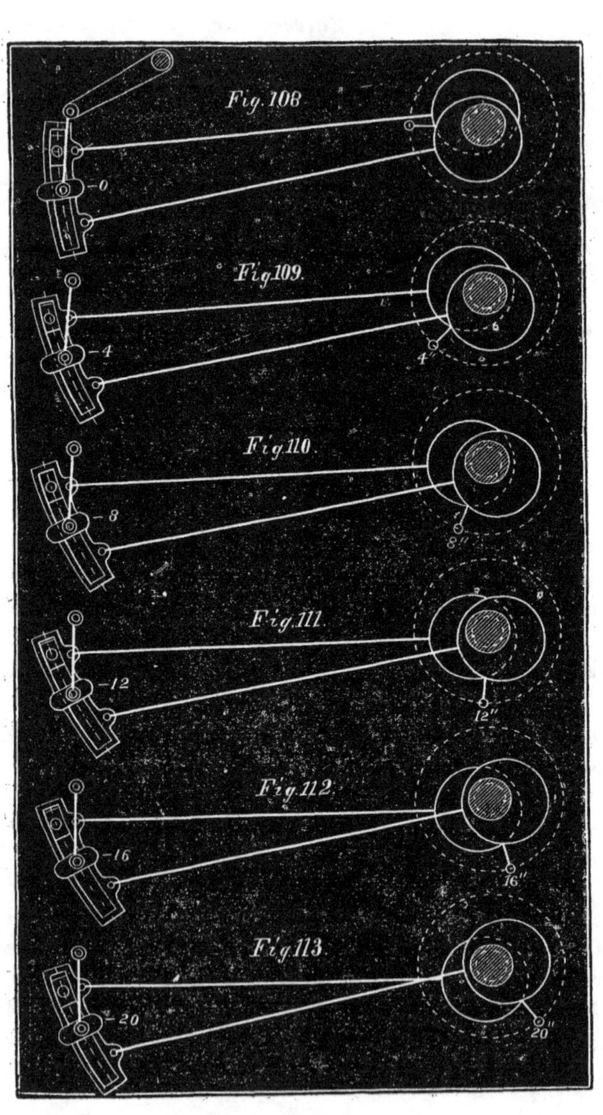
Fig. 108
-0
Fig. 109.
-4
4"
Fig. 110.
-8
8"
Fig. 111.
-12
12"
Fig. 112.
-16
16"
Fig. 113.
-20
20"

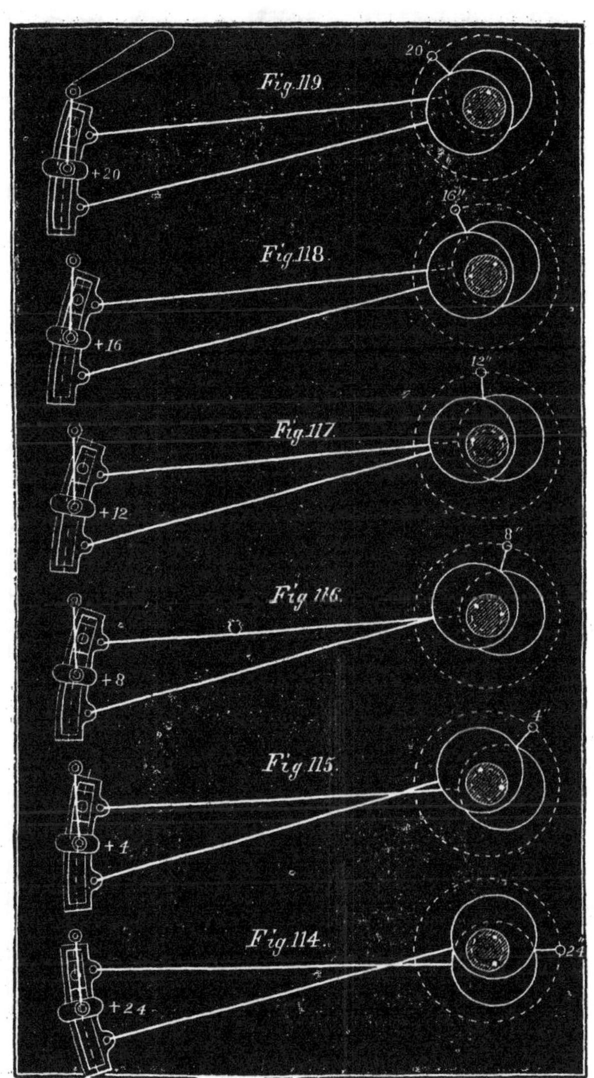

Scale ⅜ in. = 1 foot.

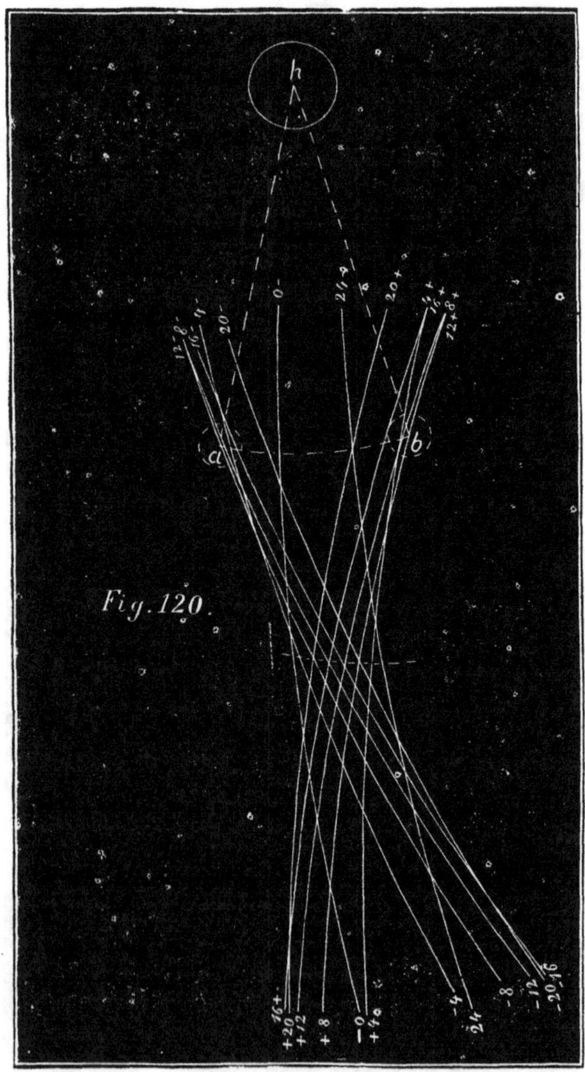

Scale $\frac{3}{16}$ in.=1 inch.

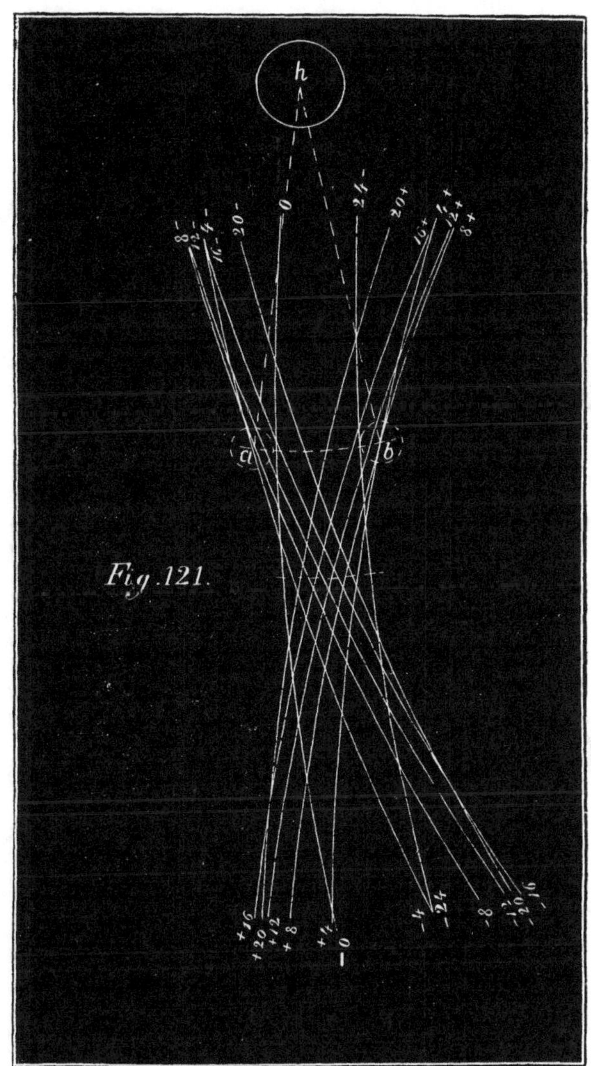

Scale $\frac{3}{16}$ in. = 1 inch.

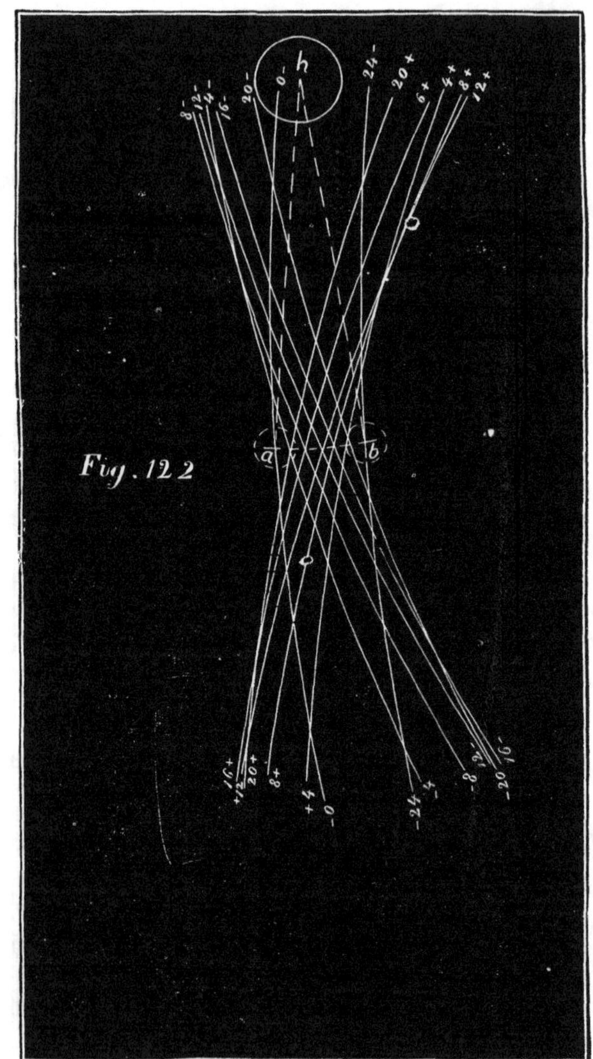

Scale $\frac{3}{16}$ in.=1 inch.

ted lines *h a* and *h b* represent the two extreme positions into which the rocker-arm would be moved by the action of the link. It will be seen that when the link is in the position shown, it imparts the full stroke of the eccentrics to the rocker-pin and consequently to the valve. We will now suppose that the link is raised up as shown in fig. 106, so that the position of the rocker-pin is just half-way between the end of the eccentric-rod and the centre of the link. This position is called *half-gear.* In fig. 121 the different positions of the centre line of the link and of the rocker have been laid out for half-gear in the same way as was done for full-gear before. From this it will be seen that the travel, *a b,* imparted to the rocker-pin and valve by the link when it is in the position shown, instead of being 5 in. is only 3½ in. In fig. 107 the link is raised up, so that the rocker-pin is in the centre of it or midway between the eccentrics. This position is called *mid-gear.* The successive positions of the centre line of the link in this position have been laid down in fig. 122 in the same way as was done for full and half-gear. The movement of the rocker, it will be seen, is, for mid-gear, only 2½ in. These diagrams show that when the rocker-pin is opposite the eccentric-rod, the valve receives the full throw of the eccentric, and that the motion imparted by the eccentric diminishes as the rocker-pin approaches the centre of the link, so that, with eccentrics having 5 in. throw and a valve with ⅞ lap and ⅛ in. lead, we can increase or diminish the travel of the valve from 2½ to 5 in. by simply raising or lowering the link, which is done by the reverse-lever.

QUESTION 189. *What is the effect of this variation of*

travel on the working of the valve and the admission and release of steam to and from the cylinder?

Answer. It is almost precisely the same as that which is effected by increasing or diminishing the throw of the eccentric, which was explained in the answer to Question 52. In order to show this effect more clearly, we have represented by motion-curves,* fig. 123, the movement imparted to the valve by the link when it is in full, half and mid-gear, as illustrated in the preceding figures. The curve for full-gear is engraved in full heavy lines; that for half-gear in lighter lines, and for mid-gear in dotted lines. From these curves it will be seen that when the valve is worked in full-gear the steam-port is opened wide at 2 in. of the stroke and steam cut off at 21 inches. When the valve is worked in half-gear the port is not at any time opened wide and steam is then cut off at 17½ in. of the stroke, and when worked in mid-gear the greatest opening of the steam-port is no greater than the lead and the cut-off occurs at 4 inches of the stroke.

It is of course possible to work the link in any intermediate position between those which we have represented. Usually the reverse-lever is arranged so that the steam will be cut off at 6, 8, 10, 12, 15, 18, and 20 inches of the stroke.

QUESTION 190. *What is the greatest and the least admission of steam possible with the ordinary link motion?*

Answer. With 24 in. stroke of piston and 5 in. travel and ⅞ in. lap, steam can be admitted as shown by the motion-curves during 21 in. or 87½ per cent. of the stroke,

* The nature of these curves was explained in answer to Question 44.

and can be cut off at about 4 in. or 16⅔ per cent. It will be seen, however, that in mid-gear the motion-curve becomes a straight line, and that the ***pre-admission*** of steam, that is the admission of steam before the piston reaches the end of the stroke, is equal to that admitted after, so that it is impossible to work the locomotive with the link in that position. Practically it is found that no useful work can be done with a link if the steam is cut off at less than six inches, or one-fourth of the stroke. Even then the opening of the steam-ports is so small that the steam which enters the cylinders is very much wire-drawn.

QUESTION 191. ***How are the curves drawn which represent the motion of the valve?***

Answer. These motion-curves as produced by the link-motion are very difficult to draw, as the motion of the link is extremely complicated. It is doubtful, therefore, whether those who have no knowledge of mechanical drawing will be able to understand the following description of the method of doing it, which we will try to make as clear as possible.

In the first place, the centre *S*, fig. 124, of the axle, *A*, of the rocker, and *B* of the lifting-shaft, must be laid down in their proper positions. If, now, the valve has ⅞ in. lap and ⅛ lead, the lower rocker-pin must be one inch ahead of its middle position when the piston is at the front end of the cylinder, and at the beginning of the backward stroke. We will, therefore, mark the centre, *a*, of the rocker-pin in this position. If from the centre of the axle a circle, ***c d e***, be drawn whose diameter is equal to the throw of the eccentrics, this circle will represent the path in which the centres of the eccentrics will revolve. If, now, the dis-

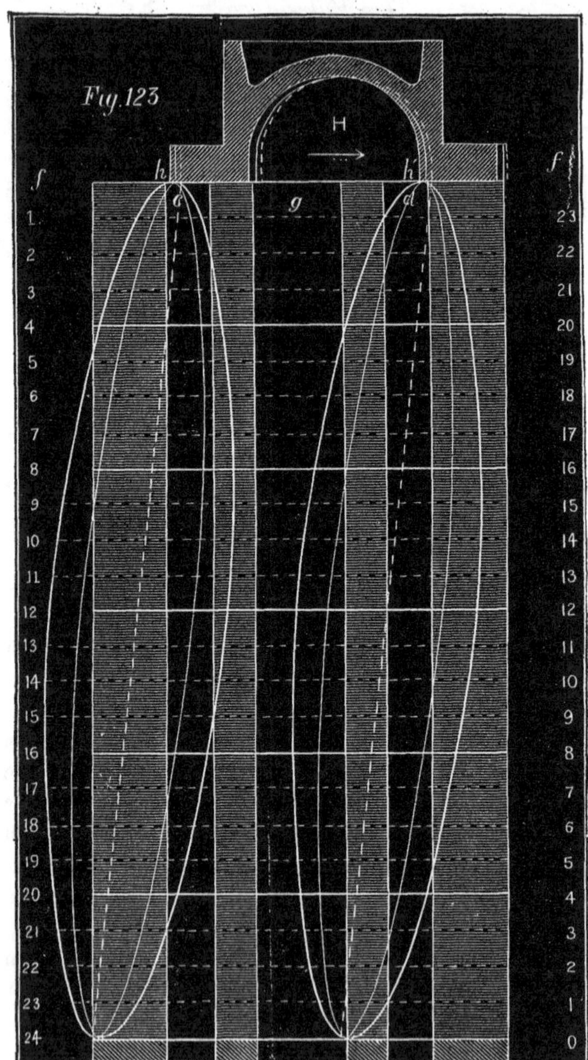

Scale $\frac{3}{16}$ in. = 1 inch.

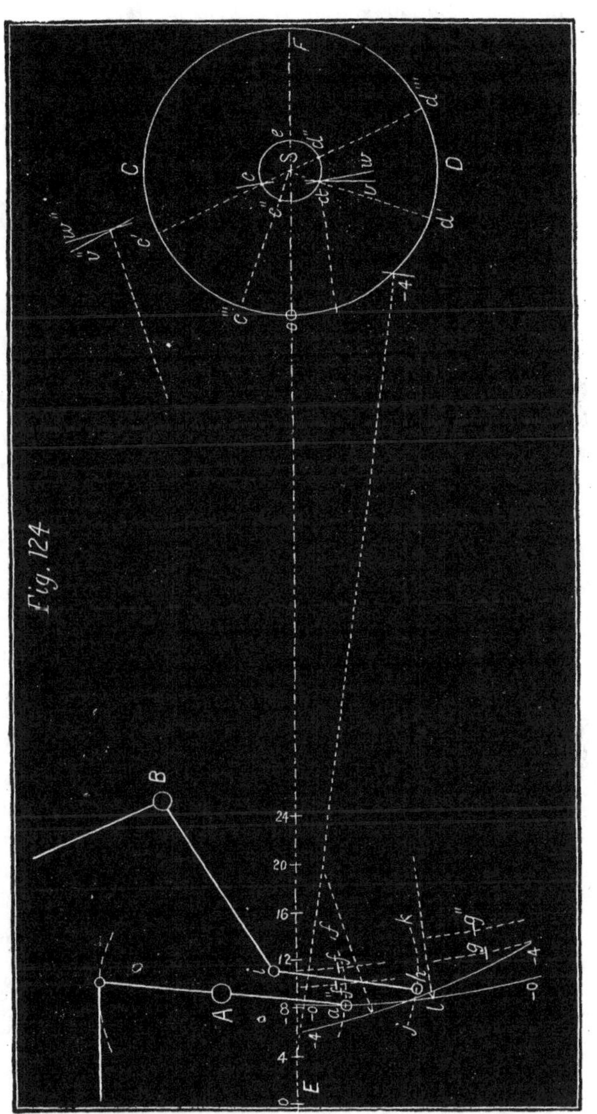

Scale ¾ in.=1 foot.

tance from the centre of the axle to the centre of the lower rocker-pin, *a*, when the latter is in its middle position, be taken for a radius,* and from the position of the rocker-pin at the beginning of the stroke as a centre, the circle representing the path of the eccentrics be intersected at two points, *c* and *d*, the points of intersection will represent the positions of the centres of the forward and backward eccentrics. Having determined these positions, draw arcs of circles, *f* and *g*, from these centres with a radius equal to the distance from the centres of the eccentrics to the centres of the pins which connect the rods to the link. It is evident that at the beginning of the stroke the centres of the pins in the link must each be in one of these arcs. But the link is suspended by the hanger, *i h*, which oscillates from the end, *i*, of the lifting-arm, which for any one point of cut-off is stationary; and therefore the point of suspension of the link must always be in the arc, *j k*, described from the centre of the pin, *i*, in the lifting-arm, with a radius equal to the length of the hanger. There are, therefore, three points in the link, each of which must be in one of the arcs which have been drawn, and which will determine the position of the link. This can be done easiest by drawing the link, *L*, fig. 125, on a stiff piece of paper, *m n*, and cutting off the back, *p q*, of it through the centres of the pins, *s* and *t*, and also cutting out a triangular piece, *u*, the apex of which will correspond with the centre of the

* This is usually the radius of the link but in some cases either a longer or shorter radius is taken to draw the link. In the following explanation it is assumed that the link is drawn with this radius, or from the centre of the axle. Of course if a greater or lesser radius is used, due allowance must be made therefor.

point of suspension, *o*. By placing this piece of paper on the drawing it can be moved, so that the three centre points, *s*, *t* and *o*, will respectively conform with the arcs, *f g* and *j k*, fig. 124. In this position the piece of paper will then be in the position of the link for the point of the stroke represented. By marking the centres of the link-pins on the arcs *f* and *g*, and from them as centres, with the length of the rods used

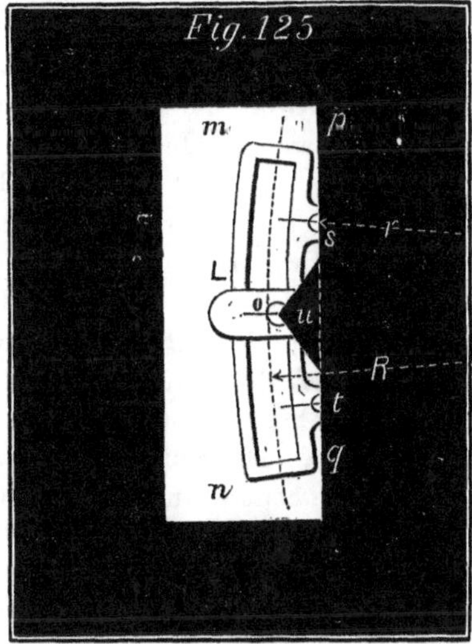

Scale, ¾ in.=1 foot.

to draw the arcs, two other arcs, *v*, *w*, be drawn intersecting each other, the point *d*, where they intersect will be the centre from which the centre line of the link can be drawn with a radius, *l d*, equal to the distance from the centre of the eccentrics to the centre of the link. This will give the first position *–o –o*, of the centre line of the link. As the rocker-pin must always be in the centre of the link, it is obvious that the point at which the centre-line of the link intersects the arc in which the rocker-pin oscillates must be the position of the centre of the rocker-pin. With this determined the position of the valve can easily be located.

In order to represent the link at any other point of the stroke, say after the piston has moved four inches, the position of the crank must first be laid down. To do this, allowance must be made for the irregularity due to the angularity of the connecting-rod, which was explained in answer to Question 54. From the centre of the axle, a circle, *C D*, whose diameter is equal to the stroke of the piston, is first drawn, which will represent the path of the crank-pin. A horizontal centre line, *E F*, should also be drawn through the centre of the axle and the centre of the cylinder. The intersection *o* of this line with the path of the crank-pin will be the position of the latter at the beginning of the stroke. If from this point a distance, *o o*, be laid off on the centre line equal to the length of the connecting-rod,* it will give the position of the wrist-pin at the beginning of the stroke, so that from this its successive positions for each inch of the stroke can be laid off. From its position after the piston has made say four inches of the stroke as a centre, and the length of the connecting-rod as a radius, if the path of the crank-pin be intersected at —4, the point of intersection will represent the position of the crank-pin at four inches of the stroke. The distance from

---

*** In order to get the engraving within the required limits, the diagram is drawn with a connecting-rod only 5½ instead of 7 feet. The latter is the length used in previous illustrations.**

o to —4 is equal to 44 degrees of the whole circle. The eccentrics, being attached to the axle, of course move the same number of degrees that the crank does, and therefore, in order to determine their position when the crank has moved any distance, it is only necessary to move them as many degrees as the crank has. This can be done very easily by extending the radii of the eccentrics, when they are in the first position, until they intersect the path of the crank-pin at c' and d'. By stepping off from the latter points of intersection a distance c' c''' and d' d''', equal to *o* —4, which the crank has moved, and then drawing other radii from the two points c''', d''', their intersection, c'' d'', with the path of the eccentrics will represent the position of the centres of the eccentrics when the crank is at —4. Having determined the position of the eccentrics, the link can be laid down as before, that is, from c'' and d'' as centres and with the length of the eccentric-rods as a radius arcs, f'' and g'', are drawn. Then with the paper template the positions of the centres of the link-pins in these arcs are determined and marked, and from them with the length of the eccentric rods as a radius, two intersecting arcs, v'', w'', are drawn, whose intersection gives the centre of the link from which its centre line, —4 —4, is drawn. This will give the position of the rocker-pin for another point of the stroke. In a similar manner its position can be determined for any number of points of the stroke, from which the position of the valve can easily be determined and laid down on the diagram for the motion-curve as was described in the answer to Question 44. Of course the valve will be moved from its middle position the same distance that the rocker-pin is,* only in an opposite direction. In order to lay down the position of the valve on the diagram for motion-curves, it is, therefore, only necessary to draw it in the same relative position as that of the rocker-pin which is given by the point of intersection of the center line of the link with the path in which the rocker-pin oscillates. To construct the motion-curves it is necessary to determine the positions of the valve for different points of the stroke and mark them on the horizontal lines which represent the respective positions of the piston. Curves are then drawn through these points, either by hand or by constructing templates. The more points there are determined, the more accurate will be the curves. It is, therefore, best to lay down the position of the valve for each inch of the stroke of the piston. They should also be drawn full size, which of course was impossible for the illustrations which are given herewith.

QUESTION 192. *Is there any other method of drawing these motion curves?*

Answer. Yes: models which show the working of the valve-gear have been constructed with a pencil, to which the reciprocating motion of the valve is imparted, and which traces a curve on a surface having the same motion as the piston. This method has been employed by the writer in an instrument which he has applied to the locomotive itself. The principle upon which it works will be understood by supposing that the steam and exhaust-ports as represented in the diagram for motion-curves, fig. 123, be drawn on a

* This will be the case when the two arms of the rocker are of the same length, as they usually are. Sometimes, though rarely, they are of different lengths.

board, *A B C D*, fig. 126, but instead of standing vertical, as in fig. 123, they are represented in a horizontal position, and the board on which they are drawn is fastened to the cross-head *L*, so that the former will move backward and forward simultaneously with the latter and the piston. A small shaft, *F*, is attached to suitable supports, *j*, which are fastened to the guides. This shaft has two arms, *G* and *E*, one vertical and the other horizontal and of the same length. The upper end of the vertical one, *G*, is then attached to the valve-stem or rocker-arm by a short connecting-rod, *H*, or other suitable means, so that the movement of the valve-stem will be imparted to the arm and shaft. Of course the end of the horizontal shaft then has exactly the same motion vertically that the valve-stem and valve have horizontally, with the very trifling inaccuracy due to the fact that the movement of the one is in a straight line, whereas the other is in the arc of a circle.

Now if a pencil, *P*, is attached to the end of the horizontal arm, *E*, and is set so that its point indicates the exact position of the steam edge, *h*, of the valve, as shown in fig. 123, it is obvious that when the piston and board have moved four inches, the pencil will have moved downward and have drawn the portion of the motion-curve from *h* to *i;* and when the piston has moved eight inches the curve will be drawn to *j*, and at 12, 16, 20 and 24 inches of the stroke the curve will be drawn to *k*, *l*, *m* and *n*. During the return stroke a corresponding curve, *n o h*, will, of course, be drawn. With such an instrument curves can be drawn for any position of the link, and they will show the exact movement of the valve during the whole

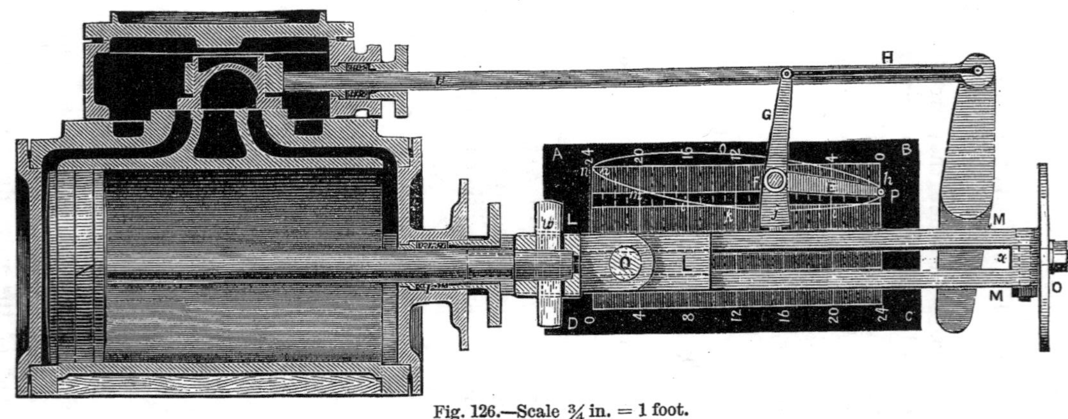

Fig. 126.—Scale ¾ in. = 1 foot.

stroke, and will indicate all the defects resulting from bad proportions or construction, lost motion in the parts, or other causes of error or irregularity.

In using this instrument, however, it is impracticable to attach a board to the inside of the cross-head, and it must therefore be fastened to the outside. The horizontal arm *E* should be made of thin steel, so as to form a spring. The end has a small *boss** with a hole in it $\frac{3}{16}$ of an inch in diameter. This hole has a screw thread cut in it, into which an ordinary hard drawing pencil is screwed. The spring is so arranged that the pencil will not be in contact with the board unless it be pressed against it. The locomotive is then placed on a smooth piece of track with steam on and run very slowly, so that a person walking alongside can press the pencil against the surface of the board, which should be covered with drawing paper. By watching the cross-head when it reaches the end of the stroke, the pencil can then be pressed against the paper and kept in contact through the whole stroke and instantly released when the motion-curve is completed. The link can then be placed in another position, and thus any number of curves can be drawn, which will furnish the most accurate means of analyzing the motion of the valve.

In practice it is best not to draw the lines which represent the edges of the ports, until after the curves are drawn and the paper removed from the board. A centre line must, however, be drawn on the engine from which to lay off the ports. This can be done by placing the valve in its middle position, and then fastening

* The term "boss" is used to imply an enlargement or increased thickness of any part.

the shaft *F* in that position with a nut which should be provided for that purpose on the end of the shaft. After it is fastened in this position, detach the connecting-rod *H*, and with one stroke of the piston a centre line can be drawn with the pencil *P*. From this centre line the edges of the ports can easily be laid off and drawn on the paper after it is taken off the engine.

QUESTION 193. *Can the position of each edge of the valve, with any given amount of travel, be shown in its relation to the ports by one motion-curve, or is it necessary to draw such curves for each edge of the valve, as shown in fig.* 28?

Answer. One motion-curve is sufficient to represent the position of any part of the valve during the entire stroke. This will be apparent if it is remembered that each motion-curve is exactly like the others, as shown in fig. 28, the only difference being that the ports occupy different positions in relation to the curves. It is, therefore, only necessary to draw lines to represent the relative positions of the ports to the other curves to show the entire motion of the valve by one curve. To illustrate this it will be assumed that a motion-curve, *h i j k l m n o p*, and a centre line, *a b*, fig. 127, have been drawn with the instrument described in the answer to the previous question. The centre line *a b*, which will be equal in length to the stroke of the piston, should then be divided into inches, and lines *ff*, 23 1, 22 2, etc., should be drawn through the points of division and at right angles to *a b*. If, now, we want to show the movement of the front steam edge of the valve in relation to the corresponding steam port, a line, *t*, should be drawn perpendicular to *f f*, to represent that edge of the valve at the beginning of the stroke. As it is impossible to determine accurately the position of this steam edge at the beginning of the stroke from the motion-curve, which is then *tangent** to the line *f f*, we must lay it off from the centre line, *a b*. This can readily be done if we remember that if a valve has $\frac{7}{8}$ in. lap when it is in the middle position, as shown in fig. 27, and $\frac{1}{16}$ in. lead at the beginning of the stroke, it must have moved $\frac{15}{16}$ in. from the middle position at the beginning of the stroke as shown in fig. 28. The line *t* must therefore be drawn $\frac{15}{16}$ in. from *a b* to represent its proper position in relation to the motion-curve, and as it has $\frac{1}{16}$ in. lead, the steam edge, *h h'*, of the steam-port must be drawn at that distance from *t*. Another line, *m m'*, can then be drawn to represent the width of the front steam-port, *c c'*. From these lines the movement of the valve in relation to the front port, *c c'*, and the admission of steam are shown as clearly as in fig. 28.

If now we want to represent the motion and relative position of the back steam edge of the valve in relation to its port, it is only necessary to assume that the line *t* represents that edge, and that the curve *h i j k l m n o h* represents its motion, and to draw the back steam-port in its proper relation to it. When the valve is in its middle position, as shown in fig. 27, the outside edge of the port *h* is $\frac{7}{8}$ in., or a distance equal to the lap, from the steam edge *q* of the valve. As the center line *a b*, fig. 127, represents the middle position of the edge of the valve, it is only necessary

* A curve is said to be *tangent* to another curve or to a straight line when the two just touch, but do not intersect or cross each other.

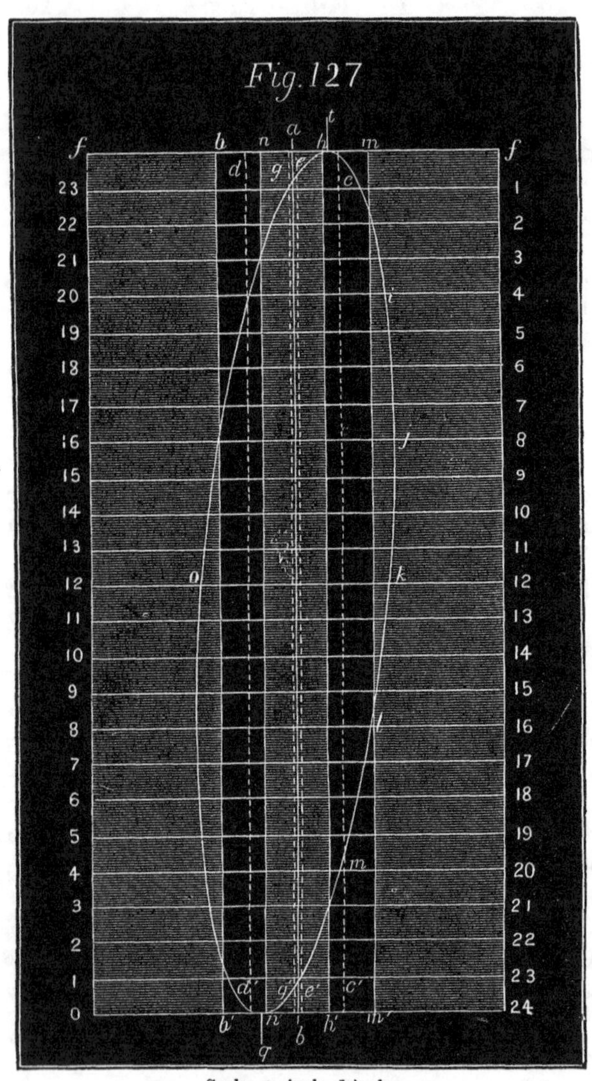

Fig. 127

Scale $\frac{3}{16}$ inch=1 inch.

to draw a line, *n n′*, $\frac{7}{8}$ in., or the same distance from the centre line *a b* that the outer edge of the port *d* is from *q* in fig. 28, to represent this edge of the port in fig. 127, and another *b b′*, at a distance from the former equal to the width of the port, to represent its inner edge. A line, *q*, below the line 0 24, will represent the edge of the valve at the beginning of the forward stroke. The curves in relation to the port *d* will then show the motion of the valve in relation to this port, in the same way that the dotted curve *d f* does in fig. 28.

If it is desired to represent the motion of the exhaust edge *h′*, fig. 28, of the valve, it is only necessary to imagine that the line *t*, fig. 127, represents that edge, and then draw in the port *d* in the same relation to it that it bears to the edge *h′*, in fig. 28. This has been done in dotted lines, *c c′* and *e e′*, in fig. 127.

If the reader will cut a paper section of a valve like that shown in fig. 27 and place the different edges, *h*, *i*, *h′* and *q*, so that they will successively correspond with the line *t* in fig. 127, the diagram will perhaps be more clear. If, for example, the paper section be placed to the right of the line *t*, so that the edge *h* will correspond with *t*, then it will be seen that the port *c* occupies the same relation to it that it does in fig. 28. If the valve be placed to the left, so that the edge *q* corresponds with *t*, then the port *d* will be in the same relation to it that it has in fig. 28. If the edges *i* and *h′* be made to correspond with *t*, then the ports drawn in dotted lines in fig. 127 will represent the ports *c* and *d* in fig. 28.

The position of the ports in relation to the centre line of the motion-curve can be determined, if it is kept in mind that the centre line *a b*, fig. 127, represents the position of the different edges of the valve when the latter is in the middle of the valve-face as shown in fig. 27, and that the ports must be on the same side, and the same distance from the centre line that they are from the edge of the valve whose motion is represented. Thus if the movement of the steam edge *h* in relation to its port, *c*, was represented, the edge of the latter must be drawn on the motion diagram the same distance from the centre line that it is from *h* when the valve is in its middle position as shown in fig. 27. This distance is of course just equal to the lap of the valve. If the motion of the exhaust edge *h'* was represented in relation to the steam port *d*, then the inside edge of the latter would be drawn the same distance from the centre line *a b* in the diagram that the inner edge of the port is from the edge *h'* of the valve, which is equal to the inside lap. The exhaust port could also be drawn in the same way, but it would be liable to confuse a diagram made to so small a scale as that which has been employed for the accompanying illustrations, and it has therefore been omitted. Diagrams of this kind which are made full size will, of course, show the movement of the valve more distinctly than is possible in the space occupied by the illustrations herewith. When they are made of full size, the lines indicating the ports should be drawn of different colors, so as to distinguish them from each other easily. Such diagrams will show the position of the valve in relation to the ports, and indicate the distribution of the steam during the whole stroke. It is only necessary to refer the curve to the proper line to determine the position of the valve in relation to either of the ports for either the admission or release of the steam. If, for example, we want to observe how the admission of steam is governed by the valve, by referring to fig. 127 we see that at the beginning of the backward stroke the valve has $\frac{1}{16}$ inch lead; that at $1\frac{3}{4}$ inches of the stroke the port *c* is wide open, as shown by the intersection of the motion-curve with the line *m m′*; that the valve has received its maximum backward travel at 9 inches of the stroke, and begins to close the port at $15\frac{1}{2}$ inches, and completely closes it at 21 inches of the stroke. By referring the motion-curve to the lines *n n′* and *b b′*, we see that the valve as shown by the line *q* at *n′* again has $\frac{1}{16}$ inch lead at the beginning of the forward stroke; that the steam port is wide open at $1\frac{3}{8}$ inches of the stroke; begins to close at $16\frac{1}{4}$ inches, and is completely closed at 21 inches. By referring the curve to the lines *e e′* and *c c′* we see that the front port begins to open to the exhaust before the piston has completed its forward stroke and when it has nearly an inch to move, that it is wide open almost immediately after the piston begins its stroke, does not begin to close until the piston has moved $19\frac{1}{2}$ inches of its stroke, and is completely closed at 23 inches of the stroke. By referring the curve to the lines *d d′* and *g g′*, almost the same phenomena will be observed for the forward stroke. In fact from such a diagram the whole motion of the valve can be studied and analyzed with the greatest accuracy; and, as has already been shown, the motion imparted to a slide valve by a link is of so complicated a nature that it is almost or quite impossible to observe its exact nature without such diagrams.

QUESTION 194. *Can a motion diagram be constructed to represent the motion of the valve with different amounts of travel?*

Answer. Yes; it is only necessary to construct motion-curves for the same diagram for each distance traveled, and they will show the movement of the valve for the given amount of travel represented by the curves. This has been done in fig. 128, which is a reduced copy of a series of motion-curves taken from a locomotive. From this diagram the movement of a slide-valve worked by the link-motion can be seen from the highest to the lowest practicable point of cut-off. For convenience of reference the curves have been numbered.

The smallest travel of the valve represented by curve No. 1 is a little less than $2\frac{1}{2}$ in., and the ports are then opened only about $\frac{5}{16}$ in., and the steam is cut off at 8 in. on the backward and $6\frac{3}{4}$ in. on the forward stroke. The exhaust is opened or the steam is released during the backward stroke at 17 in., and during the forward stroke at $16\frac{5}{8}$. When the valve works with its greatest travel, as represented by curve 8, it travels 5 in., and opens the steam port wide at 3 in. of the backward stroke and $2\frac{1}{4}$ in. of the forward stroke. The steam is cut off at $20\frac{3}{4}$ and $20\frac{1}{2}$ in., and its release takes place at $23\frac{1}{8}$ in. of each stroke. The following table gives the greatest width of opening, the point of cut-off, the point of release, and the lead for each motion-curve on the diagram. This table has been made up from the motion-curves drawn with the instrument described in answer to Question 191, on a locomotive which had been running about eighteen months and whose valve-gear consequently was con-

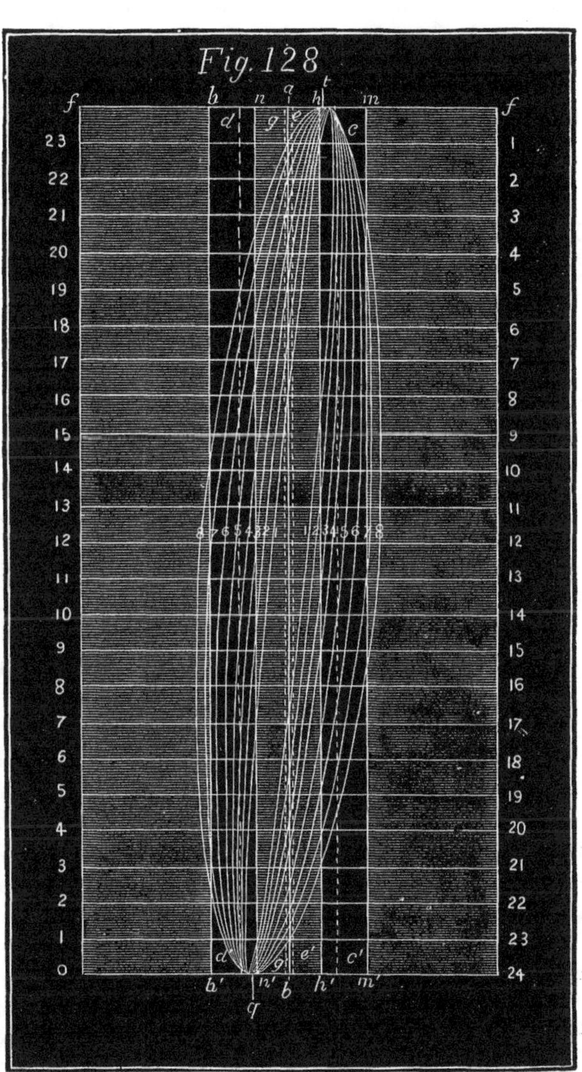

Scale $\frac{3}{16}$ inch=1 inch.

siderably worn, as is indicated by the flatness of the motion-curves on each side at the point when the motion of the valve was reversed. This flatness was

No. of curve....	Travel of valve.	Width of opening of steam-port.		Point of cut-off.		Point of release.		Lead..........
		Backwd stroke.	Forwr'd stroke.	Backwd stroke.	Forw'rd stroke.	Backwd stroke.	Forw'rd stroke.	
	in.	in.	in.	in.	in.	in.	in.	in.
1	$2\frac{1}{2}$	$\frac{11}{32}$	$\frac{5}{16}$	8	$6\frac{3}{4}$	17	$16\frac{5}{8}$	$\frac{9}{32}$
2	$2\frac{5}{8}$	$\frac{7}{16}$	$\frac{13}{32}$	$9\frac{1}{2}$	$9\frac{1}{2}$	$18\frac{5}{8}$	$18\frac{5}{16}$	$\frac{1}{4}$
3	$2\frac{7}{8}$	$\frac{9}{16}$	$\frac{1}{2}$	12	$11\frac{3}{4}$	$19\frac{3}{4}$	$19\frac{9}{16}$	$\frac{7}{32}$
4	$3\frac{1}{8}$	$\frac{11}{16}$	$\frac{41}{64}$	14	14	$20\frac{11}{16}$	$20\frac{9}{16}$	$\frac{3}{16}$
5	$3\frac{1}{2}$	$\frac{7}{8}$	$\frac{27}{32}$	$16\frac{1}{2}$	$16\frac{1}{2}$	$21\frac{11}{16}$	$21\frac{1}{2}$	$\frac{5}{32}$
6	4	$1\frac{1}{8}$	$1\frac{3}{32}$	$18\frac{1}{4}$	$18\frac{1}{8}$	$22\frac{3}{8}$	$22\frac{1}{4}$	$\frac{1}{8}$
7	$4\frac{1}{2}$	$1\frac{1}{4}$	$1\frac{1}{4}$	$19\frac{5}{8}$	$19\frac{1}{2}$	$22\frac{13}{16}$	$22\frac{3}{4}$	$\frac{3}{32}$
8	5	$1\frac{1}{4}$	$1\frac{1}{4}$	$20\frac{5}{8}$	$20\frac{1}{2}$	$23\frac{1}{8}$	$23\frac{1}{8}$	$\frac{1}{16}$

caused by the lost motion in the valve-gear, the pencil remaining for a time stationary when the motion was reversed and while the parts were moving from their bearings on one side to those on the other. The curves and the table therefore show the operation not of a theoretically perfect valve-gear, but are examples of actual practice, with such imperfections as are incidental to ordinary locomotives. It will be seen that the instrument shows not only what the valve-gear should, but what it actually does do, and delineates all its imperfections.

QUESTION 195. *What are the chief dimensions of the valve-gear represented in fig.* 128?

Answer. The throw of eccentrics was 5 in., the steam-ports were $1\frac{1}{4}$ in., and the exhaust-port $2\frac{3}{4}$ in. wide, the valve had $\frac{7}{8}$ in. outside and $\frac{1}{16}$ inside lap and $\frac{1}{16}$ in. lead at full stroke.

QUESTION 196. *What relation is there between the distance which the ports are opened by the valve, and its travel when worked by a link?*

Answer. As explained in the answer to Question 52, the width which the steam-ports are opened by the valve for the admission of steam diminishes with the travel of the valve. This is shown very clearly by the motion-curves, and also in the above table, from both of which it will be seen that when the valve travels only $2\frac{1}{2}$ in. the steam-ports are opened only $\frac{11}{32}$ in. for the back stroke and $\frac{5}{16}$ for the front. With $2\frac{5}{8}$ travel the opening is $\frac{7}{16}$ and $\frac{13}{32}$ in. With 4 in. travel the port is opened $1\frac{1}{8}$ and $1\frac{3}{32}$ in. and with $4\frac{1}{4}$ in. travel they would be opened wide. With $4\frac{1}{2}$ and 5 in. travel, as will be seen from the motion diagram, the ports are not only opened wide, but the valve throws "over" them, or travels beyond their inner edges.

QUESTION 197. *How is the point of cut-off affected by the link?*

Answer. Changing the travel of a valve with a link has a very similar effect to that produced by eccentrics of different throw—that is, the period of admission is increased with the throw of the eccentric and that for expansion lessened. This is shown clearly in both the motion diagram and the table. With the first curve and a travel of $2\frac{1}{2}$ in. the steam is cut off at 8 in. for the backward stroke and $6\frac{3}{4}$ in. for the front, and with 5 in. travel steam is admitted during $20\frac{5}{8}$ in. of the backward and $20\frac{1}{2}$ in. of the forward stroke.

QUESTION 198. *How is the point of release or exhaust of the steam affected by the link?*

Answer. As the travel increases, it is delayed until

later in the stroke. Thus, with 2½ in. travel the steam is exhausted or released from the cylinder during the backward stroke when the piston has moved 17 in., and on the return stroke at 16⅝ in., whereas, with 5 in. travel of the valve, the release is delayed until 23⅛ in. of the stroke. An examination of the diagram and table will show very clearly the relation of the point of release to the travel.

QUESTION 199. *How is the lead affected by the ordinary link motion?*

Answer. It is increased as the travel is diminished, as is shown in the table, and also by the inclination of the curves at the top and bottom of the diagram.

QUESTION 200. *What is the cause of this change of the amount of lead?*

Answer. This can be best explained by reference to fig. 129, which represents a link with very short eccentric rods. If now the centre from which the link was drawn was in the centre of the axle *S*, and the eccentric straps embraced the axle instead of the eccentrics, their ends *c* and *d* would each describe the same arc, *a b*, parallel with the centre line, *x y*, of the link, and the latter could then obviously be raised and lowered without moving the rocker-pin at all. But the eccentric straps being attached to the eccentrics, as shown by the dotted lines, when the rods are raised or lowered they describe arcs, *c e* and *g h*, from the centres *s* and *t* of the eccentrics, and not from the centre of the axle. When the link is raised then, the end of the upper rod obviously moves in the arc *c e*, and the top of the link is moved from the axle, as shown in fig. 130, a distance equal to the interval between the arc, *a b*, drawn from the centre of the axle, and

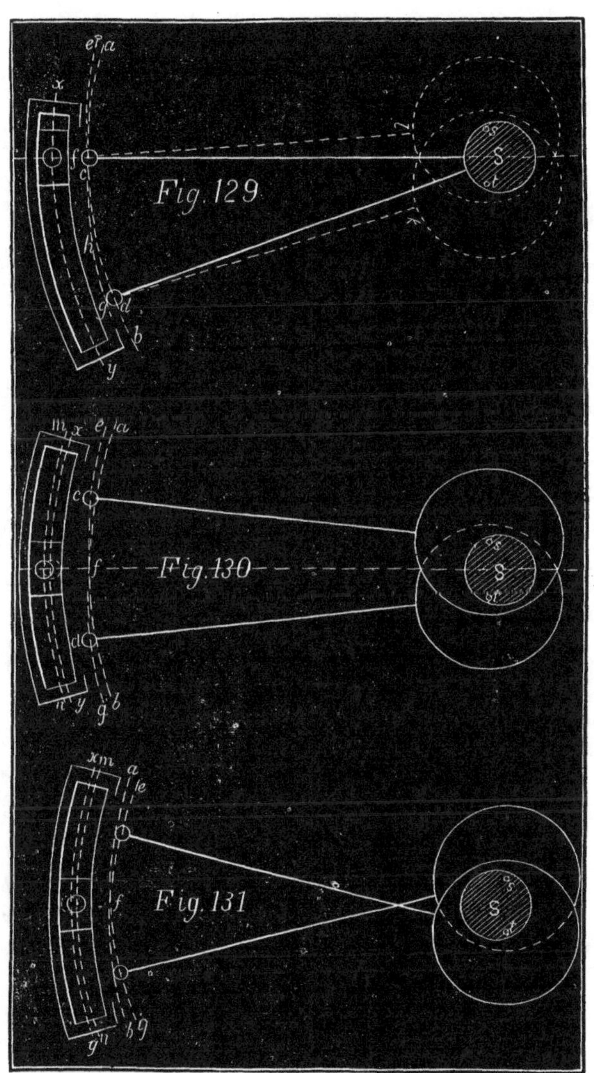

Fig. 129

Fig. 130

Fig. 131

Scale ¾ in. = 1 foot.

e f, which the rod describes from the centre of its eccentric. When the link is lowered from back to mid-gear, a similar action takes place, as the end, *d*, fig. 130, of the lower rod describes an arc, *f g*, so that the whole link is thrown from the axle a distance equal to the space between the arcs described from the centre of the axle and the centres of the eccentrics. When the position of the eccentrics is reversed, as shown in fig. 131, the link is moved towards the axle, thus causing an increase of lead on the opposite side of the valve. We have employed for our illustrations very short eccentric rods, in order to make this action apparent by exaggerating it. It is obvious from the engravings that the difference in the lead is increased as the eccentric rods are shortened, and also as the distance between the points of connection of the rods with the link is increased. It will also be plain that increasing the throw of the eccentrics, that is, increasing the distance of the centres *s*, *s*, of the eccentrics from the centre *S* of the axle will also increase the variation in the lead in full and mid-gear.

QUESTION 201. ***What is meant by the distribution of steam in the cylinder?***

Answer. It means the admission and exhaust of steam to and from the cylinder in relation to the stroke of the piston or the revolution of the crank.

QUESTION 202. ***What are the principal periods or elements of the distribution of steam by the slide-valve and link motion?***

Answer. They are:

1. The *pre-admission* or lead, that is, the admission of steam into the cylinders in front of the piston before it has completed its stroke.

2. The *admission* of steam after the piston has commenced its stroke.

3. The *expansion* of steam in the cylinder.

4. The *pre-release,* or exhaust of steam before the piston has completed its stroke.

5. The *release,* or exhaust during the return stroke of the piston.

6. The *compression* of steam, or closing the exhaust before the piston has completed its return stroke.

QUESTION 203. *What is meant by the clearance of the piston?*

Answer. It is the space between the piston and the cylinder-head when the former is at the end of the stroke. If the piston touched the cylinder-head at the end of each stroke, it would cause a concussion or "thump" which would injure these parts. Owing to the impossibility of constructing machinery with absolute accuracy, it is therefore necessary to leave a space, usually from $\frac{1}{2}$ to $\frac{1}{4}$ in. wide, between the piston and the cylinder-heads, so as to be certain that they will not strike each other should there be any slight inaccuracies in the length of the piston-rods, connecting-rods, frames or other parts.

QUESTION 204. *Why is it desirable to open the steam-port and admit steam at the end of the cylinder towards which the piston is moving BEFORE the latter has completed its stroke?*

Answer. Because it is essential, in order to insure a good action of the steam, that the maximum cylinder pressure should be attained at the very commencement of the stroke. If the steam-port was not opened until after the piston had commenced its stroke, some appreciable time would be consumed in filling the clearance space and the *steam-way* with steam.* It is also found, especially if an engine is working at a high speed, that a slide-valve worked by the ordinary link-motion will not open the steam-port rapidly enough to enable steam of the maximum boiler pressure to fill the space after the receding piston, unless the valve begins to open the port *before* the piston reaches the end of its stroke.

Another advantage resulting from the pre-admission of steam consists in the smooth working of the engine at high speeds, a circumstance which reduces greatly the wear and tear of the working gear. As the piston approaches the end of its stroke, the pre-admitted steam forms a kind of elastic cushion, which is well calculated to absorb the momentum of the reciprocating parts at that instant. The pressure due to the momentum of these parts will, of course, depend upon their weight and the speed of working, increasing directly as the square of the speed. It follows from this that the lead should increase with the speed, and that it should be greatest at high speeds. As has been shown before, this condition is fully accomplished by the ordinary shifting-link motion.

QUESTION 205. *Upon what does the admission of steam into the cylinder depend?*

Answer. It depends in the first place upon the opening of the throttle-valve, and the size of the pipes and passages through which it is conveyed from the boiler to the cylinder. In the second place, it depends upon the time and amount of opening of the steam-port by the valve.

* The *steam ways* are the passages which lead from the steam-chest to the cylinder, and are sometimes called steam-ports, but the term steam-ways is used to distinguish the passages from their openings in the valve-seat, which latter are more properly called steam-ports.

QUESTION 206. ***What should be the pressure of the steam in the cylinder during admission?***

Answer. In order that the steam may be used to most advantage, it should be admitted and maintained in the cylinder at full boiler pressure during the whole period of admission. If the opening of either the throttle-valve or the steam-ports is not sufficient to allow the steam to flow into the cylinder at full boiler pressure, the steam is said to be wire-drawn, and much of the advantage of using it expansively as has already been explained in answer to Question 59, is then lost.

QUESTION 207. ***Why is it difficult to admit and maintain steam at the full boiler pressure in the cylinder during admission?***

Answer. Because it is necessary to reduce the travel of the slide-valve in order to cut off the steam "***short,***" or soon after the beginning of the stroke of the piston. When the travel is reduced, the valve opens the port only a small distance, so that the area of the opening is not then sufficient to allow the steam to flow into the cylinder with sufficient rapidity to fill it at full boiler pressure, especially if the engine is working at a high speed. Thus, by referring to the table given on page 216 and to the motion curves in fig. 128, it will be seen that when the steam is cut off at from $\frac{1}{4}$ to $\frac{1}{2}$ stroke, the port is opened for the admission of steam only from $\frac{1}{4}$ to $\frac{1}{2}$ inch wide. From the curves it will also be seen that the valve then acquires its maximum travel and the steam-port its greatest width of opening very soon after the piston begins its stroke; after which the port is gradually closed, so that before the steam is entirely cut off the opening is so much reduced in area that the steam cannot flow through it rapidly enough to maintain the steam at full boiler pressure in the cylinder when the engine is working at high speeds.

QUESTION 208. *What means are used to overcome this difficulty and thus admit steam at full boiler pressure when the valve is cutting off short?*

Answer. In the first place, the steam-ports are made from ten to twelve times as long as they are wide, so that a narrow opening will have a comparatively large area. In the second place, by giving the valve lead, not only are the clearance space and the steam-way filled with steam when the piston begins its stroke, but the port is then open a distance equal to the lead. With the ordinary link motion, as has already been shown, this lead increases as the travel and period of admission diminish, so that the smaller the total distance that the port is opened, the greater is its opening at the beginning of the stroke. As the steam is usually cut off short when locomotives run at high speeds, it will be seen that the increased lead which is imparted to the valve by the shifting link is an advantage rather than a disadvantage. But while it is often possible in this way to secure a pressure of steam in the cylinder at the beginning of the stroke equal or nearly so to that in the boiler, yet it is almost impossible to maintain this pressure during the whole period of admission, when the steam is cut off short and the engine working at a high speed. To obviate this evil what is called the Allen valve was designed, which is represented in fig. 132. This valve has a channel or supplementary port, *a a*, which passes over the exhaust cavity, and has two openings, *b*, *b'*, in the valve-face. When the valve begins to admit or "*take*" steam at *c*, as shown in fig. 133, it will be seen that it also uncovers the opening *b′* at *e* and admits steam at *b′*, which passes through the channel *b′ a a b* and enters the steam-port *c* at *b*, and in this way there is a double opening for the admission of steam. The opening *b* of the supplementary port is closed as the valve advances, but when this takes place the steam-port is

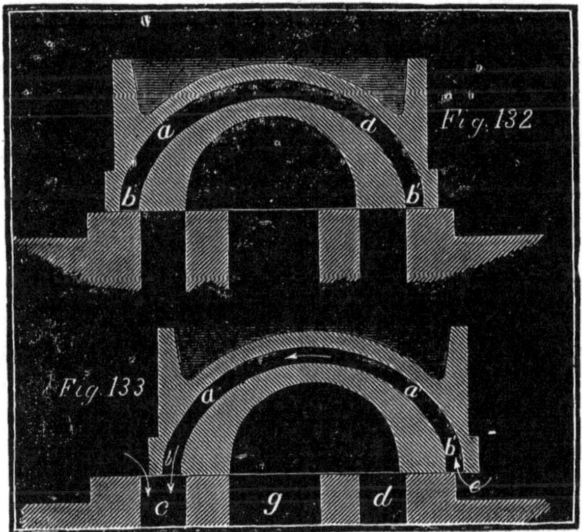

Scale $\frac{3}{16}$ in. = 1 inch.

uncovered far enough to admit all the steam that is required. This form of valve is very efficient when the travel and point of cut-off are very short. It then gives just twice as much opening as the ordinary valve for the admission of steam. This improved valve has been much used in Europe; but, although it is an American invention, has not received the attention in this country which its merit deserves.

QUESTION 209. *What is meant by the pre-release of steam?*

Answer. It is the release of the steam before the piston has completed its stroke. If it is confined until the piston has reached the end of the cylinder, there will not be time nor will it be possible, with a slide valve and link-motion, to secure a sufficiently large opening of the port to permit the steam to escape from the cylinder before the piston begins its return stroke. If there were no pre-release, there would therefore be more or less back pressure on the piston.

QUESTION 210. *Upon what does the amount of pre-release depend.*

Answer. First, as has already been explained in answer to Question 51, on the amount of inside lap; and second, on the outside lap of the valve and lead of the eccentrics; and third, on the travel of the valve. The less the inside lap, the greater the outside lap and consequent lead of the eccentrics; and the shorter the travel of the valve, the earlier will be the release. The proper amount of this pre-release depends upon the velocity of the piston and the quantity of steam to be discharged or the degree of expansion. From the motion-curves in fig. 128 it will be seen that it is a marked feature of the shifting-link motion that the pre-release occurs earlier in the stroke as the link approaches mid-gear, or as the travel of the valve diminishes. As the link is usually worked near that position when the engine is run at a high speed, it will be seen that in this respect again the link-motion is well adapted for working the slide-valves of locomotives.

QUESTION 211. *What governs the period of release.*

Answer. The release like pre-release is dependent upon the amount of inside lap, the outside lap and consequent lead of the eccentrics, and the travel of the valve.

The addition of inside lap has the effect of closing the port earlier than it would be closed without, and thus shortening the period of release and also of reducing the area of the opening of the port. This will be apparent by referring to fig. 128, in which the valve had $\frac{1}{16}$ in. lead. The dotted lines which represent the edges of the ports in relation to the exhaust edges of the valve are therefore drawn $\frac{1}{16}$ in. from the centre line *a b*. If, however, there had been no inside lap, then the edges of the ports would have conformed to the line *a b*. It will be observed that the first curve crosses the dotted line *g g′* at $15\frac{1}{2}$ in. of the forward stroke, which is the point at which the port is closed to the exhaust, or where the period of release ends and compression begins. If there had been no lap and the line *g g′* had therefore occupied the same position as *a b*, then the motion-curve would not have crossed it until the piston had reached 16 in. of its stroke, thus showing that the period of release had been lengthened and compression delayed. As the width of the opening of the port is represented by the distance of the motion-curve from the right hand side of the line *g g,′* which represents the edge of the port, it is obvious that if there had been no lap, so that the position of the line representing the edge of the port had occupied the position of *a b*, then the space between it and the motion-curve would have been greater, thus showing that the port would have been opened wider if there had been no inside lap. The width of the opening of the port to the exhaust is in fact always diminished by an amount equal to the inside lap.

With the same travel, increase of outside lap and lead shortens the period of release, but has no effect on the width of the opening of the port to the exhaust.

Increase of travel, with the same outside lap, lengthens the period of release and also increases the width of the opening of the port to the exhaust.

QUESTION 212. *What governs the period of compression.*

Answer. As compression begins when release ends, or when the port is closed to the exhaust, it is controlled by exactly the same causes, and as the two events occur simultaneously, of course whatever shortens the period of release lengthens that of compression.

QUESTION 213. *What effect do the clearance spaces and steam-ways have upon the compression of the confined steam?*

Answer. By referring to the motion-curves in fig. 128, it will be seen that the steam-port is closed by the exhaust edge of the valve, or compression begins some time before the piston reaches the end of the stroke. The result is that the remaining portion of the cylinder, through which the piston must move *after* the port is closed to the exhaust, is filled with steam of atmospheric pressure, or possibly a little above that pressure. As this is confined in the cylinder, it is compressed by the advance of the piston. If there was no room between it and the cylinder at the end of the stroke, then either the cylinder would be burst or the valve would lift so as to allow the compressed steam to flow back into the steam-chest. The clearance and the steam-passages, however, afford considerable room, into which the confined steam can be compressed without danger of bursting the cylinder, or of raising the slide-valve when there is steam in the steam-chest. As the clearance spaces and steamways must be filled with high-pressure steam at the beginning of each stroke, it must be obtained either by taking a supply of "*live*"* steam from the boiler, or by compressing into the clearance spaces the low-pressure steam that still remained in the cylinder when the port was closed to the exhaust. By the latter process, a certain quantity of steam is saved at the expense of increased back pressure. It should be borne in mind also that the total heat of the compressed steam increases with its pressure, and as this latter approaches that in the boiler, the temperature of the former must have been raised from that due to about atmospheric pressure to nearer the temperature of that in the boiler. These changes of temperature which the steam undergoes will affect the surface of the metal with which the steam is in contact during the period of compression; it follows from this, that the ends of the cylinder principally comprising the clearance spaces must acquire a higher temperature than those parts where expansion only takes place. This is an important consideration, since the fresh steam from the boiler comes first in contact with these spaces, and by touching surfaces which have thus previously been heated, as it were, by the high tempera-

* The term "live" steam means steam taken direct from the boiler and which has not been used in the cylinder or to do any work.

ture of the compressed steam, less heat will be abstracted from the fresh steam, and therefore a less amount of water will be deposited in the cylinder.*

It will thus be seen that the effect of compression is to fill the clearance spaces and steam-ways with compressed steam before pre-admission begins. As already stated, this is done at the expense of back pressure in the cylinder. It must be remembered that all the energy, excepting that part which is wasted by loss of heat, friction, etc., which is consumed in compressing the confined steam, is again given out to the piston by expansion. The confined steam also acts as an elastic cushion to receive the piston, just as the steam which is admitted before the end of the stroke would if there were no compression. Compression, therefore, has the effect of saving the quantity of live steam which it would otherwise be necessary to admit before the end of the stroke to fill the clearance spaces and steam-ways and also to "cushion" the piston. As already stated, the momentum of the piston and other parts depends upon their weight and the speed at which they are working, increasing directly as the square of the speed, from which it follows that the compression should increase rapidly with the speed, and should be the greatest at high speeds. As the ports are prematurely closed to the exhaust with the shifting-link motion, and as the lead increases rapidly as the link approaches mid-gear, and the amount of compression is at the same time correspondingly augmented, it will be seen that the shifting-link motion fulfills these conditions very perfectly.

* Bauschinger's Indicator Experiments on Locomotives, published in Vol. III. of the RAILROAD GAZETTE.

The pressure to which the confined steam will rise depends of course upon the amount of the period of compression, and also on the size of the clearance spaces. As it is possible to have such an amount of compression that it will exceed the boiler pressure, and thus raise the valve from its seat and be forced back into the steam-chest, some care must be exercised to proportion the one to the other, so that the degree of the confined steam may not be excessive.

QUESTION 214. *How can the effect of the distribution of the steam upon its action in the cylinder be determined by experiment?*

Answer. As already explained in answer to Question 55, this can be done by an instrument called a steam indicator.

QUESTION 215. *What is the construction of this instrument?*

Answer. The indicator now ordinarily used is the Richards indicator, the outside of which is represented in fig. 134 and a section in fig. 135. It consists of a cylinder, *B*, into which a piston, *C*, is accurately fitted, but so that it will move freely in the cylinder. The piston rod is surrounded with a spiral spring, *D*, the lower end of which is attached to the top of the piston, and the upper end to the cylinder cover. When steam is introduced below the piston it pushes it up in the cylinder and the spring is compressed. If there should be a vacuum below the piston, the air above it will press the piston downward and extend the spring. This latter occurs only when the indicator is used on condensing engines. Of course the distance which the piston is forced up by the steam pressure below it depends upon the amount of pressure and also on the tension of the spring; and therefore by attaching a pencil to the piston-rod so that it can mark on a moving card in front of it, a diagram will be drawn which would indicate the steam pressure, as was explained in answer to Question 55. But there are some practical difficulties in the way of doing this.

Fig. 134. Fig. 135.

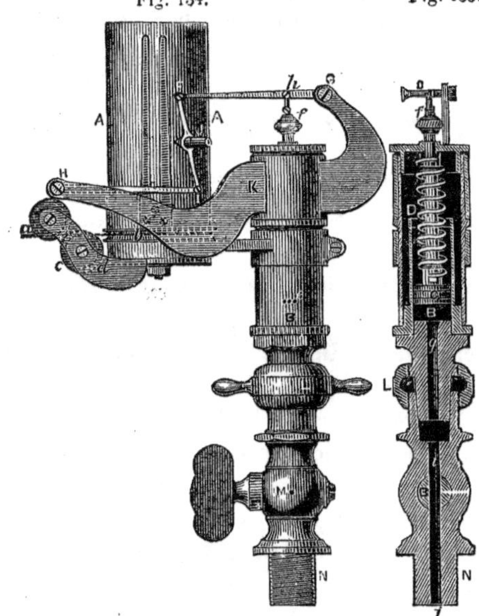

Scale 3 in.=1 foot.

It is found that if the pencil is attached directly to the piston-rod of the indicator, the distance through which they must move, in order to make the scale of the diagram sufficiently large to be clear, is so great that the momentum of the parts carries them further than the pressure of the steam alone would move them. The distance through which the pistons or instruments move, moreover, makes it impossible that the changes of pressure should be indicated simultaneously with the position of the piston; the latter must travel while the action is taking place, and thus the diagram shows changes of pressure later or more gradually than they occur.* To overcome these and other difficulties, the piston-rod of the indicator which we have illustrated is attached at *h* to the short arm of a lever, *F G*, and to the end of the long arm a piece, *F I*, is attached, which carries a pencil, *J*. By this means the piston has only one-fourth of the motion that it imparts to the pencil, so that the momentum of the moving parts is comparatively slight. If the pencil was attached directly to the end of the lever, it is obvious that it would move in the arc of a circle, and that this would be a source of error in the diagram. To avoid this the pencil is attached to what is called a "parallel motion." This consists of a coupling-rod, *F I*, which connects the ends of two levers, *F G* and *I H*. The centre of the rod *F I*, to which the pencil is attached, will with this arrangement move in a straight line. The levers and all the parts are of course all made as light as possible, so that their weight will have little effect on the motion of the indicator piston.

The paper or card on which the diagram is drawn is wrapped around a brass cylinder, *A A*. This cylinder is made to revolve part of the way around by a strong twine, *a b*, which is wrapped around a pulley, *b*, at the bottom of the cylinder. The twine is attached to a lever, similar to that shown in fig. 30, which receives a reciprocating motion from the piston of the

* Richards' Steam Indicator, by Charles T. Porter.

engine. The twine can of course move the cylinder only in one direction, and therefore a coiled spring similar to a clock spring is placed inside of the cylinder to draw it back when the twine is relaxed. In this way the paper cylinder or drum receives a part of a revolution at each stroke of the piston, and moves simultaneously with it. This drum is used instead of a flat card, on account of the practical difficulties of

Fig. 136.

employing the latter. The motion of the paper on this drum will, however, be exactly the same in relation to the pencil as the motion of a flat card would be.

The method of attaching an indicator to a locomotive is represented in fig. 136. It will be seen from this that it is placed over the center of the steam chest and connected to each end of the cylinder with

$\frac{3}{4}$-inch pipes. A globe valve was in the case represented placed on each side of the indicator, so that it could be put into communication with either end of the cylinder, or could be completely shut off from both. A better plan, however, is to have a three-way cock at the point where the horizontal pipe connects with the vertical one leading to the indicator, as the passages in a three-way cock are more direct than those in globe valves. The arrangement of the levers for giving motion to the indicator drum, and of the seat, which is very requisite for the experimenter, will be readily understood from the engraving without further explanation. It is thought by some engineers that the indicator should be applied as near to each end of the cylinder as possible. It is believed, however, that if the pipes, cocks, and their connections are made large enough so as not to impede the motion of the steam, no appreciable error will arise from the method illustrated in fig. 136.

QUESTION 216. *What should be the form of an indicator diagram, if the steam is distributed by a link motion so as to produce the best practicable action in the cylinders?*

Answer. It should approximate to that shown in fig. 136. In this diagram the vertical lines represent inches of the stroke, and the scale on the left the steam pressure in pounds per square inch. The atmospheric and vacuum lines are also indicated, as already explained in answer to Question 55. The points at which the different periods of the distribution begin are indicated by the letters *a, b, c, d, e* and *f*. These are in the order in which they occur: *a*, pre-admission; *b*, admission; *c*, expansion; *d*, pre-release; *e*, release; and *f*, compression. The lines forming the outline of the diagram will be designated for convenience of description as follows:

The line from *a* to *b*, the *admission line.*
" " " *b* to *c*, the *steam line.*
" " " *c* to *d*, the *line or curve of expansion.*
" " " *d* to *e*, the *exhaust line.*
" " " *e* to *f*, the *line of back pressure.*
" " " *f* to *a*, the *line or curve of compression.*

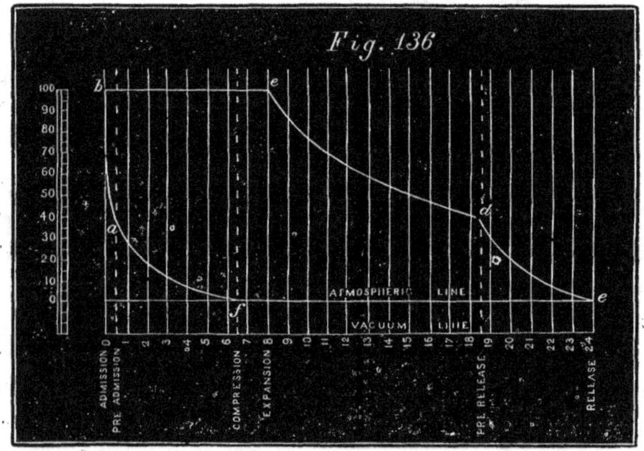

Fig. 136

The diagram represents a distribution of steam produced by a valve having $\frac{7}{8}$ in. outside and $\frac{1}{16}$ inside lap, and operated by the link motion represented in fig. 103. The eccentrics have 5 in. throw, and the steam-ports are $1\frac{1}{4}$ and the exhaust $2\frac{3}{4}$ in. wide. The valve as shown by the diagram is cutting off at 8 in., or one-third of the stroke. Pre-admission begins when the piston still has $\frac{1}{2}$ in. to move before reaching the end of its stroke. Admission of course begins with the stroke, expansion at 8 in., pre-release at $18\frac{1}{2}$ in., release at the end of the stroke, and compression at 17½ in. of the return stroke. The valve is supposed to be set without any lead, or "*line and line*,"* as it is called at full stroke. When the steam is cut off at 8 in. of the stroke, the valve has 2⅝ in. travel and $\frac{3}{16}$ in. lead. The steam pressure in the boiler is supposed to be 100 pounds above the atmosphere. Of course, when the valve cuts off at different points of the stroke, the periods of distribution will be somewhat changed; but from the above diagram the principal features of a good distribution can be explained.

These are: First, that the steam pressure should rise rapidly during the period of pre-admission, so that there will be full boiler pressure in the cylinder at the beginning of the stroke. When this occurs, the pre-admission line will rise from *a* to *b*, to such a point at *b* which will indicate full boiler pressure in the cylinder. The same pressure should then be maintained in the cylinder during the whole period of admission, and the admission line from *b* to *c* should therefore be a straight horizontal line, as shown in fig. 136. When expansion begins, the pressure will fall, as was explained in answer to Question 55. The expansion line should approximate a hyperbolic curve, but if there is much loss of heat by radiation or other causes, the diagram will fall considerably below the theoretical curve. With cylinders well protected and with dry steam the expansion line will fall slightly below a hyperbolic curve at the beginning of the period of expansion, and rise above it during the latter part of the same period. The reason of this is that the cylinder

* That is, the steam edges of the valve correspond with the steam edges of the port at the beginning of the stroke.

is heated by the admission of live steam of comparatively high pressure and temperature, so that, when the pressure becomes reduced by expansion, a part of tho water which is condensed in the cylinder will be re-evaporated by the heat in the latter. From the point of the pre-release, *d*, to the end of the stroke, *e*, the exhaust line should fall rapidly, so that there will be no pressure behind the piston during its return stroke. To explain the theoretical form of the exhaust line would lead us into a very abstruse discussion, which would be out of place here. It will be sufficient for our purpose to call attention to the fact that the pre-release should allow all the steam in the cylinder to escape before the piston reaches the end of the stroke, so that the back pressure during the return stroke may be as low as possible. It is, however, only at comparatively slow speeds that the steam in locomotive cylinders escapes during the period of pre-release, so that the back pressure is reduced to that of the atmosphere. It is necessary in locomotives, as has already been explained, to contract the area of the blast orifices or exhaust nozzles, in order to stimulate the draft through the fire, so that the steam cannot escape with sufficient rapidity to reduce the back pressure to that of the atmosphere if the engine is running fast. Of course every pound of back pressure on the piston is so much loss of energy, and a reduction of the amount of work done by the engine; but it is a sacrifice which must be made in order to be able to generate the requisite quantity of steam. In studying the distribution of steam, however, every effort should be made to reduce the back pressure as much as is practicable, and yet maintain a sufficient supply of steam, and therefore the line of back pressure should conform as closely as possible to the atmospheric line. The compression line should be a hyperbolic curve, beginning with the period of compression. In calculating both the compression and expansion, allowance must be made for the clearance space and steam-way. In a cylinder like that illustrated in fig. 92, their contents would be about equal to that of two inches of the cylinder. Therefore, when steam is cut off at 8 in. of the stroke, instead of having a quantity of steam which will fill a cylinder 16 in. diameter and 8 in. long, we have as much as would fill a cylinder of that diameter and 10 in. long. The same thing is true of the compression. This must occur in the above example when the piston has 6½ in. more to move before completing its stroke. There is therefore a quantity of steam in front of it sufficient to fill a cylinder 8½ in. in diameter. This steam is of course compressed by the advance of the piston, and if its pressure when compression begins is the same as that of the atmosphere, then it will be 0.9 lbs. above it when the piston has only 6 in. to move and 3.2, 6.2, 10.5, 16.9, and 27.5 lbs. effective pressure when the piston has 5, 4, 3, 2 and 1 inches to move respectively, and when preadmission begins, the pressure will have risen to 48.7 lbs. If the back pressure is above that of the atmosphere, of course the compression will be correspondingly increased. It will also be seen that, without any or with very little clearance space, the compression would at the end of each stroke rise above the boiler pressure. It being a peculiarity of the ordinary shifting-link motion that as the period of admission is reduced that of compression is lengthened, the latter becomes very excessive when the steam is cut off at less than one-third or one-fourth of the stroke.

Question 217. *In what respect would a diagram made by an indicator differ from the theoretical form represented in fig.* 136?

Answer. It would be drawn with less exactness; that is, the corners instead of being sharply defined, as in fig. 136, would be more or less rounded, as in fig. 137, and the curves and straight lines would vary

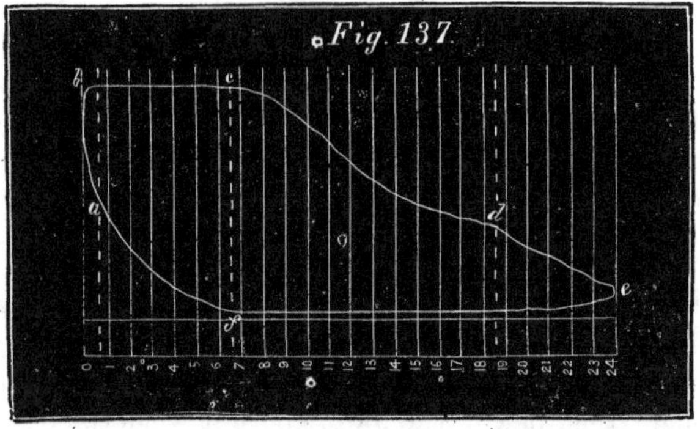

somewhat from the exact mathematical form indicated in fig. 136. The higher the speed at which the engine is working when the diagrams are taken, the greater will be the variation from the theoretical form.

Question 218. *If the amount of pre-admission is insufficient, how will it be shown in the indicator diagram?*

Answer. The effect of too little pre-admission is to lower the pressure of the steam at the beginning of the stroke, and at high speeds there will not be time enough nor sufficient opening of the steam-port to supply the deficiency after the stroke has commenced.

The corner of the diagram at *b* will then be very much rounded, as shown in fig. 138. This is apt to be the case when steam is admitted during a considerable part of the stroke, as a shifting-link motion then gives less lead than when it is worked nearer mid-gear. If the steam is cut off short, then the pressure in the cylinder during admission is very much below boiler pressure, and is apt to fall rapidly after the commencement of the stroke, as shown in fig. 138.

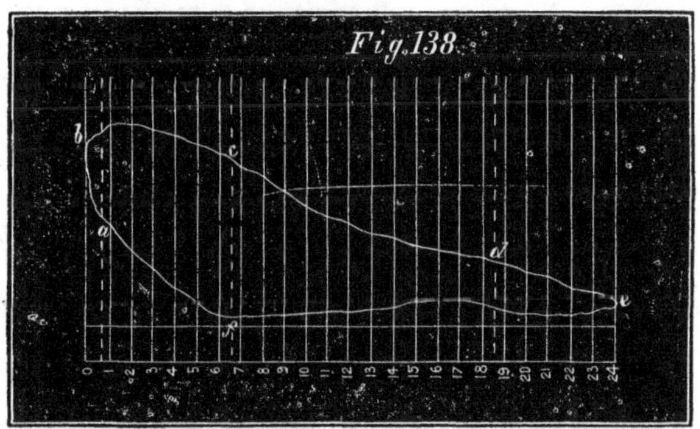

Fig. 138.

QUESTION 219. *If the opening of the steam-ports during admission is too small, what will be the form of the diagram?*

Answer. The effect will be very much the same as that produced by too little pre-admission or lead; that is, the pressure in the cylinder will be much lower than in the boiler and will fall rapidly during the periods of admission, as shown in fig. 138.

QUESTION 220. *What defects will be indicated by the expansion curve of indicator diagrams?*

Answer. If the cylinders are not well protected, and there is much loss of heat from radiation, there will be a rapid fall of pressure during the period of expansion, which will be shown by the expansion curve falling below the theoretical curve shown in fig. 136. If, on the contrary, the indicator curve is much above the theoretical curve, it may be caused by a leak in the valve. As steam is quite as likely to leak from the steam-port into the exhaust as from the steam-chest into the steam-port, a valve which is not tight may produce just the contrary effect upon the indicator diagram. As it is usually quite easy to detect a leak in the valve by other means, the use of the indicator for this purpose is unnecessary. Attention is called to it, however, to show the impossibility of getting results of any value with the indicator if the valves are not steam-tight.

QUESTION 221. ***What should be observed regarding the exhaust line of the indicator diagram?***

Answer. The most important point to be observed is, whether the pressure at the end of the stroke is reduced as low as possible, as at high speeds it is usually much more difficult to exhaust the steam from than to admit it into the cylinder. As already stated, the blast in the chimney makes it almost impossible to exhaust the steam to atmospheric pressure when the locomotive is running fast. If the steam is released too late in the stroke, as already explained, there will not be time enough nor sufficient opening of the port to allow the confined steam to escape from the cylinder before the end of the stroke, and this will be indicated on the diagram by the space between the line of back pressure and the atmospheric line during the commencement of the return stroke, as shown in fig. 138.

QUESTION 222. *What should be observed regarding the line of back pressure?*

Answer. The most important point is, that it should approximate as closely as possible to the atmospheric line, as all the back pressure not only diminishes the efficiency of the engine, but is a total loss of energy. Too much inside lap will increase the amount of back pressure, but generally it is more influenced by the area of the blast orifices than by any other cause. Every effort should be made, therefore, to have them as large as possible and yet have the boiler make as much steam as is needed.

When only one blast orifice is used for both cylinders, it often happens that when the steam is exhausted from the one cylinder it "blows" over into the other, and thus produces an additional amount of back pressure. This is shown by a rise or "hump" in the line of back pressure, as indicated in fig. 138.

QUESTION 223. *Can the amount of compression which is needed be determined by calculation?*

Answer. Yes; but it involves more abstruse principles of mathematics than it is thought best to introduce here. Some of the reasons can, however, be given, which will make the subject clearer, and enable the reader, if he has sufficient knowledge of mathematics, to investigate the subject still further.

In the first place it is a well-known fact that the motion of a piston in the cylinder of a steam engine is not a uniform one, but increases in speed from the beginning of the stroke to the middle, and diminishes in speed from the middle to the opposite end. The cause of this is that the crank revolves at a uniform speed during the entire revolution, but the piston moves much less at the beginning of the stroke, with a given amount of revolution of the crank, than it does at the middle. This is shown in fig. 140, in which *A* is a cylinder and *B* the piston and *a b c d* the path of the crank. Now while the crank moves from *a* to 1, or $\frac{1}{12}$ of a revolution, the piston has moved $1\frac{5}{8}$ in., or a distance equal to that from *a* to 1′ or to the base of a perpendicular drawn from 1 to the centre line *a c*. While the crank moves from 1 to 2, or through the second twelfth of a revolution, the piston has moved from 1′ to 2′, or $4\frac{3}{8}$ in., or $2\frac{3}{4}$ in. further than during the first twelfth of the crank's revolution. During the third twelfth of the revolution the piston moves from 2′ to 3′, or 6 in., thus showing that it continues to increase in the distance moved during each period of the revolution of the crank until the latter has made a quarter revolution. The speed of the piston then begins to diminish until it reaches the end of the stroke. It is slightly affected by the angularity of the connecting-rod, as already explained, but for the present this is disregarded. It is obvious now that if the momentum, or actual energy stored up in the piston and other reciprocating parts after they have passed the middle of the stroke, added to the pressure behind the piston, is greater than the resistance offered by the crank, the motion of the latter will then be accelerated and thus conveyed to the moving engine and train. If, however, there is any momentum in the piston when it reaches the end of the stroke, evidently it can exert no power to cause the crank to revolve, but must be expended by producing a pressure on the crank pin and thus on the axle-boxes. Not only will such a pressure not cause

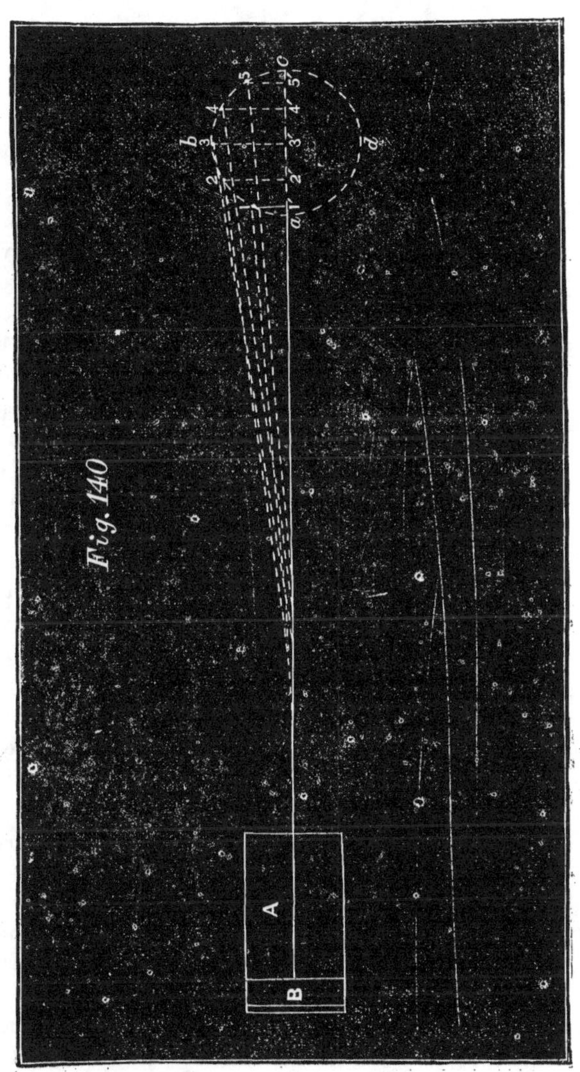

Fig. 140

the crank to revolve, but it will be more difficult to turn the crank with such a pressure against it than it would be without. The momentum of the piston and other reciprocating parts at the dead point therefore creates a resistance to the movement of the crank instead of helping to turn it. It will also be observed that after the crank has moved slightly from the dead point, any pressure on the piston will exert very little force which will tend to turn the crank. In fact the nearer the piston is to the end of the stroke the greater is the proportion which the friction of the crank-pin and axle bears to the useful effect of the strain in causing the crank to turn. Calculation shows that for about three degrees on either side of the dead points the effect of pressure on the crank-pin is actually to retard the engine. If now the piston reaches the end of the stroke with a certain amount of unexpended momentum stored up in it, if this energy is expended by producing pressure on the crank, then it will not only be a waste of energy but a double waste by retarding the motion of the crank. If, however, this energy can be absorbed by compressing steam which will fill the clearance spaces, it will not only prevent the retarding effect referred to, but the energy in the piston and other parts will be converted into steam pressure, which will be given out in useful work during the next stroke. It would, of course, be impossible to arrest the motion of the piston instantly, and therefore its momentum is gradually absorbed from the time compression begins until it reaches the end of the stroke. As the energy of a moving body is equal to its weight multiplied by the square of its speed, it is obvious that to overcome this a different amount of compression would be required for each speed, and also that it must be adjusted to the weight of the moving parts. Such exact adaptation is not practicable on locomotives, nor does the link motion enable us to alter the amount of compression with so much exactness: but the explanation shows the value of increasing the amount of compression with the speed, which fortunately the peculiarities of the shifting-link motion enable us to do without difficulty.

QUESTION 224. *What cause produces the form of diagram represented by fig.* 139?

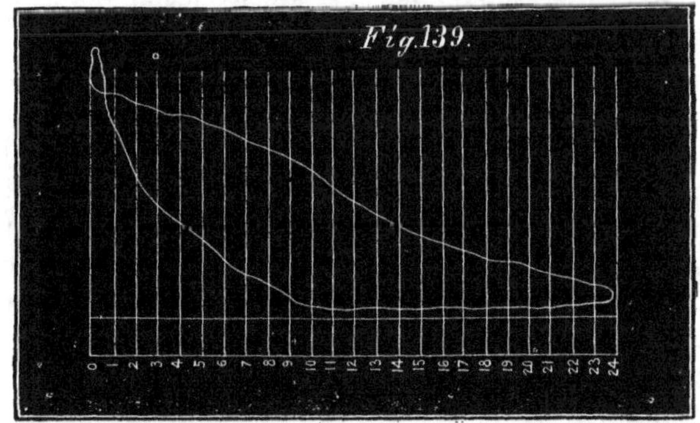

Answer. It is produced by excessive compression, which causes the pressure in the cylinder to rise above boiler pressure before pre-admission begins. As soon as the port is opened, part of the steam in the cylinder flows back into the steam-chest, and thus the pressure is reduced, as shown by the diagram.

QUESTION 225. *How can we determine whether the steam is distributed in the cylinders to the best advantage, and how can we discover the fault, if there is one, in the link motion?*

Answer. The indicator will show the action of the steam in the cylinder, and motion-curves drawn with the instrument described in answer to Question 192 will show the exact movement of the valve. By comparing the indicator diagram with the motion-curves, the one will show the defects in the other.*

QUESTION 226. *To what extent can the movement of the valve be modified by alterations in the proportions of the link motion?*

Answer. The motion of the valve is susceptible of an almost infinite number of changes, by different variations and combinations of proportions of the working parts of the link motion. These changes are, however, limited by the general laws which govern the motion of eccentrics, and therefore cannot influence the motion of the valve beyond certain limits. Hardly any variation can be made either in the proportions or arrangement of the working parts which will not have some influence upon the movement of the valve. Aside from the proportions of the valve itself, which have already been discussed, the throw of the eccentrics, the length of the rods and of the link, the point of connection of the rods with the link, the point of suspension, the position of the lifting shaft, the length of the arms, the length and position of the rocker arms will each of them effect the distribution of steam. The number of combinations of all these different proportions is of course almost infinite, and therefore any full discussion of them will be impossible here.

QUESTION 227. *What are the most important points which require attention in designing a link motion?*

---

* See description of Richards' Improved Steam Engine Indicator, with directions for its use, by Charles T. Porter, London.

Answer. It should be proportioned so that—

First, the lead and the period of admission should be the same for each end of the cylinder, for each point of cut-off, and, if possible, in back as well as forward gear.

Second, the width of opening for both admission and exhaust should be as large as possible when steam is cut off short.

Third, the exhaust or pre-release should occur early enough and be maintained long enough to reduce back-pressure as low as possible.

QUESTION 228. *How can the lead and period of admission be equalized?*

Answer. It is impossible to make the periods of admission absolutely alike for every point of cut-off in both fore and back gear. It is therefore customary to disregard the back gear, as engines are worked but little with the link in that position. Even for forward gear the periods of admission cannot be made exactly alike for each end of the cylinder and for each point of cut-off, and therefore it is usual to make the periods of admission alike for half-gear forward, in which position the link is worked most.

The periods of admission for the front and back ends of the cylinder can be changed most in relation to each other by altering the position of the point of suspension on the link. This can be done either by moving this point up or down, or horizontally. Usually links are suspended from a point halfway between the points of connection of the eccentric-rods and from $\frac{1}{4}$ to $\frac{3}{4}$ in. back of the centre line of the slot in the link. A somewhat better distribution can be secured by suspending it about 3 in. above the centre, but the suspending link must then be made so short that it is subjected to very great strains by the motion of the link, and this evil is usually considered much greater than the advantage which is gained thereby in the more equal distribution. The point at which the upper end of the suspension link is hung also influences the relative amount of admission front and back. This point, of course, varies as the end of the lifting arm is raised or lowered. In designing valve gear it is usually tested by a full-sized model, which will show the exact motion of all the parts. The best position for the lifting shaft and the length of its arm can be determined perhaps most satisfactorily by placing the link in full gear forward, then moving the point of suspension of the upper end of the link-hanger horizontally so that the front and back admission will be alike, and then marking this position. The same process should then be repeated for half gear and for the shortest point of cut-off. If the position of the lifting shaft and the length of its arm are then so arranged that the end of the latter will move through the three points which have been thus determined, the admission will be very nearly equal for each end of the cylinder. Usually, however, it is impossible to arrange the shaft and arm so that they will conform exactly to these conditions, and therefore an approximation is made which will come as near as possible to what is required. It may be stated, however, that the lifting shaft should be kept as low as possible, so as not to interfere with the eccentric-rods. In some cases the shaft has been suspended from the boiler, so that the outside eccentric-rod would work past or over the end of the lifting shaft, thus allowing the latter to be located lower than would otherwise be possible.

QUESTION 229. *Which parts of the link-motion have the greatest influence on the distribution of steam?*

Answer. The lap of the valve and the throw of the eccentrics. The effect of any change of these upon the distribution is very similar to that produced if a single eccentric is used, which was explained in the answers to Questions 49, 50 and 52.

QUESTION 230. *What is the effect upon the admission of increasing the throw of the eccentrics with the same lap?*

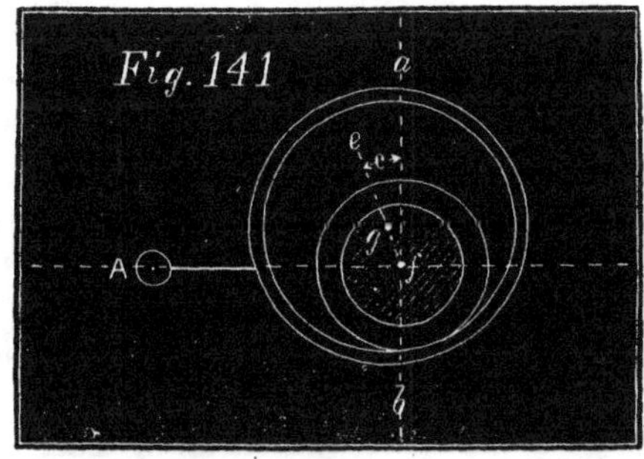

Fig. 141

Answer. As already explained, the effect is to increase the period of admission, or in other words to cut off later in the stroke, and also to increase the width of the opening of the steam-port or the distance which the valve throws over the port. This has an important influence upon the admission, when the link-motion is used.

QUESTION 231. *What is meant by the angular advance of the eccentrics?*

Answer. It is the angle which a line, *e f*, fig. 141,

drawn through the centre of the axle and the centre of the eccentric makes with a vertical line *a b*, when the crank is on one of the dead-points or centres. Thus in fig. 141 the crank *A* is represented on the front centre. In order to give the valve the necessary lead the eccentric must be moved ahead of the vertical line *a b*. The angle *c* which the line *e f* (drawn through the centre of *g* of the eccentric and *f* of the axle) makes with the vertical line is called the *angular advance.*

QUESTION 232. *What is meant by linear advance?*

Answer. By linear advance is meant the distance which the valve has moved from its middle position at the beginning of the stroke of the piston. This, when the two rocker arms are the same length, is the same as the distance of the centre of the eccentric *g* from the vertical line *a b*, fig. 141.

QUESTION 233. *Why does the cut-off occur earlier with an eccentric having a short throw than with one which gives more travel to the valve?*

Answer. Because it is necessary to give the eccentric with the short throw more angular advance in order to give the valve the required lead. This is illustrated in fig. 142, in which a section of a valve, *V*, and ports *c*, *g*, and *d*, are represented. In order to simplify the diagram as much as possible the rocker is left out and the valve is supposed to be moved by the rod *R* directly from the centre *a* of the eccentric. *The effect of the angularity of the connecting rod and eccentric rod is also neglected. The circle *a b e f* represents the path of the centre of an eccentric

*It will be seen that this causes the position of the centre of the eccentric to be reversed.

having 5 in. throw, and *h i j* the path of one having 3½ in. throw. In order to give the valve the required lead, which is supposed to be just line-and-line at the beginning of the stroke, the linear advance of the valve must be equal to the lap, or ⅞ in. If therefore we draw a line, *p a*, parallel to the vertical centre line, *e k*, and ⅞ in. from it, the intersection of *p a* at *a* and *h* with the paths of the eccentric will be the centres of the eccentrics. If through these centres and the centre of the circle, lines, *o a* and *o p*, be drawn, the angles which they make with the vertical *e k* will be the angular advance. It will be seen from these lines that in order to give the valve the required lead it is necessary to give the eccentric with the small travel more angular advance than is necessary for the one with the larger throw. It is obvious, too, that when the centre of the larger eccentric has reached the point *b* the valve will have received its greatest travel, and that when it reaches *p* the steam-port *c* will again be closed or the steam cut off. If the small eccentric is employed, the valve will then have its maximum travel when the centre *h* reaches *s*, and the port will be closed when it reaches *i*. By drawing lines, *o p* and *o n*, through *i* and *p*, it will be seen that from the beginning of the stroke until the steam is cut off, if the large eccentric is employed, it, and consequently the shaft and crank, must move over an angle measured by the arc *q t p*. If the small eccentric is used, it and the crank must move through an angle measured by the arc *u t n*. In other words, the crank must turn a considerably greater distance before steam is cut off with an eccentric having a large than with one having a small throw.

Scale $\frac{3}{16}$ in.=1 inch.

It is also quite obvious from fig. 142 why the port is opened a shorter distance with a small than with a large eccentric. The distances *o s* and *o b* are equal to half the throws of the eccentrics, or $1\frac{3}{4}$ and $2\frac{1}{2}$ in. The linear advance *o r* is in both cases $\frac{7}{8}$ in., and therefore after the port begins to open the valve will be moved by the small eccentric a distance which is equal to $1\frac{3}{4}-\frac{7}{8}=\frac{7}{8}$ in., and by the large one $2\frac{1}{2}-\frac{7}{8}=1\frac{5}{8}$ in.

QUESTION 234. *What is the effect on the admission of giving an eccentric with a small throw the same angular advance as one with a large throw, and then reducing the lap of the valve so that the lead will be the same in both cases?*

Answer. The admission and the cut-off will then occur at the same points of the stroke, but the ports will not be opened so wide. This is illustrated in fig. 143, in which the paths of two eccentrics having the same throw as those in fig. 142 are represented. The centre, *a*, of the larger eccentric is represented in the same position in fig. 143 as in fig. 142. If a line is drawn from the centre of the larger eccentric to that of the axle, and if the centre, *h*, of the smaller eccentric is located on the intersection of this line with the circle representing its path, then the smaller eccentric will have the same angular advance, but the linear advance measured by the distance *o t* will be only $\frac{5}{8}$ in. If the valve have the same lap as in fig. 142, its steam edges at the beginning of the stroke, if the small eccentric is employed, will occupy the position represented by the dotted lines *A* and *B*. If these edges are cut off, as shown by the full lines and shading, then the valve will have the same lead as in fig. 142. It is obvious, too, that if the smaller eccen-

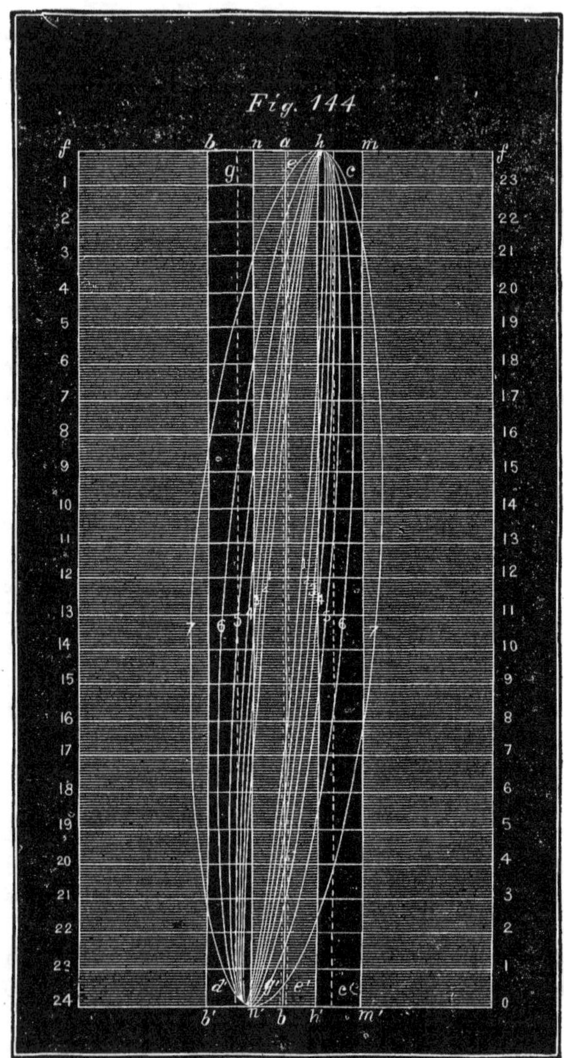

Scale $\frac{3}{16}$ in = 1 inch.

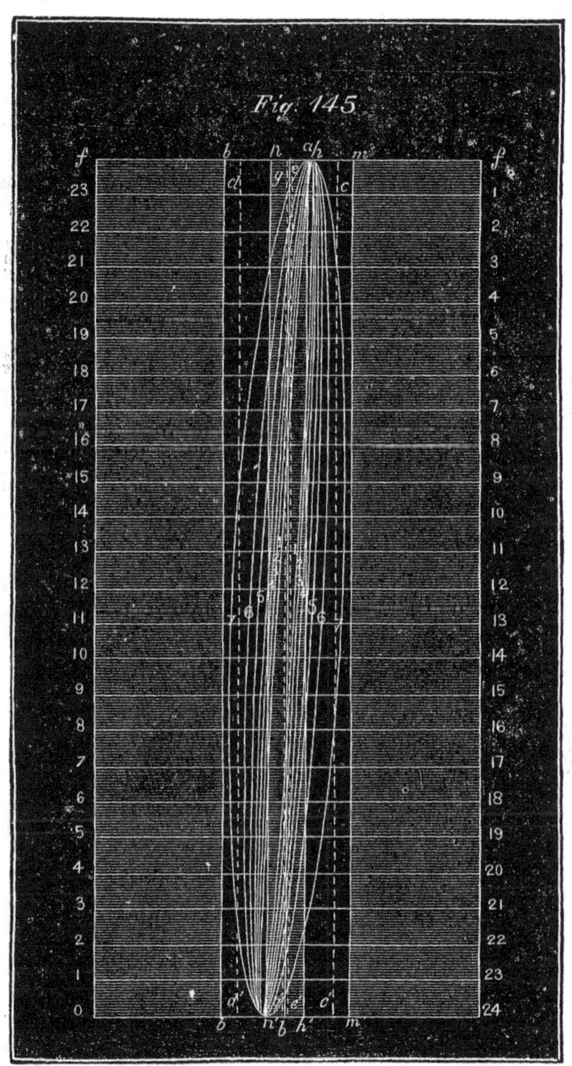

Scale $\frac{3}{16}$ in.=1 foot.

tric has the same angular advance it will reach the point *v*, at which, with the reduced lap, the steam will be cut off, at the same time that the centre, *a*, of the large eccentric will reach *p*, at which point it cuts off the steam with the valve having the large lap. There is, however, this difference in the distribution, that in the one case the valve opens the port a distance equal to *t s*, and in the other a distance equal to *r b*. As *o t* is equal to the linear advance of the small eccentric, or $\frac{5}{8}$ in., and *o s* to half the throw of the eccentric, or $1\frac{3}{4}$, *t s* is equal to $1\frac{3}{4}-\frac{5}{8}=1\frac{1}{8}$ in. The distance *r b*, as shown above, is equal to $2\frac{1}{2}-\frac{7}{8}=1\frac{5}{8}$ in., so that the effect produced upon the admission of using an eccentric with a small throw and corresponding amount of lap is, that the ports are not opened so wide as with an eccentric having a larger throw.

QUESTION 235. *How do eccentrics with a short throw, and valves with a corresponding amount of lap, affect the admission with a link motion as compared with eccentrics having a larger amount of throw and greater lap of valve?*

Answer. The chief difference is that the ports are not opened so wide for the same period of admission. Thus in fig. 144 is a series of motion-curves drawn with a model of a link motion like that illustrated in fig. 103. The eccentrics had 5 in. throw, and the valve $\frac{7}{8}$ in. lap outside and $\frac{1}{16}$ in. inside. Fig. 145 represents a series of curves, drawn with the same arrangement of valve-gear, excepting that the eccentrics had $3\frac{1}{2}$ in. throw and the valve $\frac{1}{2}$ in. lap. In both cases the curves represent the motion of the valve when cutting off at the same point of the stroke. The following table will show the relative amount of opening of the port.

Point of Cut-Off	Width of Opening of Steam-Port.	
	Eccentric 5 in. throw.	Eccentric $3\frac{1}{2}$ in. throw.
6 in.	$\frac{7}{32}$ in.	$\frac{5}{32}$ in.
8 "	$\frac{9}{32}$ "	$\frac{3}{16}$ "
10 "	$\frac{11}{32}$ "	$\frac{7}{32}$ "
12 "	$\frac{7}{16}$ "	$\frac{9}{32}$ "
15 "	$\frac{5}{8}$ "	$\frac{3}{8}$ "
18 "	$\frac{31}{32}$ "	$\frac{11}{16}$ "
21 "	$1\frac{1}{4}$* "	$1\frac{1}{32}$ "

* The valve throws over $1\frac{3}{4}$ in. at this point.

It will be seen from this that the eccentric with 5 in. throw gives a greater width of opening for every point of cut-off than the one with $3\frac{1}{2}$ in. throw. For the higher admissions this is not important, but when steam is cut off short it will be observed that the width of the opening is very small. At high speeds the small opening is a great disadvantage.

QUESTION 236. *Has it been determined what amount of opening is required for given speeds of the piston?*

Answer. Not with any degree of accuracy. It is customary to make the area of the ports about one-tenth that of the piston. It is certain, however, that with steam-ports of this proportion an opening considerably less than their whole area is sufficient to maintain steam at boiler pressure in the cylinders. One of the defects of the link motion is that the opening of the port is very small when the steam is cut off short. It is best, therefore, to secure the largest practicable opening of the ports for the lower points of cut-off.

QUESTION 237. *What are the proportions of the valves and eccentrics used in the ordinary practice in this country?*

Answer. The following report made by a committee of the Master Mechanics' Association will show the proportions used on thirty-five different railroads, and is a fair indication of the common practice.

TABLE
SHOWING THE AMOUNT OF LAP, LEAD AND TRAVEL OF THE VALVES OF LOCOMOTIVES USED ON 35 OF THE RAILROADS IN THE UNITED STATES AND CANADA.

			Outside Lap.	Inside Lap.	Travel of Valve.	Lead in full Gear
			in	in.	in	in.
For locomotives running	express pass. trains	25 use	7/8	1/8	5	1-10
" " "	" " "	6 "	3/4	1-16	4 3/4	1/2
" " "	" " "	4 "	1 1/4	1/4	5	1/8
" " "	accom. " "	20 "	3/4	3/8	5	1-10
" " "	" " "	10 "	7/8	1-16	5 1/2	1-16
" " "	" " "	5 "	5/8	3-16	4 1/2	1/8
" " "	heavy fr'ght. "	19 "	3/4	1-16	5	1-10
" " "	" " "	11 "	5/8	1/8	4 1/2	1-16
" " "	" " "	5 "	1/2	3-16	4 3/4	1-10

QUESTION 238. *What should be the width of the bridge between the steam and exhaust ports?*

Answer. It is usually made about the same thickness as the sides of the cylinder, in order to secure a good casting; but sometimes it is necessary to make it wider, in order to prevent steam from escaping from the steam-chest into the exhaust which is apt to be the case if a valve has little lap and a long travel.

QUESTION 239. *What determines the width of the exhaust port?*

Answer. The throw of the valve. This will be clear if we refer to fig. 146, which represents a valve with a travel of $5\frac{1}{2}$ in. It will be seen that when it is in the extreme position in which it is shown the width *A* of the opening of the exhaust-port is very small. If this opening is contracted too much it will of course interfere with the free escape of the exhaust steam. It is therefore best to make the exhaust-port so wide that with the greatest travel of the valve the width of its opening will be either quite or very nearly equal to the width of the steam-port.

QUESTION 240. *Where is the reverse lever located and how is it constructed?*

Answer. It is located on the *foot-board** *K′ K′*, as shown in plate II. It consists of a lever *O, O*, with the fulcrum at the lower end. The *reverse-rod l′ k*, which connects the lever with the vertical arm *k* of the lifting-shaft, is attached above the fulcrum of the reverse lever. Figs. 147 and 148 represent side and end

Scale $\frac{3}{16}$ in.=1 foot.

views of the lever on an enlarged scale and with some of the details attached which are omitted on plate II. *C, C* are two curved bars, which in this country are usually called *quadrants,* but in England are called (and more properly) *sectors.* These are placed on each side of the reverse-lever and are fastened to some portion of the engine. They have notches, *n, n, n,* cut in

* The *foot-board K′ K′*, plates 2 and 3, is a platform for the locomotive runner and fireman to stand on and is located at the back end of the engine.

them to receive the *latch L,* which slides in a clamp, *H,* and holds the reverse-lever in the notches in which it is placed. This latch is operated by a *trigger, D,* which is grasped by the locomotive runner when he takes

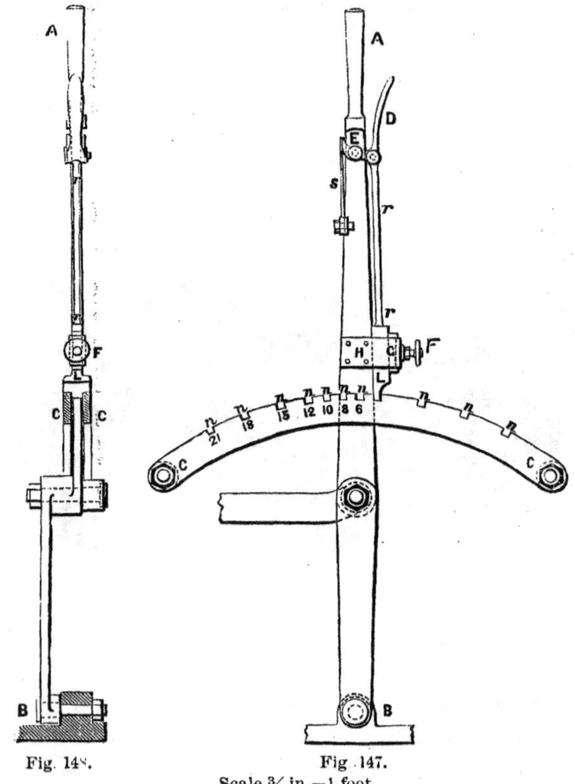

Fig. 148. Fig. 147.
Scale ¾ in.=1 foot.

hold of the handle *A* of the reverse-lever. The trigger works on a pin, *E,* as a fulcrum and is attached to the latch by a rod, *r r.* When the trigger is pressed up against the handle, the latch is raised out of the notches by the rod *r r*, and is pressed into them again by the spring *s* when the trigger is released. *F* is a set-screw which presses against a gib, *G*, and is intended to keep the latch tight and prevent the reverse-lever from shaking.

QUESTION 241. *How are the notches in the sector arranged?*

Answer. They are usually arranged so that the steam will be cut off at some full number of inches of the stroke when the reverse-lever is in each one of the notches. They are therefore located so that the steam will be cut off at 6, 9, 12, 15, 18 and 21 inches, or at 6, 8, 10, 12, 15, 18 and 21 inches of the stroke. A notch is also placed so as to hold the link in mid-gear. In some cases as many notches as there is room for are put into the sectors. The latter seems to be much the best plan, as it gives more gradations in which the valve-gear can be worked, and it is a matter of no consequence whatever in the working of an engine whether the steam is cut off at some full or some fractional number of inches of the stroke. By referring to fig. 144 it will be seen how very great the difference of the distribution of steam must be, as indicated by the 5th, 6th and 7th motion-curves.

QUESTION 242. *How long should the reverse-lever be?*

Answer. The lever should be sufficiently long so that in throwing the link from full gear forward to full gear backward the handle *A* will move *not less* than four times the distance that the link is moved. It is much better to give the end of the handle *A* five or even six times the motion of the link, as there will then be a much easier action in reversing the engine.

This will also make it possible to use longer sectors, and give room for more notches.

QUESTION 243. *What provision is made in the reversing gear for overcoming or neutralizing the weight of the link and other parts of the valve-gear?*

Answer. Their weight is counterbalanced by the pressure of a spring of some kind. In fig. 103 the two volute springs enclosed in a case, *H*, are used for this purpose. These are compressed by the rod *m*, which is attached to a short arm *l*, on the reverse shaft *A*, when the link is lowered, and consequently the tension of the spring resists the weight of the link when the latter is down or in forward gear. Different kinds of springs are used for this purpose and sometimes are attached to the reverse-lever instead of to the lifting-shaft.

QUESTION 244. *What is meant by "setting" a slide-valve?*

Answer. It is to fasten the eccentrics in the right position on the axle and to adjust the length of the eccentric-rods and valve-stem so that the valves will give the required distribution of steam.

QUESTION 245. *How are the valves of a locomotive set?*

Answer. After the wheels, axles, main connecting-rods and valve-gear are connected together, put the rocker-arm in its middle position, and lengthen or shorten the valve-stem so that the valve will be in the centre of the valve-face. Then place the crank on the forward centre and the full part of the forward motion eccentric above and that of the backward motion eccentric below the axle, and fasten them to the axle temporarily by tightening up the set-screws.

Then throw the link down until the block comes opposite to the end of the eccentric-rod, and turn the wheels,* and at the same time, observe whether the travel of the valve is equal to the throw of the eccentric and also whether it travels equally on each side of the centre of the valve-face. If its travel is greater than the throw of the eccentric, raise the link up; if less, lower it down until the two are just equal, and then mark the position for the notches on the sections or quadrants to receive the latch of the reverse-lever. If the valve does not travel equally on each side of the centre of the valve-face, either lengthen or shorten the eccentric-rod, as may be necessary. Repeat this operation for the backward motion, by raising the link up until the block is opposite the end of the lower eccentric-rod. After having done this, go over the whole process again to see whether it is all correct. Now with the crank on the forward centre, and the link in full gear forward, loosen the set-screws in the forward eccentric, and move it around the axle so that the valve will have the required lead and then fasten it again. Now raise the link up into full back gear, and set the backward eccentric in the same way. Then turn the wheels so as to bring the crank on the back centre, and observe whether the lead is correct for the back end of the cylinder. If it is not, lengthen or shorten the valve-stem or eccentric-rod so as to make the lead alike at both ends, and if it is then too much or too little, it can be increased or diminished by moving the eccentrics on the axle.

* This can be done by moving the engine on the track, or by raising it off its wheels, so that the latter can be turned without moving the former. In some shops a pair of rollers is put in the track so that by placing the driving wheels on them they can be turned without any difficulty.

Great care must be taken in setting valves to be sure that the cranks are exactly on the centres or dead points, and it is impossible to set them in that position with sufficient accuracy from the motion of the piston or cross-head, and therefore the centres of the crank-pins should always be set so as to conform to a line drawn through the centre of the cylinder and the axle. When the cylinders are horizontal, it is of course only necessary to place the cranks on a horizontal line drawn through the centre of the axle.

When the valves are set it should also be noticed whether the axle-boxes (whose construction will be explained hereafter) are in the centre of the jaws, and if not they should be moved to the centre by driving wooden wedges between them and the frames, either above or below, as may be required. The position of the boxes has a very material influence on the valve-gear.

If it is intended to lay off the notches on the sectors so as to cut off steam at certain definite points of the stroke, these points should be laid off in the guides from the motion of the cross-head. The latter being placed in any of the required positions at which steam is to be cut off, the reverse-lever should then be moved so that the link will just close the admission port. The lever can then be clamped to the sectors, and the wheels turned so as to show whether its position is correct for each end of the stroke. As before stated it is impossible to get the ordinary link-motion to cut off at exactly the same points at both ends of the cylinder, but a very close approximation can be made by proportioning the different parts properly. As has already been stated, it is believed to be a much better plan to put as many notches in the sectors as possible, than to locate them for certain definite points of the stroke.

In setting the valves of locomotives, care must be taken to turn the wheels *forward* for the *forward motion* and *backward* for the *backward motion.*

After the valves are set the position of the eccentrics on the shaft should be marked, so that in case they become loose on the road they can easily be set again. It is usual, too, to mark the position of the valves with centre-punch marks on the valve-stem and on the stuffing-box of the steam-chest, so that with a gauge made for the purpose the position of the valve can be determined without taking off the steam-chest cover.

In some cases the eccentrics are keyed on, which is done after their position is determined by setting the valves. The ends of the set-screws which are used to fasten the eccentrics should be cup-shaped and case-hardened, so as to hold as securely as possible to the axle when they are screwed down.

PART XII.

THE RUNNING GEAR

QUESTION 246. *What is meant by the running gear of a locomotive?*

Answer. It means those parts, such as the wheels, axles and frames, which carry the other parts of the engine. As the Germans express it, it is the "*wagon*" of the locomotive.

QUESTION 247. *How may the wheels be classified?*

Answer. As *driving* and *carrying* or *truck wheels.*

QUESTION 248. *What service must the driving wheels perform?*

Answer. The driving wheels, as indicated by their name, "drive" or move the locomotive on the track, as was explained in answer to Questions 64, 65 and 66. As their adhesion depends upon the pressure with which they bear upon the rails, they must carry either a part or the whole of the weight of the engine.

QUESTION 249. *What proportion of the weight of ordinary locomotives is usually carried on the driving wheels?*

Answer. Eight-wheeled "American" locomotives, which are most commonly used in this country, have about two-thirds of their weight on the driving wheels.

QUESTION 250. *What is meant by the "truck" of a locomotive?*

Answer. It means one or more pairs of wheels which are attached to a separate frame and to the locomotive by a flexible connection, so that the axles are not held rigidly at right angles to the main frame, but can assume positions which approximate to that of radii of the curves of the track. In plates I, II and III, *E E* are the truck wheels, *b′ b′* the truck frame, and *y*, plate II, and fig. 40, the centre-pin, around which the truck frame turns.

Question 251. *What service does the truck perform?*

Answer. It carries the weight of the front end of the locomotive, and also guides it into and around curves and *switches.**

Question 252. *How does it perform the latter service?*

Answer. It does it very much in the same way as the front wheels of an ordinary wagon enable it to turn around corners; that is, the truck wheels being attached to a separate frame, which is connected to the locomotive by a centre-pin, just as the front axle of an ordinary wagon is connected by the king-bolt, can turn.

Question 253. *Why are two pairs of wheels used on a locomotive instead of one, as on an ordinary wagon?*

Answer. Because it is necessary to have one pair of wheels guide the other. In an ordinary wagon the front axle is guided by the pole or shafts. Nearly every one knows the difficulty of moving a wagon when the pole or shafts are removed, especially if it be pushed from behind. The movement of the front axle is then uncontrolled, and it is impossible to direct the motion of the vehicle. The same thing would oc-

* A switch is a movable pair of rails, by which a locomotive is enabled to run from one track to another.

cur with a locomotive if a single pair of wheels were used, and attached in the same way as the front axle of a wagon. Thus if a single pair of wheels were con-

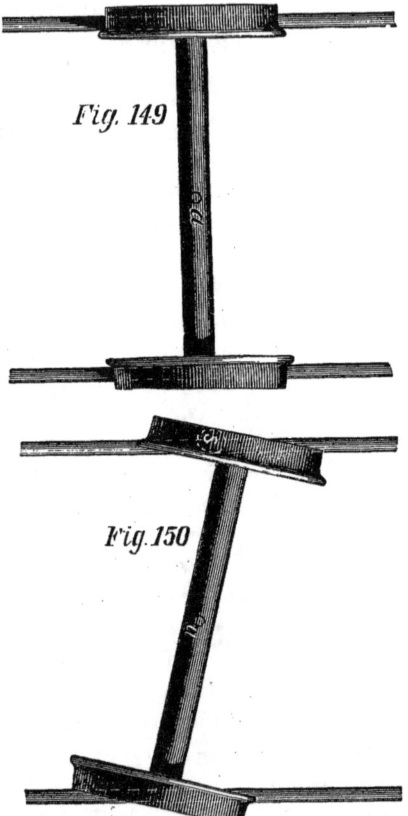

Scale, 3/8 inch = 1 foot.

nected to a locomotive by a centre-pin, *a*, fig. 149, so that the axle would be free to move around this pin, then if one of the wheels should strike an obstruction, say a stone, *s*, fig. 150, there would be nothing to prevent the axle from being thrown into the position shown in fig. 150, and the wheels would be quite sure to leave the track. When two pairs of wheels are used and both axles attached to the same frame, which is connected to the engine by a centre-pin, *s*, fig. 151, between the two axles, then the wheels in moving round the centre-pin must move around the centre *s* in arcs of circles, *m n*, *m n*, described from the centre *s*. These arcs, it will be observed, cross the rails. Now if the wheels should move in that direction, the flange of one

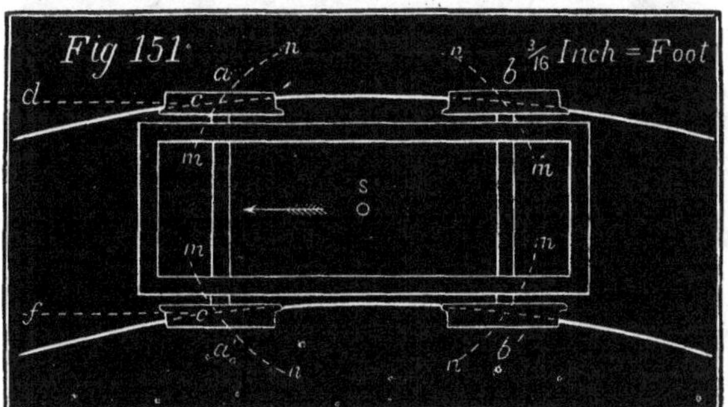

of them would come in contact with the rail and prevent it from moving any farther. It is therefore evident that wheels arranged in that way can only move about the centre-pin as far as the curvature of the track will permit. Trucks are sometimes used with only one pair of wheels, but the centre-pin is then placed some distance behind the centre of the axle, or in the same relation to it that the centre *s* is to the axle *a a′* in fig. 151. It is evident that if the frame for such a truck turns around the centre-pin,

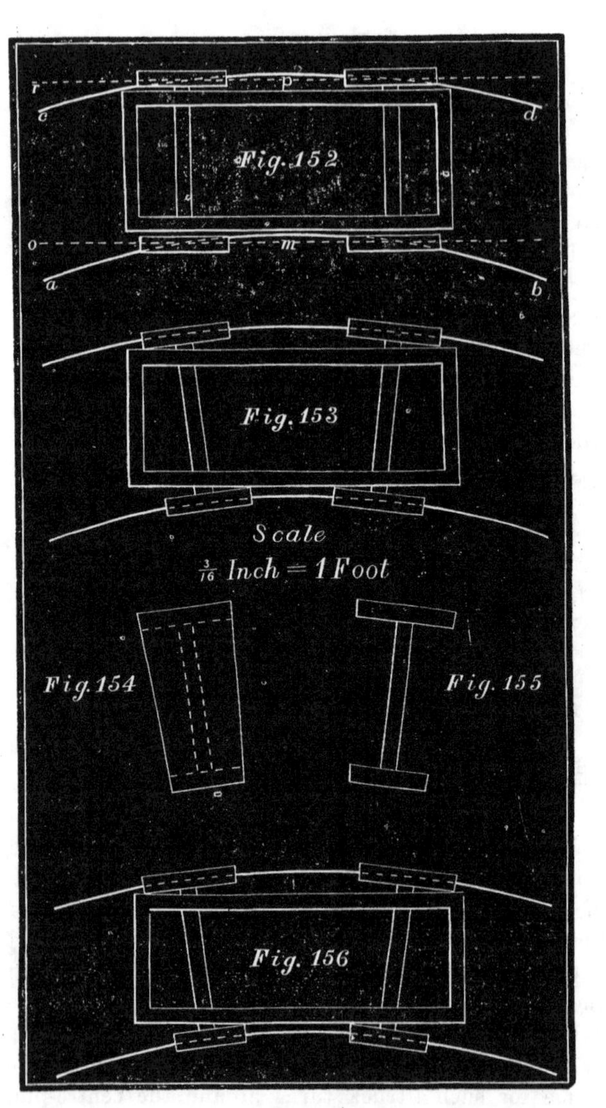
r
p
c
d
Fig. 152
o
m
a
b
Fig. 153
Scale
3/16 Inch = 1 Foot
Fig. 154
Fig. 155
Fig. 156

the wheels must move across the track in the same way as represented by the arcs *m n*, in fig. 151. The construction and operation of trucks with a single pair of wheels will be more fully explained hereafter.

QUESTION 254. *Why will a locomotive run around curves easier if the front axles are attached to a truck frame which is connected to the locomotive by a flexible connection?*

Answer. Because the truck axles can then assume positions which conform very nearly to the radii of the curves of the track, and it is well known that if two or more axles, each with a pair of wheels on it, are attached to a frame with their centre lines parallel with each other, as shown in fig. 152, they will roll in a straight line, but if the centre lines of the axles are inclined to each other, as shown in fig. 153, the tendency will be to roll in a curve, the radius of which will depend upon the degree of inclination of the axles to each other. In order to make the wheels in fig. 152 roll on the curves *a b* and *c d*, it will be necessary to slide them laterally a distance equal to that between the curves and the straight lines *m o* and *p r*, and as the length of the outside curve is greater than the inside one, if the wheels are fastened to the axles so they cannot turn on them and roll on the curves, either the wheels on the inside or those on the outside must slip a distance equal to the difference in the length of the two curves. Considerable force will therefore be required to overcome the resistance due to the combined lateral and circumferential sliding of the wheels, so that more power will be needed to make them roll in a curve than is necessary to make them roll in a straight line. If, however, the axles are inclined to each other, then the wheels will naturally roll on a curved path, and it will not be necessary to slide them sideways to make them conform to such a path. But if the wheels are all attached to the axles so that those on the same axle cannot turn independently of each other and are all of the same diameter, then either the inside or the outside ones must slip, because the path in which the outside ones roll is longer than the inside curve, so that even if the axles are inclined to each other more power will be needed to roll the truck in a curved path than to roll the wheels shown in fig. 152 in a straight line. It is, however, a fact that a cone or a portion of a cone like that shown in fig. 154 will of itself roll on a curve. It will do the same thing if the middle is cut away, as indicated by the dotted lines in fig. 154 and as shown in fig. 155. If now the wheels are made so that their peripheries* form portions of a cone and the axles are inclined to each other as shown in fig. 156, then there will be no slipping on the track, because the outside wheel, being larger in diameter than the inside one, advances further in one revolution than the latter does, and thus rolls on the longest path in the same time that the inside or smaller wheel does on the shorter one. When this is the case, such wheels will roll in a curve as easily as those in fig. 152 will in a straight line. The degree of inclination of the axles and of the sides of the cone must, however, vary with the radius of the curve. But if the axles are parallel to each other, and the wheels conical, as represented in fig. 157, they will not roll

* The periphery is the outside surface on which the wheel rolls. This part of a wheel is usually called the "*tread*."

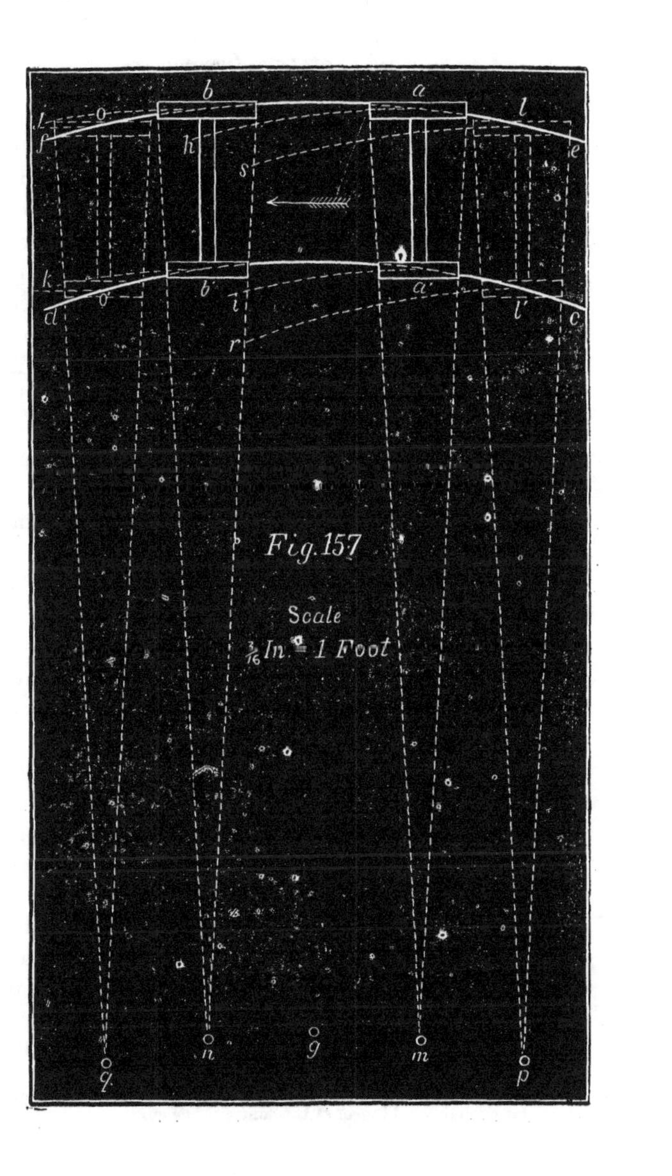

Fig. 157

Scale
$\frac{3}{16}$ In. = 1 Foot

either in a straight line or in a curve without great difficulty, because if they roll in a straight line, the wheels on one side being larger in diameter than those on the other, either the larger or the smaller ones must slip on the path in which they roll. If they roll on a curve, then each pair of wheels has a tendency to roll in a curve independent of the other, and therefore the wheels must slip laterally if both pairs roll on the same track. Thus, suppose two pairs of wheels, *a*, *a′*, and *b*, *b′*, fig. 157, to be made conical and attached to a frame so that their axles are parallel to each other. Now each pair of such wheels will have a tendency to roll in circular paths, *a′ i*, *a h*, and *b′ k*, *b j*, the centres of which are at *m* and *n*, or at the apices of the cones of which their peripheries form a part. If they are made to roll in circular paths, *c d*, *e f*, described from a point *g*, then each pair of wheels must slip laterally over the space between the paths *a′ i*, *a h*, in which they would naturally roll and that in which they are made to roll. Thus the wheel *a* would slide laterally the distance between the curve *a h* and *a f*, and *a′* that between *a′ i* and *c d*; *b* would slide from *b j* to *b f* and *b′* from *b′ k* to *b′ d*. It will thus be seen that in order that two pairs of wheels may roll with equal ease in a straight line and in curves, the wheels in the one case must be of equal diameters and the axles parallel, and in the other case the wheels must be of unequal diameters and their axles be *radial** to the curve. This is equally true of any number of pairs of wheels. If we have three, four, or any number of axles, with wheels all attached to the same frame, if their axles are parallel,

* That is, that their centre lines incline towards each other, and if extended far enough would meet at the centre of the curve.

and the wheels of the same diameter, they will roll in a straight line; but if their wheels are conical and their axles radial, they will roll in a curve.

For the preceding reasons it is therefore sufficiently obvious that if a locomotive is to run on both straight and curved tracks, on the former the wheels should be of the same diameter and the axles parallel, and on the latter the wheels should be conical and the axles radial.

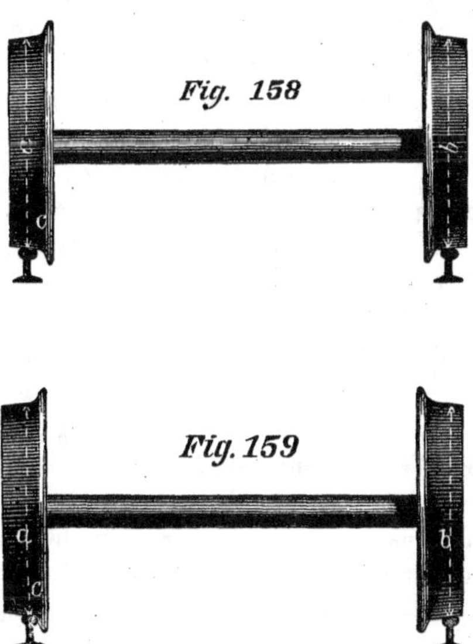

Fig. 158

Fig. 159

Scale ⅜ in.=1 foot.

QUESTION 255. *How are the wheels made so that in curves they will act as though they were of the conical form described and on a straight track all be of the same diameters?*

Answer. The periphery or tread of each wheel is made conical, but of the same size as the other, and with the small diameter of the cone outside, as shown in fig. 158. On a straight track if the position of the wheels on the rails is such that their two flanges are equally distant from the rails, as shown, then obviously at the points of contact with the rails the wheels are of the same diameter. That is, *a* is equal to *b*. But in running on a curved track, if the wheels are of the same diameter, as has been shown, they will roll in a straight line and consequently towards the outside of the curve. The flange *c*—supposing it to be at the outside of the curve—will therefore roll towards the rail, and consequently the outside wheel will rest on the rail at a point nearer the flange, as shown in fig. 159, where the diameter *a* is larger, and the inside one further from the flange where the diameter *b* is smaller than at *a* and *b* in fig. 158; and consequently the action of the wheels is the same as though their peripheries were made of the form shown in fig. 157.

QUESTION 256. *How are the axles of locomotives made to assume a position radial to the curves in the track?*

Answer. This is only done approximately, as the mechanical difficulties in the way of doing it perfectly are so great as to render it impracticable. By attaching the truck to the locomotive by a flexible connection or centre-pin, *s*, as shown in fig. 160 (which represents a plan of the wheels of an ordinary locomotive), it is plain that the truck axles *e f* and *g h*, instead of remaining parallel to the driving-axles *a b* and *c d*, will, by turning around the centre-pin, *s*, adjust themselves to the curve so as to approximate as closely to radii as is possible for two axles which are held parallel to each other. Of course the further apart they are the greater will be their divergence from the po-

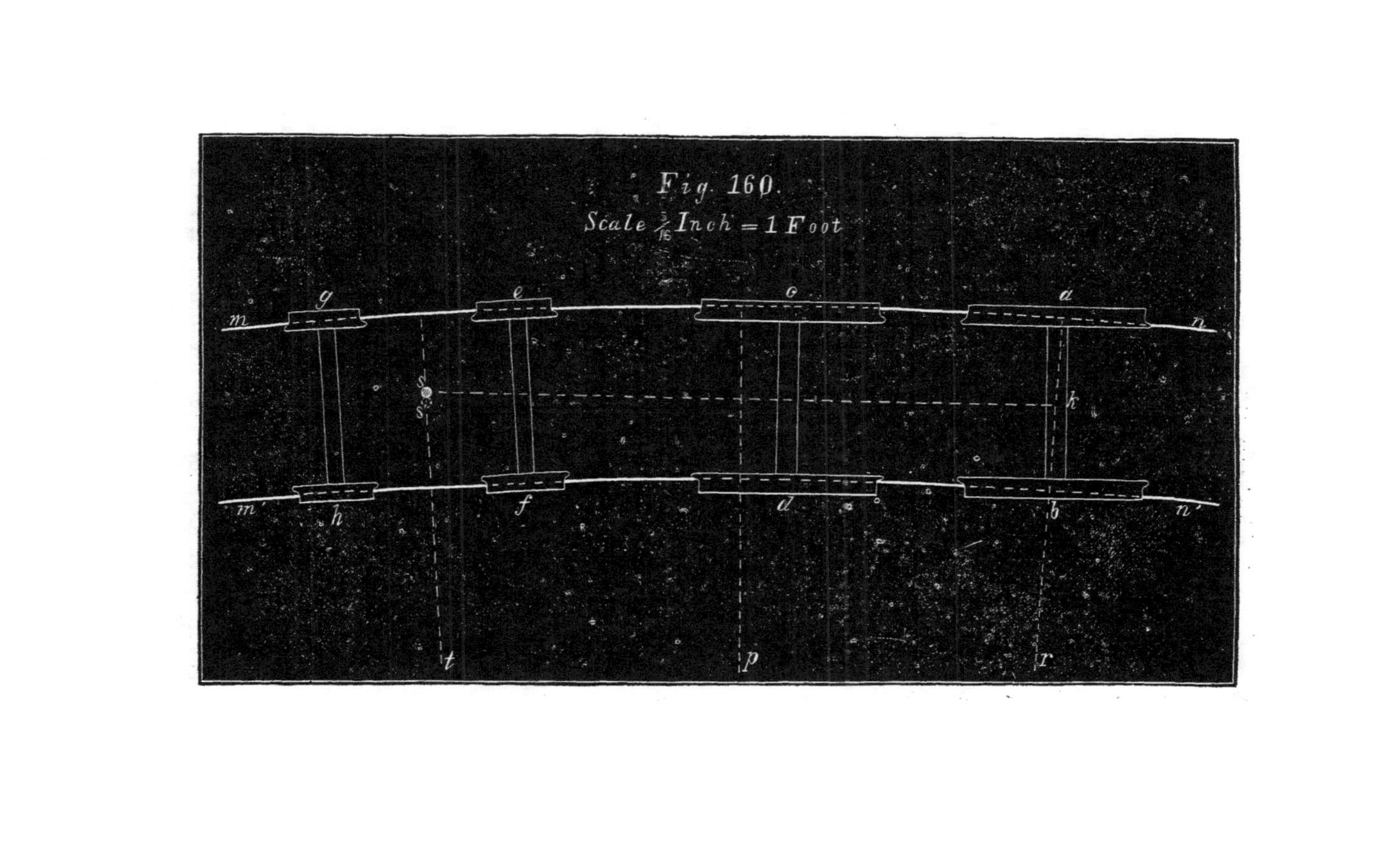

Fig. 160.
Scale $\frac{3}{16}$ Inch = 1 Foot

sition of radii, and whether the tread of the wheels be cylindrical or conical the further apart their axles are the greater will be the divergence of the paths in which they would naturally roll from that of any curve on which they must roll. Thus, if the axles were twice as far apart as they are represented in fig. 157, and in the position shown in the dotted lines *l l'* and *o o'*, the wheels, if they are conical, would then naturally roll in curves drawn from the centres *p* and *q*. If the wheels are cylindrical, they would roll in straight lines. In either case the divergence of their paths *l s* and *l r* from the curve of the track is greater than *a h* and *a' i*, the paths in which they would roll if their axles were nearer together. This divergence increases with the distance between the axles, and therefore the lateral slip of the wheels must be in the same proportion.

QUESTION 257. *Is the resistance to rolling diminished by placing the truck axles nearer together?*

Answer. It is, within certain limits. The nearer each other they are placed, the closer will the centre-pin of the truck be to the centre of the axles. The closer it is to the centre of the axle, the greater is the tendency of the wheels to become "slewed," or to assume a diagonal position to the rails as represented in fig. 150, and thus increase the resistance and also the danger of running off the track. The increase of resistance from this cause, after the axles reach a certain distance from each other, is greater than the decrease from a closer approximation to the position of radii. In ordinary locomotives it is necessary to place the truck wheels from 5 ft. 6 in. to 6 ft. apart, in order to get the cylinders between them in a horizontal position. This distance apart works very well in ordinary practice.

QUESTION 258. *What is meant by flange friction?*

Answer. It is the friction of the flanges of the wheels against the head of the rails. Thus if two pairs of wheels, *a*, *a'*, *b*, *b'*, fig. 151, be placed on a curve and rolled in the direction of the dart, the wheel *a* will roll towards the outside of the curve until the flange comes in contact with the rail. As already explained, if two axles are parallel to each other, no matter whether the wheels are conical or cylindrical, they must slip laterally in order to roll in a curved path. As the flange must follow the curve of the rail, it forces the wheel laterally and thus compels it to roll in the curved path into which the rail is bent. As the wheel offers considerable resistance to sliding there is a corresponding pressure of the flange against the rail, and consequently the revolutions of the wheel produce an abrasive action between the two. This action is obviously increased with the distance between the axles, because, as has been shown, the lateral slip of the wheels is then greater than when they are nearer together. It is also obvious that if the wheels are parallel with the rails there will be no abrasive action of the flanges, but that the greater the angle at which the wheels stand to the rails the harder will the flanges rub against the rails, and the greater will be the flange friction. With the aid of geometry it can very easily be proved that the farther apart two parallel axles are, the greater will be the angle of the wheels to the rails on a curved track, and, therefore, the greater will be their flange friction. It must, however, be remembered that if the wheels are so close together that they are liable to become "slewed," or assume a diagonal position across the rails, as shown in fig. 150, the angle at which the wheels would stand to the rails would thus be very much increased. It has therefore come to be a very generally recognized rule that the centres of axles should never be placed nearer together than the distance between the rails.

QUESTION 259. *Is the flange friction of all the wheels of a truck the same on any given curve?*

Answer. No; of the front wheels obviously only the flange of the one on the outside of the curve comes in contact with the rail. As the centrifugal force of the engine presses the back pair of wheels towards the outside of the curve, the flange of the outside wheel alone comes in contact with the rail. But as this wheel is constantly rolling *away* from the rail, as shown by the dotted lines *h g*, fig. 151, obviously the friction of its flange is less than that of the front outside wheel, which always rolls *towards* the rail. The flange of the back inside wheel is carried outwards by the centrifugal force and also by the tendency of the wheels to roll on their largest diameters on a curve, so that its flange will not touch the rail.

QUESTION 260. *Can the axles of driving wheels assume positions radial to the track?*

Answer. In ordinary engines they cannot. Various plans have been devised for the purpose of enabling them to do so, but it is only recently that they have met with any success. Some of these plans will be described hereafter. It is, however, of less importance that the driving axles, when they are behind the centre of the locomotive, should assume positions radial to a curved track than that the front wheels should. This is illustrated by a common road wagon, as all know the ease with which such a vehicle can turn a corner if we run it with the front axle ahead, and the difficulty of doing so when the back axle is in front. In the case of a locomotive the reason for it is very much the same as that which makes the flange friction of the back wheels of a truck less than that of the front ones. From fig. 160 it will be seen that the outside driving-wheels, when the engine is running with the truck in front, are rolling *from* the rail and not against it. As stated before, the centrifugal force of the engine when in motion has a tendency to throw the wheels towards the outside of the curve. It will also be noticed that the front driving axle is near the centre of that portion of the curve which lies between the centre *s* of the truck and the centre *k* of the back axle. If it were in the middle between them, it would be exactly radial to the curve; being near the middle, it approximates closely to that position, and therefore the flange friction of its wheels is very slight. It will be noticed that if the flange of the back or trailing-wheel on the inside of the curve were not kept away from the rail it would roll toward and impinge against that rail. But it will be noticed that the flange of the front driving-wheel will come in contact with the inside rail before that on the back wheel can touch it. For this reason, and also on account of the effect of the centrifugal force exerted on the engine and the tendency of the wheels to roll on their largest diameters, the flange of the inside back wheel is kept out of contact with the rail, and as the back wheel on the outside of the curve rolls away from the rail there is very little friction of the flanges of the back driving-wheels.

It will also be noticed from fig. 160, that if the radius of the curve is very short, the bend of the rails between the back pair of driving-wheels and the centre of the truck is so great that the inside rail will press hard against the flange of the front or main driving-wheel next that rail. This of course produces a great deal of friction, and if the curve is excessively short the flange will mount on top of the rail and the tread of the opposite wheel will fall off from its rail. For this reason the centre-pin of the truck is sometimes arranged so that it can move laterally, that is cross-wise of the track. In fig. 160 the centre-pin is represented as having moved some distance from the actual centre of the truck, which is represented with dotted lines. The front wheels of locomotives are also sometimes made with wide "flat" tires, that is, tires without flanges, so that there will be no friction against the one rail and no danger of falling off the other.

Another action also takes place which facilitates the motion of the driving-wheels of ordinary engines around curves. Every one knows how easy the direction in which the front wheels of a common wagon can be controlled by taking hold of the end of the tongue or pole. With the leverage which it gives the wheels and axle can easily be directed wherever it is desired. A similar action takes place in an ordinary locomotive. The front driving-axles are guided by the truck, which is attached to the frame ten or twelve feet in front of the driving-axle, and thus the truck exerts a leverage to guide the movement of the driving-axles, just as a common wagon can be guided by the pole.

If the locomotive is run backward, then none of these advantages exist, and the flange friction of the back driving-wheels is excessive. Engines such as construction locomotives, which run backward as much as forward, wear out the flanges of the back wheels very rapidly on crooked roads.

QUESTION 261. *What is meant by the "spread" of the wheels or axles?*

Answer. It is the distance between the centres of two axles.

QUESTION 262. *What is the "wheel-base" of a locomotive?*

Answer. It is the distance between the centres of the front and back or trailing-wheels. On ordinary engines, such as that illustrated in plate I, it is the distance from the centre of the front truck to the centre of the back driving-wheels.

QUESTION 263. *Is the "coning" of the tread of the wheels of much practical importance?*

Answer. There is great difference of opinion regarding it, but even if its action is very beneficial, the advantage is very soon lost, owing to the wear of the wheels. It is, therefore, believed that the advantage is more apparent in theory than in practice.

QUESTION 264. *How are the driving-wheels of locomotives constructed?*

Answer. They are made of cast iron with wrought-iron or steel tires around the outside. Fig. 161 represents a perspective view of a pair of locomotive wheels and axle. The central portion of the wheel, that is the hub, spokes and rim, are cast in one piece. Usually the hub and the rim, and sometimes the spokes, are cast hollow. The central portion of the wheel, that is the part which is made of cast iron, is called the ***wheel-centre.***

Fig. 161.

Question 265. *How are the tires fastened on the wheel-centres?*

Answer. The insides of the tires are usually turned out somewhat smaller than the outside of the wheel-centre. The tire is then heated so that it will expand enough to go on the centre. It is then cooled off, and the contraction of the metal binds it firmly around the cast iron part of the wheel. As an additional security bolts or set-screws, *a, a*, fig. 161, are screwed through the rim and into the tire to prevent it from slipping off in case it becomes loose. In some cases the wheel-centre and the inside of the tire are turned conical, and the tires are then put on cold and held on with hook-headed bolts, *C*, as shown in fig. 162, which is a

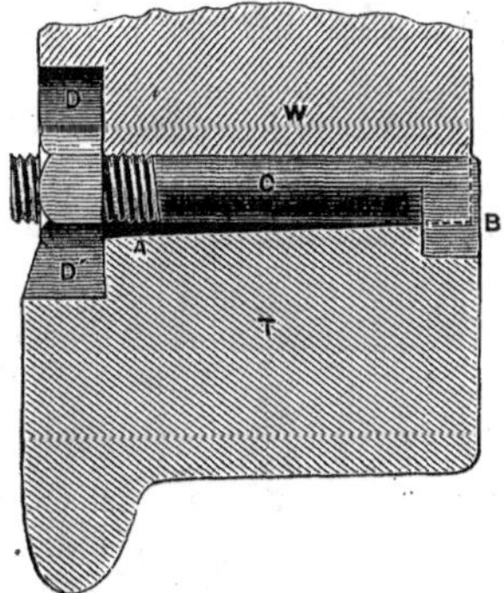

Fig. 162. Scale 3 in.=1 foot.

section of the tire and the rim of the wheel. The wheel-centre is made largest on the inside. As the strain against the flange of the tire is inward, the cone of the wheel-centre resists this strain. If it was curved or tapered the reverse way, the strain would come on the bolts, and it would also be impossible to remove the tires without first taking the wheels off the axles. This method of putting on tires has the advantage that they can be removed quickly and without heating the tires.*

---

* It is exclusively used on the Baltimore and Ohio Railroad.

QUESTION 266. *Are there any standard sizes for the inside diameters of tires?*

Answer. Yes. To avoid the great inconvenience arising from the diversity in the *inside diameters* of tires, the American Railway Master Mechanics' Association has recommended that the inside diameter of tires should be made 36, 40, 44, 50, 56 and 62 inches. The thickness for the first three sizes to be 3 in. and the last three 2½ in.

QUESTION 267. *How are the driving-wheels fastened on the axles?*

Answer. The hubs are accurately bored out to receive the axles, and the latter are turned off so as to fit the hole bored in the wheel. The axles are then forced into the wheel by a powerful pressure produced either with a hydraulic or screw press, made for the purpose. In order to prevent the strain upon the crank-pins from turning the wheels upon the axle, they are keyed fast with square keys driven into grooves cut in the axle and in the wheel to receive them. The ends of these keys are shown at *b*, fig. 161.

QUESTION 268. *How are the crank-pins made?*

Answer. They are made of wrought iron or steel and accurately turned to the size required for the journals for the connecting-rods. Fig. 164 represents one of the main crank-pins, and fig. 163 a back pin for an American engine. The main pin has two journals, one, *B*, to which the main connecting-rod is attached, and the other, *A*, receiving the coupling-rod. The back pin has only one journal, *A*, for the coupling-rod.

QUESTION 269. *How are the crank-pins fastened to the wheels?*

Answer. They are turned so as to fit accurately holes which are bored in the wheels, and are usually "straight" or cylindrical. The pins are then either driven in with blows from a heavy weight swung from the end of a rope, or else pressed in with a screw or hydraulic press. Sometimes the holes are bored tapered or conical and the pins turned to the same form. They are then ground in with emery and oil, so as to fit perfectly, and are secured by a large nut and key on the inside of the wheel.

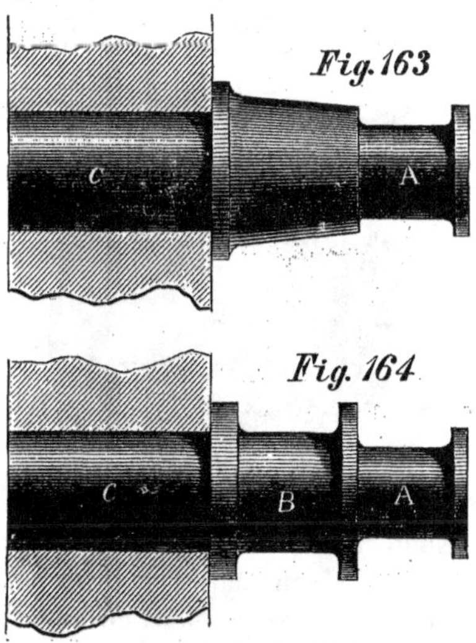

Scale 1½ in.=1 foot.

QUESTION 270. *What are the pieces A, A, fig. 161, between the spokes of the wheel for?*

Answer. They are called *counterbalance weights*, and are put in the wheels to balance the weight of the crank-pins, connecting-rods and pistons. The principle of their action will be explained hereafter.

QUESTION 271. *On what part of the axle does the weight of the engine rest?*

Answer. It rests on the driving-axle boxes *L*, fig. 161, which are placed just inside and close to the wheel.

QUESTION 272. *What are the driving-axle boxes for and how are they made?*

Answer. They are cast iron blocks, *L*, fig. 161, which embrace and rest on the axle. The part of the axle on which the box bears is called the *journal.* Each box has a brass bearing, *c*, fig. 165, which bears on top

Fig. 165.

of the journal and which is consequently exposed to the friction and wear. Fig. 165 is a perspective view of a driving-box, which shows what is called the *oil-cellar, d.* This is a receptacle underneath the axle which is filled with wool or cotton waste and saturated with oil for the purpose of lubricating the journal. The oil-cellar is held in its position by two bolts, *f, f*, which pass through it and the driving-box casting. By removing the bolts the oil-cellar can easily be removed and the box can then be taken off the axle.

QUESTION 273. *How are the truck wheels made?*

Answer. They are made of cast iron, usually in one piece. Figs. 166 and 167 represent sections of two forms of wheels used for cars. Those used for locomotive trucks are similar to these, excepting that they are usually a little smaller in diameter. They are made with a disc or plate which unites the tire to the hub, and in some cases they have ribs cast in the inside, as shown in the two figures. Some are made with single and others with double plates, as shown in

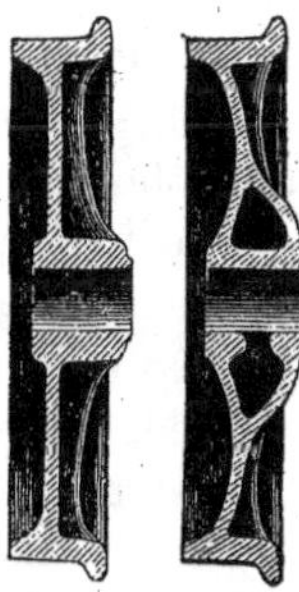

Fig. 166. Fig. 167.
Scale ½ in. = 1 foot.

the engravings, and still others with spokes similar to the driving-wheels. The tread of the wheel is hardened by a process called *chilling.* This is done by pouring the melted cast iron into a mould of the form of the tread of the wheel. The mould is also made of cast iron, but being cold cools the melted iron very suddenly, and thus hardens it somewhat as steel is hardened when it is heated and plunged into cold water.*

* It should be mentioned here that it is only certain kinds of cast iron which will be hardened in this way, or will "*chill*," as it is called. The cause to which this chilling property is due is not known.

QUESTION 274. *How are the boxes, journals and journal-bearings of the truck-wheels made?*

Answer. They are very similar to those for the driving-wheels, their chief difference being that those for the truck-wheels are smaller than those for the driving-wheels.

QUESTION 275. *How are the frames for locomotives constructed?*

Answer. The frames, *H H H*, plates I, II and III, are made of bars of wrought iron from 3 to 4 inches thick and about the same in width. They are usually made in two parts, the one at the back part of the engine, to which the driving-boxes and axles are attached, and the other at the front end, to which the cylinders are bolted. The back part, or main frame, as it is called, is represented in figs. 168 and 169, and consists of a top bar, *H H,* to which pieces, *a, a', b, b',* called *frame-legs,* are welded. Two of these form what is called a *jaw,* which receives the axle-box, as shown in fig. 169. To the bottom of each jaw a *clamp, c,* is bolted to hold the two legs together. The two legs, *a* and *b',* are united by a brace, *d d,* welded to the bottom of the legs. A brace, *m,* unites the back end of the frame with the leg *b,* and is welded to each.

The front part of each frame consists of a single bar, *e,* which is bolted to the back end, as represented in figs. 168 and 169, which show the construction clearer than any description would. These front bars extend forward to the front end of the engine, and a heavy timber, called a *bumper-timber, E E,* plates I, II and III, extends across from one to the other and is bolted to each of them. This timber is intended to receive the shock or blow when the locomotive runs

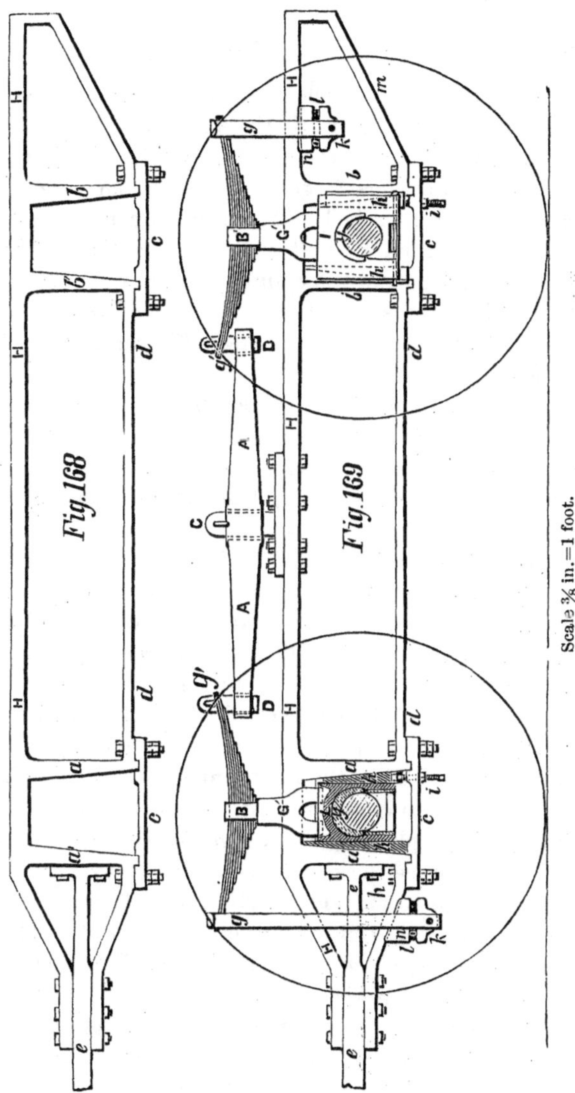

Scale 3/8 in. = 1 foot.

against any object, such as a car. The *cow-catcher* or *pilot*, *S*, is fastened to this timber.

The front bar of the frames also has usually two lugs or projections forged on it, between which the cylinders are attached. The latter are securely held in their position by wedges, which are driven in between the lugs and the cylinder castings.

The frames, as already stated, are made of wrought iron and are accurately planed off over their whole surface.

QUESTION 276. *How are the frames fastened to the boiler?*

Answer. As already stated, they are fastened to the cylinders with wedges and bolts, and as the cylinders are bolted to the smoke-box the frames are thus rigidly attached to the front end of the boiler. In order to strengthen those portions of the frames which extend beyond the front of the smoke-box and to which the bumper-timber is attached, diagonal braces, *r′ r′*, plates I, II and III are bolted both to the timber and to each of the frames at their lower ends. The upper ends are bolted to the smoke-box. Other braces, *d′*, plate II, are also fastened to the frames and to the barrel of the boiler. The frames are fastened to the fire-box by clamps, *I*, *I*, plate I, called *expansion clamps.* These clamps embrace the frames so that the latter can slide through the former longitudinally. There are also usually two diagonal braces not shown in plate II, the upper ends of which are fastened to the back end of the shell of the fire-box at about the level of the crown-sheet, and the lower ends to the back ends of the frames. There are also usually transverse braces attached to the lower part of the frames, thus uniting the two together. The guide-yokes, *j j*, plate I, are also usually bolted to the frames and to the boiler. In many cases one only is used, which extends across from one frame to the other and is fastened to the boiler.

Question 277. *Why are the frames attached to the shell of the fire-box so as to slide longitudinally through the fastenings?*

Answer. Because when the boiler becomes heated it expands, and if it could not move independent of the frames its expansion would create a great strain on both itself and the frames. The fastenings to the fire-box are therefore made so that the frames can move freely through them lengthwise, but in no other direction.

Question 278. *How much more will the boiler expand than the frames in getting up steam?*

Answer. From $\frac{1}{4}$ to $\frac{5}{16}$ of an inch.

Question 279. *Why is it necessary to support the engine on springs?*

Answer. *Because, however well a road may be kept up, there will always be shocks in running over it; these occur at the rail joints and especially when the ballasting of the ties is not quite perfect. These shocks affect the wheels first, and by them are transferred through the axle-boxes to the frame, the engine and the boiler. The faster the locomotive runs, the more powerful do they become, and therefore the more destructive to the engine and road, and consequently the faster a locomotive has to run the more perfect should be the arrangement of the springs.

*The above answer and much of the material referring to springs has been translated from "Die Schule des Locomotivführers," by Messrs. J. Brosius and R. Koch.

If we strike repeatedly with a hammer on a rail, the latter is soon destroyed, while it can bear without damage a much greater weight than the hammer lying quietly on it. The axles, axle-boxes and wheels strike like a hammer on the rails at each shock, while the shock of the rest of the parts of the engine first reaches and bends the springs, but on the rails has only the effect of a load greater than usual resting on them. Another comparison will make still plainer the lessening by the springs of the injurious effect which the weight of the boiler, etc., exercises on the rails.

A light blow with a hammer on a pane of glass is sufficient to shatter it. If, however, on the pane of glass is laid some elastic substance, such as india-rubber, and we strike on that, the force of the blow or the weight of the hammer must be considerably increased before producing the above-named effect. If the locomotive boiler is put in place of the hammer, the springs in place of the india-rubber, and the rails in place of the glass, the comparison will agree with the case above. From this consideration it will be seen how important it is to make the weights of the axles, axle-boxes and wheels as light as possible.

QUESTION 280. *How are the driving-axle boxes arranged so that the weight of the engine will rest on springs?*

Answer. They are arranged so as to slide up and down in the jaws. Springs, *B*, *B′*, fig. 169, are then placed over the axle-boxes and above the frames. These springs rest on ∩-shaped saddles, *G′*, *G′*, which bear on the top of the axle-boxes. The frames are suspended to the ends of the springs by rods or bars,

g, g', g, g', called *spring-hangers.* As the boiler and most of the other parts of the engine are fastened to the frames, their weight is suspended on the ends of the springs, which, being flexible, yield to the weight which they bear.

QUESTION 281. *How are the frames protected from the wear of the axle-boxes which results from their sliding up and down in the jaws?*

Answer. The insides of the legs, a, a', b, b', are protected with *shoes* or *wedges, h, h,* which are held stationary, and the box slides against the faces of the shoes, thus wearing the shoe or wedge but not the frame.

QUESTION 282. *Why are the shoes usually made wedge-shaped?*

Answer. They are made in that way so that when they become worn, by moving one or both of them up in the jaws, the space between them is narrowed and the lost motion is taken up. They are moved by the screws i, i. If the boxes should become loose from wear, it would cause the engine to thump at each revolution of the wheels or stroke of the piston.

QUESTION 283. *How are the springs for the driving-wheels made?*

Answer. They are made of steel plates which are placed one on top of the other. These plates are of different lengths, as shown at B, B, in fig. 169, and are from 3 to 4 in. wide and $\frac{5}{16}$ to $\frac{7}{16}$ thick. The length of the springs measured from the centre of one hanger to the centre of the other is usually about three feet.

QUESTION 284. *What determines the amount which a spring will bend under a given load?*

Answer. The number of plates, their thickness, length and breadth, and of course the material of which they are made. This can be explained if we suppose we have a spring plate of a uniform thickness, *h*, and a triangular form, of which fig. 170 is a side view and 171 a plan, and that it is clamped fast at its base, *b*. It is a well known mechanical law that any material of this form and under these conditions will have a uniform strength through its whole length to support any load, *P*, suspended at its end, and also that it will bend or deflect in the form of an arc of a circle.

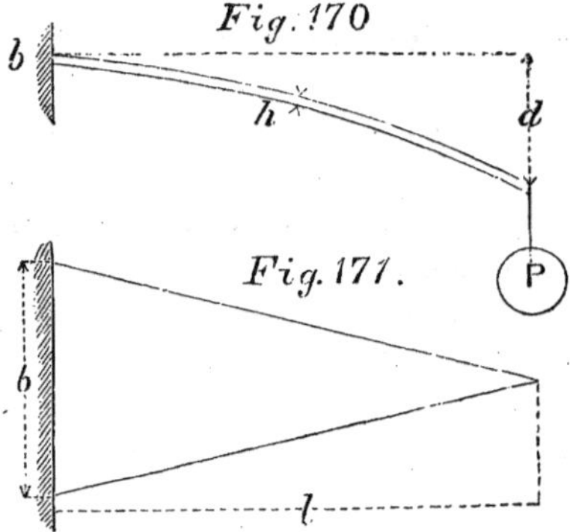

Fig. 170

Fig. 171.

QUESTION 285. *How are locomotive springs usually made?*

Answer. In locomotives the arrangement of springs is always such that they are either supported in the middle and moved at the two ends, or such that they are supported at the two ends and loaded in the middle; for our consideration it is indifferent which of the two kinds of springs is taken for the present illustration. That shown in plan and elevation in figs. 172 and 173, which is formed of a wide plate placed diagonally, and which in reality consists of two such triangular pieces as were represented in fig. 171 united at their bases *m m*, and loaded at two opposite corners, *e* and *f*, would answer the requirements mentioned if

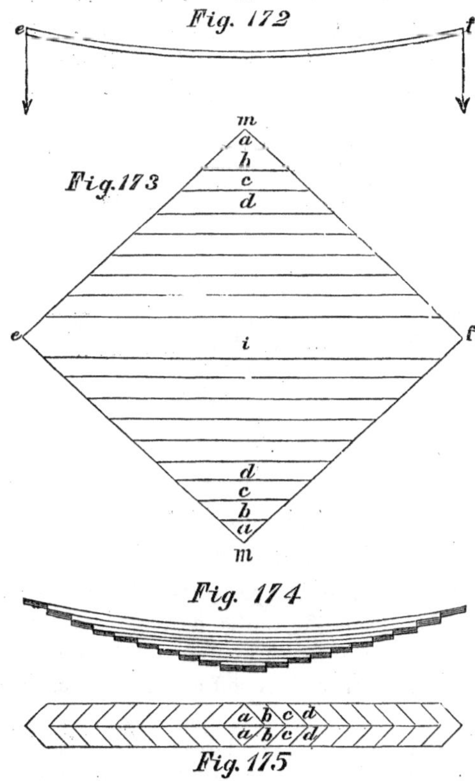

Scale ¾ in.=1 foot.

the great breadth, *m m*, were not an obstacle. This breadth is obviated by cutting the spring into several strips, *a a*, *b b*, *c c*, *d d*, ... *i*, fig. 173, of equal width, and placing these not side by side, but one over the other, as shown in figs. 174 and 175.

In order that the separate strips and layers of the spring so made, figs. 174 and 175, may not slip out of place, the strips *a a*, *b b*, etc., are made in one piece. and all the plates are inclosed with a strap, *F*, figs. 176 and 177. The plates, instead of being cut from

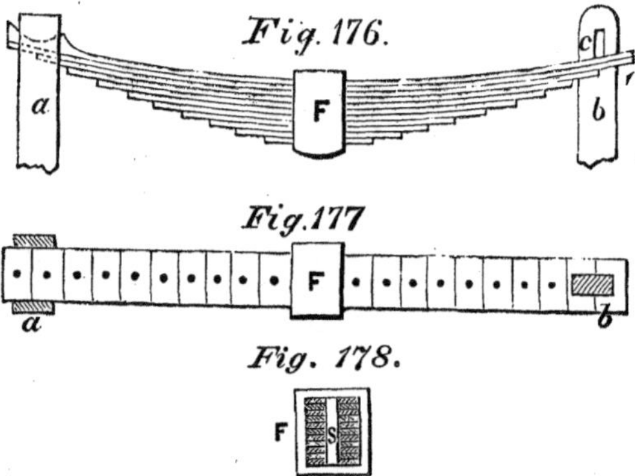

Scale ¾ in.=1 foot.

a piece like that represented in fig. 173, are, however, made out of steel of the proper width, and the ends, instead of being cut off pointed as represented, are sometimes drawn out thinner on the ends, like the point of a chisel, or oftener still cut off straight, as shown in fig. 177.

In order to hold the plates together a band, *F*, is put around the middle. This is put on hot, and becomes tight by contracting as it cools. The centre of the spring has a hole drilled through it with a pin, *s*, fig. 178 (which shows a cross section of a spring), to prevent the plates from sliding endwise. The plates at each end usually have a depression, *a*, fig. 179

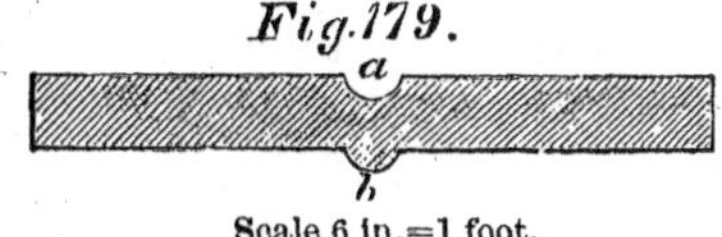

Scale 6 in.=1 foot.

(which is a cross section of a plate on a larger scale than the preceding figure), made in them on one side, and a corresponding elevation, *b*, on the other. The elevation on one plate fits into the depression on the other, and thus prevents the plates from slipping sideways.

QUESTION 286. *How should springs be curved?*

Answer. Springs should be curved so that when they bear the greatest load which they must carry they will be straight. If they are curved too much

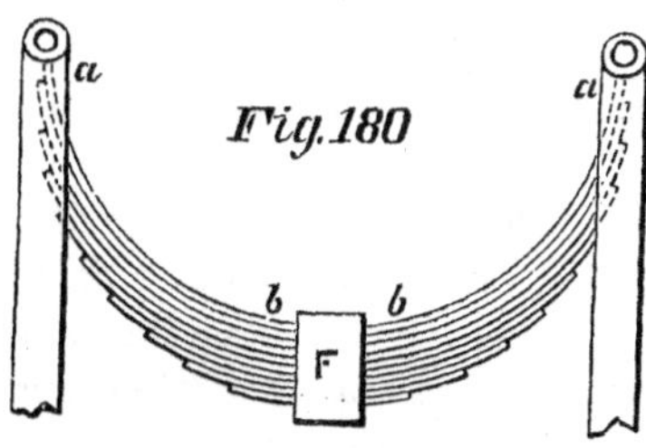

Scale ¾ in.=1 foot.

they are subjected not only to a strain which bends the plates, but to one which has a tendency to compress them endwise. Thus if a spring like that represented in fig. 180 is bent into a half-circle, it is obvious that the strain at the ends has no tendency at all to bend the plates, but only to compress them endwise. Near the middle the strain will of course bend the spring. In the one direction the spring is flexible and elastic, and in the other it is not; and as the strain of compression depends on the amount of curvature, the greater the latter is, the less flexibility and elasticity the spring will have.

Springs are often given a double curve, as shown in fig. 181. This is not to be recommended, because when a spring bends the plates must slide on each other. If they have but a single curve, they will do so and remain in contact through their whole length, but if they have two curves they will separate and therefore "gape," as it is called.

Fig. 181.

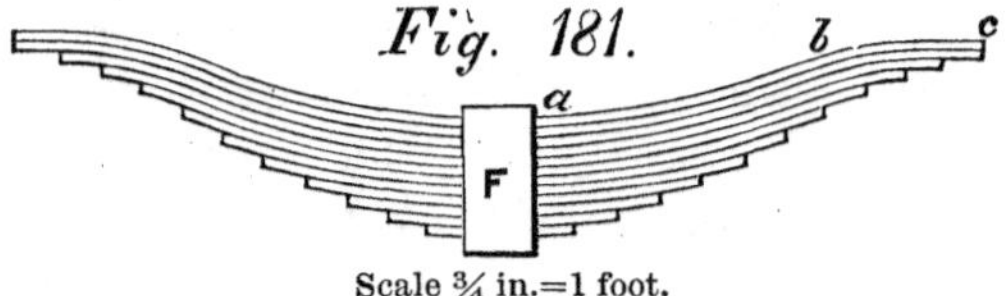

Scale ¾ in.=1 foot.

QUESTION 287. *What is meant by the elasticity of a spring?*

Answer. It is the amount which a spring will deflect or bend under a given load without having its form permanently changed. If the bending is so great that the spring does not recover its original form when the load is removed, then the strain to which it is subjected is said to exceed *the limits of elasticity*, and if repeated often it will ultimately break the spring.

QUESTION 288. *What is meant by the elastic strength and the ultimate strength of a spring?*

Answer. The *elastic strength* is the strain it will bear

without being strained beyond the limits of elasticity, and the *ultimate strength* is the strain which will break it.

QUESTION 289. *What determines the strength of a spring?*

Answer. It depends of course (1) upon the material of which the spring is made; (2) its strength increases in proportion to the number of plates, and (3) to their width, and (4) in proportion to the square of their thickness, and (5) as the length diminishes.

Thus, if we wanted to double the strength of a spring like that shown in figs. 170 and 171, it could be done in either of the following ways: (1) by making it of material twice as strong; (2) by putting another plate just like it on top; (3) by doubling the width of the base *b*, which would make the strength of the whole plate twice what it was before; (4) by making the whole plate about four-tenths thicker, which would increase its strength, as already stated, in proportion to the square of the thickness as $1.4 \times 1.4 = 2$ nearly; (5) by reducing the length to one-half what it is in fig. 170.

QUESTION 290. *What determines the elasticity of a spring?*

Answer. (1) The material of which it is made; with the same material the elasticity increases (2) as the number, and (3) as the width of the plates diminishes, and (4) with the cube of the length, and (5) decreases with the cube of the thickness of plate.

Thus, supposing the plate in figs. 170 and 171 to be $\frac{3}{8}$ in. thick and the deflection *d* $2\frac{1}{2}$ in.; the latter would be only half as much or $1\frac{1}{4}$ in. (1) if it were made of material twice as stiff, or (2) with two such plates, or (3)with one twice as wide at the base. If (4) the length were doubled, the deflection would be equal to $2 \times 2 \times 2 = 8$ times what it was before, or in proportion to the cube of the length. If (5) the thickness were doubled the deflection would be ***reduced*** in the same proportion, and would be only one-eighth of $2\frac{1}{2}$ in., or $\frac{5}{16}$ in.

QUESTION 291. ***What should be the proportion of the plates of a spring in relation to each other?***

Answer. The lower plates should diminish regularly in their lengths. The reason for this will be apparent from the fact which has already been stated, that if a

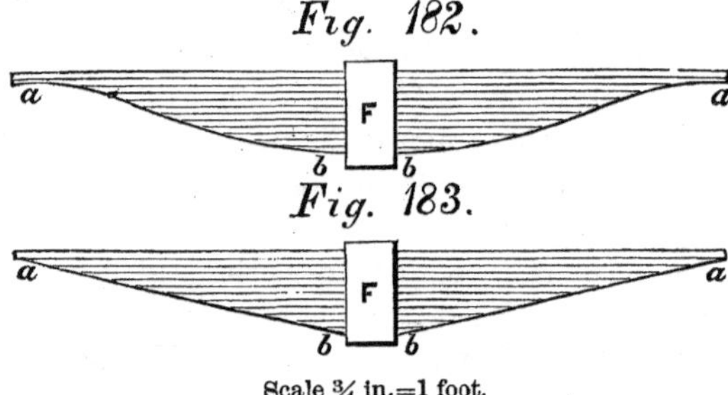

Scale ¾ in.=1 foot.

triangular plate of uniform thickness is clamped fast at its base, it will, if loaded at the end, be of uniform strength throughout its whole length. It is immaterial what the length of the base of such a triangle is, if the two sides are of equal length and the thickness of the plate is uniform, not only its strength but the amount of deflection or bending from any load will be equal all through its length. If, therefore, we make a spring by cutting a plate formed of two such triangular pieces united at their bases into strips, as has already been explained, evidently the spring made of them will have a uniform strength throughout its whole length. As the strips thus made diminish in length regularly, it is evident that if the spring plates are made of steel rolled of the requisite width, their length should be the same as that of those cut from the plate referred to above. When this is the case the lower outline, *a b b a*, fig. 183, of the spring will, when the spring is not bent, be straight lines. Sometimes the lower outline of springs is made curved, as shown in fig. 182. This gives too much strength near the strap *F*, and too little near the ends. In drawing springs, therefore, it is best to lay them out with the plates straight, as shown in figs. 182 and 183, and after determining the thickness, drawing a straight line from the strap to the end of the longest plate will give the best form of the spring and the length of each of the plates. It is necessary, however, to put a sufficient number of long plates in each spring to give it the required strength next to the attachment of the hanger. Sometimes one or more of these long plates are made heavier than the rest. The evil of this method of construction will be apparent if it is remembered that the greatest permissible deflection up to the breaking of the spring decreases with the *cube* of the thickness of the plate and its strength increases with the *square* of the thickness. Now if we have a spring with say ten plates $\frac{3}{8}$ in. thick and one on top $\frac{3}{4}$ in. thick, the thick plate will have a strength *four* times that of the thin plates, but its elasticity will be only one-eighth that of the thin plates, and therefore it will require eight times as much load to bend it any given distance as is needed to bend the thinner plates the same distance. But its strength is only four times that of the thin plates, so that for any given amount of elasticity the thick plate must bear twice as much load as it has strength to carry. This shows what a great mistake is committed if some of the plates are made thicker than others, a conclusion which is supported by practical experience, as it is found that if the top plates are made thicker than others, the thick ones break most frequently, which is the necessary result of the supposed strengthening by increasing the thickness of the top plates.

QUESTION 292. **How can we find by calculation the elasticity or deflection of a given steel spring?*

Answer. BY MULTIPLYING THE BREADTH OF THE PLATES IN INCHES BY THE CUBE OF THE THICKNESS IN SIXTEENTHS, AND BY THE NUMBER OF PLATES: DIVIDE THE CUBE OF THE SPAN† IN INCHES BY THE PRODUCT SO FOUND, AND MULTIPLY BY 1.66. THE RESULT IS THE ELASTICITY IN SIXTEENTHS OF AN INCH PER TON OF LOAD.

QUESTION 293. *How can we find the span due to a given elasticity and number and size of plates?*

Answer. BY MULTIPLYING THE ELASTICITY IN SIXTEENTHS PER TON BY THE BREADTH OF PLATE IN INCHES, AND BY THE CUBE OF THE THICKNESS IN SIXTEENTHS, AND BY THE NUMBER OF PLATES: DIVIDE BY 1.66, AND FIND THE CUBE ROOT OF THE QUOTIENT. THE RESULT IS THE SPAN IN INCHES.

QUESTION 294. *How can we find the number of plates due to a given elasticity, span, and size of plate?*

Answer. BY MULTIPLYING THE CUBE OF THE SPAN

*The following rules for calculating the proportion and strength of steel springs are from Clark's Railway Machinery.

† The span is the distance between the centres of the spring-hangers when the spring is loaded.

IN INCHES BY 1.66; THEN MULTIPLYING THE ELASTICITY IN SIXTEENTHS BY THE BREADTH OF PLATE IN INCHES, AND BY THE CUBE OF THE THICKNESS IN SIXTEENTHS: DIVIDE THE FORMER PRODUCT BY THE LATTER. THE QUOTIENT IS THE NUMBER OF PLATES.

QUESTION 295. *How can we find the working strength, that is the greatest weight it should bear in practice, of a given steel-plate spring?*

Answer. BY MULTIPLYING THE BREADTH OF PLATES IN INCHES BY THE SQUARE OF THE THICKNESS IN SIXTEENTHS, AND BY THE NUMBER OF PLATES; MULTIPLY, ALSO, THE WORKING SPAN IN INCHES BY 11.3: DIVIDE THE FORMER PRODUCT BY THE LATTER. THE RESULT IS THE WORKING STRENGTH IN TONS (OF 2,240 POUNDS) BURDEN.

QUESTION 296. *How can we find the span due to a given strength, and number and size of plate?*

Answer. BY MULTIPLYING THE BREADTH OF PLATE IN INCHES BY THE SQUARE OF THE THICKNESS IN SIXTEENTHS, AND BY THE NUMBER OF PLATES; MULTIPLY, ALSO, THE STRENGTH IN TONS BY 11.3: DIVIDE THE FORMER PRODUCT BY THE LATTER. THE RESULT IS THE WORKING SPAN IN INCHES.

QUESTION 297. *How can we find the number of plates due to a given strength, span and size of plates?*

Answer. BY MULTIPLYING THE STRENGTH IN TONS BY THE SPAN IN INCHES, AND BY 11.3; MULTIPLY ALSO, THE BREADTH OF PLATE IN INCHES BY THE SQUARE OF THE THICKNESS IN SIXTEENTHS: DIVIDE THE FORMER PRODUCT BY THE LATTER. THE RESULT IS THE NUMBER OF PLATES.

QUESTION 298. *How can we find the required amount of curvature or set of the spring before it is loaded?*

Answer: BY MULTIPLYING THE ELASTICITY, PER TON, IN INCHES, BY THE WORKING STRENGTH IN TONS; ADD THE PRODUCT TO THE DESIRED WORKING COMPASS. THE SUM IS THE WHOLE ORIGINAL SET, TO WHICH AN ALLOWANCE OF $\frac{1}{8}$ TO $\frac{3}{8}$ IN. SHOULD BE ADDED TO THE PERMANENT SETTING OF THE SPRING.

QUESTION 299. *How are the spring-hangers attached to the ends of the springs?*

Answer. A great variety of methods have been used. The most common ones are those shown in fig. 169. There the hanger embraces the spring at the ends, *g, g,* (shown on an enlarged scale at *a,* in figs. 176 and 178.) The end of the spring has two projections forged on its end to receive the upper end of the hanger, which is made to fit the groove thus formed between the two projections. The other end, *b,* of the spring, figs. 176 and 178, has an eye cut in it which receives the hanger *b.* The latter is made of a single bar, and also has an eye, *c,* to receive a key which sustains the weight suspended on the hanger *b.* The back end of the front springs and the front end of the back springs are made in this way because they come on the side of the fire-box, and if their width was increased by the thickness of the hanger, as shown at *a* in fig. 178, it would rub against and wear the outer shell of the fire-box.

QUESTION 300. *How are the lower ends of the hangers attached?*

Answer. The front hanger, *g,* fig. 169, of the front spring, and the back hanger, *g,* of the back spring have eyes and pins in their lower ends, *k,* as shown in the engraving. The pins are supported by rubber springs, *l, l,* which are held between two concave castings, *n*, *k*, one of each of which rests against the frames. The object of the rubber springs is to relieve the spring-hangers from sudden shocks and strains. The benefit derived from their use is believed to be purely imaginary, as the spring itself, if sufficiently elastic, should absorb the sudden shocks which the wheels and axles will convey to the hangers.

QUESTION 301. *Why are the ends g′, g′ of the springs attached to the lever* A A?*

Answer. Because if there is a spring for every axle and the hangers are fastened to the frame, then evidently the locomotive has as many points of support as it has axle-boxes. Every shock from the rails is transferred through the wheel and the axle to the nearest axle-box and the spring belonging to it, and the latter must be made strong enough to receive and dispose of the whole of it. If the adjacent hangers, *g′*, *g′*, fig. 169, of the adjoining springs, *B* and *B′*, are connected by an equalizing lever, *A A*, which turns on the fixed point C, then the shock which affects one wheel will be transferred first to the corresponding spring. From this spring a part of the shock will be transferred to the frame by the hanger *g*, and a part by the hanger *g′* to the equalizer, which will transfer the pressure to the adjoining spring *B′*. If by some unevenness of the road or a powerful oscillation of the locomotive, a spring is momentarily burdened, the equalizer thus causes the next wheel to receive part of this load.

The advantages of this arrangement are evident: since the springs have to receive only a part of the

* This lever is called an *equalizing lever* or *beam*, or, more briefly, an *equalizer*.

shocks, they can be made less strong and therefore more flexible. The danger of running off the track and that of breaking axles, springs and hangers, is therefore reduced by the use of equalizing levers.

QUESTION 302. *How are the equalizing levers constructed?*

Answer. They are made of wrought iron and are supported in the centre by a fulcrum, *C*, which is fastened to the frame or boiler or both. The spring-hangers *g'*, *g'* are usually attached to the lever by eyes and keys. Sometimes eyes are made in the lever, as shown in fig. 169, and the hanger is inserted into the eye and held either with a key or else with projections which are forged on the hanger below the lever. In other cases the hangers are made with an eye which embraces the end of the lever.

QUESTION 303. *How is the distribution of weight of the engine affected by the equalizing levers?*

Answer. The weight is equally distributed on all the driving-wheels. This is apparent if it is observed that the weight suspended from each of the spring-hangers of each spring in fig. 169 must be the same; for if the weights in the two hangers, *g'* and *g'*, were unequal, then the end of the spring which supports the heaviest weight would be drawn down until the pressure was equalized. If the weights suspended from the two hangers, *g'* and *g'*, attached to the equalizing lever were unequal, then the one supporting the greatest load would draw up its end of the equalizer until the weights were again in equilibrium.

Another effect of the equalizing levers is that each side of the locomotive is supported in such a way that the action is the same as it would be if it was supported on one point. If, for example, we have a heavy beam, say a piece of timber like that shown by *A B*, fig. 184, suspended at one point, *C*, in its centre, to the middle, *a*, of a long spring, *D E*, the ends

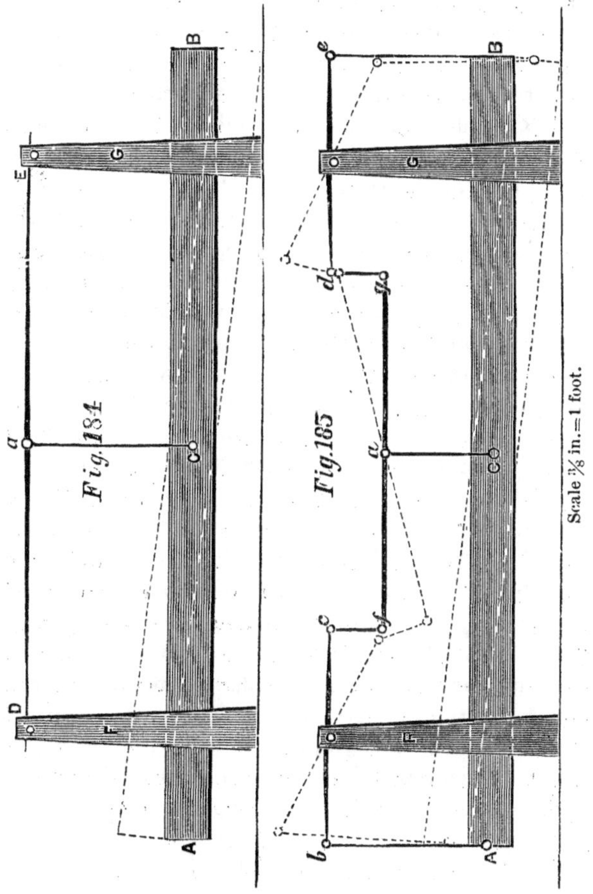

Fig. 184

Fig. 185

of which rest on two supports, *F* and *G*, it is evident that if the point of suspension is at the middle, *C*, of the timber and *a* of the spring, the weight of the timber will rest equally on the two supports, *F* and *G*, and that the ends of the timber can move up or down or vibrate about the point of suspension, *C*, without affecting the distribution of weight on the supports, *F* and *G*. If, now, the timber is suspended from three points, *A*, *C* and *B*, fig. 185, that is, its middle and two ends, as shown in fig. 185, the ends, *A* and *B*, being attached to the ends of the springs *b c* and *d e*, the latter resting on the supports *F* and *G*, and connected at their opposite ends to an equalizer, *f g*, whose fulcrum is at *a*, it is evident that each of the end hangers must support one-half of that part of the weight of the timber between it and the middle, and that the centre hanger must support one-half the weight between the middle and the two ends. Thus the hanger *A b* must support one-half the weight of the timber between *A* and *C*, and *B e* must support one-half of that between *B* and *C*; in other words, the end hangers would each sustain one-fourth of the weight of the timber and the middle one-half of its weight. If the weight of the timber is 1,000 pounds, the end hangers would each sustain 250 and the middle one 500 pounds. The weight of the middle of the timber is hung on the equalizer, and one-half, or 250 pounds of it is thus transferred to each of its ends *f* and *g*, and thence to the hangers *f c* and *g d*, and thus to the springs, so that the ends, *c* and *d*, of the springs, sustain a weight of 250 pounds, therefore, as the opposite ends also sustain the same weight, it is evident that each of the springs bears a total load of 500 pounds, or one-half of the weight of the timber, which is the same load they sustained in fig. 164. If the ends of a timber supported as shown in fig. 185 are moved up or down about the centre point of suspension, it is evident that the distribution of weight would not be affected any more than it was in fig. 164 by a similar movement, because if the ends of the timber move as shown by the dotted lines around the centre point of suspension *C*, the end *A* will ascend as much as *B* descends. The same thing is true of the ends *b* and *e* of the springs and of their opposite ends *c* and *d*, and also of the ends of the equalizer, so that when the timber, springs and equalizer are in the position shown by the dotted lines, it is in equilibrium, just as it was when the timber was horizontal; and therefore the weight on the supports is the same in both cases, thus showing that the load *A B* can move about the centre of suspension when supported as shown in fig. 185 as freely as it can if arranged as shown in fig. 184. It therefore follows that in the distribution of the weight of each side of the locomotive on the wheels and on the track, it may be regarded the same as though it was supported at one point, which is the fulcrum of the equalizing-lever.

QUESTION 304. *What advantage results from supporting the weight of the back part of the locomotive on two points?*

Answer. If the back part of the locomotive rests on only two points and the front end on the centre of the truck, then the whole weight of the engine will be sustained on three points. Now it is a well known fact that any tripod, like that on which an engineer's level is mounted, or a three-legged stool, will adjust itself to any surface, however uneven, and stand firmly in any position; whereas if there are more than three points of support, if they are all of the same length the surface on which they rest must be a plane, otherwise some of them will not touch. All railroad tracks have inequalities of surface, and therefore it is of the utmost importance that a locomotive should be able to adjust itself on its points of support to any unevenness of the track on which it must run. This is possible only when the weight rests on three points of support.

QUESTION 305. *How is the truck constructed?*

Answer. It consists, as has already been stated, of two pairs of wheels.* These are attached to a frame, *b′ b′*, plates I, II and III. The axles have boxes called *truck-boxes*, and brass bearings similar to those used on the driving-axles. These boxes work in jaws, also similar to those on the main engine frame, excepting that they have no attachment to prevent them from being worn by the motion of the boxes up and down in the jaws. Fig. 186 is a horizontal section, fig. 187 a plan, and fig. 188 a transverse section † of a truck. The frame *C D E F*, fig. 187, shown also at *h′ h′*, figs. 186 and 188, is of rectangular form and is forged in one piece. The legs *f f* which form the jaws for the boxes, are bolted to the frame as shown in fig. 186. To the lower end of these legs a brace, *g g g*, is bolted, which thus unites them together. On each side one spring, *S F S*, is placed under the

* In some rare cases three pairs of wheels are employed for locomotive trucks. Six-wheeled trucks are very commonly used under passenger cars.

† The right half is a section through the centre of the axle, or of *G g*, of fig. 186, and the left half a section through the centre of the truck, or on *g g*, of fig. 186.

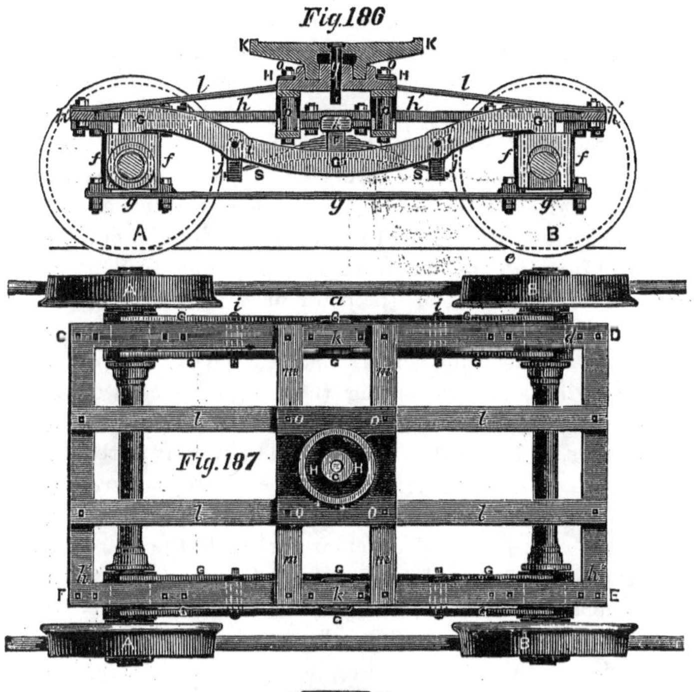

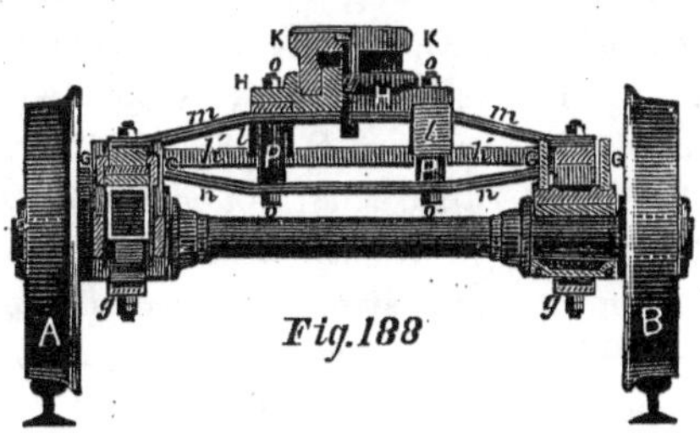

Scale, $\frac{3}{8}$ inch = 1 foot.

frame and in the reverse or inverted position to that of the driving-springs. A pair of equalizing levers, *G G G*, is placed on each side of the truck, one of them on the inside of the frame and the other on the outside, as shown in the plan. The ends of these equalizers rest on the top of the truck-boxes, and the springs are attached to the levers at *i i* by the hangers, *j j*. The truck-frame rests on the top of the spring-strap, *F*, which is made of the form of an arc of a circle, or "*rounded*," as it is termed by workmen, so that it can move freely about the point of support. It is evident that this arrangement of spring and equalizer operates in the same way as that employed for the driving-wheels in distributing the weight on each of the wheels, and that the truck-frame is supported on two points, *k*, *k*, figs. 186 and 187. The weight of the front end of the engine rests on a cast iron *centre-plate, H H.* This centre-plate rests on four bars, *l l*, *l l*, and *m m*, *m m*, two of which are bolted to the frame transversely and the other two longitudinally, as shown in the plan. These bars are elevated in the centre as shown in figs. 186 and 188. The transverse bars are trussed with two corresponding bars, *n n*, fig. 188, below. These *truss-bars* as they are called, are bolted to the upper bars with bolts, *o*, *o*, but are separated from the top-bars by distance pieces, *P*, *P*, figs. 186 and 188. The centre-plate *H H*, called the the *lower centre-plate*, has an annular groove in it, which receives a corresponding projection on the casting *K K*, called the *upper centre-plate*, which is bolted to the bed-plate of the cylinders, as shown in plate II. The upper centre-plate has a pin, *y*, called a *centre-pin*, fig. 186 and plate II, attached to it, which passes through the lower centre-plate, and has a key underneath the latter plate. This key is intended to prevent the engine from "jumping" off of the truck on a rough track or in case of accident. The annular groove and the projection which fits into it are intended to receive the strain which otherwise would bear against the centre-pin and would be liable to break or bend it.

From this description it will be seen that while the truck-frame rests on two points, *k* and *k*, the weight of the engine is supported by the centre-plate of the truck. As the back part substantially rests on the centres of the two equalizers, it will be seen that this

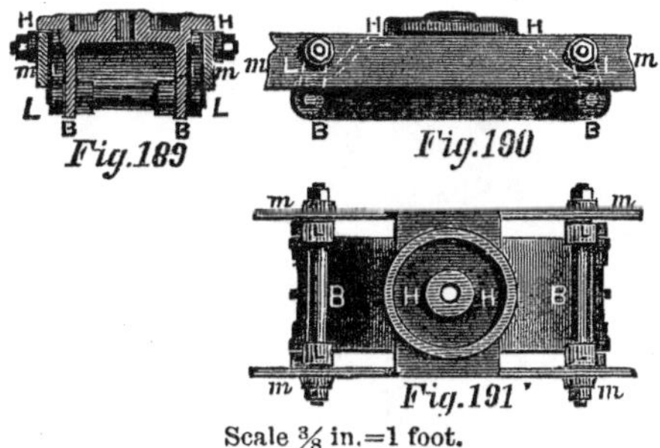

Fig.189 Fig.190 Fig.191

Scale ⅜ in.=1 foot.

distribution of the weight fulfills the conditions of the tripod, or as it has been called, the "*three-legged principle.*"

QUESTION 306. *How are trucks arranged so as to give them lateral motion?*

Answer. When this is done, the lower centre-plate is usually suspended in some way from the truck-frame on links or hangers, so that it can swing laterally. One method of doing this is shown in figs. 189, 190 and 191. Fig. 190 is a front view, fig. 191 a plan, and fig. 189 a transverse section of such an arrangement. The centre-plate *H H* has cast with it an extension, *B B*, the ends of which are suspended on links, *L, L*, called ***suspension-links***, the upper ends of which are attached to bars, *m, m*, which are set edgeways and extend across the truck-frames. It is evident that with this arrangement the lower centre casting can swing crosswise of the track on the links *L, L*, and that the front end of the engine will thus have a lateral motion independent of the truck.

PART XIII.

ADHESION AND TRACTION.

QUESTION 307. *What is meant by the "adhesion" of a locomotive?*

Answer. It is the resistance which prevents or opposes the slipping of the driving-wheels on the rails, and is due to the friction of the former on the latter.

QUESTION 308. *On what does the amount of this friction depend?*

Answer. Like all friction it depends upon the weight or pressure of the surfaces in contact, and consequently upon the load which rests on each wheel. It also depends upon the condition of the rails, and probably to some extent upon the material of which they and the tires on the wheels are made.

QUESTION 309. *How much force is required to make the driving-wheels of a locomotive slip on an ordinary railroad track?*

Answer. The force required to make them slip will, as already stated, vary very much with the condition of the rails. If they are quite dry and clean it will require a force equal to about one-fourth the weight on the wheels. That is, supposing we have a wheel, *A B*, fig. 192, attached to a frame which is fastened so that it cannot move, and that the wheel rests on a rail and is loaded with say 10,000 pounds, if now a rope or chain could be attached at a point, *B*, exactly at the tread of the wheel, and carried over a pulley, *C*, then it would require a weight, *D*, of about 2,500 pounds attached to the end of the rope to make the wheel slip. If the rails were sanded, the adhesion would be

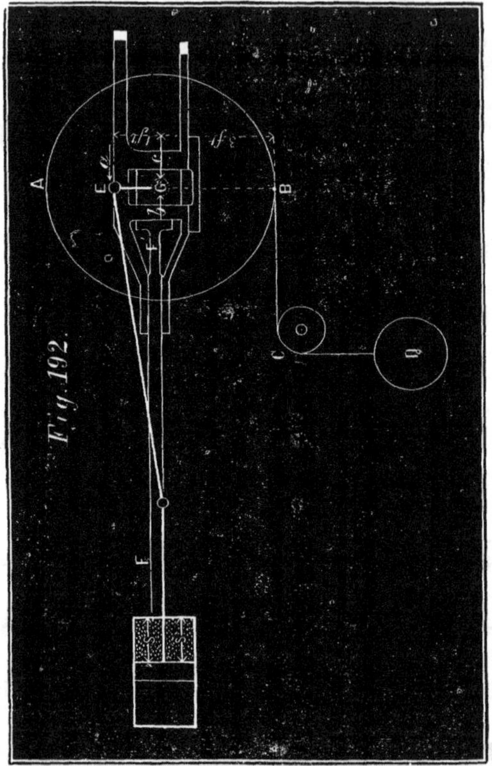

Scale ¼ in.=1 foot.

somewhat greater, and if they were wet or muddy or greasy, considerably less. For ordinary circumstances the adhesion may safely be assumed to be *one-fifth of the weight of the driving-wheels.* Of course the total weight on all the driving-wheels must be taken in calculating the adhesion. Thus, if a locomotive has four driving-wheels and each one of them bears a load of 10,000 pounds, then the total weight on the driving-wheels, or *adhesive weight,* as it is called, will be $10,000 \times 4 = 40,000$ pounds, and the adhesion will be

$$\frac{40,000}{5} = 8,000 \text{ pounds.}$$

QUESTION 310. *What is meant by the tractive power of a locomotive?*

Answer. It is the force with which the locomotive is urged in a horizontal direction by the pressure of the steam in the cylinders, and which therefore tends to move the locomotive and draw the load attached to it.

The tractive power is of course due to the pressure of steam on the piston, and therefore its amount is dependent upon the average steam pressure in the cylinder, on the area of the piston, and also on the distance through which the pressure is exerted, or, in other words, on the stroke of the piston. Thus if we have a cylinder 16 inches in diameter and two feet stroke and an average steam pressure of 50 pounds per square inch, then as the area of such a piston would be 201 square inches, the average pressure on it would be $201 \times 50 = 10,050$ pounds, and as each piston moves through four feet during one revolution of the wheels, the number of foot-pounds of energy exerted by it would be $10,050 \times 4 = 40,200$, and for the two cylinders of a locomotive double that amount, or 80,400 foot-pounds. Now if the driving-wheels are five feet in diameter, their circumference will be 15 7 feet, and therefore the locomotive will move that distance on the rails during one revolution, if the wheels do not slip. The 80,400 foot-pounds of energy is therefore exerted through a distance of 15.7 feet, and therefore

$$\frac{80,400}{15\ 7} = 5,121 \text{ pounds,}$$

which is the force exerted through each foot that the circumference of the wheel revolves and the locomotive moves. If the wheels were only half the diameter, or $2\frac{1}{2}$ feet, then their circumference would be 7.85 feet and the tractive power would be

$$\frac{80,400}{7.85} = 10,242 \text{ pounds,}$$

or double what it was before. It will be seen, then, that the tractive force of a locomotive is dependent upon (1) the average steam pressure in the cylinders, (2) the area, (3) the stroke of the pistons, and (4) the diameter of the driving-wheels.

QUESTION 311. *How is the tractive power of a locomotive calculated?*

Answer. BY MULTIPLYING TOGETHER THE AREA OF THE PISTON IN SQUARE INCHES, THE AVERAGE STEAM PRESSURE IN POUNDS PER SQUARE INCH ON THE PISTON DURING THE WHOLE STROKE, AND FOUR TIMES THE LENGTH OF THE STROKE OF THE PISTON,* AND DIVIDING THE PRODUCT BY THE CIRCUMFERENCE OF THE WHEEL. The result will be the tractive power

---

*This length may be taken in feet, inches or any other measure, but in making the calculation the circumference of the wheel must be taken in the *same* measure as the stroke of the piston.

exerted in pounds. The adhesion must of course always exceed the tractive force, otherwise the wheels will slip.

QUESTION 312. *How is the locomotive made to advance by causing the wheels to revolve?*

Answer. The pressure of steam in the cylinders is exerted in one direction against the piston, and in the opposite direction against the cylinder head, as shown in fig. 192, in which the steam is represented by the dotted shading in the back end of the cylinder, and the direction of the pressure by the darts *s*, *s*. The pressure against the piston is communicated by the connecting-rod to the crank-pin *E*, and that on the cylinder-head is carried to the axle by the frame *F F'*, and the direction of the two forces is indicated by the two darts, *a* and *b*. We may now regard the spokes of the wheels as acting as levers, and assume that the fulcrum is either at the centre *G* of the axle, or at *B*, the point of contact of the wheel with the rail.* We will assume that it is at the centre *G* of the axle and for the sake of even figures that the wheel is six feet in diameter and cylinders have two feet stroke. We will also suppose that the engine is supported so that the wheels do not touch the rails, and that a chain or rope passing over a pulley *C* is attached to the wheels at *B* and with a weight at *D*. We now have a force, *a*, of 10,000 pounds exerted on the crank-pin, or at the end of the short arm *E G* of the lever *E G B*.

* The question whether the centre of the axle or the point of contact with the rail is the fulcrum of the lever in this case has been the subject of much animated discussion and contention. As the word *fulcrum* means "a point about which a lever moves," it is believed that the dispute is due simply to a difference in the meaning assigned to the word fulcrum. If we regard the fulcrum as the point which is fixed in relation to the locomotive, then it is at the centre of the axle, but if we refer it to the surface of the earth, then it is at the top of the rail.

As *E G* is one foot and *G B* three feet long, 10,000 would be balanced by

$$\frac{10{,}000 \times 1}{3} = 3{,}333 \text{ pounds,}$$

at *B*. In other words, it would require 3,333 pounds suspended from the chain at *D* to resist the strain at *E*. But when this is the case, the pressure of the axle at the fulcrum, in the direction of the dart *c*, is equal to the pressure against the crank-pin *E* added to that exerted by the weight *D* at *B*, or 10,000+3,333=13,333 pounds.

As the pressure against the axle in the opposite direction, *b*, is only 10,000 pounds, there will be an unbalanced force of 3,333 pounds acting in the direction of the dart *c*, and tending to move it that way. As the axle is attached to the locomotive frame, this force will of course have a tendency to move the whole machine, and is really the tractive force of the engine.

If, on the other hand, we regard the point of contact *B* of the wheel with the rail as a fulcrum, we have a force of 10,000 pounds acting against a lever, *E G B*, four feet long. There would therefore be a force, *c*, of

$$\frac{10{,}000 \times 4}{3} = 13{,}333 \text{ pounds}$$

exerted at G, and as the pressure in the direction of the dart *b* is only 10,000, there would be an unbalanced strain of 13,333—10,000=3,333 pounds acting against the axle in the direction of the dart *c*, or, in other words, there is 3,333 pounds more of force pulling the axle forward than there is pushing it backward.

When the crank-pin is below the axle, in the position shown in fig. 193, then if the centre of the axle is regarded as the fulcrum we have a pressure of 10,000 pounds pushing against the front cylinder-head, which is transferred to the axle by the frames, and acts in the direction of the dart *c*, and we also have a pressure against the crank-pin *E* in the direction of the dart *a*. Now 10,000 pounds at *E* would exert a force of

$$\frac{10{,}000 \times 1}{3} = 3{,}333 \text{ pounds}$$

at *B* and

$$\frac{10{,}000 \times 2}{3} = 6{,}666 \text{ pounds}$$

at *G* in the direction of *b*. But the pressure on the cylinder-head pulls against the axle *G* in the direction *c* with a force of 10,000, so that the excess of strain in the direction *b* will be equal to 10,000—6,666=3,333 pounds. If we regard *B* as the fulcrum, the calculation is exactly the same, as 10,000 pounds at *E* exerts a force at *G* equal to

$$\frac{10{,}000 \times 2}{3} = 6{,}666 \text{ pounds,}$$

and the difference between it and the pressure exerted by the strain against the front cylinder-head is the force which urges the axle and with it the locomotive forward.

It will be seen, then, that it is immaterial which point is regarded as the fulcrum, as the result of the calculations is exactly the same.

It must not, however, be hastily supposed from what has been said that the total pressure against the axle can be greater than its resistance to the pressure. As soon as the one exceeds the other it will move. But supposing that it requires a force equal to 3,333 pounds to draw a train coupled to the engine, as soon as the difference between the force exerted

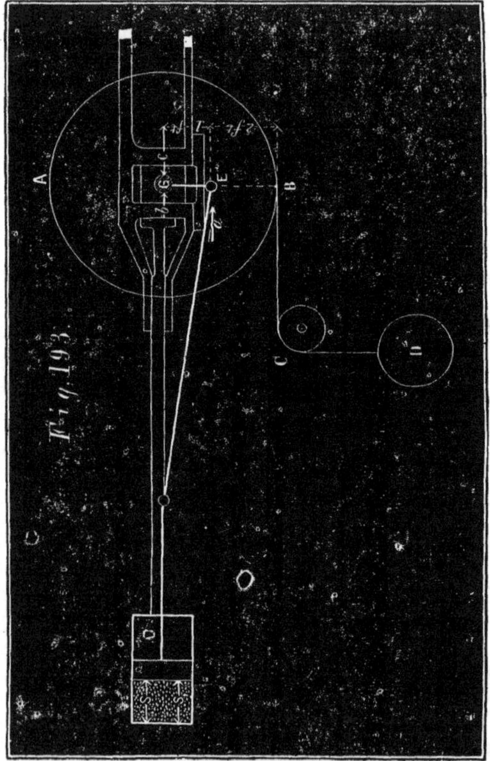

Scale ¼ in.=1 foot.

against the axle by the piston to move it forward and that which presses it back exceeds 3,333 pounds, the locomotive will move the train. If it continues to exceed it the speed of the train will be accelerated and thus the resistance which holds the engine back and that which pushes it forward will always be equal.

QUESTION 313. *Does the fact that the piston is working from the end of a longer lever E G′ B, fig.* 192, *when the crank-pin is above the axle, enable the locomotive to start a heavier train than when the crank-pin is below the axle and the piston is working against a shorter lever, G E B, fig.* 193?

Answer. No; because, as has already been shown, the pressure against the axle is the same in both cases. It is in fact only during the forward stroke that the pressure on the crank-pin moves the engine forward. The forward pressure which is exerted by the crank-pin at the axle is then greater than that exerted against the latter in the opposite direction by the cylinder-head and frames. It is this excess of crank pressure which moves the engine and which is the tractive force during the forward stroke. During the backward stroke the piston is pushing the axle backward, and the pressure against the front cylinder-head is pulling it forward. The latter then exceeds the former, and the difference between the two is the force which moves the engine forward. As has been shown, this difference is the same in both positions of the crank, and therefore the locomotive can not from this cause pull more when the crank is above the axle than when it is below.

PART XIV.

INTERNAL DISTURBING FORCES IN THE LOCOMOTIVE.

QUESTION 314. *What are the internal disturbing forces in a locomotive?*

Answer. They are: 1, the momentum of the parts which have a reciprocating motion; 2, those due to the varying pressure of the steam in the cylinder-heads; 3, those caused by the thrust of the connecting-rods against the guide-bars; and 4, those produced by unbalanced revolving parts.

QUESTION 315. *How can the effects of these disturbing forces be neutralized?*

Answer. By putting counterweights, *A*, *A*, fig. 161, in the driving-wheels opposite the crank-pins. The motion of these will then be in the reverse direction to that of the weight of the parts attached to the crank-pins, and the motion of the one will thus, to some extent, at least, neutralize the disturbing influence of the other.

QUESTION 316. *Can the weight of these counterweights be calculated for any locomotive?*

Answer. It can probably be calculated, but it is an exceedingly complicated problem, and one about which there is much difference of opinion. The difficulty is also increased by the fact that while counterweights may be heavy enough for one speed, they may be too heavy or too light for a slower or faster speed, and quite disproportioned when the engine is not working steam. The following rules are given in "Clark's Railway Machinery," and are perhaps sufficiently close to find a first approximation to the requisite position and weight of the counterweights; but the final adjustment should be made by trial. This can be done by suspending the locomotive by chains attached to the four corners of its frame, and setting the machinery in motion at the speed it is intended to run. By attaching a pencil to one or to each of the four corners of the frame, and arranging it so that it will mark on a horizontal fixed card, a diagram will be drawn, being usually an oval, which will show the amount and form of the oscillations. The counterweights can then be adjusted so that the diagram drawn by the pencil is reduced to the least possible size. When the adjustment is successful, the diameter of the diagram is reduced to about $\frac{1}{16}$ of an inch.* Another and simpler, but less accurate, way is to place a pail or other vessel filled with water on the front of the engine and run the locomotive on a smooth track at a high speed, and adjust the counterweights so that the least amount of water will be spilled.

QUESTION 317. *How can the centre of gravity of a counterweight in one segment be found?*

Answer. BY CUTTING A WOODEN TEMPLET OF UNIFORM THICKNESS TO THE FORM OF THE SURFACE, AND FREELY SUSPENDING IT BY ONE OF THE CORNERS, *a*, AS IN FIG. 194; A PLUMMET-LINE, *P a*, DROPPED FROM THE SAME POINT OF SUSPENSION

* Rankine's Treatise on the Steam Engine.

IN FRONT OF THE TEMPLET WILL INTERSECT THE CENTRE LINE *b c* AT THE CENTRE OF GRAVITY *C.*

QUESTION 318. *How can the centre of gravity of a counterweight in three segments be found?*

Answer. FIND THE CENTRE OF GRAVITY *C'*, FIG. 195, OF ONE OF THE COUNTERWEIGHTS, AS ABOVE;

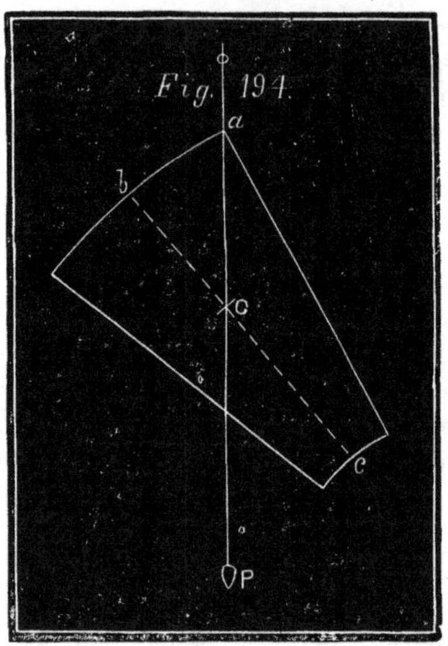

THROUGH *C* STRIKE AN ARC FROM THE CENTRE, *a*, OF THE WHEEL, CROSSING THE CENTRE LINES OF THE OTHER SEGMENTS AT THEIR CENTRES, *C' C''*; DRAW *C' C''* MEETING *A B* AT *D*, AND SET OFF *D E*, ONE-THIRD OF THE INTERVAL *D C*. THEN *E* IS THE COMMON CENTRE OF GRAVITY OF THE THREE SEGMENTS.

QUESTION 319. *How can the centre of gravity of a counterweight in two segments be found?*

Answer. This is required when the crank is opposite to a spoke, as in fig. 196. FIND THE CENTRE OF GRAVITY, C, OF ONE SEGMENT AS BEFORE, AND BY AN ARC FIND THE OTHER CENTRE C'; DRAW $C\ C'$, CUTTING $A\ B$ AT D, WHICH IS THE COMMON CENTRE OF GRAVITY.

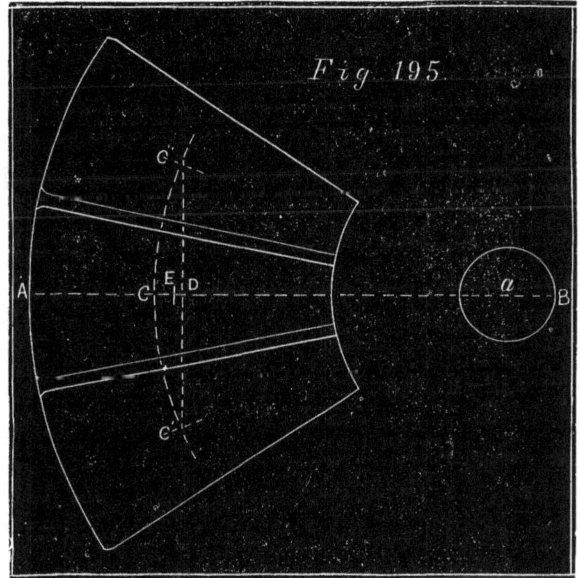

QUESTION 320. *How can the centre of gravity of a counterweight in four segments be found?*

Answer. FIND, AS BEFORE, THE CENTRES C, C', C'', C''', FIG. 197, OF THE SEGMENTS; DRAW $C''\ C'$ AND $C'''\ C$, CUTTING THE LINE $A\ B$; BISECT THE INTERVAL SO INCLOSED AT E FOR THE COMMON CENTRE OF GRAVITY.

QUESTION 321. *How is the counterweight for outside-*

cylinder engines with a single pair of driving-wheels calculated?

Answer. FIND THE TOTAL WEIGHT, IN POUNDS, OF THE REVOLVING AND RECIPROCATING MASSES FOR

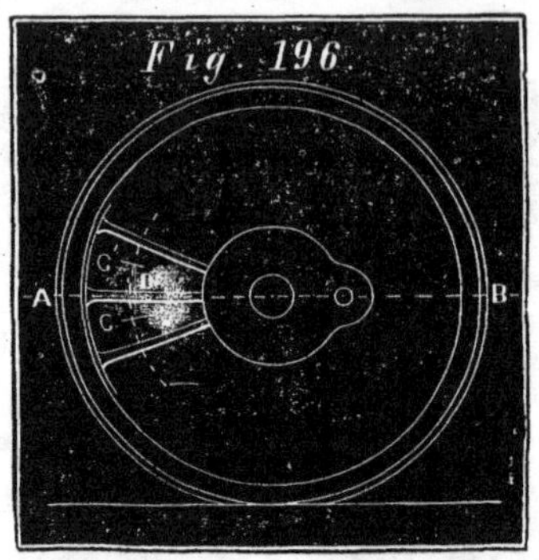

Fig. 196.

ONE SIDE, NAMELY, THE PISTON AND APPENDAGES, CONNECTING-ROD, CRANK-PIN AND CRANK-PIN BOSS; MULTIPLY BY THE LENGTH OF CRANK IN INCHES, AND

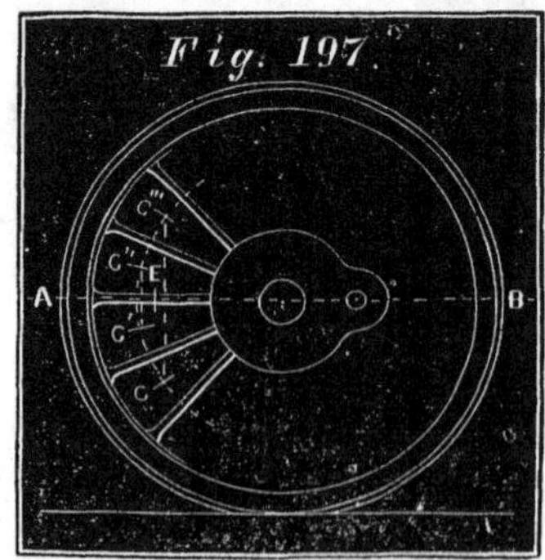

Fig. 197.

DIVIDE BY THE DISTANCE IN INCHES OF THE CENTRE OF GRAVITY OF THE SPACE TO BE OCCUPIED BY THE COUNTERWEIGHT. THE RESULT IS THE COUNTER-

WEIGHT IN POUNDS, TO BE PLACED EXACTLY OPPOSITE TO THE CRANK.

QUESTION 322. *How is the counterweight for outside-cylinder engines with coupled driving-wheels calculated?*

Answer. FIND THE SEPARATE REVOLVING WEIGHTS, IN POUNDS, OF CRANK-PIN, CRANK-PIN BOSS, COUPLING-RODS AND CONNECTING-ROD, FOR EACH WHEEL, ALSO THE RECIPROCATING WEIGHT OF THE PISTON AND APPENDAGES, AND HALF THE CONNECTING-ROD; DIVIDE THE RECIPROCATING WEIGHT EQUALLY BETWEEN THE COUPLED WHEELS, AND ADD THE PART, SO ALLOTTED, TO THE REVOLVING WEIGHT ON EACH WHEEL; THE SUMS SO OBTAINED ARE THE WEIGHTS TO BE BALANCED AT THE SEVERAL WHEELS, FOR WHICH THE NECESSARY COUNTERWEIGHT MAY BE FOUND BY THE PRECEDING RULE.

QUESTION 323. *How are the counterweights constructed?*

Answer. They are usually made of cast iron, so as to fill or partly fill the spaces between the spokes of the wheel, as shown at *A A* in fig. 161. Each of the segments consists of two pieces, one of which is put in from the outside of the wheel and the other from the inside. The two are then bolted together with bolts, which are shown in the above figure. In some cases the counterweights are cast solid with the wheels, and in others, cavities are cast in the wheels which are filled with lead, which is poured in when melted. Some locomotive builders make the rims and spokes of the wheels hollow and fill them with lead opposite to the crank-pins. It is difficult, however, to get the required weight in such wheels unless they are of large diameter.

QUESTION 324. *What effect has the strain on the draw-bar, when the engine is pulling a load, upon the distribution of the weight on the wheels?*

Answer. It has the effect of pulling the back end of the engine down, and, as it is balanced on the fulcrums of the equalizing levers, it at the same time lifts up the front end. In this way the harder a locomotive is pulling the greater will be the weight which is thrown on the driving-wheels, and that on the truck will be correspondingly diminished. The higher the draw-bar is above the rails the greater will be the tendency to pull the engine down behind and up in front.

PART XV.

MISCELLANEOUS.

QUESTION 325. *What is the sand-box, V, plates I and II for, and how is it constructed?*

Answer. It is intended to carry a supply of dry sand, which is scattered on the rails in front of the driving-wheels when the latter are liable to slip. This is done by two pipes, *e′*, *e′*, plate I, one on each side of the engine. They lead from the sand-box to within a few inches of the rail. At the upper end and inside the sand-box they each have a valve which is operated by a lever which is connected to the cab by a rod which enables the locomotive runner to open or close the valve at pleasure.

The sand-box is usually made of sheet iron with a cast iron base, and a top of a more or less ornamental design. It also has an opening on top through which the sand is supplied to the box. This opening has a loose cover to exclude rain and dirt from the sand. The sand-box is usually located on top of the boiler in front of the front driving-wheels.

QUESTION 326. *What is the bell U for?*

Answer. It is used for giving signals of the starting or approach of the engine. It also is located on top of the boiler and is usually hung on a cast iron frame and rung with a rope connecting it with the cab.

Question 327. *What is the weight of an ordinary locomotive bell?*

Answer. From 50 to 100 pounds.

Question 328. *What is a locomotive head-light?*

Answer. It is a large lamp, *T*, plates I and II, placed in front of the locomotive to signal its approach at night and also to illuminate the track for the locomotive runner.

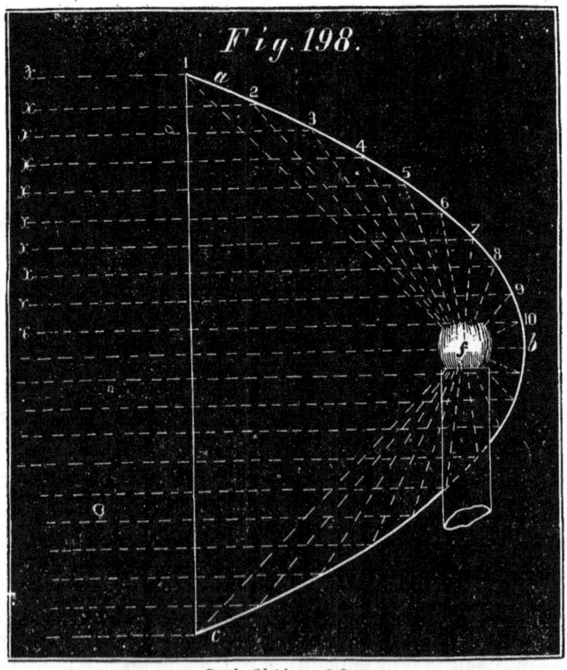

Scale 1½ in. =1 foot.

Question 329. *How is a head-light constructed?*

Answer. The lamp has what is called an Argand

burner; that is, a burner with a hollow cylindrical wick, through the centre of which a current of air circulates, which thus supplies the flame with a larger quantity of air than is possible if the latter can come in contact with the former only from the outside. The result is that the combustion is much more brilliant than with ordinary burners. In order to throw all the light on the track the burner is placed inside of a concave reflector, *a b c*, fig. 198, which is of a *parabolic* form. One of the peculiarities of this form of reflector is that if a light is placed in its focus *f* the rays will be reflected from its surface in parallel lines. Thus, let *a b c*, fig. 198, represent a section of such a reflector. Now, if a light be placed in the focus *f* the rays will strike against the reflector, be thrown in the direction of the dotted lines *f* 1 *x*, *f* 2 *x* . . . *f* 9 *x*, etc., and thus be thrown directly in front of the engine. The reflectors are usually made of copper and plated with silver.

The lamps and reflectors for head-lights are inclosed in a rectangular case which is supported on two brackets bolted to the front of the smoke-box. On these brackets a wooden shelf is fastened on which the head-light rests.

QUESTION 330. *What are the running-boards and hand-rails?*

Answer. The *running-boards* are planks, *i i*, plate I, placed on each side of the boiler to enable the locomotive runner or fireman to go from the cab to the front end of the engine when it is running. The hand-rails, *m m' m'*, are brass or iron pipes attached to the top of the boiler and extending from the cab to the smoke-box, and are placed there, as their name indicates, to support or for a hand-hold for persons on the running-board.

QUESTION 331. *What provision is made for removing from the track such obstacles as cattle or fallen rocks, which may be in front of locomotives?*

Answer. What is called a *cow-catcher* or *pilot*, *S*, plates I and II, is attached to the front of the locomotive. This is usually made of wood, and consists of a triangular frame at the bottom which is supported about four inches above the tops of the rails. Straight pieces of wood of about $2\frac{1}{2} \times 4$ inches section are fastened to this frame and also to a horizontal piece which is bolted to the bumper-timber E'. These pieces arranged in this way and only a few inches apart give to the cow-catcher a peculiar curved form somewhat resembling that of the mould-board of a plow, which is very well adapted for throwing any obstacles from the track. Sometimes these pieces are placed horizontally instead of being inclined up and down. Cow-catchers are also in some cases made of round iron bars or angle iron. They are always bolted securely to the bumper-timber and strengthened by strong iron braces attached to the bottom frame at the front and back. These braces are usually fastened at the other end to the bumper-timber, but are sometimes attached to the bed-plates of the cylinder.

There is also usually a strong *pushing-bar* attached with a bolt and hinged joint to the bumper-timber. This is shown in plates II and III in the position it occupies when not in use. It is used in pushing cars, as very often there is not room for the pilot under the end of the car. In using it is raised up, and the front end is then coupled to the draw-head of the car.

QUESTION 332. *What is the foot-board or foot-plate of a locomotive?*

Answer. It is a wrought or cast iron plate which extends across and rests upon the two frames at the back part of the locomotive and behind the boiler, and on which the locomotive runner and fireman stand. It also unites the two frames very securely, and furnishes an attachment for the draw-bar. The foot-board is often made much heavier than is necessary for strength, in order to increase the weight, and thus the adhesion, on the driving-wheels. It is a fact often not suspected that any weight placed on the back end of an ordinary locomotive will increase the load on the driving-wheels by an amount considerably greater than that of the weight itself. The

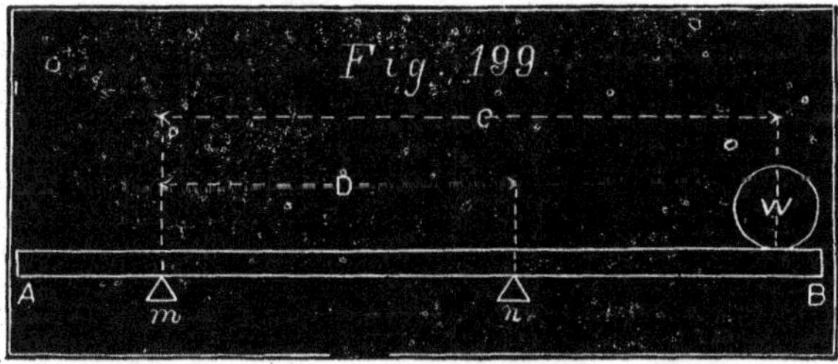

Fig. 199.

reason of this is that the locomotive rests on the centre of the truck and the centres of the equalizers, and therefore the weight, if applied to the back end of the engine, gains considerable leverage. This will be clear if we take a beam, *A B*, and rest it on two supports, *m* and *n*, fig. 199. If now we put a weight *W* on the end, overhanging the point of support, the weight which will rest on *n* will be equal to that of *W* multiplied by its distance *C* from *m* and divided by the distance *D* between *m* and *n*. Thus if a foot-board weighs 1,000 pounds, and its centre of gravity is 5½ feet behind the centre of the equalizer, and the latter 14 feet from the centre of the truck, then the weight thrown on the driving-wheels will be equal to

$$\frac{1,000 \times 19\frac{1}{2}}{14} = 1,393 \text{ pounds.}$$

The same thing is of course true of any other weight placed on the back end of the engine.

QUESTION 333. *What are the "wheel-guards" of a locomotive?*

Answer. They are sheet iron covers over the upper half of the periphery or tread of the wheels, and are placed there to protect the engine from the dirt and mud which adhere to the wheels and are then thrown off on the machinery by the centrifugal force.

QUESTION 334. *What are "check" or "safety chains?"*

Answer. There are two kinds of such chains, the one attached to the trucks and frames of the locomotive and the tender. The object of these chains is to prevent the trucks from turning around and getting crosswise of the track if the trucks should leave the rails. The other kind of safety chains connects the engine to the tender, so that, in case the draw-bar or coupling-pins should break, the two will not separate. Great care should be exercised to attach the truck chains so as to be strong enough to resist the strains to which they will be subjected in case the trucks run off the track. The grossest carelessness and ignorance are often shown in the construction of these parts.

PART XVI.

SCREW-THREADS, BOLTS AND NUTS.

QUESTION 335. *How must the screws of bolts and nuts be made, in order to fit each other?*

Answer. Each size of screw must be made of exactly the same diameter, and their threads of the same form and proportions and *pitch*.

QUESTION 336. *What is meant by the "pitch" of a thread?*

Answer. It is the distance the thread progresses lengthwise of the screw in one revolution. Thus if a single-threaded screw has one-eighth of an inch pitch, it means that the threads are $\frac{1}{8}$ of an inch apart measured from the centre of one thread to the centre of that next to it, and therefore there are eight threads to each inch in length of the screw.

QUESTION 337. *What is meant by a "single-threaded" screw?*

Answer. It means a screw with but one thread instead of two or more. Thus if we take a string and wind it around a pencil, it will represent a single-threaded screw, and if we take two or three strings and wind them parallel to each other, they will represent a double or treble-threaded screw. The latter kinds are seldom or never used on locomotives, so that in the following discussion only single-threaded screws will be referred to.

QUESTION 338. *What is the usual form of the threads of screws?*

Answer. The most common is what is called the V-thread, represented in fig. 200, which is made sharp at both the top and bottom. If such a thread for one screw is made very pointed and that for another is blunt, it is plain that the nut for the one will not fit the other accurately, and also that if a nut has eight threads to the inch, it will not fit on a bolt with nine. Owing to the fact that, until within a few years, no common standard has been agreed upon for the form, proportions or pitch of screws there has been very great diversity in these respects

Fig. 200.

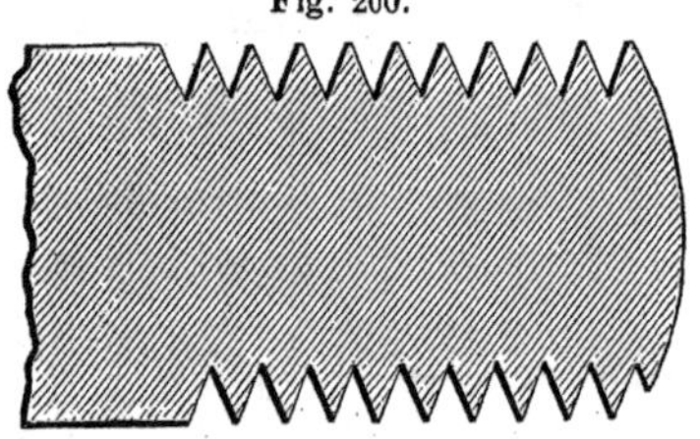

Full Size.

in the screws which have been used in the construction of locomotives and other machinery. In 1864 the inconvenience and confusion from this cause became so great that it attracted the attention of the Franklin Institute of Philadelphia, and a committee was appointed by that association to investigate and report on the subject. That committee recommended the adoption of the Sellers system of screw-threads and bolts, which was devised by Mr. William Sellers, of Philadelphia. This same system was subsequently adopted as the standard by both the

Army and Navy Departments of the United States, and then by the Master Mechanics' and Master Car Builders' associations, so that it may now be regarded, and in fact is called, the United States standard, but the design is due to Mr. Sellers.

QUESTION 339. *In establishing a standard system of screws and threads, what is the first thing which must be determined?*

Answer. The number of threads to the inch, or the pitch of the threads for screws of different diameters.

QUESTION 340. *What is the standard for the number of threads to the inch for the different sized screws of the Sellers system?*

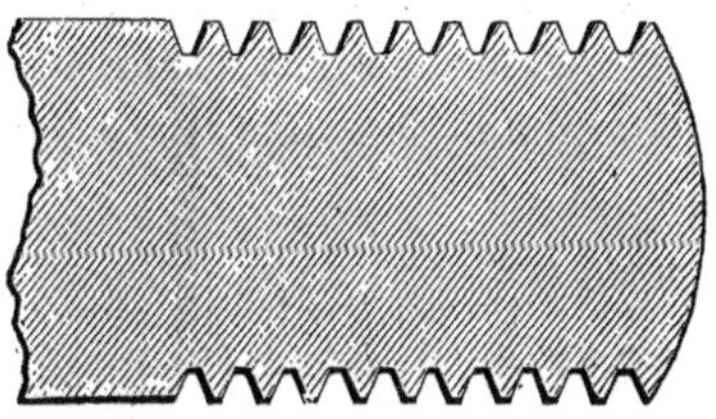

Fig. 201. Full size.

Answer. The number of threads with their other proportion is given in the table at the end of this chapter on page 348.

QUESTION 341. *What is the form of the thread of this standard?*

Answer. The form is shown in fig. 201, and is similar to the V-thread, excepting that it is flattened at the top and bottom.

QUESTION 342. *What are the reasons for the adoption of this form of thread?*

Answer. It has already been pointed out that if a

screw is made with a "blunt" thread it will not fit a nut with very acute or "sharp" threads; or, if the thread of the bolt was acute and that in the nut obtuse, they would fit imperfectly. It is therefore necessary in a standard system to fix upon the angle which the sides of the thread shall bear to each other. This in the United States standard system was determined by Mr. Sellers at 60 degrees, because that angle is easily laid off without special instruments* and is perhaps as good as or better than any other form for the threads.

It is obvious that if a tool is ground with its sides at an angle of 60 degrees to each other, if the point is made sharp after a very little use it will be worn more or less so that the bottom of the thread will not be cut perfectly sharp, and therefore it will be difficult to make bolts and nuts with sharp threads fit each other accurately. It is also plain that the sharp edge of a thread gives very little strength to the screw, and yet diminishes that of the bolt very materially. It will also be impossible to measure the diameter of the screw at the bottom of the thread if it is made sharp, as its depth will vary as the point of the tool wears, and it is almost impossible to measure the diameter of such a screw accurately with ordinary calipers. A sharp-edged thread in a bolt is also very liable to be injured and bruised by coming in contact with other objects. To obviate these evils the standard threads are therefore made flat on the top, and it is evident that a similar shape at the bottom will give increased

* This can be done by drawing a circle of any diameter, and subdividing the circumference into six equal parts with the radius. Lines, drawn from the points of division to the centre will have an inclination of 60 degrees to each other.

strength to the bolt as well as conform to and fit the thread in the nut. To give this form requires only that the point of the cutting tool shall be taken off, and then it is evident this form of thread can be cut in a lathe with the same tool and in the same manner as the sharp thread. The width of the flat top and bottom should of course bear a definite proportion to the size or pitch of the thread.

QUESTION 343. *What are the proportions of the standard threads?*

Answer. The rule given by Mr. Sellers for proportioning the thread is as follows: "DIVIDE THE PITCH, OR, WHAT IS THE SAME THING, THE SIDE OF THE

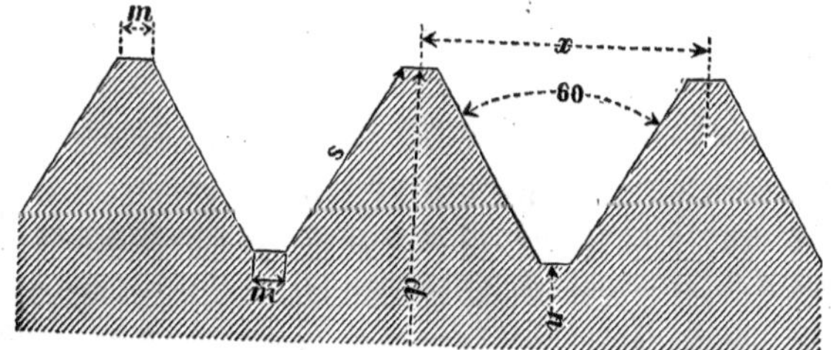

Fig. 202.

THREAD, INTO EIGHT EQUAL PARTS; TAKE OFF ONE PART FROM THE TOP AND FILL IN ONE PART IN THE BOTTOM OF THE THREAD: THEN THE FLAT TOP AND BOTTOM WILL EQUAL ONE-EIGHTH OF THE PITCH, THE WEARING SURFACE WILL BE THREE-QUARTERS OF THE PITCH AND THE DIAMETER OF SCREW AT BOTTOM OF THE THREAD WILL BE EXPRESSED BY THE FORMULA:

$$\textit{diameter} - \frac{1.299}{\textit{no. threads per inch.}}$$

In order to make the form and proportions of this standard thread as plain as possible, we have had an enlarged diagram, fig. 202, engraved, so as to represent the different parts clearly. x represents the pitch, d the diameter of the screw in inches, v the number of threads to the inch, n the diameter at bottom of thread, m the width of back part of thread at the top and bottom, and s the length of the side of thread.

From Mr. Sellers' rule the following formulæ can be deduced:

$$n = d - \frac{1{,}299}{v}$$

$$m = \frac{x}{8}$$

$$s = \frac{3x}{4}$$

From this rule any thread can be constructed, it being only necessary to know the pitch or number of threads to the inch. This, with all the dimensions of the standard threads for bolts from $\frac{1}{4}$ to 2 inch diameter, is given in the table on page 348.

For practical use in the shop a gauge like that shown in fig. 203 will be found most convenient for grinding the tools to the proper form for making the standard screws. With this gauge the screw-cutting tool can first be ground to the proper angle by fitting it to the deepest notch, and the requisite quantity should then be taken off the point by fitting it to the notch representing the form of thread for the sized bolt or number of threads to the inch which it is intended to cut.

Wherever this standard for threads is used, if any pretense at all is made to accuracy of workmanship, careful attention should be given to the form and proportion of the threads as well as to the number to the inch. In buying taps and dies the purchaser should see that they conform in every respect to the standard, and in making specifications for new work similar care should be exercised to secure the true standard, form and proportion of screws. In many shops the workmen who have the care of those tools are entirely ignorant of the peculiarities of the Sellers system, and have only the vague idea that so long as they get the

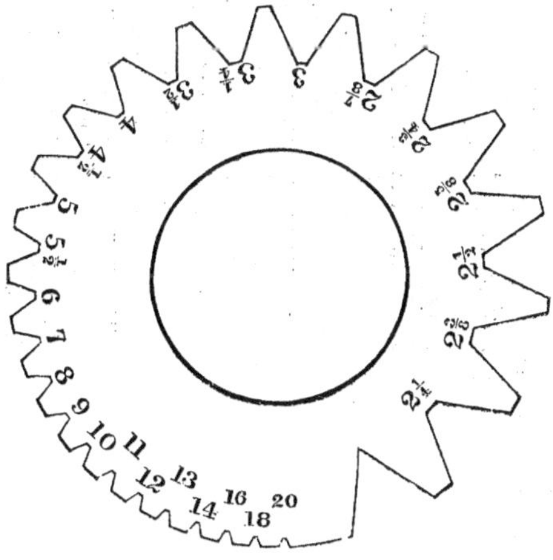

Fig. 203. Full size.

proper number of threads to the inch they are doing all that is necessary to secure uniformity. Unless, therefore, some care is exercised to insure accuracy of workmanship in this department, the adoption of a "standard" for screws will not insure the advantages which would result from uniformity of screws and threads.

QUESTION 344. *How thick must a nut be, measuring lengthwise of the bolt, so that the thread in the nut will be of equal strength to that of the bolt?*

Answer. Its thickness must be equal to the outside diameter of the screw.

TABLE GIVING PROPORTIONS OF THE UNITED STATES OR SELLERS STANDARD SYSTEM OF SCREW-THREADS.

Outside diameter of screw in inches..............	Number of threads per inch..............	Diameter of screw at the root of the thread in decimals of an inch...	Width of top and bottom of thread in decimals of an inch..............	Outside diameter of screw in inches..............	Number of threads per inch..............	Diameter of screw at the root of the thread in decimals of an inch...	Width of top and bottom of thread in decimals of an inch..............
1/4	20	.185	.0062	1	8	.837	.0156
5-16	18	.240	.0074	1 1/8	7	.940	.0178
3/8	16	.294	.0078	1 1/4	7	1.065	.0178
7-16	14	.344	.0089	1 3/8	6	1.160	.0208
1/2	13	.400	.0096	1 1/2	6	1.284	.0208
9-16	12	.454	.0104	1 5/8	5 1/2	1.389	.0227
5/8	11	.507	.0113	1 3/4	5	1.491	.0250
3/4	10	.620	.0125	1 7/8	5	1.616	.0250
7/8	9	.731	.0138	2	4 1/2	1.712	.0277

PART XVII.

TENDERS.

QUESTION 345. *What are locomotive tenders for?*

Answer. They carry a supply of fuel and water for locomotives while they are running.

QUESTION 346. *How are they usually constructed?*

Answer. Their construction is represented in figs. 204, 205 and 206. Fig. 204 is a side view, fig. 205 a longitudinal section, and fig. 206 a plan of an ordinary tender, which consists of a frame, *A A A A*, made of wood or iron,* mounted on a pair of trucks, *T, T.* The top of the frame is covered with planks, *B, B,* which form the floor of the tender. On top of this floor a sheet-iron tank, *C C C,* is placed, which carries the supply of water. This tank is made somewhat in the form of a letter ⊃, as shown in the plan. It is made in this way so that the space between the two branches, *C, C,* or "legs," as they are called, will give room for fuel. Around the upper edge of the tank a sheet-iron rim, *D D,* is riveted, so as to prevent the fuel from falling off when it is filled up above the top of the tank.

QUESTION 347. *How is the tank filled with water?*

Answer. There is a round opening, *E,* called a *manhole,* on top. Into this the end of a leather or canvas

*The frame represented in the engraving is made of wood. In the plan it is shown by dotted lines.

hose is introduced, which is attached to a stationary tank, at a water station, and a stream of water is then allowed to flow through the hose into the tank of the tender.

QUESTION 348. *How is the water conducted from the tender to the engine?*

Answer. To each side of the front end of the tank, one end of a piece of rubber hose, *F F*, is attached, which is connected at the other end to the pipe on the engine which supplies the pump with water. The opening inside the tank through which the water flows to the hose is covered with a valve, which is not shown in the engraving, but which is operated by a lever or handle, *G*. The valve is covered with a hood or strainer, perforated with small holes, which is intended to prevent dirt from entering the hose and thus getting into and obstructing the pump. The hose is connected to the supply pipe by a screw-coupling similar to that used with ordinary fire-engine hose.

QUESTION 349. *How are the flat sides of the tank strengthened so as to resist the pressure and weight of the water?*

Answer. They are sometimes braced or stayed with rods or bars, *a*, *a*, and *h*, *h*, fig. 205, extending from one side to the other and from the top to the bottom, and angle or T iron is also riveted to the sides to stiffen them.

QUESTION 350. *How is the tender connected to the engine?*

Answer. By the draw-bar, *H*, and coupling-pin, *o*, fig. 205, and also by the safety chains, *d*.

QUESTION 351. *In what respect do the tender trucks differ from the engine truck?*

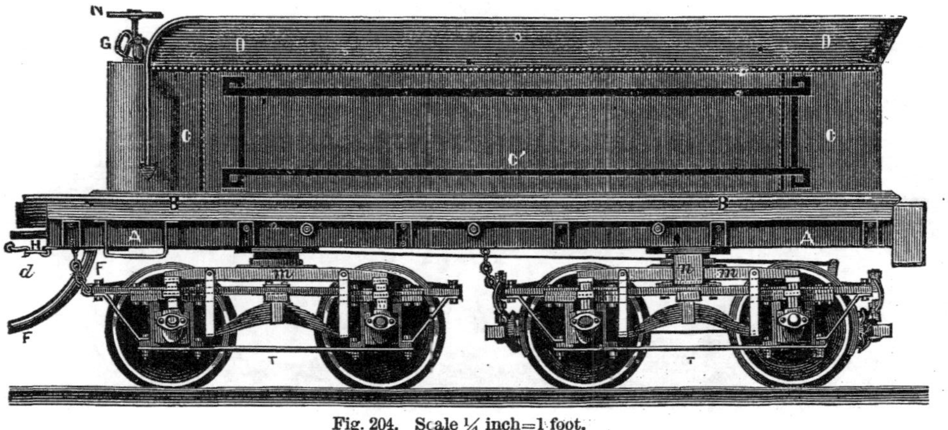

Fig. 204. Scale ¼ inch=1 foot.

Fig. 205. Scale ¼ inch=1 foot.

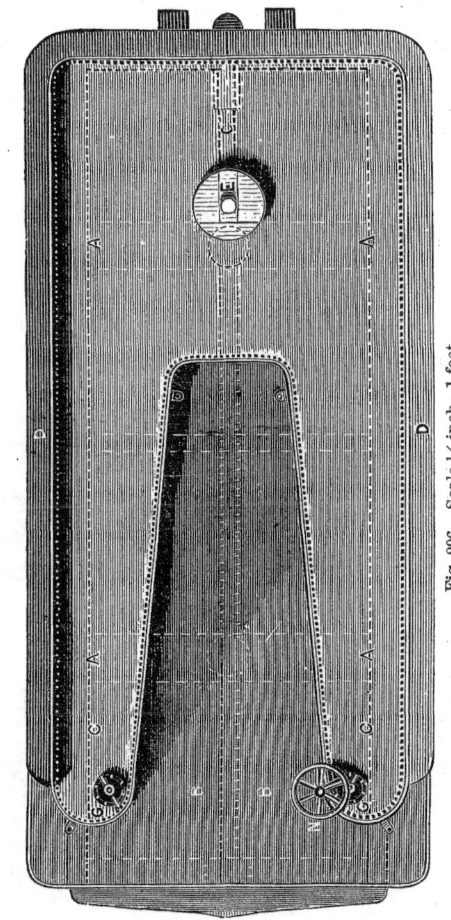

Fig. 206. Scale 1/4 inch=1 foot.

Answer. Chiefly in having the journal-bearings and frames outside of the wheels.

QUESTION 352. *Why are the bearings placed outside instead of inside?*

Answer. Because they are then more accessible than if they are inside, and the oil-boxes on the axles can be entirely closed over the ends of the axles, so that

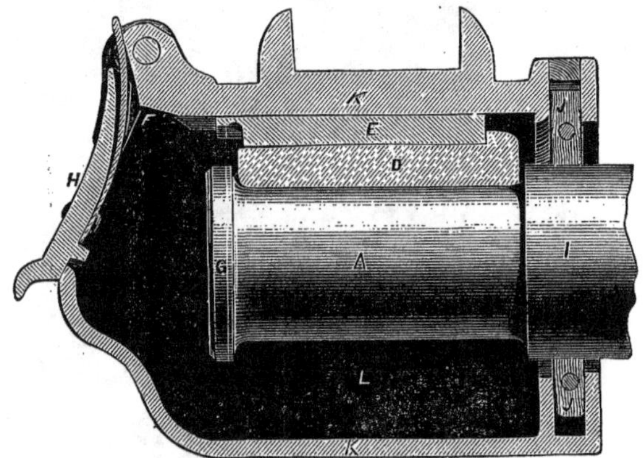

Fig 207. Scale $\frac{3}{16}$ in.=1 inch.

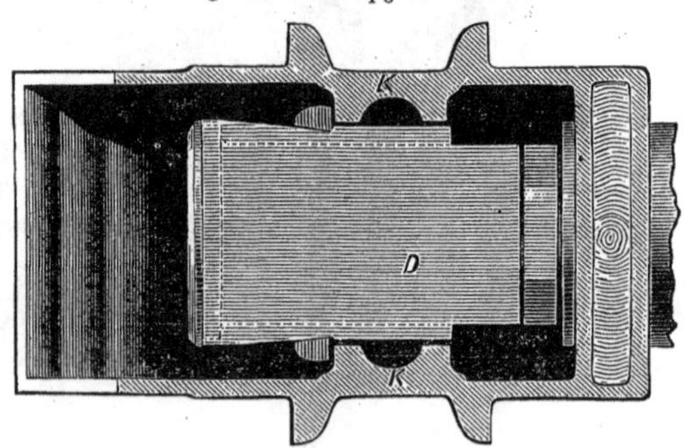

Fig. 208. Scale $\frac{3}{16}$ in.=1 inch.

no oil can leak out, whereas if the boxes are inside, they must be left open at both ends. When the boxes are on the outside, they can be oiled, or a journal-bearing can be removed and a new one put in its place, with much less difficulty than if the boxes were on the inside of the wheels. The only reason why the bearings of engine truck-axles are placed inside the wheels is because they would be in the way of the cylinders if they were outside.

QUESTION 353. *How are the axle-boxes for the tender axle constructed.*

Answer. Their construction is similar to that of a car axle-box, the standard form of which is represented in figs. 207, 208 and 209. Fig. 207 is a sec-

Fig. 209. Scale $\frac{3}{16}$ in.=1 inch.

tion lengthwise of the axle, fig. 208 a section crosswise of the axle, and fig. 209 a sectional plan. *A* is the journal of the axle, which is inclosed by a cast iron box, *K K,* which is open in front and at the back. The front has a cover, *H,* which is either fastened by a spring, as shown in the illustrations, or is bolted to the box. The axle enters the box from the back, *I*, and has either a wood or leather packing, *J J*, called a *dust-guard*, to keep the dust from getting in and the oil from leaking out of the box. *D* is a brass journal-bearing, which rests against a cast iron bearing piece or *key*, *E*, which is put in so that by removing it through the opening *F F*, the brass bearing can be raised up high enough to clear the collar, *G*, on the end of the axle and thus be removed in the same way. The lower portion, *L*, of the box under the axle is usually filled with cotton or woolen waste saturated with oil. This constantly presses against the axle, and thus keeps it oiled.

QUESTION 354. *How are the tender trucks constructed?*

Answer. They are made of various patterns, some of which have wooden frames and in other cases the frames are made of iron. The truck illustrated in our engraving, figs. 204 and 205, is made of iron and is very similar to the engine truck, excepting, as already stated, the frames are outside instead of inside of the wheels.

QUESTION 355. *How is the tender supported on the trucks?*

Answer. It rests on the centre of the front truck and on a bearing, *n*, fig. 204, on the frames on each side of the back truck. This arrangement gives three bearing points, the advantages of which have already been explained. A truck which supports the load which it carries in the centre is said to be *centre-bearing*, and if the load is carried on each side, *side-bearing*.

QUESTION 356. *How are the brakes attached to the tender?*

Answer. They are attached usually to the back truck alone, but in some cases to both trucks, and are operated by a wheel, *N*, fig. 204, and a shaft which extends below the tender frame and on which a chain attached to the brakes is wound.

QUESTION 357. ***How much water and coal does an ordinary tender carry?***

Answer. A tender for a thirty-ton engine carries from 1,500 to 2,000 gallons of water and three to four tons of coal, and weighs from 40,000 to 45,000 pounds loaded. An engine of this kind and its tender therefore weigh about 100,000 pounds, which, being even figures, can easily be remembered.

PART XVIII.

FRICTION AND LUBRICATION.

QUESTION 358. *What is meant by friction?*

Answer. Friction is the resistance between two bodies in contact which opposes the sliding of the one on the other. Thus if a brick is placed on a board with a slight inclination, it will not slide because the friction between them, or the resistance opposed to motion, is greater than the force exerted by the weight of the brick to move it downward. If, however, the inclination of the board is increased sufficiently so that a larger proportion of the weight of the brick urges it downward, then the friction will be overcome, and it will slide. When the brake-blocks of a car are pressed against the wheels, they produce friction, which resists the revolving motion of the wheels and will ultimately stop the car; and when the weight of an engine is supported on the driving-wheels and they rest on the rails, the friction between them, as has already been pointed out, resists their slipping on each other, and thus enables a locomotive to exert tractive force. Friction also resists the turning of an axle on its journal and therefore makes the tractive force of the locomotive necessary to move a train of cars.

QUESTION 359. *On what does the amount of friction depend?*

Answer. The amount of friction of two bodies in contact depends (1) UPON THE PRESSURE OF THE ONE ON THE OTHER, AND IS INDEPENDENT OF THE AREA OF THE SURFACES IN CONTACT; (2) ON THE NATURE OF THE MATERIALS IN CONTACT; (3) ON THE NATURE OF THE SUBSTANCE, SUCH AS OIL OR OTHER LUBRICANT, WHICH IS INTERPOSED BETWEEN THEM. Thus, a brick will slide down an inclined board as easily if it is laid on its broadest side as it will if placed edgewise; and if a cast iron plate, say 10 inches square, is planed and scraped, so as to be as nearly a perfect plane surface as it is possible to make it, it will, if loaded with say a hundred pounds weight, slide on a similar true surface as easily as another plate with half as much area and loaded with the same weight. A shaft resting against a long bearing will require no more power to turn it than would be needed if the bearing was short.*

QUESTION 360. *What is meant by the "co-efficient of friction?"*

Answer. It is the proportion which the resistance to sliding motion bears to the force pressing the surfaces together. Thus a smooth, clean and dry cast iron plate loaded with 100 pounds will require a force of about 15 pounds, or fifteen one-hundredths of the weight or pressure of the plates, to slide them on each other. The *co-efficient of friction* is therefore said to be 0.15, and with any other weight or pressure on the plates we could determine the force required to slide them on each other by multiplying the pressure by the co-efficient of friction. Thus, if the plates were

* In fact, ordinarily less power is required to turn it if the bearing is long than if it is short, the reasons for which will be explained hereafter.

loaded with 250 pounds, the force required to slide the one on the other would be equal to $250 \times .15 = 37.5$ pounds. The co-efficient of friction, however, varies for different materials. Thus, while the co-efficient of friction between two pieces of smooth, clean and dry cast iron is 0.15, that of a piece of brass on cast iron, under similar conditions, is 0.22, and of two pieces of wood about 0.4.

QUESTION 361. *What is the effect of introducing some unguent or lubricating material, such as oil, between the surfaces in contact?*

Answer. The co-efficient of friction is very much reduced thereby. Thus the co-efficient of friction of the cast iron plates, if their surfaces are greased with tallow, is 0.1 ; if lubricated with lard 0.07, with olive oil 0.064, and with lard and plumbago 0.055, thus showing that the amount of the friction depends very much upon the nature of the lubricant which is used, as well as on that of the materials in contact.

QUESTION 362. *What effect on the amount of friction has the manner of applying the lubricating material to the surfaces in contact?*

Answer. The more perfect the lubrication the less will be the co-efficient of friction. It has, for example, been found by experiments made with cast iron shafts turning on bearings of the same material that when the lubricating material was applied so that the surfaces were only "unctuous," that is slightly greasy, the co-efficient of friction was very little less than when they were dry, that is when there was no lubricating substance between them, and that when they were greased "from time to time" the co-efficient was reduced to 0.07 and 0.08 ; but when they were continually oiled it averaged 0.05, and sometimes fell as low as 0.025, showing that with the best lubrication the friction was only one-sixth what it was when the surfaces were only "unctuous." Between these two limits there is every degree of frictional resistance, according to the condition of lubrication. This shows how important it is that the oiling fixtures should be kept in the most perfect condition and the utmost care be exercised in keeping every part of a locomotive thoroughly lubricated.

QUESTION 363. *What effect does the pressure per square inch of the surfaces in contact have upon the lubrication?*

Answer. The tendency is, when this pressure becomes excessive, to press out the lubricant which is between the two surfaces, and ordinary experience proves that the greater the weight or the force per square inch with which two bodies are pressed together, the greater is the difficulty of keeping them perfectly lubricated.

Thus it is easier to keep the journals of a car well lubricated when it is empty than when it is heavily loaded, and the guide-bars of a locomotive are more liable to be cut when the engine is pulling a heavy load than with a light one.

QUESTION 364. *What effect has the velocity of the surfaces in contact on the friction and lubrication?*

Answer. With the surfaces in the same condition, the friction is independent of the velocity of motion of the surfaces against each other, but perfect lubrication becomes more difficult as the velocity increases, so that an increase of velocity will often increase indirectly the amount of friction. Thus, taking our previous illustrations, it is more difficult to keep the journals of a car or engine well lubricated when running fast than when running slow, and the same thing is true of the guide-bars.

QUESTION 365. *What considerations should govern the proportions of frictional bearings for locomotives and other machines?*

Answer. The dimensions to be given them should not be determined from a consideration solely of their resistance to rupture,* but they should be made so large that the pressure they must bear will be distributed over so much surface that the proportion borne by each square inch will be comparatively small, thus making good lubrication much less difficult, and consequently reducing the co-efficient of friction.

QUESTION 366. *Is not the amount of energy required to overcome the friction on a journal of large diameter greater than would be required if the journal was smaller?*

Answer. If the co-efficient of friction in the two cases is the same, undoubtedly the large journal will require the greatest expenditure of energy to turn it, because its periphery moves further than that of the small one; but the advantage attributed to large journals is that they can be lubricated more perfectly, because their surfaces being larger the pressure is not so great per square inch, and thus the gain from the reduction of the co-efficient of friction is greater than the loss attributable to the increase of the diameter of the journal. Thus if a car journal is $3\frac{1}{4}$ inches in diameter $\times$ $5\frac{1}{2}$ inches long, the available surface exposed to friction is equal to that of a longitudinal

*Morin's Mechanics.

section of the journal, or $3\frac{1}{4} \times 5\frac{1}{2} = 17.875$ square inches.* Supposing now that the journal is loaded with 5,000 pounds, and the average co-efficient of friction is 0.085. In one revolution of the wheel the journal will move 0.85 of a foot, and therefore $5{,}000 \times .085 = 361\frac{1}{4}$ foot-pounds of work. If now the journal is made, as has been proposed, $3\frac{3}{4} \times 7$ inches, then its effective surface will be equal to $26\frac{1}{4}$ square inches, but the journal will move 0.98 of a foot in one revolution. If, however, the lubrication is improved by the increased area of the journal so that the co-efficient of friction is reduced from 0.085 to 0.07, then the energy consumed in one revolution will be equal to $5{,}000 \times 0.7 \times .98 = 343$ foot-pounds, or less than was consumed with the small journals. The co-efficient of friction is assumed, and could only be determined by experiment, but the assumption shows how the resistance of the large journals may be less than that of the small ones. Of course it would be better to give the increased bearing surface by adding to the length of the journal, but nearly all locomotives and car journals must be increased in diameter as well as in length when they are enlarged, in order to have the requisite strength to carry the loads they must bear.

QUESTION 367. *Is the law that* FRICTION IS IN PROPORTION TO THE PRESSURE ON EACH OTHER BY THE SURFACES OF CONTACT *true under all circumstances?*

Answer. No; there is a limit to the exactness of the above law, when the pressure becomes so intense as to crush or grind the parts of the bodies at and near

* The reason for this is that the effective surface of the journal *A*, fig. 209. which resists the pressure of the bearing, is equivalent only to the horizontal area represented by the dotted line *a. b.* just as the surface which resists the pressure inside of a boiler is equivalent to the diameter multiplied by its length, as was explained in answer to Question 99.

their surfaces of contact. At and beyond that limit the friction increases more rapidly than the pressure;* and the friction then becomes very irregular.

QUESTION 368. *In what cases is the limit referred to probably reached?*

Answer. Probably in some locomotives the pressure of the driving-wheels on the rails is sufficient to partly crush the latter.

QUESTION 369. *What effect has the nature of the materials in contact on the friction?*

Answer. The amount of friction and also the lubrication is very much influenced by the nature of the bearing surface and also by the material used as a lubricant. Some metals, such as brass and other alloys, are much less liable to abrasion and seem to retain lubricants on their surfaces better than other metals, and are therefore much used for journal and other bearings. Some substances, especially oils, are good lubricants, while other materials of apparently similar nature are not. The reason why these materials possess these properties while others are without them is not known, and the value of any material as a lubricant, or the degree to which another will resist friction without abrasion, can only be tested by experiment.

* Rankine.

PART XIX.

COMBUSTION.

QUESTION 370. *What is meant by combustion?*

Answer. By combustion is meant the phenomenon ordinarily called burning, as when a piece of wood or coal or a candle is burnt. In reality combustion is a union of one of the "*chemical elements,*" oxygen, of which the atmosphere is composed, with the elements which constitute the fuel.

QUESTION 371. *What is meant by the term "chemical element?"*

Answer. The science of chemistry has demonstrated that nearly all substances by which we are surrounded are composed of certain other substances, which latter, as far as is now known, are not compounds, and are therefore called *elementary substances, or chemical elements.* Thus the air by which we are surrounded is composed of two gases, called nitrogen and oxygen; water is composed of hydrogen and oxygen, and coal chiefly of carbon and hydrogen. There are now over sixty of these elementary substances known. From no one of them have chemists been able to extract any material excepting the substance itself. These elementary substances will combine with others so as to form what is apparently a new material, but on weighing it it will be found that the weight of the new material is greater than the original elementary substance, showing that something was added to it which effected the change.*

QUESTION 372. *To what fact is this combination or combustion of elementary substances due?*

Answer. It is owing to the fact—the exact reason for which is perhaps not yet understood fully—that the atoms of the elementary substances of which fuel is composed, that is hydrogen and carbon, and the atoms of oxygen, which forms part of the atmosphere by which we are surrounded, attract each other with great energy when they are excited into activity by the application of heat.

QUESTION 373. *What phenomenon always attends chemical combination of substances?*

Answer. Such combination always gives out heat, whereas their separation absorbs heat. It has further been proved by actual experiment that the amount of heat liberated by the chemical union of the same quantity or number of atoms of two or more substances is always the same, and that when, by any cause, the atoms thus joined are separated, exactly the same amount of heat is absorbed.*

QUESTION 374. *In what proportions do the elementary substances combine with each other?*

Answer. It is a law of chemistry that each of the elementary substances combines with the others in certain definite proportions only. These proportions vary for the different elements, and have been determined with great accuracy by chemists. Thus, eight parts by weight of oxygen will combine with nitrogen and form atmospheric air, or the same proportion of oxygen will combine with hydrogen and form water,

* "The New Chemistry," by J. P. Cooke, Jr.

or with carbon and form carbonic acid, which is the deadly gas which accumulates at the bottom of wells.

Now oxygen always combines with other substances in the proportion of eight parts by weight, or by *some simple multiple of* eight, that is $8 \times 2 = 16$ parts, or $8 \times 3 = 24$ parts, etc. Each of the other elementary substances also has a certain fixed proportion in which it combines with others, and this proportion, which is usually given by weight, is represented by a number called its *chemical equivalent.* Thus 8 is the chemical equivalent of oxygen. Carbon combines with other elements in proportions of 6 and nitrogen in proportions of 14, so that 6 and 14 are the chemical equivalents of carbon and nitrogen. Now 8 parts by weight of oxygen can be made to combine with 14 parts of nitrogen, or $8 \times 2 = 16$ parts of oxygen will combine with 14 of nitrogen, but it is impossible to make, say 12 parts of oxygen combine with 14 parts of nitrogen. We can combine $14 \times 2 = 28$ parts of nitrogen with 8 parts of oxygen, but no chemical process can make say 10 or 20 parts of nitrogen combine with 8 parts of oxygen. If 20 parts of nitrogen are mixed with 8 parts of oxygen, then the latter will combine with 14 parts of the former, but 6 parts of nitrogen will be left, and chemical combination will then cease.

The following table will give the chemical equivalents of the principal elements which enter into the process of combustion of the fuel used in locomotives:

	Chemical equivalent by weight.
Oxygen	8
Nitrogen	14
Hydrogen	1
Carbon	6
Sulphur	16

QUESTION 375. *What effect do the proportions in which*

elements are combined have upon the substances which are produced by the combination?

Answer. A change in the proportions in which the elements are combined usually alters the entire nature of the substance, so far at least as it affects our senses. For instance, oxygen unites chemically with nitrogen in different proportions, forming five distinct substances, each essentially different from the others, thus:

14 parts of	Nitrogen	with	8	of Oxygen	forms	Nitrous Oxide.
14 " "	"	"	16	" "	"	Nitric Oxide.
14 " "	"	"	24	" "	"	Hyponitrous Acid.
14 " "	"	"	32	" "	"	Nitrous Acid.
14 " "	"	"	40	" "	"	Nitric Acid.

We here find the elements of the air we breathe, by a mere change in the *proportions* in which they are united, forming distinct substances, which differ from each other as much as *laughing gas* (nitrous oxide) does from that most destructive agent *nitric acid,* commonly called *aqua fortis.**

QUESTION 376. *What occurs when a fresh supply of bituminous coal is thrown on a bright fire in the fire-box of a locomotive?*

Answer. The fresh coal is first heated by the fire, and if a sufficient quantity is thrown in to prevent the immediate formation of flame,† a volume of gas or vapor, usually of a dark yellow or brown color, is given off. The quantity evolved will be greatest when the coal is very small. This gas or vapor is commonly called smoke, but it does not deposit soot and in reality is not true smoke. If a sheet of white paper be held over the vapor as it escapes from the coal and there is

*Combustion of Coal and the Prevention of Smoke, by C. Wye Williams.

† Usually if more than two or three shovels full are thrown in there will be no immediate formation of flame.

no flame, the sheet will become slowly coated with a sticky matter of brown color difficult to remove, and having a strong tarry or sulphurous smell; whereas if a sheet of paper is held over smoke it will quickly be covered with black soot. The color and smell left on the paper in the first case are due to the tarry matter, sulphur, and other ingredients in the gas. Deprived of the coloring matters, the vapor is a chemical mixture of 2 parts of hydrogen and 6 parts of carbon, and is called carburetted hydrogen, and is nearly the same as the colorless gas by which our houses are lighted.* A similar gas is generated at the wick of a burning candle or lamp and is consumed in the flame. Before the gas is expelled from the fresh coal the latter must be heated to a temperature of about 1,200 degrees, so that if 100 pounds at a temperature of 50 degrees is put on the fire 23,000 units of heat will be absorbed to heat the coal.† Nor is this all, as has been explained in answer to Question 38, when any substance is vaporized a certain amount of heat apparently disappears, which has been called the *heat of evaporation* or *of gasification*. Average bituminous coal contains about 80 per cent. of carbon, 5 per cent. of hydrogen and 15 per cent. of other substances usually regarded as impurities. When the coal is heated up to about 1,200 degrees, the 5 per cent. of hydrogen unites with three times its weight of carbon, and thus 20 per cent. of the coal is converted into the gas described. In this process a large amount of heat is absorbed or becomes latent, as it does when water or

---

* A Treatise on Steam Boilers, by Robert Wilson.

† The quantity of heat required to heat coal is only about one-fifth that needed to heat the same weight of water to the same temperature.

any other substance is converted into vapor. It will therefore be seen that the first effect of putting fresh coal on the fire *is to cool the fire.* This fact has an important bearing on the question of combustion and will be referred to hereafter.

QUESTION 377. *How can the process of the combustion of the gas generated from the coal be best explained?*

Answer. As this gas is substantially the same as ordinary illuminating gas, the manner in which it burns can perhaps be made clearer by examining the combustion of an ordinary gas-light. As stated before, combustion is a chemical union of the oxygen which forms one of the elements of the air with the hydrogen and carbon of the fuel, which, in this case, form gas. It should be clearly kept in mind that combustion is the result of this union, and that the oxygen is as essential to combustion as coal or gas, and in fact is the fuel of combustion just as much as coal or gas is. If we were to conduct a pipe from the external air into a vessel filled with coal gas we could *light the air* and it would burn in the gas as the gas burns in the air.

It will be noticed, however, that before either the gas or the air will burn, they must be lighted. Air and gas, even if mixed together in the same vessel, will not burn unless they are lighted. This can be done by the flame of any burning material, or with a piece of metal heated to a very high temperature, or by an electric spark. In other words it may be said that the atoms of the two gases must be excited into activity by the application of heat, that is, what is called an *igniting temperature* must be communicated to them before chemical combination will begin. The chief feature which distinguishes combustion from other chemical union is the circumstance that the heat generated during the combination is sufficient to maintain an igniting temperature, and the necessity of doing so in order to continue the process is of very great importance in the combustion of coal in locomotive boilers, as will be shown hereafter.

QUESTION 378. *How does an ordinary gas-light burn after it is lighted?*

Answer. Under ordinary conditions the hydrogen, which is the most combustible of the two elements of which coal gas is formed, is the first to burn. This part of the combustion forms the lower bluish part of the flame. The combustion of the hydrogen thus separates it from the carbon, which is then set free; and as carbon is never found in a gaseous condition when uncombined with other substances, it at once assumes the form of fine soot when the hydrogen is burned away from it. This fine soot, or pulverized carbon, is, however, intensely heated by the combustion of the hydrogen. Now carbon when heated to an igniting temperature will, if brought into contact with a sufficient quantity of oxygen, combine with it or be burned. Each particle of carbon thus becomes a glowing centre of radiation, throwing out its luminous rays in every direction. The sparks last, however, but an instant, for the next moment they are consumed by the oxygen which is aroused to full activity by the heat, and only a transparent gas rises from the flame. But the same process continues; other particles succeed, which become heated and ignited in their turn, and it is to this combustion of the solid particles of carbon that the light which is given out by a gas-burner or candle is due.*

QUESTION 379. *Why does a gas-burner, candle or other flame sometimes smoke?*

Answer. Because the supply of oxygen is then insufficient to consume the particles of solid carbon which are set free and which then assume the form of

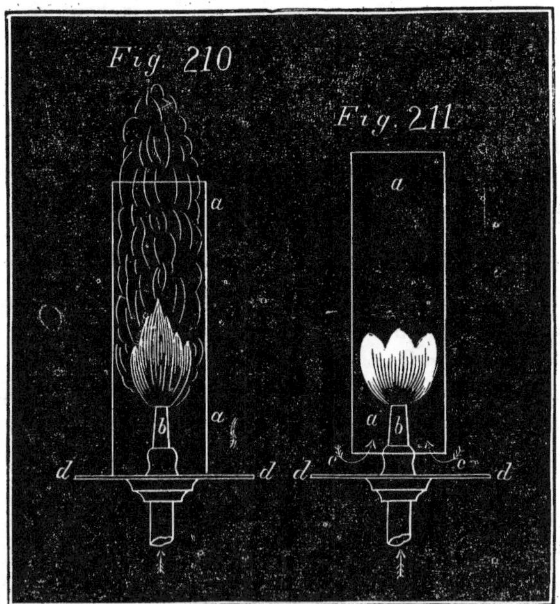

soot. This can be illustrated if we cut a hole in a card, *d d*, fig. 210, so as to fit over an ordinary gas-burner, *b*. If we then light the gas and place a glass chimney, *a a*, over the burner and let it rest on the card, it will be found that the flame will at once begin

* "The New Chemistry," by J. P. Cooke, Jr.

to smoke, because very little air can then come in contact with the flame, and therefore when the fine particles of carbon are set free by the combustion of the hydrogen, instead of being burned as they would be if the air with its supply of oxygen were not excluded from the flame by the chimney, they escape unconsumed in the form of fine black powder or soot. If we raise the chimney up from the card, as shown in fig. 211, so as to leave enough space between them at the bottom of the chimney to permit air to enter so as to supply the flame with oxygen, the smoke will instantly cease, as the particles of carbon are then consumed. The same principle is illustrated in an ordinary kerosene lamp. It is well known that without a chimney the flames of nearly all such lamps smoke intolerably, whereas with a glass chimney and the peculiarly formed deflector which surrounds the wick the light burns without smoke unless the wick is turned up high. The effect of the chimney is to produce a draft, which is thrown against the flame by the deflector, and thus a sufficient supply of oxygen is furnished to consume all the particles of carbon, whereas without the draft produced by the chimney the supply of oxygen is insufficient to ignite all the carbon, which then escapes in the form of smoke or soot.

It must not, however, be hastily assumed that if the flame does not give out a bright light, therefore the combustion is not complete. As has already been stated, the light of the gas flame is due to the presence of burning particles of solid carbon, which is set free by the combustion of the hydrogen with which it is combined. After it is separated from the hydrogen it immediately assumes a solid form. If the coal gas is mixed with a sufficient quantity of air before it is burned, the oxygen in the latter will be in such intimate contact with the former that the difference of affinity of oxygen for the carbon and hydrogen does not come into play, and as there is enough oxygen for all, the carbon is burnt before it is set free, and as there are then no solid particles in the flame, there is no light. This is illustrated by a "Bunsen burner," fig. 212, which is much used in chemical laboratories.

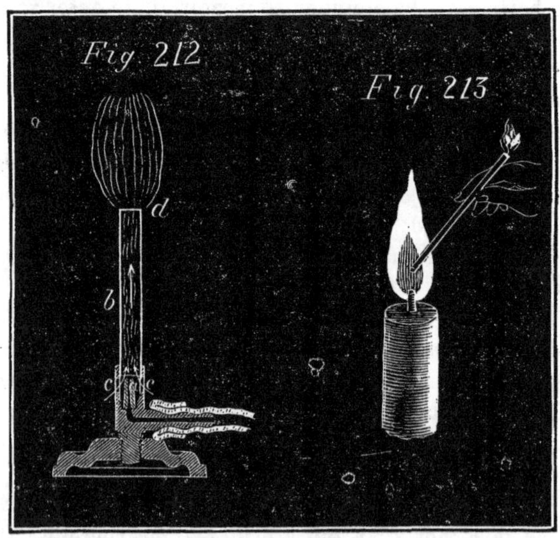

It consists of a small tube or burner, *a*, which is placed inside of another larger tube *b*. The latter has holes, *c*, *c*, a little below the top of the small tube. The current of gas escaping from the small tube produces what is called an *induced current* of air in the large tube. This air enters through the holes *c*, *c*, and is mixed with the gas in the tube *b*, and the mixture is burned at *d*. The flame from such a burner gives hardly any light, but the heat is intense, as is shown if a metal wire is held in it for a few seconds, as it will very soon glow with heat.

QUESTION 380. *What important difference is there in the structure of the flame of a Bunsen burner and that of an ordinary gas-burner or candle?*

Answer. The gas which escapes from the mouth *d* of the pipe *b*, fig. 212, is mixed with air, and therefore contains within itself the elements which only need to combine to produce combustion; whereas with an ordinary gas-burner or candle the air comes in contact with the flame only from the outside, or on its surface. This is shown better perhaps in the flame of an ordinary candle. The heat of such a flame distils a gas from the melted tallow, which is similar in nature to that which escapes from coal at a high temperature. Now by observing the candle very closely it will be seen that at the bottom close to the wick there is very little combustion, as the gas there first escapes from the wick and is not heated to a sufficiently high temperature to burn freely. A little above the lowermost part the flame is of a pale bluish color, which is due to the combustion of the hydrogen. Above that, where the carbon is set free, its particles glow with heat imparted by the burning hydrogen and are then consumed by uniting with the oxygen of the air. The combustion occurs only at the surface of the flame, the inside being a mass of combustible gas which cannot burn until it in turn comes in contact with the oxygen of the air. This can be proved by inserting one end of a small tube, fig. 213 (a pipe stem will do), which is open at both ends, into the flame. The combustible gas will then escape at the other end and can easily be lighted with a match.

It will be found that the flame from the Bunsen burner is much more intense than that of an ordinary candle or gas-burner. The reason of this is that combustion, as already stated, takes place through the whole mass of its flame, whereas an ordinary flame burns only at its surface. Common gas-jets are therefore arranged so that the flames will be flat, thus exposing as much surface to the air as possible, and, as explained in answer to Question 329, in describing the lamps for head-lights, their burners are usually made with a circular wick, through the centre of which a current of air circulates. This arrangement exposes a larger surface of the flame to the air, and also with the aid of a chimney furnishes an abundant supply for combustion. In stationary boilers with long flues of a large sectional area the flame will often extend for thirty feet, showing that while combustion is going on only at the surface of the flame, it takes a long time to complete the process. The same thing is shown if a gas-burner is made with a single round hole. The flame will then be very long and liable to smoke at the top.

QUESTION 381. *From the preceding considerations what may we infer to be necessary in order to consume coal gas perfectly?*

Answer. In the first place, that there must exist a certain degree of what chemists call "molecular activity," which is produced by heat, or what we have called the *igniting temperature.* The necessity of this is sufficiently obvious with ordinary gas-burners, as they must always be *lighted* before they will burn. Now imagine that it was required to burn gas which was issuing from a hundred jets, of every variety of size, in a violent wind storm, or gusts of wind. Obviously it would be necessary to keep a lighted torch all the time to relight those which would be blown out. The gas in a locomotive fire-box is in reality burnt in a storm of wind more violent than any natural one. It is therefore necessary to be constantly ready to relight the streams of gas which the faintest breath would extinguish, or those of larger volume which have absorbed a great deal of heat and thus reduced the temperature at the time and place of their birth, when they assumed the gaseous form, as was explained in answer to Question 376. To relight them with certainty it is necessary to keep a constant temperature in the fire-box high enough to ignite the gas which escapes or is distilled from the coal.

Second. That the chemical change in combustion consists simply in the union of the elements burned with the oxygen of the air; and therefore, to burn the gas perfectly, without smoke or waste, ***enough*** air must be furnished to supply all the oxygen which will combine with the fuel.

Third. That the air must be mixed with the gas, otherwise combustion will occur only at the surface of the flame, and will therefore be so slow that much of the gas will escape unconsumed.

It must be clearly kept in mind that no one or two of these requirements alone, without the third, will burn coal perfectly. What is needed is all three in combination. A very common error is to suppose that passing smoke over a hot fire, or in other words, maintaining an igniting temperature, will alone effect perfect combustion; or that if a sufficient supply of air is admitted, without an igniting temperature in the fire-box, the fuel will be burnt completely. Neither of them will accomplish the object alone, and the gas and air must at the same time be thoroughly mixed with the burning gas in the fire-box.

QUESTION 382. ***What substances are produced by the combustion of coal gas?***

Answer. The hydrogen of coal gas unites during combustion with oxygen in the proportion, as indicated by their chemical equivalents, of 1 part by weight of hydrogen with 8 parts of oxygen, the product of which is water. Of course at the high temperature at which the gases combine or burn the water is produced in the form of steam. That water or steam is one of the products of combustion is shown every cold evening, when the insides of shop show-windows are covered with moisture, which is due to the steam that is given off by the burning gas-lights or lamps inside, and is then condensed against the cold glass.

Carbon combines with oxygen in two proportions: first, 6 parts of the former will unite with 8 of the latter, forming what is called *carbonic oxide;* or 6 parts of carbon will combine with 16 parts of oxygen, forming *carbonic acid gas* or *carbonic dioxide,* as it is called in some of the new books on chemistry. It is probable that the former compound, that is carbonic oxide, is never or very rarely formed in the flame of coal gas; but, as will be seen hereafter, is a very common and wasteful product of the combustion of the solid portion of the coal which is left after the gas is expelled from it. When there is not enough oxygen for the perfect combustion of the carbon in the flame, it smokes, and the carbon escapes in the form of soot. This, as will be shown, may in a locomotive fire-box help to form carbonic oxide after it leaves the flame.

QUESTION 383. *What remains in the coal after all the gas is expelled by heat?*

Answer. What remains is ordinarily called coke, which, with the exception of some incombustible substances, such as sand, ashes and cinders, which the coal contains, is nearly pure carbon.

QUESTION 384. *What is the chemical process of the combustion of coke?*

Answer. The solid carbon of the coke when raised to an igniting temperature; or, in other words, on being lighted, unites with the oxygen in one of the two proportions already given; that is, if the supply of oxygen is sufficient, 6 parts of the carbon of the coke unite with 16 parts of oxygen, forming carbonic acid gas, or carbonic dioxide. If, however, the layer of fuel on the grates is thick, or the supply of air is comparatively small, there will not be enough oxygen to supply 16 parts of the latter to each 6 parts of the carbon, so that when that occurs, instead of combining in that proportion, and thus forming carbonic dioxide, 8 parts of oxygen will unite with 6 parts of carbon and form carbonic oxide. Now it should be carefully kept in mind that the heat of combustion is due to the union, or, as it is sometimes expressed, it is the clashing together of the molecules of the two elements which unite. If, therefore, only half the quantity of oxygen unites with 6 parts of carbon, evidently there will be less heat evolved than there would be if twice that amount of oxygen combined with the carbon. From carefully made experiments it was found that the total heat of the combustion of one pound of carbon when converted into *carbonic oxide* was 4,400 units, whereas when it was converted into *carbonic dioxide* 14,500 units were given out. It will thus be seen that it is extremely wasteful to burn coal without a sufficient supply of air to produce carbonic dioxide. The danger of waste from this cause is also increased by the fact that carbonic oxide is colorless and odorless, and therefore its production is not apparent, especially as most persons have the impression that when there is no smoke from a fire combustion is then complete. It burns with a blue or yellowish flame when air is admitted into the fire-box, and its presence can often be detected by these phenomena when the furnace door is opened.

QUESTION 385. *How can the requisite quantity of air be supplied to the fire in a locomotive fire-box?*

Answer. It is done in two ways: one is to keep but little coal on the grates, or in the phraseology of firemen, to "carry a light fire." The other method is to admit fresh air above the fire. If the latter plan is adopted when the supply of air through the grates is insufficient for perfect combustion, the carbonic oxide will unite with the oxygen of the air above the fire, and thus a second combustion will take place, the product of which will be carbonic dioxide. It must be kept in mind, however, that not only must there be enough air supplied to the fire to consume the coke, but the gases which are distilled from the coal must also be supplied with oxygen in order to effect their perfect combustion. Even if enough air is admitted to consume the coke perfectly, if the carbonic dioxide thus formed is mixed with large quantities of smoke above the fire, the solid carbon or soot of the smoke may then combine with the dioxide and thus form carbonic oxide, if there is not enough fresh air present to furnish the requisite oxygen for the carbon in the smoke. A very common error is to suppose that smoke can be burned by passing it over or through a very hot fire. The smoke may thus be made invisible, it is true, but it does not therefore follow that it is perfectly consumed.

QUESTION 386. *Is it possible to admit too much air into the fire-box of a locomotive?*

Answer. Yes; probably all the air that is admitted which is not necessary for combustion, or, in other words, the oxygen of which does not combine with the fuel, instead of increasing diminishes the amount of water converted into steam. It does this in two ways; first, by reducing the temperature of the gases in contact with the heating surfaces, and second, by increasing the volume or quantity of the gases which must pass through the tubes. Heat is transmitted through the heating surface of a boiler in proportion to the *difference* of the temperature of the products of combustion on one side and the water on the other.* Thus, if the temperature of the water on one side is 250 degrees, and the hot gases on the other is 500, there will be only half as much heat transmitted to the water in a given time as there would be if the gases had a temperature of 750 degrees. If the volume of gases is doubled by the admission of too much air, then obviously in order to pass through the tubes

* This law is perhaps not absolutely correct, but is near enough for our present illustration.

they must move at double the velocity, so that not only is their temperature diminished, but the time they are in contact with the heating surface is diminished in like proportion. This is shown by the effect of opening the furnace door, or of allowing the fire to burn away so that portions of the grate are left uncovered. The volume of cold air which will in either of these cases enter the fire-box will be so great that the pressure of the steam in the boiler will begin to fall at once.

QUESTION 387. *What determines the amount of air which must be admitted to the fire-box of a locomotive to effect perfect combustion?*

Answer. This depends chiefly upon the *rate of combustion,* that is, the number of pounds of coal consumed per hour on each square foot of grate surface. Of course if 100 pounds is burnt it will require twice the supply of air that would be needed if only 50 pounds were burnt.

QUESTION 388. *How should the air be admitted so as to burn the coal perfectly?*

Answer. In burning bituminous coal it has been shown that there are two distinct bodies to be dealt with, the one coke, a *solid,* the other coal gas, which is of course a *gaseous body.* The combustion of each of these is necessarily a distinct process. If the requisite quantity of air is supplied to the burning coke, or solid portion of the coal, it will, as has been shown, be converted into carbonic dioxide, and thus be perfectly consumed. If the supply of air is insufficient, the product of the combustion will be carbonic oxide, which is very wasteful. If, for example, there is a thick layer of coke on the grate, the air will enter and unite with the lower layer of coal and form carbonic dioxide, but as it rises there will not be enough air to supply oxygen to the carbon, and another equivalent of the latter will therefore combine with the carbonic dioxide and form carbonic oxide. It is evident, though, that the thinner the fire, the easier it is for air to pass through it, and consequently the greater will be the quantity which will enter the fire-box. Nothing would seem easier then than to regulate the thickness of the fire on the grates so that just the needed amount of air would pass through it. If coke alone was to be burned, undoubtedly very perfect combustion would be (and has been) effected in this way, but if a charge of fresh coal, say 100 pounds, is thrown on the fire, the coal gas is very soon generated and escapes into the fire-box. This gas needs an additional amount of air for its combustion. It would seem that this could be supplied by reducing the thickness of the fire still further, so that more air would pass through it than was needed for the combustion of the coke alone. If this was done then too much air would pass through the coke after the gases had all escaped from the fresh coal and were burned. Besides, the passage of the air would be the most restricted after the fresh charge had been put on the fire, just at the time when the most is needed. This difficulty might be overcome if a constant supply of fresh coal just equal to that consumed were kept on the fire all the time, and the thickness of fuel on the grates was then regulated so as to admit just air enough for the combustion of the coke and also that of the gases, the production of which would then be uniform. An approximation to this method of feeding the fire is, in fact, what is aimed at on most locomotives, and probably the best practical results are produced by that method.

Two difficulties are, however, encountered in this method. In the first place it is impossible to feed a fire continuously with a shovel. There will be intervals between the charges which are thrown in, so that the supply is not uniform, even if the charges do not consist of more than a portion of a shovel-full at a time; and if the fire was fed in this way as uniformly as possible it would then be necessary to open the furnace door every time fresh coal was put on the fire, and so much cold air would thus be admitted that more would be lost by lowering the temperature of the boiler than would be gained by the improved combustion.

Another difficulty also is encountered in this method of burning coal in locomotives. In order to admit enough air through the fire it is necessary to keep the latter so thin on the grates that the violent draft produced by the blast lifts the coal from the grate-bars and carries the lighter particles through the flues unconsumed. It is thus extremely difficult to keep the grate uniformly covered with coal, and if it is not, the air will enter in irregular and rapid streams or masses through the uncovered parts, and at the very time when it should be *there* most restricted. Such a state of things at once bids defiance to all regulation or control, so that it is found almost uniformly that firemen of locomotives keep enough coal on the grates to avoid the danger of "losing their fire," as they express it; that is, having all the burning coal drawn through the tubes by the blast. *Now, on the control of the supply* *of air depends all that human skill can do in effecting perfect combustion and economy;* and unless the supply of fuel and the quantity on the bars can be regulated, it will be impossible to control the admission of the air.*

Another method of feeding locomotive boilers is to pile up the coal in the back part in a thick layer and slope it downward towards the front, so that there is a comparatively thin fire in front. The mass piled up at the door becomes converted into coke, and the production of gas from the coal is more gradual and uniform than it is when only a small quantity is thrown in at a time, and therefore a more uniform supply of air is needed for its combustion. But it is apparent that very little air can pass through the thick heap of coal at the back part of the fire-box, and that therefore all, or nearly all the air which enters it must come in through a comparatively small portion of the grate. It will of course be difficult to admit the requisite quantity, for the reasons already stated.

It is consequently apparent that it is practically impossible to admit enough air through the grates to effect a constantly perfect combustion of bituminous coal. It is, therefore, necessary to admit a portion of the air above the fire. In doing this, however, in order to effect perfect combustion the air thus admitted must be thoroughly mixed with the gases, and in order to be able to enter into chemical combination, or in other words, to burn, the gases must combine with the air at an igniting temperature. If too much air is admitted, it will reduce the temperature in the fire-box so much that the gases will not ignite; or, if it is

* The Combustion of Coal, by C. Wye Williams.

admitted in strong currents, the air and the gases will flow side by side like the currents of two streams of water, the one muddy and the other clear, which, as is well known, mingle very slowly. Besides, if a hot stream of gas encounters a strong stream of cold air and comes in contact with it only at its surface, the latter will be cooled down below the igniting temperature; whereas if the two had been intimately mixed in the right proportion, the whole mixture would have been hot enough to burn. It is therefore of the utmost importance that the air which is admitted above the fire should enter the fire-box in many small jets. None of the openings for its admission should exceed $\frac{1}{2}$ inch in diameter. With the violent draft in a locomotive fire-box there is an extremely brief period of time for chemical combination to take place after the gases are expelled from the coal and before they are hurried into the tubes. As the chemical action between the gases and the oxygen can only take place when the two are in intimate contact, too much pains cannot be taken to distribute the currents of admitted air and thus mix them with the combustible gases. In many cases means are adopted to delay the air and the gases in the fire-box so as to give them time for chemical combination or combustion before entering the tubes.

QUESTION 389. *Does any combustion take place after the gases enter the tubes?*

Answer. Very little; as the flames are extinguished soon after they enter.

QUESTION 390. *Why are the flames extinguished in the tubes?*

Answer. They are then in contact with large quantities of incombustible gas and beyond the reach of a supply of air; besides, the temperature of the tubes which are surrounded with water is so low that the flame is soon cooled down below an igniting temperature.

QUESTION 391. *What temperature is necessary to ignite coal gas or produce flame?*

Answer. A temperature considerably hotter than red-hot iron is needed, as can easily be shown by the fact that a gas-light can not be ignited with a red-hot poker.

QUESTION 392. *Are there any parts of the fire-box where the temperature is probably below the igniting point?*

Answer. Yes; along the sides and ends near the plates, which are covered with water on the opposite side. At these points the coal is usually "dead" or incandescent, as it remains at too low a temperature to burn. For this reason, in some cases a space of from 8 to 12 inches on each side and still more at the ends of the grates, is made of solid plates, without any openings, and therefore called "*dead-grates,*" so that no cold air can enter at those points. These plates are made sloping downwards from the sides towards the centre of the fire-box, so that the coal which falls on them and is thus coked, can easily be raked towards the middle of the fire. This arrangement of dead plates often improves the combustion and results in greater economy of fuel. The reduction of the area of the openings between the grate-bars can usually be compensated by making the bars narrower or the spaces between them wider.

QUESTION 393. *What should be the condition of the coal when it is put on the fire?*

Answer. It is true of the coal as well as of the gases that the chemical action between it and the oxygen can only take place when the two are in intimate contact, and therefore the rapidity and completeness of combustion and intensity of heat will be increased by increasing the number of points of contact, or by reducing the size of the fuel. The coal should therefore be broken up, but not so small as to fall between the grate-bars or be carried out of the fire-box by the blast.

QUESTION 394. *What amount of air must be admitted to the fire to effect perfect combustion?*

Answer. It was stated that average bituminous coal contains about 80 per cent. carbon, 5 per cent. of hydrogen and 15 per cent. of other substances. As a large proportion of the latter are incombustible, we will confine ourselves for the present to the consideration of the combustion of the hydrogen and carbon alone.

The hydrogen, as has been explained, unites with oxygen in the proportion by weight of 1 part of the former to 8 parts of the latter, and the product of this union is water, or steam. As 36 parts of air contain only 8 of oxygen, IN ORDER TO BURN THE HYDROGEN IT MUST BE SUPPLIED WITH 36 TIMES ITS WEIGHT OF AIR.

In order to burn the carbon perfectly it must, as has been explained, be converted into carbonic dioxide, which consists of 6 parts of carbon and 16 of oxygen; and as air consists of 28 parts of nitrogen to every 8 of oxygen, we must furnish 72 parts of air to every 6 of carbon, or, in other words, CARBON NEEDS 12 TIMES ITS WEIGHT OF AIR FOR ITS PERFECT COMBUSTION.

Every pound of average bituminous coal therefore requires 1.8 lbs. of air to burn its hydrogen, and 9.6 lbs. for the carbon, or 11.4 for both. As a portion of the other substances of which coal is composed, besides the oxygen and hydrogen, which others have been classed as impurities, are combustible, there will be no material error if we estimate the amount of air required for the combustion of bituminous coal at 12 POUNDS PER POUND OF FUEL. As each cubic foot of air weighs 0.08072 lb., 12 pounds will be equal to

$$\frac{12}{0.08072} = 148.6 \text{ cubic feet of air,}$$

or for the sake of even figures and a quantity which can easily be remembered, we will say 150 CUBIC FEET OF AIR ARE NEEDED FOR THE COMBUSTION OF EACH POUND OF COAL. This is the theoretical quantity of air which is needed for combustion. Now, unfortunately, the process of combustion in the fire-boxes of locomotives is one in which any very exact combination of the substances which unite is not possible with the appliances which are now employed. If, therefore, we admitted the exact amount of air given above, while some portions of the fire where combustion was not very active might have more air than is needed, other portions would have too little; and if the air is not very thoroughly mixed, the flame and burning coal may be surrounded with the products of combustion, which would exclude the air and thus reduce its effect upon the fire. For this reason, besides the air required to furnish the oxygen necessary for the complete combustion of the fuel, it is also necessary to furnish an additional quantity of air for the ***dilution*** of the gaseous products of combustion, which would otherwise prevent the free access of air to the fuel. The more minute the division and the greater the velocity with which the air rushes among the fuel, the smaller is the additional quantity of air required for dilution. In locomotive boilers, although this quantity has not been exactly ascertained, there is reason to believe that it may on an average be estimated at about *one-half* of the air required for combustion.* We would therefore have as the quantity of air needed for combustion

$$150 + \frac{150}{2} = 225 \text{ cubic feet.}$$

This estimate is roughly made, but it is the nearest approximation at present attainable. It is probable that the supply of air required for dilution varies considerably in different arrangements of the fire-box and for different kinds of fuel, and it is possible that by admitting the air for combustion in small enough jets, and deflecting the currents of smoke and gases so as to cause them to mingle with the air, the quantity required for dilution might be reduced below that indicated by the above calculation. Undoubtedly all the air which is admitted into the fire-box which does not combine with the chemical elements of the fuel lessens the amount of steam generated in the boiler, both with reference to time, that is to say per minute, and to fuel, that is per pound of coal consumed. But with the present locomotive boiler it is simply a choice of two evils. If no more air is admitted than theory indicates to be needed for combustion, then, owing to

*Rankine.

the imperfect means which are usually employed to cause the air and fuel to combine, a portion of the latter will escape unconsumed; and if *more* air is admitted, the temperature of the products of combustion is lowered and their volume increased, the evils of which have already been pointed out. It therefore becomes a matter in which we are obliged to consult experience and determine by experiment what amount of air it is necessary to admit to the fuel to produce the most economical results.

QUESTION 395. *What proportion of the air should be admitted through the grate, and how much above the fire?*

Answer. This, too, is a question which can probably be answered best by consulting experience. The relative quantity of air required above and below the fire depends very much on the nature of the fuel. Coal which "runs together" or cakes very much or has a great deal of clinker in it, doubtless, will need more air above the fire than other coal which is said to be "dryer," for the reason that it will be found impossible to admit so much air through the caking coal in the grate as through the other kind. An idea of the relative quantity which should be admitted above and below the fire may be found if we know how much air is needed to burn the solid carbon or coke which is left after the gas is expelled from it, and how much for the gas itself. The gas which is expelled from a pound of coal consists of about 0.05 lb. of hydrogen and 0.15 lb. of carbon. Now, it has been shown that hydrogen requires 36 times its weight of air to burn it perfectly, so that 0.05 lb. would need $0.05 \times 36 = 1.8$ lbs.; and carbon requires 12 times its weight of air, so that for 0.15 lb. of carbon $0.15 \times 12 = 1.8$ lbs.

is needed, so that for both 3.6 lbs. of air is required for perfect combustion. As has been shown, 12 lbs. is needed to consume the whole of the fuel, so that 30 per cent. of the whole supply is required for the combustion of the gas alone. If this is diluted in the same proportion as that required for the combustion of the carbon, and it probably should be even more so, we would have 30 per cent. of 225 = 67.5 cubic feet of air required for the combustion of the gas. It is certain, however, that the solid coke on the grates is not perfectly consumed, or, in other words, converted into carbonic dioxide, especially when the layer of it on the grates is very thick. When this is the case the air coming in contact with the lower layer of coke forms carbonic dioxide, but as it rises through the burning coke another equivalent of carbon unites with the carbonic dioxide, and thus forms carbonic oxide. If, now, enough air is admitted above the fire, this carbonic oxide will combine with it, and, as has been explained before, a second combustion will take place if there is time and opportunity for combination before the gases enter the flues. It is therefore probable that more than 30 per cent. of the whole supply of air should be admitted above the fire. It is at any rate best to provide the means for admitting more, and also appliances for regulating the supply, so that it can be governed as experience may indicate to be best.

QUESTION 396. ***Is it not possible by enlarging the grate to admit enough air to the fire to produce perfect combustion?***

Answer. Yes; when no air is admitted above the fire, large grates are found to produce the best combustion. But while it is true that the same amount of heat will be produced by the union of each equivalent of oxygen and fuel, yet if we can force *more* air and fuel to unite in the *same place,* a higher temperature is produced in that place, just as a fire in a blacksmith's forge is hotter because of the forced blast than that in an ordinary stove, or a smelting furnace than a parlor grate. If, then, we can concentrate the draft in the fire of a locomotive, we secure a greater *intensity* of combustion; and when the air is urged against the solid carbon with considerable force, it comes in contact with every point of its surface, and therefore less dilution of the air is needed, and consequently the products of combustion have a higher temperature; and, as has been explained, a larger proportion of the heat is then transferred to the water than if the temperature is lower and the volume greater.

Intensity of combustion also has the effect of maintaining an igniting temperature; whereas, if the same amount of fuel is burned slowly, its heat may not be high enough to ignite the gases as they are produced.

It is desirable, however, to have all the space that is possible in the fire-box, so as to give room for the mixing of the gases; but with a large fire-box and large grate a decided improvement and economy will often result by diminishing the effective area of the grate by covering a part of it with dead plates, but at the same time making provision for the admission of air above the fire.

QUESTION 397. *What is meant by the "Total Heat of Combustion?"*

Answer. It is the number of units of heat given out by the combustion of a given quantity (usually a pound) of fuel.

QUESTION 398. *How is this determined?*

Answer. The heat given out by the combustion of one pound of the chemical elements of which coal is composed has been determined by experiment, and from such data, knowing the substances of which fuel is composed, we can determine the amount of heat which would be developed if they were each perfectly consumed. Thus the total heat of combustion of one pound of hydrogen is 62,032 units, and of the same quantity of carbon 14,500 units.* Therefore, if a pound of coal contains 5 per cent. of hydrogen, the heat given out by the combustion of that element will be $62{,}032 \times 0.05 = 3{,}101.60$ units, and if it has 80 per cent. of carbon, the combustion of the latter would develop $14{,}500 \times 0.80 = 11{,}600$ units, so that the total heat of the combustion of these two elements would be $3{,}101.6 + 11{,}600 = 14{,}701.6$ units. It was shown in answer to Question 40 that it required 1,213.4 units of heat to convert water at zero to steam of 100 pounds pressure. As steam is usually generated from water at a temperature of about 60 degrees, the total heat required to convert it into steam of 100 pounds pressure would be $1{,}213.4 - 60 = 1{,}153.4$ units. A pound of average bituminous coal, therefore, contains heat enough to convert $12\frac{1}{4}$ lbs. of water into steam of 100 lbs. absolute pressure. Ordinarily only about half that amount of water is evaporated in locomotive boilers per pound of fuel.

QUESTION 399. *What are the chief causes of this waste of heat?*

Answer. It is due, *first,* to the waste of unburnt fuel

* The experiments which have been made to determine these amounts do not agree exactly, but those given are thought to be the most trustworthy.

in the solid state. This occurs when fuel which is very fine falls through the grates, or is carried through the tubes and out of the stack in the form of cinders.*

Second, to the waste of unburnt fuel in the gaseous or smoky state. The method of preventing this waste by a sufficient supply and proper distribution of air has been explained in the answer to preceding questions.

Third, to the waste or loss of heat in the hot gases which escape up the chimney or smoke stack. The temperature of the fire in a locomotive fire-box in a state of active combustion is probably from 3,000 to 4,000 degrees. This heat is in part radiated and conducted to the heating surface of the fire-box, and it is found that more water is evaporated by this portion of the heating surface in proportion to its area than by any other in the boiler. The gases when they enter the tubes transmit a portion of their heat to the surfaces with which they are first in contact. The amount of heat thus transmitted, as has been stated, is in proportion to the *difference* in temperature of the gases inside the tubes and that of the water outside. After passing over the part of the tube with which the gases are first in contact, they then arrive at another portion of the tube surface with a diminished temperature, and the rate of conduction is therefore diminished; so that each successive equal portion of the heating surface transmits a less and less quantity of heat, until the hot air at last leaves the heating surface and escapes up the chimney with a certain remaining excess of temperature above that of the water in the boiler, the heat corresponding to which excess

* It should be remarked here that some and perhaps most of the cinders which are carried out of the stack are not combustible but are composed of the same materials that form clinkers on the grate.

is wasted.* It is, therefore, desirable to extract as much heat as possible from the gases before they escape from the tubes. Now it will be impossible to heat the water outside of the tubes hotter than the gases inside. When the temperature of the water is equal to that of the gases, no more heat will be transmitted from one to the other. If the temperature of the water is 350 degrees, that of the gases in the tubes will never be any lower, but will escape into the smoke-box with not less than that amount of heat. If, however, the cold water is introduced at the front end of the tubes, so that the surface with which the gases are last in contact has a temperature considerably lower than 350, then an additional amount of heat will be transmitted before they escape. It is, therefore, important that the cold feed-water should be admitted near the front end of the boiler, so that the products of combustion will be in contact with the coldest part of the heating surface last, and thus give out as much of their heat as possible before they escape. As a matter of fact, the gases escape at a much higher temperature. Experiments made by the writer showed that the temperature in the smoke-box of a locomotive when first starting was 270 degrees, and when working at its maximum capacity on a steep grade and with a heavy train it was as high as 675 degrees. The average temperature while running was, in three trials on different parts of the road, as follows:

Average steam pressure, 98.8 lbs.; average temperature, 499.8 lbs.
Average steam pressure, 106 lbs.; average temperature, 535.1 lbs.
Average steam pressure, 112.2 lbs.; average temperature, 554 lbs.

In making these experiments a record was made of

* Rankine.

the indications of a pyrometer and of the steam gauge once every minute while the engine was running. The distance run was 19 miles for the first experiment, 13 for the second and 6 for the third, with 30 loaded freight cars in the train. The last experiment was made while the engine was working on a heavy grade and very nearly up to its maximum capacity.

It will thus be seen that a great deal of heat is wasted by escaping up the chimney.

Fourth, by external radiation from the boiler. This occurs chiefly from the fact that it is not sufficiently well protected or covered with non-conducting material. The practice, or rather the neglect, of not covering the outside of the fire-box with lagging doubtless causes a very considerable loss of heat by radiation and convection from the hot boiler plates.

QUESTION 400. *What is the ordinary form of fire-box employed for burning bituminous coal?*

Answer. It is that represented in plate II and figs. 41 and 44, and is simply a rectangular box, and for that reason it is called a *plain* fire-box. Sometimes provision is made for admitting air into such fire-boxes through hollow or rather tubular stay-bolts, which are put into the sides and front. In most cases, too, the fire-box door has perforations for admitting air.

QUESTION 401. *What other appliances are used for burning bituminous coal?*

Answer. The most common appliance which is added to the plain fire-box is what is called a *fire-brick arch.* This is shown in fig. 214. *B C* is the arch which, as its name implies, is formed of fire-brick and extends backward and upward from a point in the tube-sheet below the tubes. In order to be self-supporting it is built in the form of an arch, the two sides of the fire-box acting as abutments for its support. The engraving represents with sufficient clearness the direction of the flames and smoke. These must take a more circuitous "*run*," as it is called, after leaving the fire, in order to reach the tubes. Time is thus given for the gases to combine and combustion to take place.

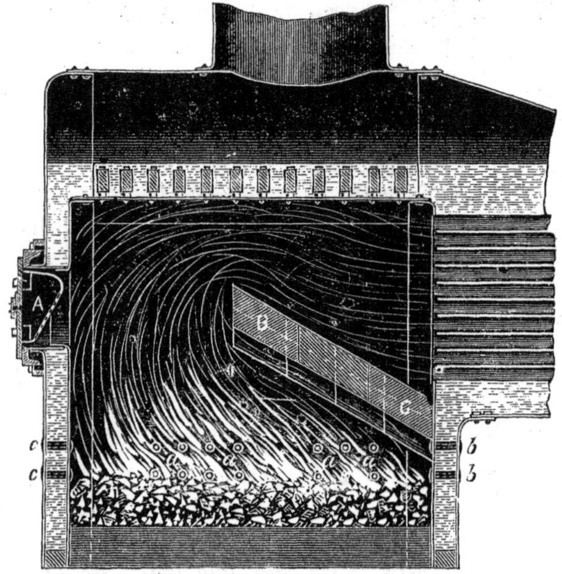

Fig. 214. Scale 3/8 in.=1 foot.

The fire-brick becomes heated, and thus to some extent prevents the gases from being cooled down below an igniting temperature by contact with the cold surface of the fire-box before combustion is complete. The fire-brick, however, soon burns out, and must be replaced, but owing to its cheapness and the ease with which it can be removed, this does not make a serious objection to its use. Air is nearly always admitted above the fire when the brick arch is used, either by tubular stay-bolts, *a*, *a*, *a*, or perforations in the door, or both.

In order to avoid the inconvenience and expense of replacing the fire-brick arch, what is known as the

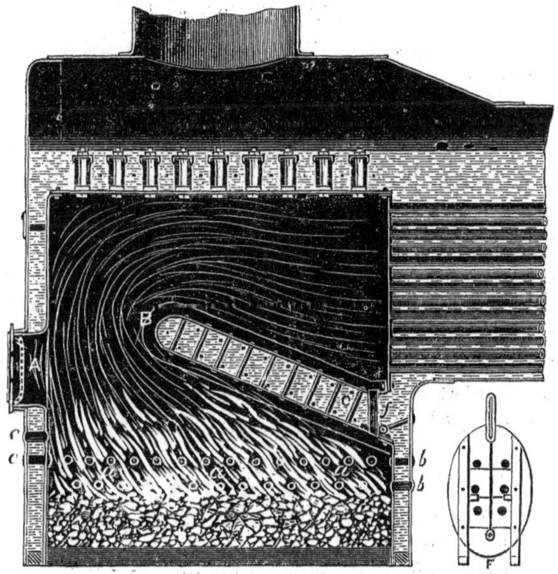

Fig. 215. Scale ⅜ in.=1 foot.

"Jauriet water-table" has been extensively used on some roads. This is the invention of Mr. C. F. Jauriet and is represented in fig. 215, and consists of a flat "table," *B C*, formed of two boiler plates placed about 4½ in. apart, with the space between filled with water. The two plates are stayed with ordinary stay-bolts in the same way as the sides of the fire-box. The form of the water-table is similar to that of the fire-brick, excepting that it is not arched, this form not being necessary, as the plates are riveted to the sides of the fire-box. Air is admitted above the fire both by hollow stay-bolts and holes in the door, as shown at *A*. Tubes, *f*, are put into the front and lower portion of the water-table to allow the ashes and cinders, which would otherwise be deposited above, to fall down on the grates.

When air is admitted at the furnace door of an ordinary fire-box, it is very apt to rush directly into the tubes without mingling with the gases. It was found by some of the firemen on English railroads that by placing a shovel over the top of the furnace door, the current of air which entered could thus be deflected downward, and in this way smoke could be almost entirely prevented. This led to the adoption of a hood or deflector, *A*, fig. 216, which is made of sheet iron and is placed over the fire-box door and is arranged with a lever, *B*, so that it can be raised in order to be out of the way when coal is thrown on the fire. It is suspended from a hook, *C*, from which it can easily be detached and taken out for repairs. This is frequently necessary, as the intense heat of the fire-box burns away the sheet iron of which it is made very rapidly. It can be made of old boiler plate, so that the expense of renewal is very slight. When this plan is used, a double sliding door, shown in fig. 217, is commonly used with it. These doors are opened by the levers *f d*, and *e g*, which are all connected together. With these sliding doors the opening for the admission of air can easily be regulated, and the opening through which the lever, *B*, is attached to the deflector, *A*, can be arranged more conveniently than with a swinging

Fig. 216.

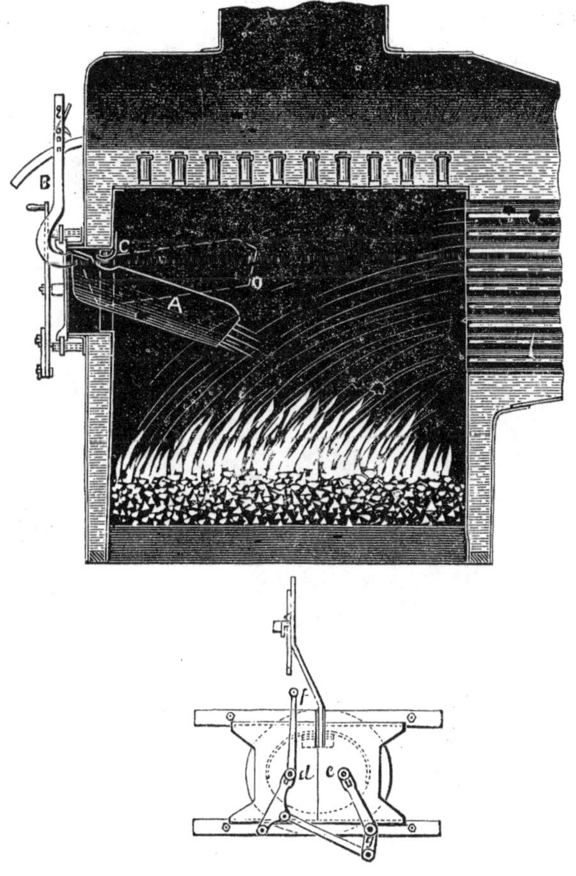

Fig. 217.
Scale ⅜ in. = 1 foot.

door. This plan has been employed by the Rogers Locomotive Works.

Another plan of fire-box, which was designed and patented by Mr. William Buchanan, Master Mechanic of the Hudson River Railroad, and used extensively on that line, is shown in fig. 218. This consists of a

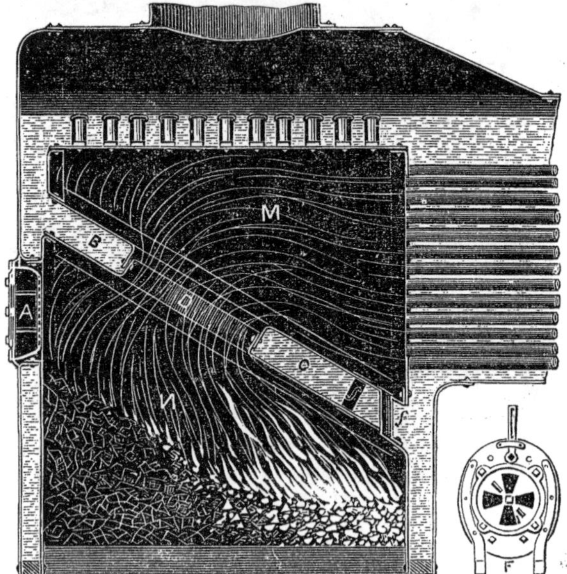

Fig. 218. Scale ⅜ in. = 1 foot.

water-table, but it extends completely across the fire-box from the tube sheet to the back-plate, thus dividing the fire-box into two compartments, *M* and *N*. In order to afford communication from the lower one to the upper one a round hole, *D*, about 24 in. in diameter, is put in the water-table in the position shown. It will thus be seen that all the currents of gas, smoke and air must unite in passing through this opening, and are thus brought into close contact with each other. After they enter the upper chamber and before they enter the tubes, there is room and time for combustion. The position of the lower side of the table, it will be seen, is similar to that of the deflector shown in fig. 216, so that it acts in somewhat the same way, by directing the currents of air, which enter through the furnace door, downward on the fire.

QUESTION 402. *How do these different plans operate?*

Answer. They will all burn coal more perfectly, and therefore more economically, if they are carefully and skillfully managed, than is possible in ordinary plain fire-boxes; but it is probable that more economy in the consumption of coal would result from the improvement of the practice and knowledge of firemen than can be expected from the use of any of the appliances described, if they are used without care, or knowledge of the principles of combustion.

QUESTION 403. *In what respect does anthracite coal differ from bituminous?*

Answer. It differs chiefly in the fact that it contains a much larger proportion of carbon and less of hydrogen, and in the fact that it consequently gives off very little or no coal gas. Its combustion is therefore more simple than that of bituminous coal, as there is very little else than solid carbon to burn.

QUESTION 404. *In what kind of a fire-box is anthracite usually burned?*

Answer. It is usually burned in a very long grate, and as the heat is very intense, the grate-bars are usually made of iron tubes, through which a current of water circulates, so as to prevent them from melting.

QUESTION 405. *Is it important to admit air above an anthracite fire to facilitate combustion?*

Answer. As there are no gases to be burned, it is not so important as it is with bituminous coal, but if the layer of anthracite on the grates is very thick, it will be impossible to get enough air through the coal to convert all the carbon into carbonic dioxide, and the carbon and oxygen will therefore unite so as to form carbonic oxide. If air is admitted above the fire, as has already been explained, another equivalent of oxygen will unite with the carbonic oxide, and a second combustion will then take place above the fire, and the carbonic oxide will thus be converted into carbonic dioxide. If, under these circumstances, no air was admitted above the fire, the second combustion would not occur, and all the heat produced thereby would be lost.

QUESTION 406. *How can we determine the relative value of different kinds of fuel for use in locomotives?*

Answer. This can only be determined satisfactorily by actual experiment. The chemical composition, excepting so far as it indicates the presence of deleterious substances, such as sulphur, ashes, clinkers, etc., affords but little assistance in determining the value of fuel. Nearly the same quantities of elements in different fuels may arrange themselves, before and during combustion, so as to produce very different series of compounds. It is true that the composition of coal gives us some indication of its heat-producing *capacity*, but the extent to which that capacity can be converted into actual steam in locomotive boilers, depends to a very great extent upon the conditions under which the fuel is burned. It should also be remembered that the rapidity with which steam can be generated is a very important matter in locomotive practice. Whether a heavy freight train can be taken up a given grade, or a fast express make time, often depends upon the amount of steam which can be generated by the fuel in each second of time that the boiler is worked to its maximum capacity. Therefore any appliance for improving combustion, which reduces the quantity of steam which can be generated by the boiler in a given time, is quite sure to fall into disuse or be abandoned. It is of course often necessary to adapt the appliances for burning fuel to the fuel itself; and when a poor quality of the latter must be used, more boiler capacity must be given than is needed to do the same work with better fuel.

The table in the appendix will no doubt be valuable as indicating the properties and relative value of several different kinds of fuel used in this country. The table is copied from a report made to the Navy Department of the United States by Professor Walter B. Johnson in 1844, and the conclusions are deduced from a series of very elaborate experiments made for the Navy Department. This report furnishes the most full and reliable data regarding the value of American fuel thus far (1874) published; but it contains little or no information concerning the fuels which are now used on railroads in our Western States. The first eight specimens of coal given in the table are anthracite; all the rest are bituminous coals.

PART XX.

THE RESISTANCE OF TRAINS.

QUESTION 407. *What is meant by the resistance of trains or cars?*

Answer. It is the power required to move them on the track. Thus if a rope, fig. 219, was attached to a car at one end, and the other passed over a pulley, *a*, and a sufficiently heavy weight, *W*, was hung on the end of the rope, it would move the car. The weight *W* would then be equal to the resistance of the car.

QUESTION 408. *How can the resistance of cars under different circumstances be determined?*

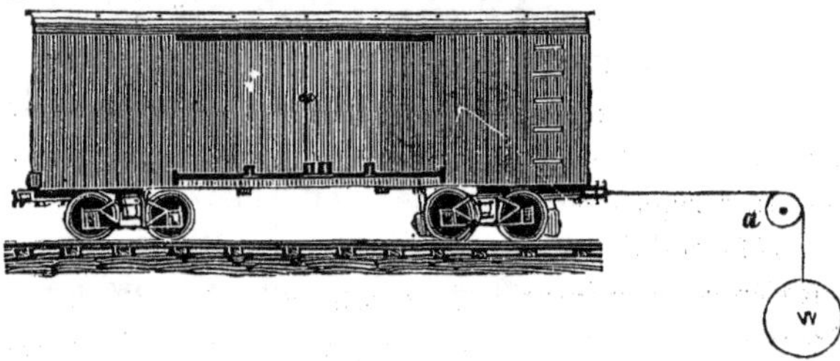

Fig. 219

Answer. It has been found that it takes a force of about 6 lbs. per ton (of 2,000 lbs.) to move a car slowly on a level and straight track after it is started. That is, if a car weighs 20 tons and a rope, fig. 219, is attached to it at one end and the other passed over a pulley, *a*, with a weight, *W*, suspended to it, it will require a weight equal to 20 × 6 = 120 lbs. to keep the car moving slowly. If two cars of the above weight were coupled together, it would require twice 120 or 240 lbs., and if three were attached to each other, three times 120, or 360 lbs., and so on. In other words, MULTIPLYING THE TOTAL WEIGHT OF THE CARS IN TONS (OF 2,000 LBS.) BY 6 WILL GIVE US THEIR RESISTANCE, OR THE FORCE REQUIRED TO KEEP THEM MOVING ON A LEVEL AND STRAIGHT TRACK AT A SLOW SPEED AFTER THEY ARE STARTED. The resistance is represented by the weight above, and the locomotive must exert a force equal to that weight to keep the train moving. As the speed increases the resistance increases, as is shown by the following table. It should be stated here, however, that our knowledge regarding this whole subject of the resistance of American cars and trains is exceedingly inaccurate and imperfect, and the data given in the books are nearly all based on experiments made in Europe, with cars of a different construction from those used here. There is reason for believing, however, that the resistance of American cars is less than that of European cars, and we have assumed it to be 6 lbs. per ton on a level at very slow speed, which is less than the resistance which is usually given, but the following figures should be regarded merely as an approximation to the actual facts, of which we are still in ignorance:

Velocity of trains in miles per hour.....	5	10	15	20	25	30	35	40	45	50	60	70
Resistance on straight line in lbs. per ton (of 2,000 lbs.).......	6.1	6.6	7.3	8.3	9.6	11.2	13.1	15.3	17.8	20 6	27	34.6

Now, if we want to get the resistance at 30 miles an hour of a train of ten cars weighing each 20 tons, the calculation would be $10 \times 20 \times 11\frac{1}{4} = 2,250$ lbs. This will give the resistance on a level and straight track. On an ascending grade the resistance is greater than that given above, because, besides pulling the car horizontally, it is necessary to raise it vertically a distance equal to the ascent of the grade. Thus if we have a grade with a rise of forty feet in a mile, the amount of energy required to simply raise the weight of a car would be equal to its weight in pounds multiplied by the vertical height of the ascent. Thus, supposing a car which weighs 40,000 lbs. to be run one mile on a grade of forty feet ascent in that distance, then the energy expended in simply raising the car will be equal to $40,000 \times 40 = 1,600,000$ foot-pounds. Now, if it was necessary to raise that weight by a direct vertical lift or pull, it would require a force equal to or a little greater than the load to do it. But in pulling a car or train up a grade, which is an inclined plane, the force, which is the locomotive, instead of being exerted through the vertical distance is exerted through the horizontal distance, which in this case is one mile, or 5,280 feet. Therefore, if we divide the number of foot-pounds of energy required by the distance through which the power is exerted, it will give us the force exerted through one foot. That is,

$$\frac{1,600,000}{5,280} = 151.5 \text{ lbs.}$$

The resistance due to the ascent alone of a train on a grade or incline can therefore be calculated by MULTIPLYING THE WEIGHT OF THE TRAIN IN POUNDS BY THE ASCENT IN ANY GIVEN DISTANCE IN FEET AND DIVIDING THE PRODUCT BY THE HORIZONTAL

DISTANCE IN FEET. Thus in the above example the rate of the ascent is given in so many feet per mile; we therefore multiply by 40 and divide by 5,280, which is the number of feet in a mile. If the rate of the gradient had been given, as it sometimes is, as 1 in 132, we would simply have divided the weight of the train by the latter number. If we want to get the resistance per ton of train we substitute for its weight that of one ton in pounds; thus:

$$\frac{2{,}000 \times 40}{5{,}280} = 15.1 \text{ lbs.}$$

If, now, we have the resistance which is due to the *ascent or gravity alone*, we must add to this the resistance on a straight and level track, at the speed at which the train runs, in order to determine the total resistance on the grade. On a level road at a speed of 5 miles per hour it would be 6.1 lbs. per ton, so that on a grade of forty feet to a mile at that speed the resistance would be $6.1 + 15.1 = 21.2$ lbs., per ton, and at 10 miles it would be $6.6 + 15.1 = 21.7$ lbs., and at 30 miles per hour on the grade the resistance would be $11.2 + 15.1 = 26.3$ lbs. per ton. To get the total resistance on a grade for any speed, we ADD THE RESISTANCE FOR THAT SPEED ON A STRAIGHT AND LEVEL LINE TO THE RESISTANCE DUE TO THE ASCENT ALONE. The resistances for various rates of speed and grades has been calculated, and is given in the table in the appendix.

The top horizontal row of figures of that table gives the rates of speed. The left-hand vertical row gives the rise of grade in feet per mile. The resistance for any given grade and speed is given where the vertical row of figures under the rate of speed and the horizontal row opposite the rise of the grade intersect each other. Thus, for a grade of 30 feet per mile and a speed of 45 miles per hour, we follow the vertical column under the 45 downward, and the horizontal column opposite 30 to the right, and where the two intersect the resistance, 29.1 lbs. is given.

QUESTION 409. *What effect do curves have on the resistance of trains?*

Answer. They increase the resistance, but in what proportion or to what degree is not known accurately. European authorities say that the resistance is increased, over what it would be in a straight and level line, about 1 per cent. for every degree of the curve occupied by a train. It is probable, however, that the resistance of American cars, which nearly all have double trucks, is not so great on curves as that of European cars, which nearly all have long and rigid wheel-bases, and whose wheels therefore can not adjust themselves so easily to the curvature of the track as they can when the American system of double trucks is used.

QUESTION 410. *What is meant by a degree of a curve?*

Answer. In order to measure circles, they are all supposed to be divided into 360 equal parts, which are called degrees. One degree of a curve is therefore $\frac{1}{360}$ of a complete circle; but if the curve has a long radius, one degree of such a curved track will be longer than one degree of a curve with a short radius, but each will have the same amount of "bend" or curvature. It is this latter which increases the resistance of trains, and the greater the number of degrees of a curve occupied by a train of cars, the greater will be the "bend" of the track, and therefore the greater the resistance.

QUESTION 411. *What other causes affect the resistance of trains?*

Answer. The condition of the track and the force and direction of the wind. On a rough track the resistance is very much greater than on a smooth one, and a strong head-wind makes it much more difficult to pull a train than it is in calm weather.

PART XXI.

PROPORTIONS OF LOCOMOTIVES.

QUESTION 412. *In proportioning a locomotive to any given kind of work, what are the first facts which should be known?*

Answer. We should first know the weight of the train which the locomotive must draw; second, the speed at which it must run; and third, the steepest grades and the shortest curves of the road on which it must work. From these data the resistance of the train which the locomotive must overcome can be at least approximately determined.

QUESTION 413. *When the greatest resistance of the train is known, what is the next thing to be determined?*

Answer. As was stated in answer to Question 66, if the wheels revolve and their adhesion is greater than the resistance opposed to the movement of the locomotive, the latter will overcome the resistance; but if the latter is greater than the friction, the wheels will slip. It therefore follows that the adhesion must be somewhat greater than the resistance. As the adhesion is equal to about one-fifth* of the adhesive weight or pressure of the driving-wheels on the rails, obviously this weight should be five times the resistance. Thus, if we have a train weighing 400 tons which we want to take up a grade of 40 feet per mile at a speed of 20

* See answer to Question 309.

miles per hour, its resistance, calculated from the table given in the previous part, would be 9,360 lbs. Therefore, 9,360 × 5 = 46,800 lbs. = the required adhesive weight.

QUESTION 414. *What considerations determine the manner of distributing this weight on the wheels?*

Answer. It is found by experience that if too much weight is placed upon one wheel, the material of which the rails are made is partly crushed and injured, and they then wear out much more rapidly than they would if the weight was distributed on more wheels, and thus a smaller amount of weight rested on each point of contact with the rails. The amount of weight which can be carried on a single wheel depends upon the material of which the rails are made, and to some extent on their form and size, or as the latter is usually expressed, on their weight per yard.

QUESTION 415. *When the adhesive weight and the number of driving-wheels are known, how is the size of the latter and of the cylinders determined?*

Answer. The size of the wheels will to a certain extent depend upon the speed, because the larger the wheels, the further will the locomotive move in one revolution; but no exact rule can be given for their size. At present there is still a great diversity of opinion among engineers regarding the best sizes of wheels and cylinders for any given service. Probably the safest plan will be to consult the best practice, and in the absence of any better reasons be guided for the present by that. In this country the most common size of locomotives used is that which we have selected for our illustrations, that is, what are called five-feet wheels, and cylinders of 16 inches diameter and 24 inches stroke. More engines of these dimensions are used than of any other. For freight service the wheels are sometimes made of smaller and for passenger trains of larger diameter; but locomotives with driving-wheels and cylinders of the dimensions given are used for both passenger and freight service. It should be stated here that what are called five-feet wheels are usually about 1½ in. larger in diameter than five feet. This arose from the fact that the tires which are now used are made thicker than they were on the first engines, and the practice thus established has been continued. We will therefore take the diameter of what is called a five-feet wheel at what it really is, 61½ in. Such locomotives also have about 40,000 lbs. of adhesive weight. Now, the circumference of such wheels is 193.2 in., and therefore in one revolution of the wheels, if they do not slip, the locomotive will move that distance on the rails. At the same time each piston will sweep through the cylinder twice, and therefore in one revolution 4 times one cylinder full of steam is used. Now a cylinder of 16 in. diameter and 24 in. stroke contains or will hold 4,825½ cubic inches, so that in one revolution of the wheels $4,825\frac{1}{2} \times 4 = 19,302$ cubic inches of steam are used. As has been stated, in one revolution of the wheels, if they do not slip, the locomotive will move 193.2 in. If, now, we divide 19,302 by 193.2 it will give us the amount of steam used to move the locomotive and train one inch. Now, $19,302 \div 193.2 = 99.9$, which, for the sake of even figures we will call 100. We thus see that a locomotive with 40,000 pounds or 20 tons (of 2,000 lbs.) of adhesive weight requires 100 cubic inches of cylinder capacity* to move it one inch. Now, if a locomotive had only half as much weight on the driving-wheels, it could pull only half as much load, and would therefore use only half as much steam, and consequently need only half the cylinder capacity of the other locomotive. If there was three-quarters or a third as much adhesive weight, the cylinder capacity should also be three-quarters or a third. We thus see that the cylinder capacity should be proportioned to the total adhesive weight. Now as 100 cubic inches of cylinder capacity are needed to move an engine with 20 tons adhesive weight one inch, if we divide 100 by 20 we will get the cylinder capacity needed for each ton. That is, $100 \div 20 = 5$ CUBIC IN. CYLINDER CAPACITY PER TON (of 2,000 lbs.) OF ADHESIVE WEIGHT IS NEEDED TO MOVE ANY LOCOMOTIVE ONE INCH. This quantity we have named the *modulus of propulsion.*

Supposing now that it is required to calculate the cylinder capacity for a locomotive with 15 tons adhesive weight, and wheels $4\frac{1}{2}$ feet or 54 in. in diameter. We will first multiply 15 by the modulus of propulsion, $15 \times 5 = 75$ = the number of cubic inches of cylinder capacity required to move such a locomotive one inch. Multiplying the length of the circumference of the wheels, which in this case is 169.6 in. by 75, will give us the total cylinder capacity for one revolution. That is $169.6 \times 75 = 12{,}720$ cubic inches of cylinder capacity, or the space which should be swept through by the two pistons. Dividing this by 4 will give us the cubical contents in inches of one of the cylinders.

---

*The cylinder capacity is the space swept through by the two pistons. In the above illustrations what is meant is, that the average space in the cylinder swept through by the piston is 100 cubic inches for each inch that the locomotive advances.

Thus, 12,720 ÷ 4 = 3,180 cubic inches = the capacity of one cylinder. Now as the capacity of a cylinder is calculated by multiplying the area of the piston by the length of the stroke, if we have the one we can easily determine the other. Thus, supposing it was intended to make the stroke of the pistons 22 in., dividing 3,180 by 22 will give us the area of the piston. Thus, 3,180 ÷ 22 = 144.5 square inches. Now by the well-known rule in mensuration, if we DIVIDE THE AREA OF A CIRCLE BY 0.7854, THE SQUARE ROOT OF THE QUOTIENT WILL BE THE DIAMETER OF THE CIRCLE. Thus, 144.5÷0.7854 = 183.9. The square root of 183.9 is 13½ nearly, which should be the diameter of the cylinder. Instead of calculating the diameter of the circle, a more convenient way is to refer the area to a table of areas, and from it find the diameter. Of course if we have the diameter of the piston and want to get the stroke, we DIVIDE THE CUBICAL CONTENTS OF THE CYLINDER BY THE AREA OF THE PISTON. Thus, in the present illustration, if it was intended to have the piston 13½ in. diameter, we would have divided 3,180 by the area of a piston 13½ in. diameter, which is 143.1, so that we would have 3,180 ÷ 143.1 = 22 nearly, = inches of stroke of piston.

From the above considerations we can deduce the following RULE FOR CALCULATING THE CAPACITY OF THE CYLINDERS WHEN THE ADHESIVE WEIGHT IS KNOWN:

MULTIPLY THE TOTAL WEIGHT ON THE DRIVING-WHEELS IN TONS (of 2,000 lbs.) BY 5, AND THEN BY THE CIRCUMFERENCE OF THE WHEELS IN INCHES, AND DIVIDE BY 4. THE QUOTIENT WILL BE THE CUBICAL CONTENTS IN INCHES OF EACH CYLINDER.

From this, if either the diameter or stroke is given the other can easily be found, as has been explained.

It should be remarked here that it is unimportant, so far as the power of the locomotive is concerned, whether the cylinders have a large diameter and a short stroke or a small diameter and a long stroke, provided the cubical contents are the same. Thus cylinders 17½ in. in diameter and with 20 in. stroke would have almost exactly the same capacity and the same power would be exerted with them as with cylinders 16×24 in.; the only difference would be that with the cylinder of the largest diameter the pressure on the piston and consequently on the crank-pin journal and the strain on the parts would be greater than with the smaller cylinder. The difference in pressure would, however, be exactly compensated by the loss or gain in the leverage exerted through the driving-wheels on the rails.

QUESTION 416. *What circumstances should determine the size of locomotive boilers?*

Answer. They should be proportioned to the amount of adhesive weight, and to the speed at which the locomotive is intended to work. Thus, a locomotive with a great deal of weight on the driving-wheels could pull a heavier load and would, by the above rule for proportioning the cylinders, have a greater cylinder capacity than one with little adhesive weight, and would therefore consume more steam, and therefore should have a larger boiler. It is also obvious that if a locomotive like that shown in plates I and II should have a boiler just large enough to furnish steam when running at the rate of 20 miles an hour, it would be too small if the locomotive ran 40 miles an hour, the train resistance being the same in both cases. Driving-wheels 5 feet in diameter would at 20 miles per hour make 112 revolutions per minute, and would therefore consume 448 cylinders full of steam. At 40 miles per hour double the number of revolutions would be made, and consequently twice the quantity of steam would be used, and therefore the boiler should have twice the steam-producing capacity. If, therefore, we know the size of a boiler required for a given amount of adhesive weight and a given speed, we can easily calculate the boiler capacity for any other weight and speed.

QUESTION 417. *How can we determine the boiler capacity needed for an engine with a given amount of adhesive weight and for a given speed?*

Answer. This must be determined empirically, that is from experience.

QUESTION 418. *On what does the steam-generating capacity of a boiler depend?*

Answer. First, upon the size of its grate and fire-box, because more fuel can be burned in a large fire-place than in a small one; second, on the amount of heating surface to which the products of combustion are exposed, and third, on the draft produced by the blast or exhaust steam. Of course the amount of steam generated is also dependent upon a great variety of other circumstances, such as the nature of the combustion, the firing, the arrangement of the fire-box, grates, etc., and the condition of the heating surfaces; but these have nothing to do with the proportions or size of the boiler.

QUESTION 419. *What are the proportions of boilers used in locomotives like that which has been illustrated in these articles and represented in Plates I and II?*

Answer. The area of the grate is about 2,100 square inches and the total heating surface about 800 square feet, and the water capacity about 5,000 lbs., and the total weight of the boiler, including all the boiler attachments and appliances for promoting combustion, about 30,000 lbs.

QUESTION 420. *At what speed are such engines usually run?*

Answer. The speed varies so much under different circumstances, that it is impossible to give even approximately the average speed of such engines.

QUESTION 421. *How then can we determine the proper proportions of a boiler for a locomotive intended for any given service?*

Answer. As stated before, this can only be done empirically. The safest method is to select a locomotive which is doing the best service, and learn the average speed at which it runs, the size of its grate and the amount of its heating surface, and its adhesive weight. NOW MULTIPLY THE ABOVE SPEED IN MILES PER HOUR BY THE ADHESIVE WEIGHT OF THE LOCOMOTIVE IN TONS (of 2,000 lbs.) AND DIVIDE THE PRODUCT INTO THE AREA OF THE GRATE IN SQUARE INCHES. THEN MULTIPLY THE ADHESIVE WEIGHT OF THE LOCOMOTIVE FOR WHICH THE BOILER IS TO BE PROVIDED BY ITS SPEED, IN MILES PER HOUR, AND BY THE QUOTIENT OBTAINED ABOVE: THE PRODUCT WILL BE THE AREA OF THE GRATE IN SQUARE INCHES FOR THE NEW ENGINE. To illustrate this, suppose an engine of the dimensions given to run at an average speed of 20 miles per hour. Now, multiplying that speed by the number of tons of adhesive weight and dividing the product into the area of the grate, we have $20 \times 20 = 400$ and $2100 \div 400 = 5.25$. We now want to determine the size of a grate for the boiler of a locomotive with 30 tons adhesive weight and to run at a speed of 15 miles per hour. We therefore multiply 15 by 30 and the product by the above quotient, or $15 \times 30 \times 5.25 = 2{,}362.5 =$ square inches of grate surface for the boiler. The required heating surface can be obtained in a similar way, by substituting it instead of the grate surface in the calculations.

QUESTION 422. *How is the size of locomotive boilers usually limited?*

Answer. By the weight of the locomotive and to some extent by the distance between the rails. It will be found often that it is impossible to make the boiler of the size indicated by a calculation similar to the above without at the same time making the weight of the locomotive and the adhesive weight greater than was assumed. The result of such a calculation indicates, therefore, that too large a proportion of the weight of the locomotive is on the driving-wheels for the speed at which it is intended to work, and that either they should bear less weight or the speed be reduced.

QUESTION 423. *In what respects is the operation of locomotive boilers different from that of nearly all other steam boilers?*

Answer. The amount of steam generated in proportion to the amount of heating surface is much greater in locomotive boilers than in any other kind. To produce combustion which will be sufficiently active to generate the requisite quantity of steam, the fire must be stimulated by the blast created by the exhaust steam to a degree unknown in other kinds of boilers. So rapid is the movement of the products of combustion that a smaller proportion of the heat is imparted to the water contained in the boiler, and consequently a less amount of water is evaporated in proportion to any given amount of fuel than in boilers in which combustion is less violent. The combustion is also less perfect, because the strong draft does not allow time for a perfect combination of the gases which produce combustion.

The supply of steam which a locomotive boiler must furnish is also much more irregular than the demands made upon any other kind of boiler. At one time the fire must be urged to the greatest possible intensity in order to furnish steam enough to pull a train up a steep grade. When the top is reached the demand ceases, and the boiler can be cooled. The load which a locomotive can pull over a given line of road is usually limited by the utmost capacity of the boiler to supply steam at these critical periods.

QUESTION 424. *What relation is there between this irregular action and the size of the boiler?*

Answer. The smaller the boiler, or rather the larger the amount of steam which must be generated in a given time in proportion to the heating surface, the more must the fire be urged; and therefore the smaller the boiler in proportion to the work it must do, the less will be its economy. In order to produce a rapid combustion in a small boiler, it is necessary to contract the exhaust nozzles in order to create a draft strong enough. In doing this the back pressure on the pistons is very much increased, and when the blast becomes very violent a great deal of solid coal is carried through the tubes and escapes at the smoke-stack unconsumed. At the same time large quantities of unconsumed gases escape, because there is not time for combustion to take place in the fire-box. The fact that with a violent draft the flame and smoke are in contact with the heating surface for a sensibly shorter period of time also has its influence; as less heat will be imparted to the water if the products of combustion are only $\frac{1}{100}$ of a second instead of $\frac{2}{100}$ in passing through the tubes.

There is another consideration which should be taken into account in this connection, which is, that if a boiler is so small that it is worked nearly up to its maximum capacity at all times, it will be impossible to accumulate any reserve power in it in the form of water heated to a high temperature to be used as occasion may require. With a boiler having a great amount of heating surface and capacity for carrying a large quantity of water, the latter can be heated at times when the engine is not working hard, and the heat thus stored up in the water can then be used when it is most needed. Thus we will suppose that to pull a train of cars on a level 250 lbs. of steam are consumed per mile. On a grade of 30 feet per mile the resistance will be three times what it is on a level, and therefore three times the quantity of steam will be consumed, so that the boiler must then evaporate 750 lbs. of water per mile. Now to convert 250 lbs. of water heated up to a temperature due to 130 lbs. of effective pressure, or 355.6 degrees, into steam of that pressure will require 216,575 units of heat. If at the same time that this steam is being consumed, we pump into the boiler 250 lbs. of water of a temperature of 60 degrees, 73,900 more units of heat will be needed to raise the water to the temperature due to 130 lbs.

effective pressure, so that on the level part of the road it would be necessary to transmit to the water in the boiler 216,575+73,900=290,475 units of heat in a mile. If there is no room in the boiler for storing a surplus quantity of hot water, it will be necessary on a grade as fast as the steam is consumed to feed an equivalent amount of cold water to take the place of that which was converted into steam, so that on a 30 feet grade it would be necessary to convert at the rate of 750 lbs. of hot water into steam in a mile, which would require 649,725 units of heats, and at the same time heat an equal amount of cold water to a temperature due to the pressure of the steam, which would require 221,700 more units. So that it will be necessary to transmit at the rate of 871,425 units of heat to the water per mile. Now if the boiler was so large that more water could be pumped into it and heated than was used on the level portion of the road, and could there be stored up for future use, the pumps might be either partly or entirely shut off when the engine was working the hardest on the grade. In this way, instead of being obliged to convert hot water into steam, and at the same time heat an equal amount of cold feed-water, there would be a surplus of hot water stored up already heated. It would therefore only be necessary to convert this hot water into steam, which will require a transmission of heat to the water at the rate of 649,725 units of heat instead of 871,425. It must be remembered that on nearly all roads there are certain difficult places which practically limit the capacity of the locomotives on that line. If therefore the capacity of the engines can be increased at those points, their capacity over the whole line is increased.

It will be seen by the above illustration that by having a large boiler it is necessary for it to do very much less work at the critical period, when, as every locomotive runner knows, it is often of the utmost importance to make use of every possible available means in order to pull the trains. It is true that on a very long grade the supply of surplus hot water would soon be exhausted, but even in such cases there is usually one place, owing to a curve or other cause, which is more difficult to surmount than any other, in which case it will be necessary to use more steam for a short time than the locomotive can generate if the boiler is fed continuously. For such cases a surplus of water can be used. But even if the resistance is equal over the whole length of the incline, still the large boiler will have the advantage, because it can at all times generate more steam than a smaller one. It may therefore, we think, safely be assumed that locomotive boilers should always be made as large as the weight of the locomotive will permit.

QUESTION 425. *What effect does the size of the driving-wheels have upon the combustion and evaporation of locomotive boilers?*

Answer. As small wheels make more revolutions in running a given distance than large ones, there will be more strokes of the piston with the former than with the latter, if the locomotive in both cases runs at the same speed. As smaller cylinders are usually employed with small wheels, the blast up the chimney is then composed of a larger number of discharges of steam, but each one of less quantity, than when larger wheels and cylinders are used. In the one case the "puffs" of steam are many and small, and in the latter few and large. If the cylinders are proportioned by the rule which has been given for that purpose, the amount of steam discharged in running any given distance will be the same with engines having large and those with small wheels, the only difference being that it will be subdivided into a greater number of discharges in the one case than in the other. Now, it is found that the draft of engines is much more effective on the fire when the blast is thus subdivided, that is when small wheels and cylinders are used, than it is with large ones, and therefore more steam is generated with the former than with the latter.

QUESTION 426. *What relation is there between the size of the wheels and that of the boiler?*

Answer. As has been explained, the size of the boiler is limited by the weight of the locomotive. The boiler and its attachments of an American locomotive, when the former is filled with water, weigh about half as much as the locomotive; therefore unless we increase the weight of the latter or decrease the weight of the machinery, we can not increase the size of the boiler. Now, large wheels are heavier than small ones; they require larger cylinders, stronger connections, heavier frames, and in fact nearly all the parts of the machinery used with large wheels must be heavier than are required when small wheels are used. Therefore, by decreasing the size of the wheels all the other parts of the engine proper can be made lighter than is possible if large wheels are used, and thus the size and weight of the boiler can be increased without increasing the whole weight of the locomotive. There is of course a practical limit below which the size of the wheels can not be reduced, because the speed of the piston would become so great as to be injurious to the machinery. By reducing the stroke, however, with the diameter of the wheels, the evil referred to may be obviated to a great extent. A cylinder with a large diameter and comparatively small stroke has also the advantage that there is less surface exposed to radiation of heat than there is in a cylinder in which these proportions are reversed.

PART XXII.

DIFFERENT KINDS OF LOCOMOTIVES.

QUESTION 427. *Into what classes may locomotives be divided conveniently?*

Answer. 1. Locomotives for "switching," "shunting" or "drilling" service, that is, for transferring cars from one place to another at stations; 2, for freight traffic; 3, for ordinary passenger traffic, and 4, for suburban or metropolitan railroads, where a great many light trains are run.

QUESTION 428. *What kinds of locomotives are used in this country for switching cars at stations?*

Fig. 220.

Answer. Four-wheeled locomotives similar to that shown in Plate IV. In some cases they are made with six driving-wheels. Engines like that shown in Plate IV have separate tenders, but they are sometimes made so as to carry the water-tank and fuel on the locomotive itself, as shown in fig. 220, and are then called tank locomotives. Fig. 220 represents a switching engine built by the Taunton Locomotive Manufacturing Company.

QUESTION 429. *Why are four-wheeled locomotives used for switching?*

Answer. Because in such service it is constantly necessary to start trains, many of which are very heavy, and therefore a great deal of adhesion is needed. For this reason the whole weight of the locomotive and in the case of tank locomotives that of the water and fuel is placed on the driving-wheels. It is also necessary for such locomotives to run over curves of very short radius and into switches whose angle with the main track is very great, and therefore in order that they may do this and remain on the track, their wheel-bases must be very short, and consequently the wheels are all placed near together between the smoke-box and fire-box.

QUESTION 430. *Why are such locomotives not suited for general traffic?*

Answer. Owing to the shortness of their wheel-bases they become very unsteady at high speeds, and acquire a pitching motion, similar to that of a horse-car when running rapidly over a rough track. This unsteadiness not only becomes very uncomfortable to the men who run the locomotive, but there is danger of the engine running off the track. As nearly all switching is done at very slow speeds, it is not so objectionable for that service as it would be on the "open road"* at high speeds.

* The term "*open road*" is a literal translation from the German, for which there is no corresponding English term, and means the road between stations where trains run fast.

QUESTION 431. *What kinds of locomotives are used for freight service?*

Answer. The greater part of the freight service of this country is performed by locomotives like that selected for the illustrations of these articles, and represented in Plates I, II and III. Such locomotives have been called "American" locomotives because they first originated in this country and are now more generally used here than anywhere else. Side elevations of locomotives of this kind, built by the Baldwin Locomotive Works, the Grant Locomotive Works, the Danforth Locomotive and Machine Company, the Mason Machine Works and the Hinkley Locomotive Works are represented in Plates V, VI, VII, VIII and IX. Such locomotives have been described in the preceding pages.

QUESTION 432. *What are the dimensions of such engines?*

Answer. The principal dimensions of the engines illustrated are given in the table in the appendix, but locomotives of this plan are built of much smaller and also of larger sizes than those represented by the engravings. In some cases such locomotives do not weigh more than 35 or 36,000 lbs., with cylinders from 8 to 12 inches in diameter. In other cases they weigh as much as 66,000 lbs., with cylinders 17 or 18 inches in diameter. The wheels vary from 4 to 6 feet in diameter, but the most common sizes are 4½ and 5 feet

QUESTION 433. *When it is desirable to pull heavier loads than is possible with the adhesive weight that can be placed on four driving-wheels, what is done?*

Answer. One or more pairs of driving-wheels are

added, as in the ten-wheeled locomotive represented in Plate X, the "Mogul" engine, Plate XI, and the "Consolidation" engine, Plate XII. The ten-wheeled locomotive, it will be seen, is similar in construction to an ordinary American locomotive, excepting that it has another pair of driving-wheels in front of the main driving-wheels. It will be seen, however, that it is necessary to keep these close to the latter, because if they are brought further forward they will be too near the back truck-wheels. For this reason a truck consisting of a single pair of wheels, *A, A,* is placed in front of the cylinders, as represented in Plates XI and XII, is now much used. The front driving-wheels are then placed further forward, and thus bear a larger proportion of weight than they do in locomotives like that shown in Plate X.

QUESTION 434. *How are trucks with a single pair of wheels constructed?*

Answer. The truck frame is extended some distance behind the truck-axle, as shown in fig. 221, and the centre-pin, *a,* about which it vibrates, is placed at the back end. The weight of the locomotive, or that portion to be carried on the truck, is then made to rest over the centre of the axle, but in such a way that it can move laterally or crosswise over the track. Such trucks were first made so that the weight of the engine rested on slides on the truck frame, but recently they are nearly always suspended on links, so that they can swing like a pendulum, as shown in figs. 190 and 191. The weight of the engine then rests on the centre-plate, *H H,* which forms part of the plate, *B B.* This is suspended by links, *L L,* represented by dotted lines, which are attached by bolts to the cross-pieces, *m m*, which are fastened to the truck frame. In this way the truck-wheels can move sideways independent of the engine itself. As the wheels and axles, *A A*, must move about the centre-pin, *a*, fig. 221, the axle assumes a radial position to the curves of the track. It does this, too, quite independent of the driving-wheels, as is shown in fig. 221, which represents a

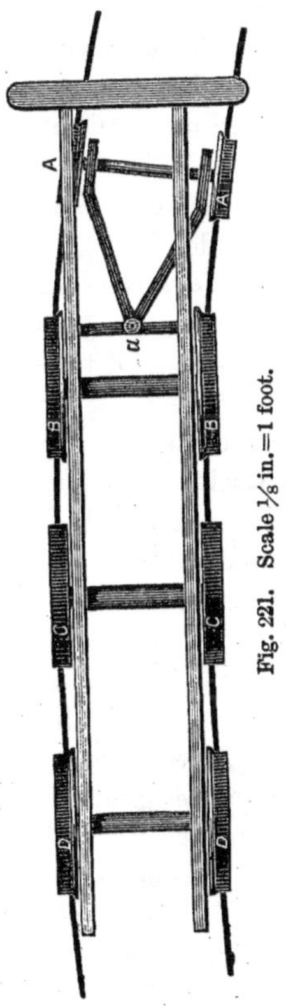

Fig. 221. Scale 1/8 in.=1 foot.

plan of the wheels on a curve. It will be seen that the truck is not at all influenced by the position of the driving-wheels. This arrangement therefore gives great flexibility to the wheel-base, and enables the wheels to adjust themselves to any lateral curvature or alignment of the track.

QUESTION 435. *For what purpose are locomotives like that shown in Plates XI and XII used?*

Answer. "Mogul" locomotives are often used for ordinary freight service where heavy trains must be hauled, and also on steep grades. Consolidation locomotives, represented in Plate XII, which have eight driving-wheels, are employed almost exclusively for traffic over heavy mountain grades.

QUESTION 436. *What other kinds of locomotives are used for freight traffic?*

Answer. Various kinds of tank locomotives, that is, locomotives which have no separate tenders, but carry the water-tanks and fuel on the frame and wheels of the locomotive itself, have been devised and are to some extent used. Plate XIII represents a locomotive of this kind on which the tanks are placed on each side of the boiler, and the fuel on a Bissell truck at the back end. A similar truck is placed at the front end, so that a locomotive of this kind can run equally well either way. The lateral movement of the two trucks also gives great flexibility to the wheel-base, so that such an engine will adjust itself easily to the curvature of the track. If, however, the two pairs of truck-wheels should both stand on an elevated part of the track, and the driving-wheels on a depression, the latter would evidently not carry as much and the truck-wheels would carry more of the weight of the engine than they did on a level part of the track. If the reverse condition of things should occur, that is, if the driving-wheels should be on an elevation and one or both pairs of the truck-wheels on a depression, then the latter would bear less weight than they did and the driving-wheels more. For this reason, in order to distribute the weight evenly on all the wheels, it is necessary to equalize the weight on the truck and driving-wheels, by connecting them with equalizing levers, similar to those which were described in answer to Question 301. These levers distribute any undue weight which may come on one wheel to that next to it. This is important, because if the driving-wheels bore less weight at some times than at others, their adhesion and their capacity to draw loads would be reduced in like proportion.

It is evident, however, that if the water-tank or fuel is carried on the driving-wheels, there will be a greater weight on them when the tank is full than when it is empty, and that therefore there will either be so much weight on the wheels at one time as to be injurious to the rails, or else there will be too little for adhesion at another. Of course cases are conceivable, and doubtless exist in practice, where more adhesion is required to start a train and haul it during the first part of the "run" than will be needed during the latter part. In such cases doubtless the variable character of the weight might be an advantage instead of the reverse, but for ordinary practice a variable load on the driving-wheels would have the disadvantages which have been described. For this reason tank locomotives have been built like that represented in Plate XIV. In this it will be seen that the weight of the water-tank rests on a four-wheeled truck at the back end. A Bissell or two-wheeled truck is, however, placed in front in the same position as in the engine represented in Plate XIII, and carries a portion of the weight of the boiler and machinery.

In order to get all the advantages which a four-wheeled switching engine possesses in having its *whole* weight on the driving-wheels, and at the same time avoid the disadvantages which result from a short wheel-base, and also from a varying amount of weight on the driving-wheels, a locomotive like that represented in Plate XV was designed by the writer with the whole weight of the boiler and machinery resting on the driving-wheels, and the water and fuel on a truck. By this means not only the objections to carrying the weight of the water on the driving-wheels is overcome, but at the same time the disadvantages arising from the short wheel-base of the switching locomotive, Plate IV, are also obviated. That is, all the *permanent weight* of the boiler and machinery of such a locomotive rests on the driving-wheels, and is therefore all *adhesive weight,* as it is in the switching engine, and at the same time by extending the frame beyond the fire-box and placing the water-tank and fuel on this extension of the frame and supporting their weight on a truck, the engine has a wheel-base which is as long and as flexible as that of ordinary American engines, represented in Plates V, VI, VII, VIII and IX, and as the latter have only about *two-thirds* of their weight on the driving-wheels, locomotives like that represented in Plate XV, of the same weight as the others, have fifty per cent. more adhesion, or they may be one-third lighter and have the same adhesion. As was explained in answer to Question 260, if an ordinary American locomotive runs backwards, that is, with the driving-wheels in front, the friction of their flanges against the rails on curves of short radius will be very excessive. To avoid this with locomotives of the design last described, they are run with the truck first, which, being at the opposite end of the boiler from the position which it usually occupies, reverses the position of the boiler and other parts relative to the motion of the engine. That is, the fire-box is then in front and the smoke-stack behind. Engines of this kind have been built and are now working and doing excellent service; but the prejudice which exists against running locomotives in the reverse direction to what has been customary seems to be the chief obstacle in the way of their use.

Another plan which possesses all the advantages of the locomotive described above and is free from the last objection is represented in Plate XVI. This plan was first adopted by Mr. Robert Fairlie in England, but has been introduced into this country and very much improved by Mr. William Mason, of Taunton, Mass. In these locomotives, the driving-wheels and cylinders are attached to a truck frame which turns around a centre-pin like any ordinary truck. The steam and exhaust pipes are connected to the boiler and cylinder with pipes which have flexible joints. By this means the truck can move independently of the boiler, and thus the driving-wheels can adjust themselves to the curvature of the track, just as the wheels of any other truck do, and therefore the driving-wheels can be run ahead just as well as the truck-wheels which carry the tank. This plan possesses the additional advantage that the fire-box can be made as wide and as long as may be desired without interfering with the driving-wheels. The flexible pipes are, however, usually considered an objection; but with the improvements which have been made in their design and construction, the difficulties which were at first encountered have probably been overcome. At any rate if there is no other objection to the use of such locomotives, ingenuity and care should in time overcome that one. Plate XVII represents a locomotive of this plan, with six driving-wheels and a six-wheeled carrying truck under the tank. This latter plan of locomotive is intended for heavy freight traffic.

QUESTION 437. *What kind of locomotives is used for passenger trains?*

Answer. Eight-wheeled American locomotives are used almost exclusively for passenger service. Usually the driving-wheels of such locomotives are larger in diameter than are used for freight traffic. Their size varies from 5 feet to 5 ft. 9 in. in diameter. The locomotive by the Mason Machine Works represented in Plate VIII has $5\frac{1}{2}$ feet driving-wheels. For very heavy express trains locomotives with 17×24 inch cylinders and weighing 34 tons are now used on many through lines.

QUESTION 438. *What is meant by suburban and metropolitan railroads, what is the nature of their traffic, and what kinds of locomotives are needed for it?*

Answer. The traffic of suburban railroads consists chiefly of the transportation of passengers who do business in the city to the latter in the morning and to their homes in the evening. As the largest number of passengers must be carried during a few hours in the morning and evening, it is necessary to run very heavy trains at those times. As the passengers must be distributed at many stations which are near together, it is necessary to stop often; and in order that the average speed may be reasonably fast the trains must run very rapidly between these stations. It is therefore necessary to have heavy locomotives, with more than the usual proportion of adhesive weight, so that the trains can be started quickly without slipping the wheels. The main valves should also have a liberal amount of travel, so that steam will be admitted to and exhausted from the cylinders quickly. In some cases it is thought desirable to have locomotives which will run equally well either way, so that it will not be necessary to turn them around at each end of the "run."

By metropolitan railroads are meant railroads in large cities. They may be divided into two classes, one for carrying freight cars from the outskirts of cities to the warehouses and stores at their business centres, and also from the terminus of one road to that of another. Metropolitan railroads of this kind are usually branches of lines which extend from the city. Locomotives for such traffic must have great tractive power, in order to pull heavy trains, and as the speed is usually slow the wheels and the boiler capacity may be small. They must generally be capable of running through curves of very short radius; and as the traffic is usually carried through streets in close proximity to buildings, the locomotives should be as nearly as possible noiseless. The other class of metropolitan roads is for carrying passengers. The traffic of the latter is similar to that usually carried on horse railroads, and consists almost exclusively of passengers. At present (1874) there are only one or two metropolitan railroads in this country for carrying passengers which are operated by steam power. It seems certain, however, that their use will soon become very general in all large cities. Their traffic will consist of many light trains run at short intervals and at comparatively slow speeds, and therefore very light locomotives are required.

QUESTION 439. *What kinds of locomotives are used for suburban railroads?*

Answer. The ordinary American eight-wheeled locomotive is used more than any other kind; but a number of locomotives like that represented by fig. 222 have been built and are used for this traffic. These have one pair of driving-wheels in front of the main pair and a Bissell truck in front of the cylinder. With this arrangement the driving-wheels bear a larger proportion of weight than they do if arranged on the ordinary American plan with a four-wheeled truck. Another plan is that shown in Plate XVIII. Such engines, as will be seen, have a Bissell truck at each end, and therefore they run equally well either way. In some cases the tanks of such engines are carried on the top and sides of the boiler. When they are obliged to run only a short distance, and a small supply of water is needed, this arrangement answers very well; but it is impossible to carry a large supply of water in this way without overloading the wheels of the locomotive, and at the same time increasing the evils of a varying load on the driving-wheels.

Fig 222.
LIGHT PASSENGER AND FREIGHT LOCOMOTIVE,
BY THE GRANT LOCOMOTIVE WORKS, PATERSON, N. J.

Locomotives like that shown in Plate XIV are also used for suburban traffic. As shown in the engraving they have a four-wheeled truck at one end and one with two wheels at the other, so that it is thought that they can be run safely either way. The four-wheeled truck carries the weight of the water and fuel.

The plan of engine represented by Plate XV is very well adapted for this kind of traffic. Excepting on curves with a very short radius it could be run in either direction at any required speed, without encountering any other difficulty excepting the prejudices of those who run it.

As double-truck locomotives similar to that shown in Plate XVI can adjust themselves to any curve, this objection could not be urged against their use.

QUESTION 440. *What kinds of locomotives are used on metropolitan railroads?*

Answer. For freight traffic ordinary switching locomotives like that represented in Plate IV are often employed. In some cases these have the tanks on the locomotives. It often happens, though, that such traffic must be conducted in the streets of a city, and that the noise, especially of the exhausting steam, is thus liable to frighten horses and disturb the occupants. It is, then, necessary either to condense the exhaust steam or render its escape noiseless, which is done by allowing it to escape into the water-tanks. Street locomotives which have a condenser similar to the surface condensers used on marine engines are used on the Hudson River Railroad in New York. The exhaust steam passes through these and then escapes into the tanks. The latter are long and narrow, so as to expose a great deal of surface to radiation, and in this way cool the water which becomes heated by the steam. The engines have four driving-wheels and vertical boilers. The cylinders are connected to a crank shaft with a pinion on it, which gears with another wheel of larger size on the driving-axle. In this way the speed is reduced and great tractive power can be exerted. The whole of the engine is enclosed so as to hide the machinery, the sight of which is supposed to frighten horses. The engines were designed and patented by Mr. A. F. Smith, formerly Master Mechanic of that road.

For roads in cities carrying passengers almost exclusively, an entirely different class of locomotives is needed. To suit passengers it is of course necessary to run a great many trains at very short intervals. When this is done the trains are necessarily very light, and therefore only light locomotives are needed. Plate XIX represents the locomotives employed on the Greenwich Street Elevated Railroad in New York. These engines weigh only 10,000 lbs., and the wheels are 30 in. diameter and the cylinders 7×10 in. The peculiarity in their construction consists in their having an intermediate shaft between the two pairs of driving-wheels. This shaft has two cranks inside of the frames and two outside. The cylinders are connected to the inside cranks, and the coupling-rods to those on the outside. The water is carried in a tank on top of the boiler. The fuel is anthracite coal.

PART XXIII.

CONTINUOUS TRAIN BRAKES.

Question 441. *What are meant by automatic or continuous train brakes?*

Answer. Continuous train brakes are brakes which can be applied to all the cars of a train by the locomotive runner on the locomotive. In some cases such brakes are arranged in such a way that they can also be applied from any car in the train, or are made self-acting in case of an accident, such as a car getting off the track or a train breaking in two.

Question 442. *What are the principal systems of brakes of this kind in use?*

Answer. What is called, after its inventor, the Westinghouse atmospheric brake is now used more than any other. Next to this, Smith's vacuum brake is used most. Besides these two, Creamer's, Ward's, Loughridge's and Henderson's systems of brakes are used to a limited extent. The two first are, however, the only ones which have come into sufficiently extensive use as yet to justify us in describing them here.

Question 443. *How does the Westinghouse brake act and how is it constructed?*

Answer. As its name indicates, the medium employed for transmitting the power for operating the brakes is atmospheric air.

This is compressed to any required density by a

steam pump which is located between the driving-wheels, or in any other convenient place on the locomotive. This pump is shown in section in fig. 223 and consists of two cylinders, the upper one, *A*, the steam cylinder, the piston of which is connected by its rod with the piston in the lower cylinder, *B*. This latter is operated by the steam piston, and at each

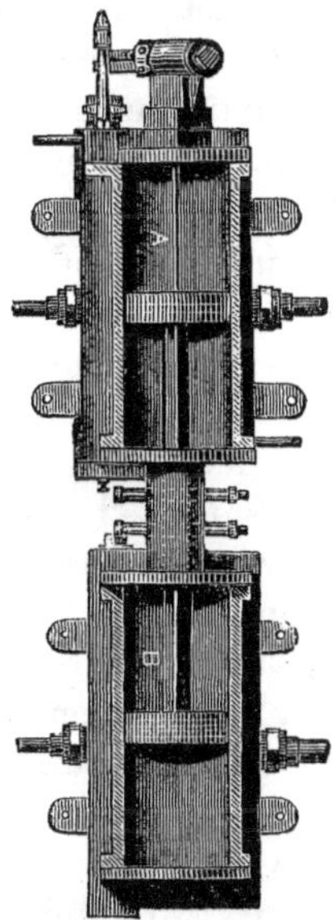

Fig. 223. Scale ½ in.=1 foot.

stroke a quantity of air, equal to the space swept through by the lower piston, is compressed and thus forced into a cylindrical reservoir, which is usually placed under the foot-board of the locomotive, in which it is stored for use at any time when the brakes are to be applied. The air and steam cylinders are supplied with suitable valves for admitting and releasing the air and steam. From this reservoir it is conducted back under the tender and cars by pipes, which are connected together between the engine and tender and between the cars by India rubber hose. Two pieces of hose are attached to the engine and also to each end of the tender and cars, so that in case one piece should break the others will act. Each of these pieces is united or coupled to the corresponding piece opposite to it by a peculiar coupling made for the purpose, so that they can be quickly disconnected if the cars, engine or tender are uncoupled.

Under the tender and also under each car is a cylinder and piston. The compressed air is conducted to this cylinder in front of the piston when the brakes are to be applied. As the piston-rod is connected by a bell crank to the brake levers when the piston is forced out by the pressure of the air, the brakes are at once applied to the wheels. As the reservoir under the foot-board is connected by the pipes which have been described with the cylinders under each car and the tender, by simply opening communication between the reservoir and the pipes, the air at once rushes from the reservoir back through the whole length of the train, and so rapid is its motion and quick its action that only a second or two intervenes between the opening of communication and the application of the brakes. To relieve or "let off" the brakes it is only necessary to close the reservoir cock and open communication from the air-pipes to the external atmosphere, when the compressed air in the brake cylinders will escape, and the springs ordinarily used on car brakes will cause the pistons to resume their former positions.

For the purpose of opening the connection from the reservoir to the brake cylinder, and closing this connection and opening one from the latter to the external air, a single three-way cock is commonly used. This is arranged at such a point as to be under the control of the engineer, so that he can at pleasure turn

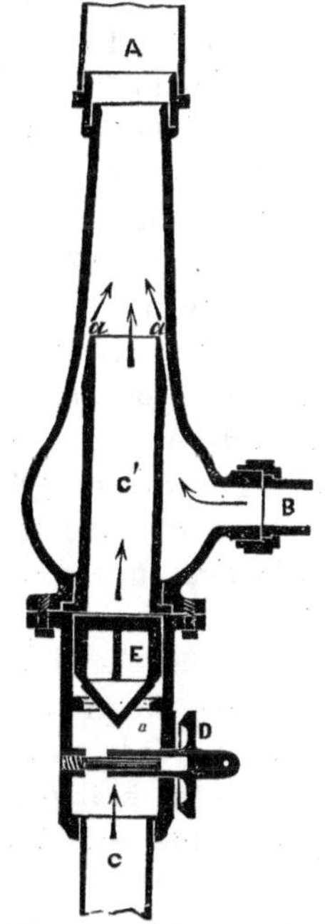

Fig. 224. Scale 1½ inch=1 foot.

on the compressed air with any degree of force, instantaneously, or slowly, or with a varying power, or by another turn of the cock let it off as freely, still keeping it under the same complete control.

QUESTION 444. *How does the vacuum brake act and how is it constructed?*

Answer. The power is applied to the brakes of the cars in this system by exhausting instead of compressing the air. This is done by means of an ejector, of which fig. 224 is a section. This operates somewhat like an injector. Steam is admitted into the pipe *B*, and escapes through the annular or circular opening *a a*. The effect of this is to create what is called an "induced current," or to draw the air from the pipe *C' C*, which, with the steam, escapes at *A*. This produces a partial vacuum in the pipe *C*, which extends back under the cars. The pipes under the cars are connected together by rubber hose, which are prevented from collapsing by coils of wire inside. Under the tender and under each car are India rubber cylinders with cast iron ends, one fastened to the car and the other movable. The rubber cylinders can be extended or compressed somewhat like the bellows of an accordeon. The rubber is supported by iron rings inside, placed from 4 to 6 inches apart, so as to prevent them from collapsing when the air is exhausted from them. When this is done the pressure on the movable cast iron end draws it towards the fixed one, and by attaching the former to the brake levers by a rod, the force of the pressure on the head is communicated to the brakes.

The ejector is placed on top of the boiler, and when the brakes are to be applied the locomotive runner opens a valve, which admits steam into the ejector, which instantly begins to produce a partial vacuum and thus apply the brakes. When the pressure of the brakes is to be released, the release valve, *D*, is opened, which admits air into the pipe, *C*, through which it is conducted back to each of the India rubber cylinders, and thus counteracts the pressure on the ends and releases the brakes.

Both the atmospheric and the vacuum brakes have recently been applied to the driving-wheels of locomotives with very excellent results.

PART XXIV.

PERFORMANCE AND COST OF OPERATING LOCOMOTIVES.

QUESTION 445. *What is the cost of operating ordinary locomotives per mile run?*

Answer. The average cost at the present time (1874) is from 20 to 25 cents per mile.*

QUESTION 446. *What items of cost are included in this, and what proportion do they each bear to the total cost?*

Answer. The items of cost and the percentage of each to the whole expense of operating locomotives, and also to the total of all the expenses of operating locomotives are given in the following table:

	Approximate average cost per mile run.	Percentage of total cost of operating locomotives.	Percentage of total cost of all the operating expenses of railroads.
Fuel	6.0 cts.	0.30	.03
Oil and waste	0.4 cts.	0.02	.004
Wages of locomotive runners and firemen	6.0 cts.	0.30	.06
Repairs of locomotives	7.0 cts.	0.35	.07
Cleaning locomotives	0.6 cts.	0.03	.006
Total	20.0 cts.	1.00	.20

From this table it will be seen that the locomotive

* Deducting 10 per cent. from this amount will give very nearly the gold value of the cost. The figures given above represent the cost in the depreciated promises to pay of the United States Government.

expenses are 20 per cent. of the whole cost of operating railroads. This cost of course varies under different circumstances. The above is probably somewhat lower than the average cost in this country.

QUESTION 447. *How many miles do locomotives ordinarily run per ton of coal and per cord of wood?*

Answer. This also varies greatly under different circumstances. An average taken from the monthly reports of 52 different roads gives 38 miles run per ton of coal, and an average from the reports of 16 roads gives 47½ miles run per cord of wood. No deductions should, however, be made from this of the relative value of wood and coal for fuel, because the trains which are run with wood for fuel are usually lighter than those hauled with coal-burning engines. The above figures are the average results during the month of May, 1871, of all the trains on the roads from whose locomotive reports it has been compiled. The following report of experiments, which were carefully made by the writer, will give the performance of a locomotive when great care is taken to produce good results. It should be stated, however, that the engine with which these experiments were made had been in service eighteen months, without receiving thorough repairs, and that the boiler at times primed badly, so that the rate of evaporation of water per pound of coal is not a fair indication of the performance of the engine in that respect. The coal used was known as Brazil coal, from Indiana, and in order to compare the performance of two engines only lumps of coal were used, so as to leave no room for question regarding the relative amount of fine coal used by each engine. The maximum grades on the road on which the experiments were made were 30 feet per mile, and the total ascent from the lowest to the highest point on the road was 374 feet.

LOCOMOTIVE EXPERIMENTS.

	1873.	1873.	1873.
Date of experiment	July 21.	July 28.	August 2.
Number of miles run	145	145	145
Number of cars hauled	41	31	41
Total weight of cars, lbs.	1,497,240	1,119,650	1,508 860
Total amount of coal burned, lbs. . .	8 676	5,102	7,221
Total am'nt of water consumed, lbs .	63.531	45.719	52,609
Water evaporated per lb. of coal, lbs. .	7.32	8.02	7 04
Miles run per ton (of 2,000 lbs.) of coal .	33.4	50 8	38 8
Coal consumed per car per mile, lbs. .	1 45	1.13	1 21
Average speed, including stops, miles .	11.1	13	13 8

QUESTION 448. ***How can we determine the speed at which an engine is running?***

Answer. In the absence of any special instruments for the purpose, BY COUNTING THE NUMBER OF REVOLUTIONS OF THE DRIVING-WHEELS PER MINUTE, THEN MULTIPLYING THE LENGTH OF THEIR CIRCUMFERENCE IN INCHES BY THE NUMBER OF THEIR REVOLUTIONS PER MINUTE AND THE PRODUCT BY 60, AND DIVIDING THE LAST PRODUCT BY 63,360. THE QUOTIENT WILL BE THE SPEED IN MILES PER HOUR. Thus, supposing driving-wheels which are $61\frac{1}{2}$ in. in diameter, and whose circumference is therefore 193.2 in., should make 164 revolutions per minute, then $193.2 \times 164 \times 60 \div 63{,}360 = 30$, (nearly) miles per hour.

PART XXV.

WATER-TANKS AND TURN-TABLES.

QUESTION 449. *How are locomotive tenders or tanks supplied with water?*

Answer. At suitable points, called *water stations*, along the line of the road, large tanks or reservoirs are

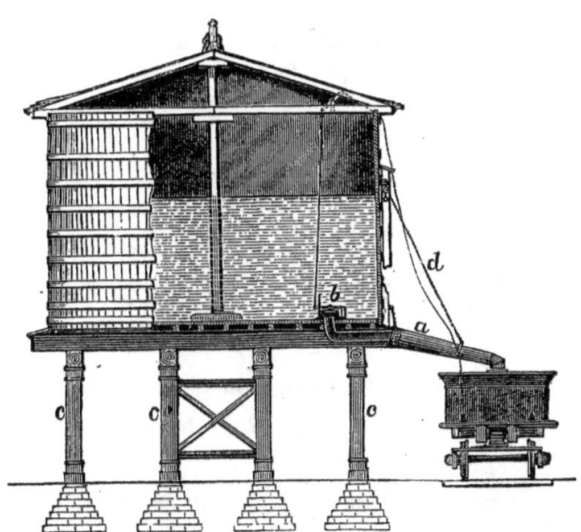

Fig. 225. Scale $\frac{1}{16}$ in.=1 foot.

located, which are filled either from a natural stream which is higher than the tank and thus flows into the latter, or else the water is pumped in, either by hand or by horse, wind, water or steam power.

These tanks are usually, when there is room for them, located near the track, as shown in fig. 225, so that the water can be conducted by a spout, *a*, direct from the tank to the man-hole of the tender. Communication to and from this spout is opened and closed by a valve, *b*, inside of the tank. The spout is usually attached to the tank by a hinged joint, so that it can be lowered to the tender and then raised up out of the way of the engine and train. It is generally balanced by a counterweight, suspended to one end of a rope, which passes over a pulley and is fastened to the spout at the other end. Such tanks are now generally made of wooden staves like a tub or pail, and supported on a heavy frame, *c c c*, made of wood, as shown in the engraving, or on stone or brick masonry.

Fig. 226. Scale $\frac{1}{16}$ in.=1 foot.

When there is no room for the tank or reservoir near the track, it is placed in any convenient position at some distance from it, and the water is then conveyed by an underground pipe to the place where the locomotive must take water. At the end of this pipe what is called a *water-crane*, fig. 226, is located. This consists of a vertical pipe, *A*, with a horizontal arm, *B*, which is made so as to swing around over the man-hole of the tender when the latter is to be filled with water. In some cases the horizontal arm alone swings around, but in others the vertical pipe turns with the horizontal one in a joint, *C*, underneath the surface of the ground. The latter plan is thought to be preferable to the first, as the pipe is less liable to freeze fast in the joint when the latter is underground than when it is exposed above. A suitable valve, *D*, is also attached to the pipe below ground, so that the stream of water can be turned off or on at pleasure by the wheel *E*.

QUESTION 450. *What considerations should determine the source from which a supply of water should be drawn?*

Answer. The first must of course be its convenience to the point where the water is to be used; but more attention should be given to the quality of the water than it ordinarily receives, as the use of impure water, or that which contains a considerable amount of mud or solid matter mixed with it, or in suspension as it is called, or has lime or other mineral substances chemically combined with it, will very soon coat the inside of the boiler with a covering of scale, which is a very bad conductor of heat, and consequently the boiler is much less efficient and much more heat is wasted than if the heating surfaces were clear. Besides this loss of efficiency, when boiler plates are covered with non-conducting scale, they are much more liable to be injured by the action of the fire than when the water comes directly in contact with the metal of the plates. Some water, too, has a corroding effect on the metal of the boiler which is very destructive.

QUESTION 451. *How can the relative amount of in-*

crustating substances in different kinds of water be determined?

Answer. The relative quantity of solid matter or mud which is held in suspension can be at least approximately determined by simply filling vessels, say large clear glass bottles, with different kinds of water and letting them stand for some time until the solid matter settles to the bottom.

An easy method of precipitating the lime and some other salts which are held in solution and which will not settle until they are converted into a solid form is the following: Dissolve in a goblet of pure water (distilled or freshly caught rain water) two or three teaspoonfuls of the *oxalate of ammonia.* Have equal quantities, say a goblet-full of each of the waters to be tested, ranged side by side and marked so as to be identified. Into each of these goblets stir equal quantities of the solution mentioned—about three teaspoonfuls will be enough—and let them stand for a day. The lime and some other salts will be precipitated and fall to the bottom as a powder; and the quantity of this precipitate in each glass will form a very good index of its relative injuriousness in the formation of scale.

When the oxalate of ammonia cannot easily be procured, an experiment may be tried, in the same way, by dissolving common white soap, or other pure soap, in a goblet of pure water, and then stirring into the glasses of water to be tested a few teaspoonfuls of this solution. The comparative amount of lime in the water will be shown by the amount of coagulated matter which will be thrown down.*

*Correspondent of the Railroad Gazette.

QUESTION 452. *How are locomotives turned around on the track?*

Answer. The most common means employed for that purpose is a *turn-table*, fig. 227. This consists of two heavy beams made of wood, cast or wrought iron, placed side by side and resting on a pivot in the centre, on which they turn. They are placed in a circular pit below the level of the track, so that when rails are laid in the ordinary way on top of the beams they will be exactly level with the track which leads up to the pit. By turning the beams on the central pivot so that the rails will come exactly in line with the permanent track which leads up to the pit, the locomotive can be run on the turn-table, which is then revolved a half-revolution, which of course reverses the position of the locomotive and brings it opposite

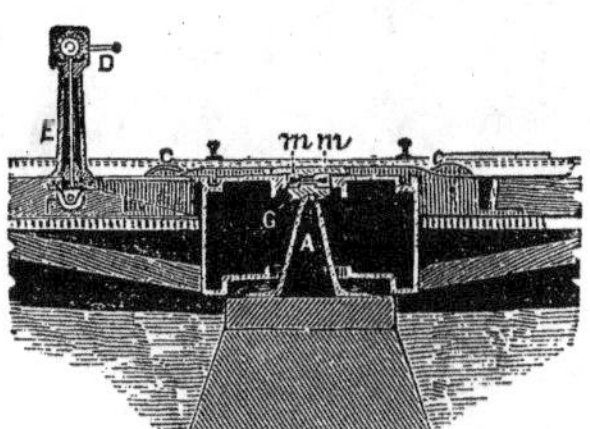

Fig. 228. Scale $\frac{3}{32}$ in.=1 foot.

the permanent track so that it can be run off from the table. In order to prevent the beams from tipping down when the engine first runs on or off of the turn-table, wheels are placed at their outer ends which run on a circular track and bear any inequality of weight that may be thrown on them if the locomotive is not equally balanced on the central pivot.

QUESTION 453. *How is the central pivot constructed?*

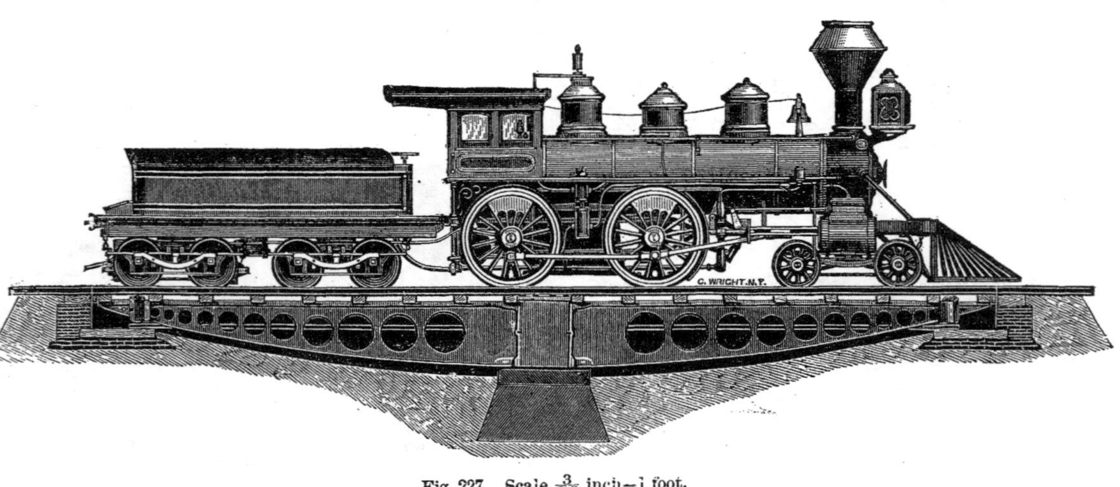

Fig. 227. Scale $\frac{3}{32}$ inch = 1 foot.

50-FOOT TURN-TABLE, BY WILLIAM SELLERS & CO., PHILADELPHIA.

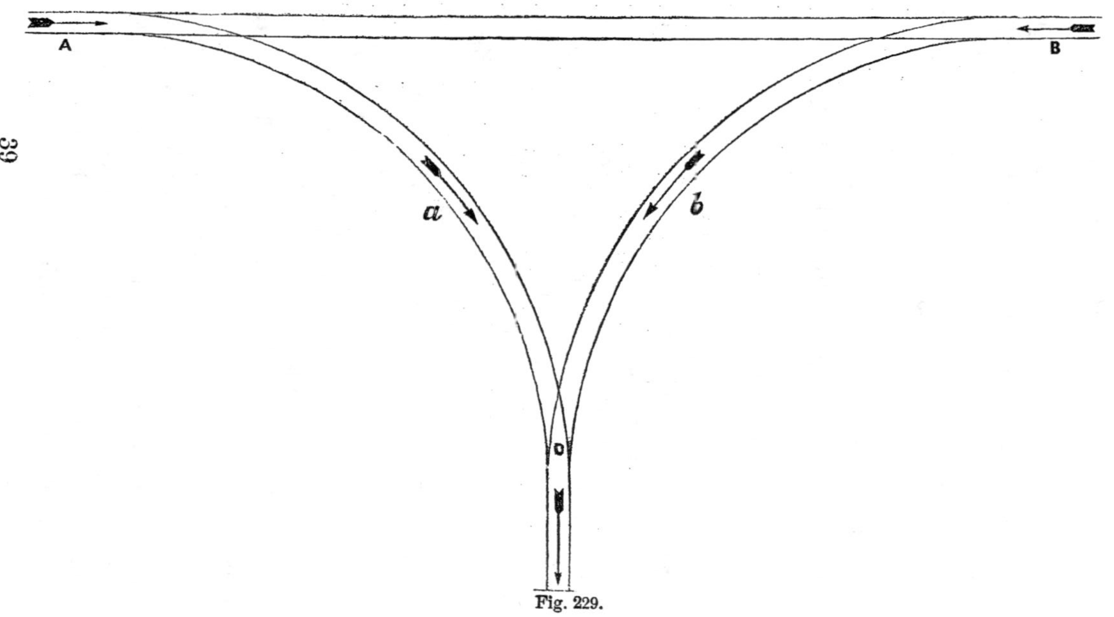

Fig. 229.

Answer. It usually consists of a vertical post, *A*, shown in fig. 228, which is a transverse section through the centre of the turn-table, the end of which rests on hard cast iron or steel bearings. In some cases, as shown in figs. 227 and 228, which represent a turn-table built by William Sellers & Co., of Philadelphia, the weight rests on conical steel rollers, *m m*, which revolve in a circular path formed in the top plates. Sometimes turn-tables are fitted with gearing and cranks, *D*, fig. 228; but if they are made so that the whole weight rests on the centre, and if they are of sufficient length so that an engine and tender can be moved on them sufficiently to be balanced over the centre, gearing will not be needed; but a simple lever fastened to the turn-table will be all that will be required to turn the table and the engine and tender on it. The tables should be of such a diameter or length across the centre as will enable the class of engine in use on any road to be balanced. With light engines the 50-feet table is large enough; with the long, heavy engine now used on the great trunk lines, the engine and tender quite fill up the entire length of 50 feet, leaving no margin for adjustment. In such cases, the 54 feet, 56 feet, or, better, the 60 feet, should be employed. These large tables are also made heavier in proportion. The table should be of such a length that engines, with tender either empty or full, when run on the table can be so placed as to bring the centre of gravity immediately over the centre. When so balanced, one man can turn the loaded table with ease.

In setting up turn-tables it is necessary that the foundation at centre, upon which the pivot rests, should be of the most substantial character, so as not to be liable to settle. The circular track, which may be made of light rails, say 28 or 30 lbs. to the yard, should be level, and the table should be so adjusted as to swing clear of the circular track when loaded. The pit required is quite shallow near the edge and deepens towards the centre. Provision is made for covering the entire pit by a platform turning with the table, but this should be avoided whenever possible, as the best constructed cover does offer some resistance in turning. Even in roundhouses, where a covered pit might be considered preferable as presenting a smooth floor for crossing in any direction, it has been found advisable, in view of the greatest ease in turning and the facility offered by the open pit for cleaning, to dispense with the cover. The centre upon which the table turns is constructed of the best cast steel, and consists of conical rollers of steel between two steel plates grooved out to receive these rollers. This part of the table must be kept clean and well oiled, say with best sperm or lard oil and tallow of such a consistency as not to harden in cold weather. The top cap at centre is held in place by a circle of bolts. These bolts take the entire weight of the table and load; by slacking off the bolts the table can be lowered on the wheels on the circular track and the cap lifted off to gain access to the plates and rollers. These should be opened, examined and cleaned at least once every three months.

Under the cap and between it and the top of the centre box are segments of wood. These can be altered in thickness to bring the table in proper adjustment. If the centre foundation settles, these segments should be thinned sufficiently to enable the table to be screwed up to a proper height. With proper care such tables are practically indestructible.*

QUESTION 454. *Is there any other method of turning locomotives?*

Answer. Yes; what is called a Y is sometimes used. This consists of a system of tracks laid somewhat in the form of the letter Y, as shown in fig. 229, in which *A B* is the main track, with two curves, *A C* and *B C*, laid as shown. If now it is desired to turn a locomotive which is standing in the position of the dart *A*, it is run on the curve *A C* to the position of the darts *a* and *C*. It is then run backward from *C* on the curve *C B*, as represented by the dart *b*, and when it reaches the main track in the position of the dart *B* it is evident that its position will be reversed, as is shown if we compare the direction of the dart *A* with that of *B*.

---

* Wm. Sellers & Co.

PART XXVI.

INSPECTION OF LOCOMOTIVES.

QUESTION 455. *What are the principal divisions of the work of operating or running a locomotive?*

Answer. They are: 1. Inspection and lubrication; that is, an examination of the parts to see that they are in good working order, and the application of oil to the journals and other parts subjected to wear. 2. Setting the engine in motion and starting the locomotive and train. 3. Management while running. 4. Stopping the engine and train. 5. Laying up. 6. Management in case of accident. 7. Cleaning the engine.

QUESTION 456. *When the locomotive is inspected, what should be especially observed about the boiler?*

Answer. In the first place, all new boilers should be tested by pressure before being used, and ALL boilers, whether new or old, SHOULD BE TESTED PERIODICALLY. The oftener the better. The ways of applying the pressure test are: 1, the cold-water test, that is, by filling the boiler with cold water and then forcing in an additional quantity with a force-pump so as to raise the pressure to that at which it is intended to test the boiler; 2, the warm-water test, by filling the boiler entirely full of cold water and then kindling a fire in the grate so as to warm this water. As water expands about one twenty-fourth in rising from 60 to

212 degrees, the rise in temperature will cause a corresponding increase in pressure; 3, by steam pressure.

If the latter method were not so commonly used, it would seem the height of madness to test a boiler—which is neither more nor less than an attempt to explode it—in the shop where it is built or repaired, and where the results of an explosion would be more disastrous and fatal than anywhere else, in order to see whether it will explode when put into service on the line of the road. The danger of explosion is also increased at such times by hammering and caulking at leaky rivets and joints.* It would seem, therefore, very much more rational to test boilers first by hydraulic pressure. For a first test this is preferable, because cold water will leak through crevices which would be tight when the boiler is heated, so that leaks can be more surely detected with cold than with warm or hot water. It is, however, doubtless true that boilers are often strained much more by the unequal expansion of the different parts than by the actual pressure. It is therefore thought that after the hydraulic test has been applied the second or warm-water test should be used. This can be easily done, as the boiler must be filled full of water for the first test. When the boiler is subjected to the test pressure, it should be carefully examined to see whether any indications of weakness are revealed. Any material change of form or any very irregular change of pressure is indicative of weakness The flat stayed surfaces should be carefully examined by applying a straight edge to them before and after they are subjected to pressure,

* Wilson on Boiler Construction.

to see whether they change their form materially. One of the greatest dangers and most common accidents to locomotive boilers, as has been pointed out in a previous chapter, is the breaking of stay-bolts, to detect which, a locomotive runner and master mechanic should exercise constant vigilance. While the pressure is on, the outside surface of the boiler should be thoroughly examined with slight blows of a hammer, which will often reveal a flaw in the metal or a defect in workmanship. After the hydraulic and warm-water tests have been applied, the boiler should be emptied, and the inside examined carefully to see whether any of the stays and braces have been broken or displaced by the test. After this has been done, and not until then, should steam be generated in the boiler. In making the latter test it would doubtless be more safe to employ a pressure somewhat lower than that employed with the cold and warm water. There is great diversity of opinion regarding the maximum pressure which should be employed in testing boilers. It is doubtless true that a weak boiler might be injured and thus made dangerous by subjecting it to a very severe pressure, while without such a test it would have been safe. Recent experiments have indicated, however, that in most cases the ultimate strength of material is actually increased by subjecting it to a strain which even *exceeds* the elastic limit, provided such a strain is imposed only a few times. Although no absolute rule can be given to govern all such cases, it is thought that for the hydraulic and warm-water tests, a pressure about 50 per cent. greater and for the steam test 25 per cent. greater than the maximum working pressure should be employed.

Before old boilers are tested, they should be very carefully examined, both inside and outside, to see whether they are injuriously corroded. It is to be regretted that the insides of locomotive boilers are usually made so difficult of access that it is impossible to discover the extent and the effects of corrosion without the most careful examination. This is not possible without getting inside of the boiler. Whenever this can be done, a prudent locomotive runner should use the opportunity of inspecting the boiler of his engine himself, and not depend upon the boiler-makers who are employed for that purpose. He should remember that it is his life and not theirs which is exposed to danger by any weakness or defect in the construction of the boiler of the locomotive which he runs.

Before starting the fire in a locomotive, the fire-box should be carefully examined to see if there are any indications of leaks, which will often reveal cracked plates, defective stay-bolts or flues. If the latter simply leak at the joints, they can generally be made tight by caulking or the use of the tube expander. This is easily done when the engine is cold, but if not attended to may be very troublesome on the road. Leaks at other parts of the boiler should be examined, as they may reveal dangerous fractures.

It is of the utmost importance, both for safety and for economy of working, that boilers should be kept clean, that is, free from mud and incrustation. In some sections of the country, especially in the Western States, this is the greatest evil against which locomotive runners and those having the care of locomotives must contend. The cures which have been proposed are numberless, but that which is now chiefly relied upon is, first, the use of the best water that can be procured, and second, frequent and thorough washing out of the boiler.

QUESTION 457. *What sort of examination should be given to the boiler attachments?*

Answer. It should be observed whether the grate-bars or drop-doors of the grate are properly fastened, and whether the ashes have been cleaned out of the ash-pan, and also whether the fire is clean, that is, whether the grates are free from cinders or clinkers. The height of water in the boiler should be observed by testing it with the gauge-cocks and by noticing it in the glass gauge, if one of the latter is used. It is also well to blow out the sediment and mud from the latter before starting, and to see that the valves which admit steam and water to the glass are open. They should, however, be opened only a very short distance, so that only a small quantity of steam or hot water will escape in case the glass tube should be broken. The injector, if one is used, should be tested to see that it is in working order, and as soon as the engine starts out of the engine house both of the pumps should also be tested, in order to see whether they are in good working condition. The safety-valves should be raised, so as to be sure that they are not rusted or otherwise fastened to their seats. There is no part of a locomotive more liable to disorder than the steam gauge. For this reason it should be frequently tested, and whenever there is any indication of irregularity in its action it should be examined. As the wire netting on the smoke-stack often has holes cut into it by the action of the sparks, it should be frequently examined to see whether it is in good condition. It is also liable to be "gummed up," especially if too much oil is used in lubricating the cylinders and valves. As soon as holes are cut into the netting there is danger that the sparks which escape will set fire to the combustible material near the track, and if the netting is gummed up the draft will be obstructed and the engine will not make steam. The gummy matter can often be removed by building a wood fire on top of the netting. In this way the oil in the gummy matter is burned up, which leaves a dry material which can then, at least to some extent, be beaten out of the netting.

QUESTION 458. *How can it be known whether the pumps are working well?*

Answer. Their operation is indicated by the force of the stream which escapes from the pet-cock when it is open. When the pump is in good condition the water begins to escape promptly in a strong stream as soon as the pump-plunger begins its inward stroke, and continues to escape until the plunger completes its stroke. If the pump is not in good condition, this escaping stream is weak and is apt to continue during the outward stroke of the pump-plunger. It is difficult to tell, however, when the engine is running slowly, whether the pump will work well at higher speeds, and therefore a locomotive runner should always test the condition of the pumps during the previous run.

QUESTION 459. *What should be noticed in connection with the throttle-valve?*

Answer. As a failure of the throttle-valve to work may be the cause of a most serious accident, it should be certain that it is in good working condition, that all the bolts, pins and screws and other accessories are in good working order. It should also be known whether the throttle-valve is steam-tight. This can be learned by observing whether steam escapes from the exhaust-pipes or cylinder-cocks when the latter are open, the reverse lever in full gear, and the throttle-valve closed. If the throttle-valve leaks, enough steam may accumulate in the cylinder, when there is no one on the engine, to start it, and in this way cause a serious accident. The throttle-lever should always be fastened with a set-screw or latch of some kind when the engine is standing still.

QUESTION 460. *In inspecting the cylinders, pistons, guides and connecting-rods, to what points should the attention be directed?*

Answer. It should be known whether the piston packing is properly set out, that is, whether it is so tight that it will not "*blow through,*" or leak steam from one end of the cylinder to the other, which of course will waste a great deal of steam. Of the two evils, it is, however, better to have piston-packing too loose than too tight, because if it is too tight, it is liable to cut or scratch the cylinders so as to make it necessary to rebore them, and at the same time if the packing-rings are lined with Babbitt metal, the heat created by the intense pressure and friction will melt the metal. In some cases the cylinders become heated to so high a temperature from this cause that the wood-lagging with which they are covered on the outside is burned.

The packing of the piston-rods should be steam-tight, and it should be observed whether the rod and the pump-plunger are securely attached to the cross-head.

The utmost care must be exercised to keep the guides well oiled. The oil cups on the guide-rods or cross-heads, when they are placed on the latter, must be kept clean, so that the oil will flow freely, and yet not too rapidly, on the surfaces exposed to friction. The same thing is true of the oil-cups on the connecting-rods. Attention should be given to the brass bearings of the connecting-rods to see that they are not so loose as to thump, nor keyed so tight on the crank as to be liable to heat. The latter can be easily known by moving the stub-end lengthwise of the journal. They should never be so tight that they cannot be thus moved with the hand. Especial attention should be given to seeing that all the bolts and nuts on the connecting-rods are tight. There are no parts of a locomotive which require more careful attention in order to keep them lubricated, and thus prevent them from heating and being "cut," than the bearings on the crank-pins and the slides of the cross-head. Examination should be made to see that neither the piston-rods, pump-plungers, guides, connecting-rods nor crank-pins are bent or sprung.

QUESTION 461. *How can it be known whether the piston-packing is too loose or "blows through?"*

Answer. It can usually be noticed in the sound of the exhaust, which can be heard very distinctly on the foot-board when the furnace door is opened. If the packing is not tight, it produces a peculiar wheezing sound between and after each discharge of steam. If the packing leaks, it will also be indicated by the escape of steam from *both* the cylinder-cocks, if they are open, just after the crank passes the dead point. This will usually show in which of the cylinders the packing is too loose. The same thing will occur, however, if either or both of the main valves leak, so that it is often hard to determine whether the "blow" is due to a leak from the valve or from the piston. Of course, it may sometimes happen that both leak, or that the piston on one side and the valve on the other leak, so that often the diagnosis of the disease, as the doctors say, is extremely difficult. Careful observation and experience will, however, aid a locomotive runner in detecting such defects much more than any directions which can be given here.

QUESTION 462. *What is meant by "setting out packing," and how should it be done?*

Answer. "*Setting out packing*" is simply expanding the rings when they get too loose. With ordinary spring packing, figs. 96 and 97, which is now generally used, this is done by screwing up the nuts *b, b, b,* which, as was explained in answer to Question 169, compresses the springs *a, a, a,* and thus expands the rings *A, A.* In doing this, as already stated, great care must be exercised not to screw the nuts up too hard, and it is always better to have the packing too loose than too tight. Care must also be taken to keep the piston-rod in the centre of the cylinder, otherwise there will be undue pressure and wear on the stuffing-box. After the nuts are screwed up, the position of the piston-head should be tested with a pair of callipers. This is done by placing one leg of the callipers against the side of the cylinder, and setting them so that the other leg will just touch the edge of the projection *E,* fig. 96, or the end of the piston-rod. Then by placing the callipers above and below, and on each side of the piston, it will appear whether it is too high or too low or too near either side; then by loosening the nuts on one side and tightening them on the other it can be moved to a central position. Ordinarily this work is intrusted to persons who are employed for the purpose. A young locomotive runner, fireman or mechanic will, however, always do well to familiarize himself with such duties, and, if possible, do it himself, under the direction of those who are skilled in that kind of work.

QUESTION 463. *If the stuffing-box of the piston-rod leaks, what should be done?*

Answer. If the packing in it is in good condition, it can usually be made tight by simply screwing up the gland. In doing this, the nuts on the bolts should not be screwed up more than is necessary to make the packing steam-tight. Any greater pressure only increases the friction on the piston-rod unnecessarily. In doing this, the two bolts must be screwed up equally, otherwise the gland will be "canted," that is, inclined so as to "bind" or bear unequally and very hard against the piston-rod, and thus be liable to cut or scratch it. After packing has been in the stuffing-box a long time, it becomes very hard and compact, and sometimes partly charred. Then either it must be removed and new packing be put in, or, if in tolerably good condition, it can often be made to work well by simply reversing it, that is, by putting that which was at the bottom of the stuffing-box on top and *vice versa*. Before packing is put into a stuffing-box, the former should always be thoroughly oiled.

QUESTION 464. *When the slides of the cross-heads wear, how is the lost motion taken up?*

Answer. When there are gibs on the cross-head, the lost motion can be taken up by putting "*liners*" or "*shims*," that is, thin pieces of metal, between them and the cross-head, so that they will fill up the space between the guide-bars. When there are no gibs, the guide-bars must be taken down, and the blocks between them at each end must be reduced in thickness so as to bring the bars nearer together. In doing this, great care must be taken that the guides are accurately "in line" with the centre line or axis of the cylinder. This work should never be intrusted to any excepting skilled workmen, from whom those who are inexperienced should seek instruction.

QUESTION 465. *When the brass bearings of the connecting-rods become too loose on their journals, what should be done?*

Answer. They must be taken down, and the two surfaces in contact must be filed away so as to bring them closer together. In doing this they must be filed square with the other surfaces, otherwise they will not bear equally on the journals when they are keyed up. Before attaching them permanently to the rods, they should be keyed on the journal in the strap alone, so that it can be known by trial whether they move freely and yet are tight enough to prevent thumping on the journal. When they are attached to the rod, it is very important, especially with coupling or parallel-rods, that the correct length from centre to centre of the bearings be maintained. It is much better to leave coupling-rods loose on their journals, because, if the bearings are keyed up tight, the rods are sure to throw an enormous strain on the crank-pins, as the distance between the centres of the axles is not always absolutely the same, owing to the rise and fall of the axle-boxes in the jaws. It is therefore always best to have a little play in the coupling-rods, and it is safe to say that much more mischief is done by meddling with the coupling-rod brasses than by neglecting them.

QUESTION 466. *What part of the valve gear should receive attention when the engine is inspected?*

Answer. All the bolts, nuts and keys should be carefully examined to see that they are properly fastened. The bolts and nuts in the eccentric straps are especially liable to become loose, and as they are between the wheels, and therefore not easy of access, are often neglected. The oil-holes should all be seen to be clear, otherwise it will be impossible to keep the journals well oiled. The eccentric straps and the link blocks are very liable to be imperfectly oiled, and when the former become dry and cut, they throw a great strain on the eccentric-rods, which is liable to break them. When this occurs the strap and the portion of the rod which is attached to it revolve with the eccentric, and frequently a hole is thus knocked into the front of the fire-box, which disables the engine. The valve gear is, with the exception, perhaps, of the pumps and injector, the most delicate part of the locomotive, and more liable to get out of order than any other, and should therefore be watched with the greatest care.

QUESTION 467. *How can it be known whether the main valves of a locomotive are tight?*

Answer. As already indicated, the symptoms which manifest themselves when a valve leaks are very similar to those which appear when the piston packing leaks. If the valve is moved to its middle position and steam is admitted into the steam-chest, and it then escapes from both cylinder-cocks, it is apparent that the valve is not tight. But the valve faces of locomotives usually wear concave, because the valves are worked most about half-stroke, so that they will often be tight when in the centre of the face, but will leak at the ends of the full stroke. This will become apparent by the peculiar wheezing sound, already referred to, when the engine is at work. As has been explained, it is, however, often very difficult to determine whether this sound is due to a leak at the pistons or the valves. If the packing of the valve-stem leaks, it can be remedied in the manner described for making that of the piston-rod tight.

QUESTION 468. *To what points of the running gear should attention be directed during inspection?*

Answer. All the wheels of the engine and tender should be carefully examined to see that they are sound. A fracture in a driving-wheel is usually apparent if the wheel is carefully examined. The condition of ordinary cast iron tender and truck-wheels is revealed on striking them with a hammer, when if they are sound they will give out a peculiar clear ring; whereas if they are fractured, the sound produced by the blow of the hammer will be dead, like that of a cracked bell. The flanges of the wheels should also receive attention to see that they are not broken, as such a fracture is not always revealed by the sound produced by a blow from a hammer. The axles too should be examined to see that the wheels have not worked loose on the wheel-seat. When this occurs it often becomes apparent by the oil from the axle-boxes working through between the hubs of the wheel and the axle. This can be observed on the outside of the wheels when the bearings are inside, and inside the wheels when the bearing is outside.

The springs should be examined to see that they are in good condition, and the oil-holes in the boxes must be kept clear, so that the oil can reach the bearings. The tender boxes are kept oiled by packing them with cotton or woolen waste saturated with oil. This should be taken out occasionally and renewed and the boxes cleaned. The working of the driving-boxes up and down the jaws will in time wear them so that there will be some lost motion in the jaws. This will be indicated by a thump when the cranks pass the dead point. A similar thump will, however, be produced by lost motion in the boxes of the main connecting-rod, so that it is difficult to determine, without special examination, the cause which produces the concussion. It is therefore best when an engine works with a thump at each revolution for the runner to stand by the side of it where he can touch the connecting-rods and driving-wheels, and then have the fireman open the throttle-valve so as to move the engine slowly. If the lost motion is in the connecting-rods it can be felt by the jar as it passes the dead points. The same is true of lost motion in the jaws, which can be felt by touching the driving-wheels. When the jaws become worn the lost motion can be taken up by moving up one or both of the wedges. When this is done, great care must be taken to keep the centres of the driving-axles the same distance apart on both sides of the engine, and also to keep their centre lines square with the frames. There should always be centre-punch marks placed on the frames or guide-yokes on each side of the engine in front of the main axle, and at equal distances from its centres, so that when the boxes or jaws become worn the position of the axle can be adjusted with a tram from these marks. Of course, if the main axle is square, it is easy to adjust the trailing axle from it with a tram. If the axles are not square with the frames and parallel with each other, the engine will run towards one side or the other of the track, according to the inclination of the axles. It sometimes happens that the bolts which hold up the wedges in the jaws are broken. When this occurs the wedge drops down, and of course the box has so much lost motion that it soon manifests itself in the working of the engine. These bolts, and also those which hold up the clamps on the frames at the bottom of the jaws, should be examined when the engine is inspected, so as to be sure they are in good condition. The bolts and nuts about both the engine and tender trucks should be watched to see that none are lost or work loose. The engine and tender should occasionally be lifted up from the centre plates of the truck, and the latter be lubricated with tallow. It often happens that these become dry, so that they are difficult to turn when the weight rests on them, and therefore they will not adjust themselves easily to the curves of the track.

QUESTION 469. *What other parts of a locomotive should be examined before starting?*

Answer. It should be certain that the brakes on the tender are in good working condition, that is, that the bolts, nuts and keys are all secure, the levers, rods and chains properly connected, and the shoes fastened and not too much worn. If either an atmospheric or vacuum brake is used, it should be tested before starting, to see that the pump or ejector is in good working condition. It is also well to apply the brakes to the train before starting, so as to see whether the connections are in good condition and properly connected. It is always best for the locomotive runner to examine the connections of the brake hose through the whole train himself, to be sure that they are properly made.

The inside of the water-tank should also be examined occasionally, to see whether it is clean, and if not it should be thoroughly washed out. The man-hole should always be covered before starting, in order to prevent cinders and coal from falling in, which are liable to obstruct the pump valves. It is hardly necessary to say that it must always be certain before starting that there is enough water in the tank to feed the boiler until the next point is reached at which a supply can be obtained. The sand-box must also be filled, the bell rope in good condition, and if running at night the reflector of the head-light must be polished and the lamp supplied with oil and the wick trimmed so as to burn brilliantly. The locomotive runner must also see that the proper signals are displayed in front of his engine.

QUESTION 470. *What tools, etc., should every locomotive runner on the road carry?*

Answer. A coal shovel, coal pick, long-handled hoe* and poker, a pair of jacks, either screw or hydraulic, chains, rope and twine to be used in case of accident,

* These are of course not needed on wood-burning engines.

a heavy pinch-bar for moving the engine, a small crow-bar, oil-cans with short and long spouts and another smaller one with spring bottom, a steel and a copper hammer, a cold and a cape chisel, a hand-saw, axe and hatchet, one large and one small monkey-wrench and a full assortment of solid wrenches for the bolts and nuts of the engine, cast iron plugs for plugging tubes, with a bar for inserting them, two sheet iron pails or buckets, different colored lanterns and flags, according to the colors used for signals on the line, and a box with a half-dozen torpedoes.

QUESTION 471. *What duplicate parts should be carried with the engine?*

Answer. Keys, bolts and nuts for connecting-rods, split-keys, wedge bolts, bolts for oil-cellars of driving and truck boxes, driving and truck spring-hangers, wooden blocks for fastening guides in case of accident, blocks for driving-boxes and links, a half-dozen $\frac{3}{4}$-in. bolts, from six inches to two feet long, to be used in case of accident, two extra water-gauge glasses, two glass head-light chimneys.

QUESTION 472. *What should be observed in lubricating a locomotive or any other machinery?*

Answer. The most important thing to observe is that the oil reaches the surface to be lubricated. It is of much greater importance that the lubricant should reach the right place than that a large quantity should be used. A few drops carefully introduced on a journal will do much more good than a large quantity poured on the part carelessly. For this reason all oil-cups and oil-holes should be kept clean so as to form a free passage for the oil.

PART XXVII.

RUNNING LOCOMOTIVES.

QUESTION 473. *Before starting the fire in a locomotive, what must be observed?*

Answer. It must always be noticed, before kindling the fire, whether the boiler has the requisite quantity of water in it; that all cinders, clinkers and ashes are removed from the grates and ash-pan; that the grates and drop-door are properly fastened, and that the throttle-valve is closed and the lever secured. Locomotive boilers are sometimes seriously injured by building a fire in them when there is no water in the boiler. In filling a boiler it must be remembered, however, that when the water is heated it will expand, and that when bubbles of steam are formed they will mix with the water and thus increase its volume, so that after the water is heated its surface will be considerably higher than when it is cold.

QUESTION 474. *How should the fire in a locomotive be started?*

Answer. It should be started very slowly, so as not to heat any one part suddenly. Probably the greatest strains which a locomotive boiler has to bear are those due to the unequal expansion and contraction of its different parts. When the fire is started, of course the parts exposed to it are heated first, and consequently expand before the others. Now, if the fire is kindled rapidly, the heating surfaces will become very hot before the heat is communicated to the parts not exposed to the fire. Thus the tubes, for example, will be expanded so as to be considerably longer than the outside shell of the boiler, and therefore there will be a severe strain on the tube-plates, which will be communicated to the fire-box, stay-bolts, braces, etc. The inside plates of the fire-box will also become much hotter than those on the outside, and as it is rigidly fastened to the bar to which both the inside and the outside shells are fastened at the bottom, its expansion will all be upward, which thus strains the stay-bolts in that direction. As the motion due to this expansion is greatest near the top of the fire-box, the top stay-bolts are of course strained the most, and it is those in that position, as has already been pointed out, which are the most liable to break. When steel plates are used the expansion or contraction often cracks them, and sometimes, hours after the fire is withdrawn from the fire-box, the inside plates will crack with a report like that of a pistol. It is therefore very important both to heat and cool a locomotive boiler very slowly, and the fire should always be kindled several hours before the engine starts on its run.

QUESTION 475. *What should be done when the locomotive leaves the engine-house and before the train is started?*

Answer. Before leaving the engine-house the cylinder cocks should be opened, so that all the water or steam which is condensed in warming the cylinders can escape. Before the engine is started from the engine-house the bell should be rung and time enough allowed for any workmen employed about the engine to get out of the way. This rule must be scrupulously obeyed under *all circumstances,* and a locomotive should *never* be started without first giving such a signal. Without it there is always danger that some one about the engine will be hurt or killed. While running from the engine-house to the train the runner should observe very carefully the working of all the parts of his engine, and as far as possible see that they are in good working condition. The fireman should stay on the tender to handle the brake, as may be necessary, and should assist in coupling the tender to the first car of the train. The junction with the train, especially when it is a passenger train, should be made very gently, as otherwise passengers may be injured by the shock. Before starting the runner should see *himself* that the engine and tender are securely coupled together, and the latter to the train, that the frictional parts are properly lubricated, as explained heretofore, that the fire is in good condition and that the requisite quantity of steam has been generated. If the steam is too low, the blower is started, which stimulates the fire.

QUESTION 476. *When the train is ready, how should the engine be started?*

Answer. After the signal to start is given by the conductor, the runner also gives a signal by either ringing the bell or blowing the whistle. The latter should, however, be used, especially at stations, as little as possible, on account of the risk of frightening horses and the shock which it produces on persons who are unaccustomed to hearing it, or are suffering from any nervous disorder. After giving the requisite signal, the runner places the reverse-lever so that the valve will work either in full gear or very near it.

He then opens the throttle ***slowly*** and ***cautiously*** so as to start the train gradually. If the train is a very heavy one, it is best to back the engine so as just to "take up the slack of the train," that is, to push the cars together so that there will be no space between them and thus compress the car draw-springs. When the cars stand in this way, those at the front end of the train are started one after another, which makes the start easier than it would be if it were necessary to start them all at once. If the throttle is opened too rapidly, the driving-wheels are apt to slip, but with a very heavy train, even with the greatest care, this is liable to occur. If the train can not be started otherwise, the rails must be sanded by opening the valves in the sand-box. As little sand should be used as possible, because the resistance of cars running on sanded rails is greater than on clean rails, and thus the train is more difficult to draw after it reaches the rails to which sand has been applied. Thus the difficulty to be overcome may be increased by the means employed to overcome it.

While the train is slowly set in motion the fireman and runner must ascertain by watching whether the whole train moves together, and that none of the couplings are broken in starting, and also whether any signal is given to stop, as is sometimes necessary after the train has started. On leaving the station he should observe whether all the signals indicate that the track is clear and that the switches are set right, and also look out for obstructions on the track. The train should always be run slowly and cautiously until it has passed all the frogs, switches and crossings of the station yard, and not until then and when the runner has seen that everything is in order should he run at full speed. As the engine gains in speed the reverse lever should be thrown back and nearer the centre of the quadrant or sector, so as to cut off "shorter."

QUESTION 477. *After the engine is started, how can it be run most economically?*

Answer. The advantage of using steam expansively has already been explained in Part V.; it is more economical to use steam of a high pressure which is done by keeping the throttle-valve wide open, and then regulating the speed by cutting off shorter—that is, expanding it more. If the speed is reduced by partly closing the throttle-valve, the steam is wire-drawn and, as was shown in answer to Question 59, it then produces much less useful effect than it would if it was admitted into the cylinder at full boiler pressure.

It is found, however, that in many cases if the steam is cut off very short the final pressure when it escapes is so low that it does not produce blast enough to stimulate the fire, and therefore the boiler will not make enough steam. This is more liable to occur with engines which have small than with those which have large boilers, or when the boilers are in bad condition or the fuel is of poor quality. When it does occur it is necessary to work steam during a longer portion of the stroke, so as to increase the final pressure when it is exhausted and regulate the speed with the throttle-valve. Of course this is very wasteful, but it is often the best which can be done and pull the train.

There is also another practical difficulty in using

steam of a high pressure and running with the throttle wide open and regulating the speed with the reverse lever alone. The link motion, as has already been explained, will not be effective in cutting off at a point below about one-quarter of the stroke. Now it often happens, even when cutting off at that short point, with light trains on a level or slightly descending grade, that the speed will be too great if the throttle is wide open and with full steam pressure in the boiler. When this is the case, it is absolutely necessary to reduce the speed either by partly closing the throttle, or reducing the pressure in the boiler. Undoubtedly if valve-gear for locomotives was so constructed that steam could be cut off effectively at a shorter point of the stroke, it would result in increased economy in the use of steam.

The runner should aim to run at as nearly uniform speed as possible, and in order to do so should divide the distance between stopping points and the time given for running it into as small divisions as he conveniently can, so as to be able to tell as often as possible whether he is running too fast or too slow, and thus travel over the shorter spaces in corresponding periods of time.

QUESTION 478. *How should the boiler be fed?*

Answer. The feeding of the boiler should if possible be continuous, and the quantity of water pumped into it should be adjusted to the amount of work which the engine is doing. Ordinarily one pump is more than sufficient for feeding the boiler, so that usually only the one on the right side of the engine, where the runner stands, is used. The flow of the water is regulated by partly opening or closing the feed-cock. The injector is commonly used only when the engine is standing still, when the pumps will not feed. In feeding the boiler it must be seen that the water is neither too high nor too low. If it is too low there will be danger of overheating the crown-plates or even of an explosion; if it is too high, the steam space in the boiler is diminished unnecessarily, and will cause the water to rise in the form of a spray, and thus be carried into the cylinders with the steam, or the boiler will *prime* or *foam,* as it is called. This water, if it collects in the cylinder as already explained, may by the concussion produced by the motion of the piston break the cylinder.

Question 479. *What is the cause of priming in a boiler.*

Answer. It is often caused by the difference in temperature and pressure in the water below and the steam above. Thus, if we have a boiler in which the water is heated to a temperature due to 100 lbs. effective pressure, or 338 degrees, and we then open the throttle-valve suddenly, so as to relieve the pressure on top of the water, there will at once be a rapid generation of steam in the water which will rush to fill the space from which the steam has been drawn. This newly generated steam will be formed at the hottest part of the boiler first, that is, next to the heating surface. It will therefore happen that as soon as the pressure is relieved, bubbles of steam from all parts of the heating surface of the boiler will flow to the point at which the steam escapes. The motion of these bubbles will be so rapid that large quantities of water will be carried with them. The same thing will also occur if the heat of the water is increased very rapidly.

The water will then become hotter than the temperature due to the pressure of the steam above it, and consequently there will be a rapid formation and escape of bubbles of steam from the water, which will thus have the same effect as they would have if the steam pressure was reduced.

The amount of water carried up with the steam is increased if the escape of the latter is obstructed in any way, owing to imperfect circulation of water in the boiler, or by floating impurities, such as oil, on the surface. When this condition of things exists, the ebullition is, as it were, convulsive, and the water is thus carried up with the steam when it escapes. Priming is also probably due in some measure to the flow of steam over the surface of the water to the point of outflow,* carrying particles of water with it just as a high wind will, when blowing over the crests of the waves of the sea.

When steam is drawn, as it usually is in locomotives, from the top of the dome to which the safety-valves are attached, the tendency to prime is very much increased when they are blowing off, so that some engineers advocate the use of two domes, from both of which the supply of steam is sometimes drawn, and in other cases the safety-valves are mounted on one, and the steam-pipe is placed in another dome. Whenever the safety-valves begin blowing off steam, the pressure in the boiler should be reduced as soon as possible, not only because when they are blowing off it tends to produce priming, but because the steam which escapes from them is wasted. The pressure can be most economically reduced either by increasing

* Wilson on Steam Boilers.

the amount of water which is fed into the boiler or by opening the heater cocks and allowing the steam to escape into the tank and thus warm the water. If the boiler is too full, the former method cannot be employed, and in heating the water in the tank the runner must be careful not to get it too hot, because in that case neither the pumps nor the injectors will work satisfactorily, and the paint on the tenders is also liable to be blistered and destroyed by the heat. By feeling the tank with the hand it can soon be discovered whether the water is too hot. If the steam pressure cannot be reduced in any other way, the furnace door must be partly opened.

The use of muddy water will also sometimes cause a boiler to prime. It is probable that priming is sometimes due to the formation of foam on the surface of the water, and therefore all priming is often called foaming; whereas it is thought that often a boiler will prime when the water does not foam. More accurate information regarding the priming of boilers is, however, much needed, as many of the phenomena have thus far not been satisfactorily explained. The principal causes of priming in ordinary practice are, however, undoubtedly owing to defective circulation, too little steam room, impure water, or too much water in the boiler.

QUESTION 480. *How can it be known whether an engine is priming, and what should be done to prevent it?*

Answer. The priming of a boiler can be known by the white appearance of the steam which escapes from the smoke-stack and the cylinder cocks. Dry steam always has a bluish color. When an engine primes or works water into the cylinders, it is usually indicated by a peculiar dead sound of the exhaust, which from this cause loses its distinctly defined and sharp sound. This can be observed best when the furnace door is opened. It is also indicated by the discharge from the gauge-cock, as the water which then escapes from the lower cocks is mixed with steam, or, as runners say, is not "solid," and the steam from the upper cocks is not clear, but mixed with water. To use a phrase employed by practical men, the priming or foaming of the boiler may be known by the "flutter" of the gauge-cocks. As soon as there are any indications of priming, foaming, or that water is working into the cylinders, the cylinder cocks should be opened at once, otherwise the cylinders, cylinder heads or pistons may be broken. The throttle-valve should be either partly or entirely closed. When the latter is done the foaming will in most cases cease for the time, so that the runner can tell how much solid water there is in the boiler. If he finds that the boiler has too much water in it, it is best to shut off the pumps, and in many cases the blow-off cock is opened. The latter is, however, attended with some danger, because if any obstruction should get into the blow-off cock, or it should stick fast, so that it could not be closed, all the water would escape from the boiler, and with a heavy fire in the fire-box there would be great danger of overheating, and thus injuring the boiler or of "burning" it, as it is ordinarily termed.

A much better method of affording relief in such cases is to place what is called a *surface-cock* in the back end of the fire-box, about half way between the upper and lower gauge-cocks. With such a cock, the water can be blown off from the surface instead of from the bottom. As foaming or priming is often caused by oil, or other floating impurities on the surface, they can be blown out of the boiler with this arrangement, whereas, if the water escapes from the bottom of the boiler, the floating impurities will always remain after it is blown off. A perforated pipe, which extends for some distance along the surface of the water inside the boiler, is sometimes attached to the surface-cock, so that the water which is blown off will be drawn from a number of points along the surface.

If the steam is rising rapidly when foaming begins, it will be well to cool the boiler off by opening the furnace door part way. This means of relief should, however, be used as little as possible, because there is always danger of causing the tubes or other parts of the boiler to leak, by either heating or cooling suddenly or rapidly. If the engine primes when there is but little water in the boiler, and at a time when the steam is rising rapidly, it may sometimes be remedied by increasing the amount of feed-water, and thus partly cooling the water inside. The use of pure water, careful firing so as to keep the steam pressure regular, feeding the boiler so that the level of the water will be nearly uniform, and then starting the engine carefully, that is, opening the throttle-valve gradually, are the most effective means in practice of preventing a locomotive boiler from priming.

QUESTION 481. ***What is the economical effect of priming on the consumption of fuel in locomotives?***

Answer. It causes a great waste of heat, first by the escape of that contained in the hot water which passes through the cylinders and which does no work, and second, when steam is mixed with a great deal of water, it will not flow either to or from the cylinders as quickly or easily as dry steam will. Consequently the initial pressure on the piston, if the engine is running even moderately fast, and is cutting off short, will not be so great as it would be if dry steam was used. Wet steam is also more difficult to exhaust from the cylinder than that which is dry, and therefore the back pressure on the piston is greater when the boiler primes than when dry steam alone is used.

QUESTION 482. *When running on the open road, what should the locomotive runner observe?*

Answer. Either he or the fireman should *constantly* watch the track in front of them, and also observe, from time to time, whether the train of cars, especially if it is a long one which he is handling, is in good condition. HE MUST OBSERVE EVERY SIGNAL SCRUPULOUSLY, AND SHOULD NEVER PASS ONE UNTIL HE IS SURE THAT HE IS AUTHORIZED TO DO SO. The well-known maxim, "be sure you are right; then go ahead," should be changed for locomotive runners to, DON'T GO AHEAD UNTIL YOU ARE SURE YOU ARE RIGHT, AND WHEN IN DOUBT ALWAYS CHOOSE THE SIDE OF SAFETY. In running through curves, the speed of the train should always be moderated in proportion to the sharpness of the curve, and before reaching it. In running through curves, the tendency of the train is to continue in a straight line, and there is thus danger of running off the track. The higher the speed, of course, the greater is the resistance which is required to prevent the train from running in a straight line, and consequently the greater is the strain which is thrown on the flanges of the wheels and on the rails and axles. In running through curves, it is also impossible, usually, to see further than a short distance ahead, and therefore, if the train is running very fast, it cannot be stopped in time, should there be any obstruction or danger on the track.

QUESTION 483. *What precautions should be observed in running over steep grades?*

Answer. On approaching an ascending grade the runner should see that the fire is in good condition, and as much coal should be put on it as can be burned to advantage. He should also fill the boiler as full of water as he safely can, without danger of priming, and should heat this water as hot as possible without blowing off steam at the safety-valves. The object of this is to have a supply of water already heated before reaching the grade. If, as often happens with a heavy train, the boiler will not make as much steam as the engine consumes, if there is a large supply of hot water in the boiler it can be used as a reserve, should it be necessary to do so, without danger of injury to the boiler. If there was so little water in the boiler that it would be dangerous to allow it to get lower, then it would be necessary to feed cold water as rapidly as the hot water escaped in the form of steam. It is often impossible to heat all this cold water as fast as it is pumped into the boiler, without reducing the steam pressure until there is then not sufficient power to pull the train. If, however, there is a supply of hot water in the boiler, at the critical point on the grade, where the engine is most liable to fail, the pump can be partly shut off, and thus less water will be pumped into the boiler, and the steam pressure be maintained without danger. Undoubtedly it is better to feed locomotive boilers uniformly, if that is possible, but it often happens that a reserve supply of hot water in the boiler enables an engine to pull a train up the most difficult place, whereas, without such a supply, the locomotive would stick fast. As the capacity of locomotives is rated on nearly all roads by the number of cars they can "pull up the hill," of course whatever aids them at the critical point increases their capacity. It is this fact which gives engines with large boilers so much advantage over those with small ones.

In running up steep grades, allowance should always be made for the effect of the inclination of the track upon the position of the water surface in the boiler, and also the fact that as soon as the throttle-valve is closed, and steam shut off, the surface of the water will be considerably lower than when the engine was working hard. On a grade of 50 feet to a mile, the front end of the tubes of an ordinary locomotive would be about $1\frac{3}{4}$ inches higher than the back end of the crown-sheet. If, then, on working hard up such a grade, it is succeeded by another of equal descent, the front ends of the tubes would be $1\frac{3}{4}$ inches *lower* than they were while coming up, so that if the back end of the crown-sheet was covered with $1\frac{3}{4}$ inches of water just before reaching the top, it would be exposed to the fire as soon as the engine reached the descent. This exposure would be dangerous, because not only would the water be $1\frac{3}{4}$ inches lower over the crown-sheet, but it would fall considerably more when the throttle-valve was closed. These considerations will show the danger of running the water too low while ascending steep grades.

In pulling trains up steep grades, especial caution should be exercised to prevent any of the cars from breaking loose from the train, because such an accident may cause great disaster.

As soon as the engine reaches the top of the grade, the fireman should oil the main valves, because it can only be done when steam is shut off, as the oil will not run into the steam-chest when there is a pressure of steam in it; and as the valves are always subjected to the severest wear while pulling up a steep grade, the valves and valve-faces are apt to become dry. As saturated steam to some extent prevents valves from cutting, it is not so important that they be lubricated while the engine is working with steam, but as soon as steam is shut off they should be oiled, otherwise there is danger of their being injured by their friction on the valve-seats.

In running down grades, the runner has the greatest possible cause for using every precaution, because not only is the train much more difficult to control, but usually frequent sharp curves prevent a view of the track for any considerable distance ahead. He should, therefore, watch the track in front of him with the greatest vigilance, so as to be ready to give the requisite signals to the brakemen to apply the brakes, or, if the engine and train are provided with continuous brakes, to apply the latter, or even reverse his engine, in case of danger.

Question 484. *How should an engine be run past those stations where the train does not stop?*

Answer. The speed of the train should be slackened in passing stations, especially if a clear view of the track and switch signals can not be obtained at some distance before reaching the station. There is always a possibility that the switches may be turned wrong, or that there may be some obstruction on the track at stations, so that some caution should be exercised in running past them. The proper signal, either by the whistle* or the bell, should be given on approaching stations, and also at all common road crossings.

QUESTION 485. *What must be done on approaching a draw-bridge or a crossing of another railroad at the same level?*

Answer. In many of the States it is provided by law that all trains must come to a *dead stop* before crossing a draw-bridge or another railroad at the same level. Whether such a law exists or not, the rule should always be observed. After coming to a stop, the train should under no circumstances be started until the signal has been given to start the train by the signal-man at the bridge or crossing. A runner should *never assume* that the signal has been given, nor take another person's word for it, but should see and know it himself. In some conditions of the weather and with the light falling on a signal in certain directions, it is sometimes difficult to determine its color or form. If there is any doubt about it, the testimony of another person should always be sought. There is good reason for believing that color-blindness, that is, an incapacity for distinguishing one color from another, is a much more common infirmity than is usually supposed. It is certain, too, that people who ordinarily distinguish colors very accurately are subject to color-blindness in certain condi-

* The methods of giving signals vary so much on different roads that no general direction that will suit all cases can be given.

tions of health, and that it is sometimes the result of overwork or great weariness; and a case is recorded of a person who was always color-blind after a debauch. There are, therefore, good reasons why a locomotive runner should not always place too implicit confidence in what he "sees with his own eyes," but if he has any doubt, he should take the "benefit of the doubt," which should always lead him to take the side of safety.

QUESTION 486. *How should the engine and train be managed in running into a station?*

Answer. First of all when running into a station when the train stops, the speed must be checked so that the train will not enter with very great momentum. Therefore, at a distance varying from one to three-quarters of a mile, according to the nature of the grades and track, the steam should be shut off, so that the speed will be reduced so much that the train under any circumstances will be under full control. It is always better to enter a station at too low a speed than to run in too fast, because if it is necessary, more steam can always be admitted to the cylinders to increase the speed before coming to a stop; whereas it is not so easy to stop the train if it is running too fast, and it becomes necessary to check it before entering the station. This will sometimes be necessary, because it may readily happen through negligence or accident at stations that in switching cars one or more may be left standing wholly or partly on the track, which the arriving train must run over, in which case a collision with its terrible consequences may be unavoidable.

When a train is equipped with continuous brakes,

the control which they usually give to a locomotive runner over the train is so great that he is apt to approach stations, crossings or draw-bridges at a high rate of speed, and rely on such brakes to stop the train. This practice is always attended with great danger, because if it was found, on getting near to the station, crossing or draw-bridge, that the track was not clear, and that it was obstructed by a car or train, or the draw was open, if the runner should attempt to apply the brakes and from some cause they should fail to work, as sometimes occurs, then a collision or other disaster would be inevitable, because it would be impossible to stop the train with the ordinary hand brakes. For this reason a locomotive runner should always approach such places cautiously and with his train under sufficient control, so that if he finds there is danger ahead he can stop the train with the ordinary means, or at the worst by reversing the engine. Continuous brakes should always, excepting in cases of imminent danger, be applied gradually, so as not to check the cars with a jerk or too suddenly. The practice of opening the cock which admits air to atmospheric brakes suddenly, and then turning it back again as quickly, is almost sure to produce disagreeable and dangerous shocks to the cars. The cock should be opened gradually, so as to check the cars slowly at first.

QUESTION 487. *What must be attended to when running a locomotive at night?*

Answer. As soon as it begins to grow dark, the head-light must be lighted and properly trimmed, and the proper lamp signals placed in front of the engine, if the rules of the road require the display of such signals. A lamp should always be placed in the cab, so as to throw its light on the steam-gauge, but not into the runner's face, because he is unable to see distant signals so well if his eyes are exposed to the glare of a light near him.

At night, as objects which are passed can not be seen distinctly, it is more difficult to tell the speed at which an engine is running than it is in the day time. A runner should therefore consult his watch frequently, and by counting the revolutions of the wheels, which he can do by the sound of the pump valve or other part of the machinery, he can tell from the rule given in the answer to Question 438 the speed at which the locomotive is running. From this rule a table can easily be constructed for an engine with any size of driving-wheels, showing the speed for any given number of revolutions per minute. It will be a good exercise for a young locomotive runner to construct such a table, which will be found very convenient for reference if placed in a conspicuous place in the cab.

QUESTION 488. *What must be attended to in very cold weather?*

Answer. Great care must be exercised to prevent the water in the pumps, pipes and in the tender from freezing. If it does it will be almost certain to break the pump or burst the pipes. To avoid this the heater cocks must be opened so as to keep the water in the tender warm. In excessively cold weather the engine should be run with greater caution than at other times, as iron is then more brittle, and also more liable to break, owing to the frozen condition and consequent solidity of the track.

QUESTION 489. *In running a locomotive in severe snow or rain-storms, what should be observed?*

Answer. Whenever it snows the pilot or cow catcher should be covered with boards, or, better still, with sheet iron, so as to act like a snow plow. Brooms made of steel wire should be placed in front of the front wheels of the engine, so as to sweep the snow from the rails. The front damper on the ash-pan should be kept closed so as to exclude the snow from the ash-pan, which would soon fill it up, and in this way obstruct the draft. If the fall of snow is very heavy or it blows into drifts, the train must of necessity run very slowly, and even if a part of the track is clear of snow, it is unsafe to run fast on it, as there would be danger of throwing the engine off the rails if it should run into a heavy drift at a high speed.

In severe rain storms bridges, culverts and such portions of the track as are liable to be washed away should be approached cautiously, especially at night. In both snow and rain-storms, and also in fogs, great caution is required, owing to the difficulty of seeing signals.

QUESTION 490. *What is meant by a reserve engine or "helper?"*

Answer. A *reserve engine* is a locomotive which is not employed in hauling a regular train, but is kept as a "reserve" to go to the help of an engine which may be compelled to stop on account of an accident of any kind, or to assist engines in moving trains up heavy grades, or is used in clearing away a wrecked train, rebuilding bridges or other structures.

QUESTION 491. *What must be observed in running a reserve engine.*

Answer. As no special arrangements are usually made in preparing time-tables* for the running of reserve, or as they are usually called by railroad men, "*wild*" engines, it may very probably happen that it will be called upon to assist other engines when the road is not clear, and therefore its runner must constantly be on the look-out for signals to stop, which are often given suddenly. He must switch off with special caution in order to be sure to keep out of the way of regular trains running in the opposite direction on the same track. When he reaches the train or place where the assistance of the reserve engine is needed, he must approach it *slowly* and *carefully*, in order to avoid a violent shock. On the return from the assisted train, he incurs the same danger, and must pay close attention to any signal to stop made to him by any opposite train on the same track, and also on his part warn such trains by the proper signals.

When a train is run with two engines, both in front of it, the forward one always takes the management of the train. The runner of the hind engine must be guided by the signals of the runner of the forward engine. In starting, the forward engine must be set in motion first and then the one behind it. In stopping, the steam must be shut off first in the hind engine. Likewise in decreasing the speed during the trip, the hind engine must first regulate the flow of steam. If these precautions are not observed the forward engine may easily be thrown from the track by the faster motion of the hind one.

When a train is assisted by a "helper" placed *be-*

---

* A *time-table* is a table which gives the time when each train shall arrive at the stations it passes, the stations at which it shall stop, and all the regulations by which it shall be run.

hind the train, and therefore pushing it, the forward engine must likewise be set in motion first, and steam should be let on in the hind engine only after a signal has been given by the runner of the head engine. During the run both engines must move with the same speed.*

QUESTION 492. *How should switching engines be managed?*

Answer. In pushing and switching the freight cars in the station-yard, they should be moved carefully and severe shocks must be avoided, as the cars, the goods with which they are loaded and the persons employed about them may be injured by violent concussions. The runner must also follow the instructions of his superior *strictly* and *cheerfully*, and should examine patiently and observe with discretion the suggestions of employes who are not his superiors.

In this service it is also of special importance that the runner give a *distinct* signal with the whistle or bell before every movement of his engine, in order to warn in time those who at such times often stand on the track in the way of the engine or cars, or the persons engaged in loading, cleaning or repairing the cars, and thus give them time to get out of the way.†

QUESTION 493. *In firing a locomotive, what are the most important ends to be attained?*

Answer. That which is of first and chief importance is to make steam enough, so that the locomotive can pull its train and "*make time*"‡; second, it must

---

* Katechismus der Einrichtung und Betriebes der Locomtive, by Georg Kosak.

† Georg Kosak.

‡ The term *make time* means to run at the speed indicated on the time-table.

make the requisite quantity of steam with the least consumption of coal, and third, with the least production of smoke, although the latter, independent of the economy of combustion, is considered of importance only with passenger trains. What is frequently lost sight of in considering this subject is the fact that with all locomotives it often happens that it is a matter of extreme difficulty to make enough steam to do the work required of the engines. When a freight train is struggling up a grade with a heavy train, or an express engine is obliged to make time under similar conditions, it often depends entirely upon the quantity of steam which can be generated in the boiler in a given time whether the engine will fail or not. In firing, therefore, the most important end to be aimed at is often simply to produce the largest amount of steam possible in a given time, even at the sacrifice of economy or by producing any quantity of smoke. Any means of economizing fuel or of smoke prevention, which reduces the steam-producing capacity of boilers, is therefore quite sure to be abandoned in time.

QUESTION 494. *How can a boiler be made to produce the largest quantity of steam in a given time?*

Answer. By burning the greatest quantity of fuel possible on the grate in that time. This can be done by keeping the grates free from clinkers and the ash-pan from ashes, and then distributing the coal evenly over the grates in a layer six to twelve inches thick. The thickness of the layer which will give the best results will, however, vary with the quality of the fuel, and must be determined by experience. If the layer is too thick, not enough air will pass through it to burn the coal. If it is too thin, then so much air will pass through that the temperature in the fire will be reduced. The rapidity of combustion will also be promoted by breaking up the coal into lumps the size of a man's fist or smaller. If fine coal is used it should be wet, otherwise it will be carried into the flues by the blast before it is burned or caked or even reaches the grate. Experience will indicate the amount of air which can advantageously be admitted above the fire in order to secure the maximum production of steam. The best size of the exhaust nozzles and the position of the petticoat pipe must also be determined by experience. It will usually be found, however, that if enough air is admitted above the fire to prevent smoke, it will reduce the maximum amount of steam which can be generated in a given time. The fire should also be fed regularly and with comparatively small quantities of fuel at a time, although if the feeding is too frequent there is more loss from the cooling effect which results from the frequent opening of the furnace door than is gained from the regularity of the firing. In this, too, a fireman must consult experience to guide him.

QUESTION 495. *How can a locomotive be fired with the least consumption of coal?*

Answer. Two systems of firing are practiced in this country, one known as the "banking system" and the other the "spreading system." When the banking system is employed, the coal is piled up at the back part of the fire-box, as shown in fig. 218, and slopes down towards the front of the grate, where the layer of coal is comparatively thin and in an active state of incandescence. The heap of coal behind is gradually coked by the heat in the fire-box and the gases are thus expelled. Openings in the furnace door admit air which mingles with the escaping gases, which then pass over the bright fire in front, and are thus supposed to be consumed. When the "bank" of coal behind becomes thoroughly coked, it is pushed forward on the bright fire and fresh coal is again put on behind to be coked. This system of firing is practiced on some roads with good results, but it is doubtful whether it could be used successfully with coal which cakes and clinkers badly.

The spreading system is most commonly employed in the Western States, where the coal contains a great deal of clinker. When this is practiced, the coal is spread evenly over the whole of the grate in a thin layer, and its success and economy depend upon the regularity and evenness with which this layer of coal is maintained and the fire fed. The thickness of the coal must be adapted to the working of the engine. When it is working lightly, the layer of coal should be thin, but when the engine is pulling hard the layer of coal must be thicker, otherwise the violent blast may lift the coal off the grates. The success of this system, as was explained in answer to Question 388, depends upon the manner in which the thickness of the fire is regulated, on the admission of the proper amount of air above the fire, and on the frequency with which the fire is supplied with coal. When this system of firing is employed not more than two shovels-full of coal should be put into the fire-box at once, and if the engine is not working hard, one or even less will be sufficient. The firemen must, however, determine by experience the thickness of fire, amount of air which should be admitted and the frequency of firing which will give the best results in practice. Doubtless these will vary with different kinds of fuel and the construction of engines. Usually the greatest obstacle in the way of producing good results is the fact that firemen would rather "take things easy" than exercise that diligence and observation which will alone insure success in any occupation.

QUESTION 496. *How can smoke be most effectually prevented?*

Answer. The means of preventing smoke were very fully explained in answer to Questions 379 and 388. It may be said briefly that this can be done only by properly regulating the supply of air which is admitted to the fire. The means of doing this have already been explained.

QUESTION 497. *What method of firing is employed when anthracite coal is used?*

Answer. The spreading system alone is then used.

QUESTION 498. *How may the rules which firemen should observe when bituminous coal is used be briefly stated?*

Answer. 1. Keep the grate, ash-pan and tubes clean. 2. Break the coal into small lumps. 3. Fire often and in small quantities. 4. Keep the furnace door open as little as possible. 5. Consult the steam gauge frequently, and maintain a uniform steam pressure, and if necessary to reduce the pressure do it by closing the ash-pan dampers rather than by opening the furnace door.

QUESTION 499. *On arriving at a station where a train stops longer than a few minutes, what should the locomotive runner and fireman attend to?*

Answer. The runner should examine thoroughly all the parts of his engine, as has been heretofore explained. He should especially examine all the journals and wearing surfaces to see whether they are hot. This he can discover by feeling them. If any of them have become very much heated, they must be cooled by throwing cold water on them, and then thoroughly oiled. In oiling a hot journal mineral oil should never be used, as it is easily evaporated by the heat and then takes fire. Animal oil should therefore always be used on a hot bearing. The working parts should be thoroughly lubricated, as already explained.

The fireman should examine the tank and see whether it is necessary to take in a fresh supply of water. He should then examine the grates and ash-pan, and clean the cinders and clinkers from the former, and the ashes from the latter. Neglecting to clean the ash-pan may result in melting and destroying the grate-bars, and by obstructing the admission of air to the grates the ashes prevent the combustion from being as complete as it would be otherwise. With some kinds of fuel it is necessary to clean the tubes frequently, which must often be done at stations where the train stops.

During the stop, as thorough an inspection of the engine should be made by the runner and fireman as the time will permit; but any unnecessary waste of time must be avoided, and the firing should be so managed that nothing need be done about it during the halt at the station. On starting again the same precautions should be exercised as on making the first start.

QUESTION 500. *After reaching the end of its run, how should an engine be cleaned and repaired?*

Answer. Before reaching the last station the firing should be so managed that there will be as little fire as possible remaining in the fire-box at the end of the run. After the arrival the engine should be run over a pit which is usually provided for the purpose, and the fire should be raked out of the fire-box by dropping the drop-door if there is one to the grate, or turning the grate-bars edgewise, or withdrawing one or more of them if it is necessary to do so. In this way the fire will fall into the ash-pan, from which it can easily be raked. After all the fire is withdrawn the dampers and furnace door should be closed so as not to allow the cold air to cool the fire-box and tubes too rapidly.

In order to keep the boiler clean, that is as free as possible from sand, sediment or incrustation, it is necessary to blow it out frequently if the water which is used contains much solid or incrustating matter. With "bad water" the boiler should be blown out as often as possible. On some roads this is done after each trip. In blowing a boiler out, the blow-off cocks must be left open, and after all the water has escaped the engine should be left to stand until it is cooled off. If there is any considerable accumulation of mud or sediment the hand-holes at the bottom of the fire-box and the cover to the mud-drum should be taken off, and as much of the mud removed as can be scraped out through those apertures. A hose pipe attached to the hose of a force pump should then be inserted through these same openings, and a strong stream of water forced into the boiler. By this means much of the loose mud and scale will be washed out. The oftener this is repeated of course the cleaner can a boiler be kept. If a large amount of incrustation or mud has accumulated about the tubes, some or all of them must be taken out, so as to be able to remove the dirt.

After an engine is blown out, under no circumstances excepting absolute necessity should it be filled with cold water until it is entirely cooled off. It should be remembered that any sudden change of temperature in a boiler subjects it to very great strains and incurs the danger of cracking the fire-box plates, or causing the tubes to leak.

The tender should also be cleaned of the mud which settles in it from time to time, but it is not necessary to do this as often as it is to clean the boiler. All the plates and flues should have the soot which sticks to them thoroughly cleaned off.

Although the cleaning of the boiler and the grates is usually committed to a special set of men, yet the locomotive runner should examine them personally to see that it is properly done. He should pay attention to the condition of the grate, and see whether it is level and smooth. As soon as one or more of the bars are bent crooked, they usually burn out. If one of the bars is burnt out the fire falls through the hole that it leaves into the ash-pan, and then the fire under the grate will heat it red hot, and finally may melt every bar. Every grate-bar which is only a little damaged or bent must therefore be removed as quickly as possible and replaced with a new one.

As soon as the engine is run into the engine-house, all superfluous grease which has escaped from the wearing surfaces and the dust or mud which adheres to the engine should be wiped off with cotton waste or rags. This is usually done by men employed for the purpose. While they are doing this, they should examine every part thoroughly and observe whether it is in good condition, and if any defects are found they should be reported to the proper person whose business it is to have them repaired. As the faithfulness and skill of a fireman are often estimated by the good or bad condition of his engine, he should, if for no other reason, take pains to keep it clean and everything in as good condition as possible.

If the engine is taken to pieces in order to be thoroughly repaired, the runner, if he does not help to do this, should watch carefully the taking it apart and the putting it together again, as in this way he can become thoroughly familiar with the construction of the machine he runs.

QUESTION 501. *What precaution must be taken to prevent the water in a locomotive from freezing, if it is laid up?*

Answer. In very cold weather, if engines are laid up for any considerable time, no water must be left in the tender, boiler or any of the pipes. If, however, the engine must be soon used, and it is impracticable to let the water out of the boiler and tender, then, if exposed to the cold, a light fire must be kept in the boiler sufficient to make steam enough to warm the water in the tender. The water should, however, be drawn out of the pumps and the feed and supply pipes. This can be done by opening the pet-cocks, and closing the tender valves and uncoupling the hose, which will allow the water in the supply pipes to run out. By running the engine a few revolutions the pumps will then be emptied. The pipes and the pumps can also be prevented from freezing without uncoupling the hose if the tender valves are closed and the pet-cocks opened, and steam is then admitted into the supply pipes by the heater-cocks. This forces part of the water which is in the pumps out of the pet-cocks and warms the rest. This, however, requires constant watchfulness to prevent freezing, and in excessively cold weather, if the engine must lay up for any considerable time, it is always best to empty the pumps and pipes.

PART XXVIII.

ACCIDENTS TO LOCOMOTIVES.

QUESTION 502. *What are the most serious accidents which may happen in running a locomotive?*

Answer. The most serious accidents are:

1. Collision of two trains approaching each other.
2. Collision of a moving with a standing train.
3. Collision of trains at the crossing of two railroads.
4. Running a train into the opening left by an open draw-bridge.
5. Escape of an engine without any one on it.
6. Running off the track.
7. Explosion of the boiler.
8. Bursting or rather collapse of a flue.
9. Blowing out of a bolt, stud or rivet from the boiler.
10. Failure of the feed-pumps, injector or check-valve.
11. Breaking or bursting of a cylinder, cylinder-head, steam-chest, or steam-pipe.
12. Breaking or getting loose of the piston or cross-head or bending of the piston-rod.
13. Breaking or bending of a connecting-rod or crank-pin.
14. Breaking of a tire, wheel or axle.
15. Breaking of a spring, spring-hanger or equalizer.

16. Breaking of a frame.

17. Breaking or getting loose of a part of the valve-gear.

18. Failure of the throttle-valve.

19. Breaking of a coupling.

QUESTION 503. *What should be done to prevent a collision when two trains are approaching each other?*

Answer. The obvious thing to do is to stop the trains as soon as possible. This is done by applying the brakes at once with all their power, and then reversing the engine, although it is best not to do the latter until the train is somewhat checked, as there is always danger of bursting the cylinder or breaking the cylinder-heads, piston or connections if an engine is reversed suddenly at a high speed. Of course the higher the speed, the greater is the danger of injury from this cause, and therefore it is best, if there is time, first to check the speed of the train before reversing the engine. When the engine is reversed, the sand-valves should be opened so as to increase the adhesion of the wheels, so that when their motion is reversed they may check the speed of the train as soon as possible. On perceiving danger ahead the order of procedure should be as follows:

1. Shut the throttle-valve.

2. If the train is equipped with hand brakes alone, blow the danger signal for their application, or if the train has a continuous brake, apply it with its full force.

3. Reverse the engine and open the throttle and the sand valves.

4. If a collision is inevitable, shut the throttle-valve before the engines meet, because if it is left open, after

the collision and when the speed of the train is checked, the engine, if not disabled, will by its own power crush through the wreck and thus do additional damage.

QUESTION 504. *What should be done if a standing train should see another train approach it and there should be danger of a collision?*

Answer. The locomotive runner of the standing train should start his engine in the same direction as the approaching train is running, as quickly as possible, because the shock of the collision will be very much lessened if both trains are moving in the same direction compared with what it would be if one was standing still.

QUESTION 505. *What should be done to avoid a collision at a railroad crossing?*

Answer. As was explained in answer to Question 485, trains should always come to a dead stop before crossing another railroad on the same level. If, however, through any means danger of such a collision should be incurred, then evidently the one train should be stopped and the other moved out of the way as soon as possible.

QUESTION 506. *How can an accident by running into the opening at a draw-bridge be avoided?*

Answer. First by ALWAYS coming to a dead stop before reaching it, and second by not starting again until it is absolutely certain that the draw is closed. Of course if a locomotive runner of an approaching train finds a draw open, the only thing he can do is to stop as soon as possible.

QUESTION 507. *What measures should be taken to prevent locomotives from escaping without a responsible person on them?*

Answer. In the first place when a locomotive is left standing the throttle-valve should always be *closed* and *fastened*, the cylinder cocks should also be opened so that if any steam leaks into the cylinders it will not accumulate there, but will escape, and the reverse lever should be placed in the centre of the sector, so that if by any accident the throttle should be opened the engine will not start.

QUESTION 508. *If a locomotive should escape, what should be done, and how may it be captured?*

Answer. The first thing to be done is to telegraph to the stations towards which the escaped engine is running, either to keep the track clear, or, if there is a train approaching, to open a switch and thus let the engine run off the track. An escaped engine may be captured by a swifter engine following it, but this is always attended with great danger, as the first engine may leave the track or become wrecked. A safer plan is to telegraph ahead of the escaped engine and have an engine placed in a position where the track can be seen for a long distance in the direction in which the runaway is expected. As soon as the latter comes in sight, the waiting engine should start in the same direction, so that when they get near to each other they will both be running in the same direction and at nearly the same speed. By regulating the speed of the front engine, the following one may be allowed to come up to it quite gently, and then a man can easily climb from the one engine to the other, and thus both be stopped.

QUESTION 509. *What should be done in case an engine gets off the track?*

Answer. The first thing to do is to close the throttle-valve and "signal for brakes,"* or apply the continuous brakes if the train is equipped with them, and then reverse the engine. If its position after it stops is much inclined, it is generally necessary to draw the fire to prevent injury to the heating-surface, a part of which is then usually exposed to the steam, and therefore not covered with water.

QUESTION 510. *How is a locomotive replaced on the track in case it gets off?*

Answer. It is impossible to give any directions for replacing locomotives on the track which will meet the great variety of circumstances which occur in practice. If the engine has not run far from the rails, it can usually be run on again by placing blocks of wood under the wheels and thus running them up to their proper position, but if the engine falls on its side or runs down an embankment, it is usually necessary to send for the appliances which are now provided on nearly all roads for removing wrecks and replacing engines on the track. These appliances are generally stored in what is called a wrecking or tool car, which is placed at a convenient point on the road, from which it can be sent to any place where its services are likely to be needed. Such cars are generally provided with ropes, jack-screws, chains, crowbars, levers, etc., to be used in such cases, and generally a special set of men is sent with the wrecking car to direct and assist in replacing engines and cars on the track. It would lead us too far to describe all the methods of doing this employed under various circumstances; and as such work seldom forms part of the duties of a lo-

* This expression means, among railroad men, to signal to brakemen by blowing the whistle to have them apply the brakes.

comotive runner, a complete description would be out of place here.

QUESTION 511. *After an accident which disables the engine, what is the first thing to do?*

Answer. The first thing to do is always to "*protect the train;*" that is, to send out signal men in each direction to stop approaching trains; otherwise they might run into the wrecked train, and thus cause a double accident.

QUESTION 512. *What is the chief cause of boiler explosions?*

Answer. The cause of all boiler explosions, as happily expressed by a prominent American engineer,* is THAT THE PRESSURE INSIDE THE BOILER IS GREATER THAN THE STRENGTH OF THE MATERIAL OUTSIDE TO RESIST THAT PRESSURE. This may occur in two ways: first, and most frequently with locomotives, from insufficient strength of the boiler to bear the ordinary working pressure; and second, from the gradual increase of heat and pressure until the latter is greater than the boiler was calculated to bear.

Insufficient strength may be due: 1, to defects of the original design, owing to the ignorance of the strains to which the material of the boiler will be exposed, and its power of resistance; 2, to defective workmanship and material, which can usually be discovered by careful inspection; 3, to the reduction of the original strength of the boiler by ordinary wear and tear or neglect, which can also usually be discovered by careful inspection.

The first two causes have been fully discussed in

* See Fifth Annual Report of the American Master Mechanics' Association. page 196.

the part relating to boiler construction, and the last under the head of inspection of locomotives.

Over-pressure is nearly always due to some defect of the safety-valve, or to the fact that it is overloaded. This latter often occurs when safety-valves are set by a defective steam gauge, which indicates too little pressure. Over-pressure may also occur by letting an engine stand alone with a large fire in its fire-box and possibly with the blower turned on.

A boiler may, by suddenly opening the throttle-valve, undoubtedly be subjected to very severe strain that may possibly be sufficient to cause its destruction, even though it had sufficient strength to bear the ordinary pressure at which the safety-valve blows off. Suddenly opening or closing the throttle-valve may produce a violent rush of steam and water against the part of the boiler whence the steam is drawn. The percussion of the water and steam in such cases has been known to shake the whole boiler, and to lift the safety-valve momentarily right off its seat.* The weakest parts of a locomotive are the two sides where the barrel joins the outside fire-box. Many boilers, especially those with a high wagon-top, have flat spaces at this point, which it is impossible to stay properly. It is at this point, too, that the expansion and contraction of the tubes and the outside shell exert their greatest strains, and it will therefore be found, generally, that the seams at this point begin to leak before any others, and for these reasons it is believed that all the seams which join the outside shell of the fire-box to the barrel should be double-riveted.

* Wilson on Boiler Construction.

The practice of ascribing steam-boiler explosions to obscure causes has been productive of much mischief, as it engenders a carelessness on the part of those having charge of them, who have been led to believe that no amount of care will avail against the mysterious agents at work within the boiler. Explosions are also, in the absence of other convenient reasons, very generally attributed to shortness of water. This is often nothing more than a convenient method of shifting the responsibility from the builder or owner of the locomotive to the runner or fireman, who, if not killed by the explosion, in many cases might just as well be, so far as his ability to defend himself is concerned.*

QUESTION 513. *What should a locomotive runner and fireman do to avoid and prevent explosions?*

Answer. 1. The height of the water in the boiler should always be maintained so as to cover the heating surfaces. 2. The boiler should be kept as clean, that is, as free from scale, mud and other impurities, as possible. 3. It should never be subjected to strains from sudden heating or cooling. 4. The steam-gauge and safety-valves should be examined and tested frequently, to be sure they are in order; and 5, they should examine every part of the boiler which is accessible, but especially the stay-bolts, to see that there is no fracture of any part or any injurious corrosion or other dangerous defect.

QUESTION 514. *What should be done in case of the bursting or collapse of a tube?*

Answer. As soon as possible after it occurs, the runner must stop the train, and close first the end of

* Wilson on Boiler Construction.

the flue in the fire-box, and then that in the smoke-box, by driving in *iron plugs*, which are usually provided for the purpose. These plugs are attached to the end of a bar, with which they are inserted into the tubes. If the escape of water and steam from the tube is so great as to make it difficult to see the end of the tube, the steam may sometimes be drawn up the chimney by starting the blower. If, however, the escape is so great as to make it impossible to insert the plug, then the steam pressure must be reduced by running with both pumps on, or by starting the injector; or it may be necessary to draw the fire and cool off the engine. When a flue collapses, the front end of which is behind the steam or petticoat pipes, it is usually necessary to cool off the engine before a plug can be inserted, especially if any considerable amount of water and steam escape from it. While driving in the plug, the runner and fireman should always keep themselves in such positions that the plug can not hit them in case it is blown out by the steam. If the engine is not supplied with iron flue-plugs, a wooden plug can be cut of the proper size and driven in. This can be attached to the bar referred to and inserted; but if no such bar is carried with the engine, the wooden plug can be made on the end of a long pole and then cut nearly off. It is then inserted into the flue and driven in and broken off. It will be found that such plugs will burn off even with the end of the flue, but will not burn entirely out.

QUESTION 515. *What should be done in case a bolt, stud or rivet blows out of the boiler and thus allows the steam or hot water to escape?*

Answer. If it is accessible, cut a plug on the end of a long pole and drive it in in the same way as described above. This will avoid the necessity of cooling off the engine; but in some cases it will be found that a plug can not be inserted or driven in without drawing the fire and cooling off the boiler.

QUESTION 516. *In case it is found necessary to draw the fire and cool off the boiler, and if so much water has escaped as to uncover the crown plate, what must be done?*

Answer. If the leak has been stopped or the fault remedied, one of the safety-valves should be taken off and water poured into the boiler with pails or buckets through the opening left by the removal of the safety-valve until the crown sheet is covered. The fire may then be kindled again and the engine complete its journey. When bituminous coal is used for fuel, the necessity for drawing the fire in case of accident may often be avoided by completely covering or "banking" the fire with fine coal which has been wet, and closing the dampers and opening the furnace door. In this way the fire may be smothered and the boiler cooled without putting the fire out, so that after the defect is remedied it will not be necessary to rekindle it.

QUESTION 517. *What must be done in case of the failure of one or both of the feed pumps or of the injector or check-valve?*

Answer. If one of the pumps fails the other one may be used, but the defect or obstruction to the first should be remedied as soon as possible, because the second may also fail. It will then be necessary to depend upon the injector alone, if there is one, for feeding the boiler. Only after all the appliances for feeding the boiler have failed and the water is so low as to be in danger of exposing the crown sheet, should the fire be drawn or banked, and the runner should then at once give the proper signals for warning and the protection of his train, and if he is unable to repair the pumps or injector, he must send for aid to the nearest accessible point.

QUESTION 518. *In case a pump fails, how should it be examined in order to discover the defect?*

Answer. As explained in the answer to Question 458, the working of a pump is usually indicated by the stream which escapes from the pet-cock. If, when this is opened, steam and water escape, it is an indication that the check-valve is not working properly. When this occurs hot water will escape if the pet-cock is opened when the engine is standing still, but the pump may still feed the boiler if the upper or pressure-valve works properly. When the check-valve does not work as it should, it is also indicated by the heating of the feed-pipe, owing to the escape of hot water from the boiler through the check-valve when the pet-cock is opened. If, when the plunger is drawn out of the pump, air is sucked in through the open pet-cock, then the upper or pressure-valve of the pump does not work, but the working of the pump may still be secured by the working of the check-valve; but if the pump, air-chamber and feed-pipe then get filled with air, the plunger may compress this air at each stroke, and as it can then follow the plunger during its outward stroke, the latter will not suck water, but will simply compress the air during the inward stroke, which will then expand during the outward stroke. This will be indicated by the escape of air from the pet-cock when the plunger is moving inward, and the suction of air when the plunger is moving outward. This can be known by holding the hand in front of the pet-cock. Usually, however, the air is mixed with water so that the stream which escapes from the pet-cock is broken or irregular. If air escapes from the pet-cock during the inward stroke of the plunger, but none is sucked in during the outward stroke, it shows that there is a leak somewhere in the pump or pipes, and that it is pumping air instead of water. The leak may be in the stuffing-box of the plunger, the joints of the pump or pipes, in the hose or their connections with the supply-pipe or tender. If neither air nor water escapes from the pet-cock during the inward stroke of the pump plunger, or, if the stream of water at that time is weak, then it indicates that the suction or lower valve of the pump is not working properly. The same thing will occur if the pipe, pump or tender-valve is obstructed. If there is a cock, as there always should be, just above the suction-valve, it will aid us very much to discover the fault when the pump will not work. If, when this cock is opened, cold water escapes from it, the fault is in the suction-valve; if hot water, then it is the pressure and check-valves which are leaky, obstructed or broken, and consequently the hot water from the boiler leaks back into the pump. In the absence of such a cock, the fault can often be discovered by feeling the pump barrel with the hand. If the pump can not be made to work, and the fault is found to be in the lower valve, it must be taken out and examined; or if the fault is in the pipes, it can usually be easily remedied. If the pipes are burst with only a small fracture, it can usually be remedied by covering the aperture with canvas or rubber and wrapping twine around it tightly. The upper valve of a pump must, however, never be taken down without first being sure that the check-valve is tight, because if it is not, the person will be likely to be scalded in taking the pump apart.

Directions for managing an injector, and also for taking care of pumps in cold weather, have already been given in the answers to Questions 142 and 488.

QUESTION 519. *What should be done in case of the breaking or bursting of a cylinder or cylinder-head?*

Answer. The main connecting rod must be taken down on that side of the engine. The piston should then be moved to the front or back end of the cylinder and wooden blocks be placed between the guides so as to fill up the space between the cross-head and the end of the guide-bars, and thus prevent the cross-head and piston from moving. The valve stem should then be disconnected from the rocker, and the valve moved to the middle of the valve face, so as to cover up both steam-ports. It must then be fastened in that position by screwing up *one* of the bolts of the stuffing-box of the valve stem, so as to make the gland bind against the valve stem. The train should then be run cautiously to the next station with the use of *one* cylinder. If the engine is not able to haul the train with one cylinder, then it should be uncoupled from the train and run to the first telegraph station or other point where the aid of a helping engine can be obtained or telegraphed for. In the meanwhile the train must be protected by the proper signals. Should the engine continue its journey with one cylinder, it must be started, if it should happen to be standing at the dead point, by *pushing* or by means of *crow-bars.* In so doing, however, the bars should not be put between the spokes of the wheels, as they may easily be caught in the wheels when the engine starts, and in this way the spokes be broken or the persons who are using the crow-bars be badly hurt.

QUESTION 520. *What must be done in case a steam-chest or steam-pipe is broken?*

Answer. If a steam-chest is broken a block of wood should be bolted over the mouth of the steam passage, so as to prevent the escape of the steam from the steam-pipe on that side. It will sometimes require considerable ingenuity to devise means of fastening such a block or blocks of wood so as to cover the mouth of the steam passage. As cylinders are now usually made, the blocks can be fastened by cutting them to the proper form and size, and then placing a thick block on top, and bolting the steam-chest cover down on top of it. If the cover is broken, a part of it may be used or a piece of plank with a few holes bored into it be employed instead. In some cases a piece of board can be bolted over the end of the steam-pipe. When the latter is broken, it should be taken down and a piece of board or plank bolted over the opening of the T-pipe to which the steam-pipe was attached. The engine can then be run with one cylinder as before, although usually in such cases it is not necessary to disconnect any other parts than the valve stem.

QUESTION 521. *What must be done if a piston, cross-head, connecting-rod or crank-pin is broken or bent?*

Answer. If the piston, cross-head or main connecting-rod is broken, the same course must be pursued as when a cylinder is broken. If a coupling-rod or a crank-pin of a trailing-wheel is broken, then it is necessary to take down both the coupling-rods, but not to disconnect the main connecting-rods or their attachments, unless they are injured.

QUESTION 522. *If one coupling-rod is broken or taken down, why must the other be taken down also?*

Answer. Because if only one rod is used there is then nothing to help the cranks of the trailing wheels past the dead-points, so that in starting, or if they are moving slowly when they reach these points, they are quite as likely to revolve in one direction as the other. If they happen to turn in the reverse direction to that in which the wheels to which they are coupled are moving, then the crank-pins of one or the other pair of wheels are very liable to be broken or bent.

QUESTION 523. *What must be done if a driving-wheel tire or driving-axle breaks?*

Answer. If a tire on a main driving-wheel or the wheel itself breaks, the driving-box of the broken wheel or tire should be held up by putting a wooden block under the box. An ordinary American engine can then be run on three driving-wheels, but it must be run with the utmost caution. If the engine has more than four driving-wheels there is usually less difficulty in running it, if one of the main wheels is injured, than if there are only four. But it is almost impossible to give directions which will be applicable to all the accidents of this kind that may occur to different kinds of engines. If none of the connecting-rods, crank-pins or crank-pin bosses are injured, it is not necessary to disconnect either side, but if the injury is of such a nature that the coupling-rod must be taken down on one side, the one on the other side must be taken down too. If the main crank-pin and connecting-rod are not disabled, both cylinders may be used even if one of the main wheels or tires is broken. But even if one side of the engine must be entirely disconnected, the engine may still be run with one cylinder and by driving one wheel. If a main axle breaks the engine can usually be run, but great caution must be exercised. In such cases, however, if assistance or a telegraph office is near where the accident occurs, it is usually best to send for assistance at once, rather than take the risks which attend the attempt to run an engine so seriously injured.

QUESTION 524. *What must be done when a trailing or leading driving-wheel, tire or axle breaks?*

Answer. Very much the same course must be pursued as was described in the previous answer, although it is generally less difficult to run with a trailing or leading axle broken than it is when the main axle has met with such an accident.

QUESTION 525. *What must be done if an engine-truck wheel or axle breaks?*

Answer. It is usually best to chain up the end of the truck-frame over the broken axle or wheel to the engine frame and place a cross-tie across the other end of the truck-frame, between it and the engine frame, so that the weight of the engine may rest on the cross-tie. If a part of the flange or a piece of the wheel is broken out, the wheels should be turned around so that the unbroken part will rest on the rail, and they should then be chained or otherwise fastened so that they cannot revolve, and thus be made to slide on the rails and carry the weight of the engine in that way. The same plan is employed if a tender wheel breaks, but one end of a tender-truck frame must be chained up. It is usually necessary to place a cross-tie across the top of the tender, and fasten the chains to it.

QUESTION 526. *What must be done in case a driving-spring, spring-hanger or equalizing-lever breaks?*

Answer. As the breaking of a spring or spring-hanger may cause a more serious accident, the engine and train should be stopped as soon as possible after it occurs. If the hanger is broken and there is a duplicate on hand, it should be substituted in place of the broken one. If there is no duplicate, then the spring should be taken down, and a wooden block be placed between the top of the driving-box and the frame to support the weight which before rested on the spring. In order to insert this block, if it is a front spring which is broken, it is usually best to raise the engine with jack-screws or run the back wheels on inclined blocks of wood placed under each of the back wheels. This raises the weight off from the front-wheels, and the block can then be inserted between the box and frame. If it is one of the springs over the back wheels which is broken, the front wheels should be run on the wooden wedges. Such wedges can soon be cut out of a cross-tie with an axe, or by sawing a square stick of wood diagonally it will make two such wedges. The end of the equalizing lever next to the broken spring must be supported by inserting a piece of wood under it. This will usually be held securely by the weight which is suspended from the opposite end, bearing the blocked end down on the block.

QUESTION 527. *What should be done if an engine-truck or tender spring breaks?*

Answer. Very much the same course must be pursued that is employed when a driving-spring breaks, excepting that usually the weight can be lifted off from a truck-box easier by placing a jack under the end of the truck-frame than by the method described. Usually, too, each of the truck-springs supports the weight on two of the wheels, so that the two boxes must be blocked up.

QUESTION 528. *What must be done in case the engine-frame is broken?*

Answer. Usually very little need be done excepting to exercise more than usual caution in running, and to reduce the speed. Of course the breakage of a frame may disable the engine, but ordinarily in such accidents that is not the case.

QUESTION 529. *How can it be known if an eccentric has slipped on the axle?*

Answer. It is indicated at once by the irregular sound of the exhaust, or, as locomotive runners say, the engine will be "*lame.*"

QUESTION 530. *When it is known that an eccentric has slipped, how can it be learned which is the one that is misplaced?*

Answer. This can usually be learned by examining the marks which should always be made on the eccentrics and on the axles. If no such marks have been made by the builder of the engine, the runner himself should make them, after the valves have been set correctly. The effect upon the valve when an eccentric slips is either to increase or diminish the lead. Therefore, by running the engine slowly with the link first in full forward and then in full back gear, and observing whether steam is admitted at each end of the cylinder just before the crank reaches the dead points, it can be known which eccentric has moved. If it has slipped in one direction the lead will be increased and steam will be admitted to the cylinder some time before the piston reaches the end of the stroke. If it has moved the opposite way, the lead will be diminished and steam will not be admitted until after the piston has reached the end of its stroke. The admission of steam will be indicated by its escape from the cylinder cocks.

QUESTION 531. *If by any means the valve stem or either of the eccentric rods should be lengthened or shortened, how can it be known?*

Answer. The crank on one side should be placed at one of the dead points and the cylinder-cocks opened; then admit a little steam to the cylinder, by opening the throttle-valve slightly, and throw the reverse lever from full gear forward to full gear backward, and observe whether steam escapes all the time from the end of the cylinder at which the piston stands. Then repeat the operation with the crank at the other dead point. If either of the eccentric rods or the valve stem have been lengthened or shortened, it will cause the valve to cover the steam-port either at the front or back end of the cylinder, so that no steam will escape from the cock at that end. If the length of one of the eccentric rods has been changed, then when the altered rod is in gear the valve will have too little or no lead at one end of the cylinder and too much at the other. If, therefore, this occurs when the forward rod is in gear and *not* in back gear, it indicates that the length of the forward rod has been altered. If the reverse occurs it shows that it is the back-motion rod whose length has been changed. It must be observed that if the length of an eccentric rod is altered the lead will be changed only at that part of the link which is operated by the altered rod. That is, if the forward eccentric rod is too long or too short, the lead at the front and back ends of the cylinder in forward gear only will be affected. If the back eccentric rod is changed the valve will be affected only in back gear. If, however, the length of the valve stem is changed, the lead will be changed in both forward and back gear. The valves on each side of the engine can, of course, be tested in the same way.

QUESTION 532. *When it is discovered which eccentric has slipped, how should it be reset?*

Answer. If it has been marked, it is simply turned back so that the marks correspond with each other again. This is done by first loosening the set-screws, and, after the eccentric is turned to the proper place, tightening them up again. When an eccentric slips it is often caused by the cutting of the eccentric-straps, valve or other part of the valve-gear, so that these should always be examined to see whether they are properly oiled. If the eccentrics have not been marked, the valve may be set by placing the crank at the forward dead-point, and the reverse lever in the front notch of the sector and the full part of the forward-motion eccentric *above* the axle. Then admit a little steam into the steam-chest, open the cylinder cocks, and move the forward-motion eccentric slowly forward until steam escapes from the front cylinder cock, which will show that the steam-port is opened and the valve has some lead. To set the backward-motion eccentric the crank is placed in the same position, but the reverse lever is thrown into the back notch and the full part of the eccentric is placed *below* the axle. Then move this eccentric forward until steam escapes from the *front* cylinder cock as before. In order to verify the position of the eccentrics the crank may be placed at the back dead-point and the reverse lever moved backward and forward, at the same time observing whether steam escapes from the back cylinder cock when the link is in back and forward gear.

QUESTION 533. *What should be done in case an eccentric-strap or rod, or rocker arm or shaft, or the valve stem breaks?*

Answer. If an eccentric-strap or rod breaks, the broken rod and strap should be taken down, and the valve stem disconnected from the rocker and the valve fastened in the middle position of the valve face, and the engine should be run with one cylinder only. The same course must usually be pursued if a rocker breaks. If the valve-stem breaks, it is not necessary to disconnect the link and eccentric rods, but simply to fasten the valve in the centre of the valve face.

QUESTION 534. *If a link hanger or saddle, or a lifting arm should break, what may be done?*

Answer. The valve-gear may be used on that side of the engine by putting a wooden block in the link slot above the link block, so as to support the link near the position at which it works the valve full stroke forward. Of course the engine can then be run in only one direction, and should therefore be run with the utmost caution. If, however, it should be necessary to back the train on a side track, it can be done by taking out the wooden block and substituting a longer one, so that the link will be supported in a position near that at which it works the valve full stroke backward. These blocks must be fastened in some way, either with rope or twine, so that they will be held in their position when the engine is at work.

QUESTION 535. *If the lifting shaft itself or its vertical arm, the reverse lever or rod, should break, what can be done?*

Answer. If it is impossible to devise any temporary substitute or method of mending them, both links can be blocked up as described above.

QUESTION 536. *In case the throttle-valve should fail, what should be done?*

Answer. If such an accident occurs, especially if it happens about a station, it is attended with great danger. If it is found that steam can not be shut off from the cylinders with the throttle-valve, then the reverse lever should be placed in the middle of the sector. If this does not prevent the engine from moving, the reverse lever should be alternately thrown into forward and then into back gear, and at the same time every aperture, such as the safety-valve and heater cocks, should be opened, and every means be taken to cool the boiler as quickly as possible. The fireman should open the furnace door, close the ash-pan dampers, and start the blower so as to draw a strong current of cold air into the furnace and through the tubes. At the same time the injector should be started and the fire drawn as quickly as possible. After the boiler is cooled, the cover of the steam-dome may be removed and the valve examined if the defect can not be discovered in any other way. Of course if the accident occurs on the open road, the train must be at once protected by sending out signals in each direction.

QUESTION 537. *What must be done in case a coupling breaks?*

Answer. When a coupling between the cars or tender breaks, if the front end of the train is immediately stopped, there will be danger that the back end of it, which is broken loose, will run into the front end, and thus do great damage. As it always occurs, when a coupling of a passenger train breaks, that the signal bell in the cab is rung, the first impulse of a runner under such circumstances is to stop the engine. He should, however, be careful not to do so if on shutting off steam he finds that the train has broken in two, but should at once open the throttle in order to get the front end of the train out of the way of the rear end. The ease with which the speed of a train is arrested with continuous brakes has increased the danger of accident from this cause. Usually a runner learns by the sudden start of the engine that the train has separated, and when that occurs he should never apply the brakes.

QUESTION 538. *If from any cause the supply of water in the tender becomes exhausted, what must be done?*

Answer. It is best, if it can be done without risk of injury to the engine, to run the train on a side track and then draw the fire. If no water can be obtained near enough to supply the tender with buckets, help must be sent for; but if there is a well, stream or pond of water near, the tender can be partly filled by carrying water.

Question 539. *In case an engine becomes blockaded in a snow storm with plenty of fuel, but runs out of water, what can be done?*

Answer. Snow should be shoveled into the tender and steam admitted through the heater cocks so as to melt the snow.

Question 540. *If a locomotive without an injector should be obstructed in a snow storm or in any other way so that it could not move, and therefore could not work the pumps, what should be done in case the water in the boiler should get low?*

Answer. The weight of the engine should be lifted off from the main driving-wheels and the coupling rods disconnected from the main crank-pin, so that the main wheels can turn without moving the engine. These can then be run and the pumps thus be worked. The weight can usually be most conveniently taken off from the main wheels by running the trailing wheels on wooden blocks, and thus raising up the back end of the engine.

Question 541. *If it is impossible, in a snow storm or in very cold weather, to keep steam in the boiler without danger, what should be done?*

Answer. Draw the fire, blow all the water out of the boiler, empty the tanks, disconnect the hose and slacken up the joints in the pumps and injector so that all the water in them can escape, and thus prevent them from freezing up.

PART XXIX.

ACCIDENTS AND INJURIES TO PERSONS.

QUESTION 542. *In case an accident occurs and one or more persons are seriously injured, what can be done by those present?*

Answer. In such cases it very often happens that with knowledge and sufficient coolness to apply that knowledge, one or more non-medical persons who are present when an accident occurs can do as much or more toward saving life and allaying pain, *before* a doctor comes, than he can *afterwards.* The following cases cited by Dr. Howe in his book on "Emergencies" will illustrate this:

"*Case* 1.—A machinist was admitted to a New York hospital suffering from wounds of the wrist and palm of the hand. On arriving at the hospital the entire clothing on one side of his body was saturated with blood, from the loss of which he was partly insensible. On making an examination, it was found by the surgeon that a folded handkerchief was bandaged over the centre of the wrist, and that the wound in the palm of the hand was untouched. The pad was placed on the wrist, as if the greatest care had been exercised to avoid pressing on either of the two arteries. The bleeding in this case could easily have been controlled if the bandage and pad had been properly applied. The patient, however,

45*

developed erysipelas, and, not having sufficient vitality to carry him through, died the fifth day."

"*Case* 2.—A laborer fell from the front platform of a car at Harlem, and had his right foot crushed by one of the wheels. An ordinary bandage was placed on the limb without any compress over the vessels. In bringing the man to the hospital, the rough jolting of the carriage set the wound bleeding, and by the time he reached his destination he was apparently lifeless. The vessels were tied and stimulants administered, but he never rallied. Death occurred six hours after his admission. His injuries, independent of the bleeding, might indeed have terminated his life; still the chances would have been in his favor if a compress had been applied to the limb to prevent bleeding. The fact that such a thing was not done shows either culpable negligence or deplorable ignorance."

Many similar cases constantly occur where a little intelligent timely action of those present would save the life of an injured person, who without such help must die before professional surgical aid can be obtained.

QUESTION 543. *When it is found that one or more persons are seriously injured, what is the first thing to be done?*

Answer. The first thing to do is to extricate the person or persons from the danger, and at the same time send a messenger for a doctor. If it is doubtful if one can be obtained by sending in one direction, send two or more messengers in different directions.

QUESTION 544. *To what kind of injuries are locomo-*

tive runners and other persons employed or traveling on railroads exposed?

Answer. They are liable to be bruised or crushed in case of collision or running off the track, or of injury from falling off the train, or of being run over by a moving train. Brakemen and others whose duty it is to couple cars are liable to have their hands, arms or bodies crushed between the cars, and locomotive runners are sometimes burned or scalded if an accident happens to their engines. Train-men are also frequently exposed to very great cold in winter and heat in summer, and are thus liable to be frost-bitten or sun-struck. Passengers are seldom injured excepting through their own carelessness, unless in cases of collision or running off the track and the destruction of the cars. Strangers and even railroad employes are frequently run over by trains while walking on the track, and frequent accidents occur to deaf people in this way, and it is not very unusual to hear of train-men who sit on the main track at night while their trains are waiting on the side-track for another train to pass, go to sleep while in that position, and then are run over by the passing train.

QUESTION 545. *When persons are crushed or dangerously wounded, what are the chief immediate sources of danger and death when their wounds are not necessarily fatal?*

Answer. First, excessive bleeding in case an artery is ruptured; second, the shock to the whole system, from which the sufferer may not have the strength to recover.

QUESTION 546. *When does bleeding from a wound become dangerous?*

Answer. Profuse bleeding is always dangerous, but it should be remembered that bleeding occurs from two sources: first from the arteries, which are the vessels which convey the blood *from* the heart, and second from the veins, through which the blood flows back to the heart. The first is called *arterial* bleeding and the second *venous* bleeding. Now it must be remembered that the heart is the great force-pump of the body, and that it supplies all parts of the body with blood, somewhat as the feed-pump of a locomotive supplies the boiler with water. The arteries referred to fulfill the same purpose that the feed-pipe does to a locomotive pump—they convey the fluid from the pump to the place where it is needed. Now the blood is forced into these arteries with a certain amount of pressure, so that if any of them are cut or injured the blood will flow out in a jet or spurt just as the water will escape from a feed-pipe if that is ruptured. The blood which flows through the veins back to the heart may, on the other hand, be compared to the water in the supply pipes of a locomotive pump, that is, there is very little pressure on it, and therefore if they are injured the flow of blood from them is less rapid than from the arteries. It will therefore be seen that arterial bleeding is much more dangerous, because the blood flows from them under a pressure.

QUESTION 547. *How can arterial bleeding be distinguished from venous bleeding?*

Answer. The blood is of a bright scarlet color, and is forced out in successive jets; each jet corresponds with the movements of the heart. This characteristic spurting is caused by the intermittent force-pump action of the heart, driving out the blood. Venous bleeding is distinguished from arterial by the dark-blue color of the blood when flowing from the wound. It never flows in repeated jets, but oozes slowly from the wounded surfaces. Venous blood is traveling toward the heart, and there is consequently little force behind to cause a more rapid flow. This form of bleeding is comparatively harmless, unless occurring from very large veins.*

QUESTION 548. ***How can the bleeding be stopped in case an artery is cut or ruptured?***

Answer. The most efficient and available method is the application of PRESSURE on the artery BETWEEN THE WOUND AND THE HEART. Under ordinary circumstances this can be most effectively done with what is called a *field tourniquet,* which is simply a handkerchief passed around the limb above the wound, the ends of which are then tied together. A pad is then made, either of cloth rolled up, a piece of wood, or a round stone about the size of a hen's egg well wrapped, or any substance from which a firm pad can be quickly made, which is placed over the artery. The handkerchief is then placed over the pad and a short stick put through it on the opposite side of the limb and twisted around until the pad compresses the artery firmly. While the tourniquet is being prepared, some one should compress the artery with his fingers or thumb, so as to prevent as much loss of blood as possible.

QUESTION 549. ***What is the position of the arteries in the body and how can their location be known?***

Answer. The position of the principal arteries is

* "Emergencies and How to Treat Them," by Joseph W. Howe, M. D.

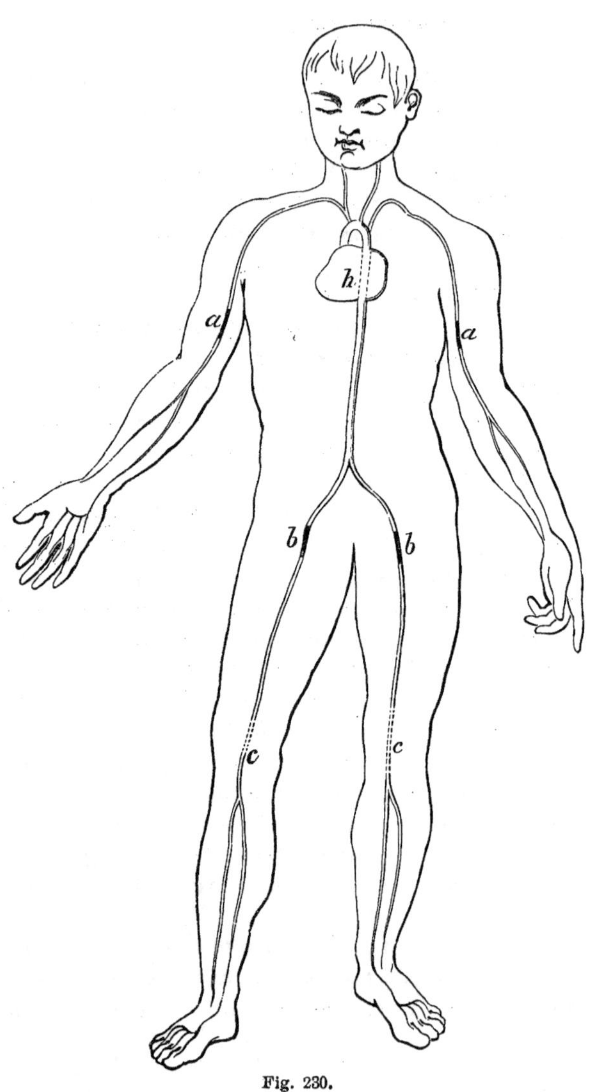

Fig. 230.

shown in fig. 230. They proceed from the heart *h* with branches, *a, a,* and *b, b,* which extend along each limb. These branches subdivide again below the knees and elbows, and again in the hands and feet. The position of the arteries can be felt by their pulsation at almost any part of them, but when they are buried below the muscles it is more difficult than when they are near the surface.

QUESTION 550. *In case of a wound and rupture of the arteries in the arm, what should be done?*

Answer. The artery at *a* should be firmly compressed with the thumb until a bandage and pad from which a tourniquet can be made are prepared. The pad should then be applied over the artery and compressed as explained in answer to Question 548. The bleeding can also be stopped by placing a round piece of wood or other form of pad between the arm at *a* and the body and then tying the arm tightly against the body, so that the pad will be pressed against the arm.

QUESTION 551. *In case of rupture to an artery below the knee, where should the pressure be applied?*

Answer. The artery approaches near the surface at *c, c,* immediately back of the knee, where it is represented in dotted lines in fig. 230. Pressure should therefore be applied at that point first with the thumb until a tourniquet can be applied. The bleeding can also be stopped by elevating the leg and allowing it to rest on the back of a chair or other similar support. The weight of the leg will then bring sufficient pressure on the artery to stop the bleeding. A towel or other soft material should be placed over the back of the chair, so that the pressure will not be too painful to the sufferer.

QUESTION 552. *If an artery is ruptured in the leg above the knee, where should the pressure be applied?*

Answer. In the thigh at *b*, where the beating or pulsations in the artery can be distinctly felt. The reader should familiarize himself with the position of the arteries by feeling their location in his own body. By doing so he may be able to save the life of a companion or other person in case of accident, whereas without such knowledge the injured person would die.

QUESTION 553. *After the arterial bleeding has been stopped, if blood should continue to ooze out of the wound, what should be done?*

Answer. The wound should be filled with lint or cotton waste; and the limb then be bandaged by beginning at its extremity and wrapping the bandage closely and evenly around it so as to bring, as nearly as possible, an equal pressure on the whole of it. Bandaging the limb in this way up to the point where the pressure is applied to the artery, will prevent swelling, and the veins will be compressed so that the blood will not flow from their torn extremities.

QUESTION 554. *When the bleeding has been stopped, what should be done?*

Answer. The injured person should be laid in as comfortable a place as can be procured for him, and should be given a moderate drink of water. If much exhausted, two or three tablespoonsful of brandy or whisky, mixed with an equal quantity of water, should be given first, and smaller quantities, *of not* MORE THAN A TABLESPOONFUL at a time, should then be given every half hour. Usually wounded persons are given too much stimulant, so that frequently they are injured more than they are benefited thereby.

After a person has lost much blood, he feels an intolerable thirst, but if too much water is given him, he is apt to become sick and vomit, which weakens him still more. It is therefore best to give him very little water, say a teaspoonful at a time, after the first drink, or if ice can be obtained, give the sufferer pieces of ice frequently, which can be allowed to melt slowly in his mouth.

QUESTION 555. *When a person is insensible, what should be done for him?*

Answer. Lay him down in as comfortable a place as the circumstances will permit, and protect him from cold, rain or hot sun, as may be needed. A common error is to place injured and insensible persons in an erect position or in a chair. If he is insensible he should *always* be laid down with his head slightly lower than his body. Then water should be dashed two or three times on his face, and warm bricks, stones or pieces of iron, such as coupling links or pins, applied to his feet and in the arm-pits and between the thighs, being careful that the warm objects applied are not hot enough to burn. Then cover the person with blankets, heavy coats or anything else which will keep him warm. Wounded persons soon become cold and chilled, the effects of which are very injurious, and therefore especial pains should be taken to keep them warm. In very cold weather there is great danger that injured persons will be frost-bitten, which must be carefully guarded against.

In case of shock, when the injured person lies pale, faint, cold and sometimes insensible, with feeble pulse and labored breathing, anything like excitement must be avoided, as it tends to exhaust the patient.

All assistance and attention should be given to a wounded person with the least noise and excitement, and all crowds and idle spectators should be driven away and every effort made to keep the sufferer comfortable and quiet. If food is given it should be in the form of beef tea or broth, and in small quantities at a time.

QUESTION 556. *In case any bones are broken, what should be done?*

Answer. The limb should be supported as comfortably as possible until a doctor's services can be obtained. There is danger with a broken limb that the bones will protrude through the flesh and skin, to avoid which the limb should be placed in a natural position and laid on a pillow, car cushion or other soft object. This should then be wrapped around the limb and tied in this position, so as to prevent any movement of the broken bones.

QUESTION 557. *If a person is crushed or severely burned, what should be done?*

Answer. The immediate danger from such injuries arises from the "shock" to the system. It is usually best to bandage the part which is crushed until surgical aid can be obtained, and the sufferer treated as explained in answer to Question 548.

QUESTION 558. *What should be done for a person who has been burned or scalded?*

Answer. Lint or cotton waste saturated with molasses and water should be applied to the wound, or the latter should be dusted with wheat flour, and then dressed with lint or cotton waste, and loosely bandaged.

If the injury should be severe, a shivering followed by depression is very likely to come on. To check this, warmth in the form of hot applications and stimulants should be used, as already explained.

QUESTION 559. *What should be done for a frost-bite?*

Answer. Warmth should be applied to the frozen part very gradually by rubbing with snow or pouring cold water on it. The occurrence of stinging pain, with a change in color, is a signal to stop all rubbing or other measure which might excite inflammation. If the frozen part turns black the next day, a poultice should be applied.

If persons exposed to the cold become very much exhausted or sleepy, stimulants should be given, as explained in answer to Question 554, and the body briskly rubbed with the hands and warm flannel or other woolen material.

QUESTION 560. *How should a person be treated who has been sun-struck?*

Answer. Apply cold water or ice to the head, place the sufferer in a cool place, and make him comfortable. After being sun-struck the person should not work for some days or weeks thereafter, until his health and strength are fully recovered.

PART XL.

RESPONSIBILITY AND QUALIFICATIONS OF LOCOMOTIVE RUNNERS.*

QUESTION 561. *What are the dangers to which the runner and the fireman are exposed by their work on the engine?*

Answer. Runners and firemen are not only exposed to great bodily injury or even death by every accident which may happen to their engine, but unless they are very careful to preserve their health it is quickly destroyed by the constant changes of the weather to which their position exposes them, and also by the effect of the heat of the fire and by the smoke by which they are often surrounded.

In order to protect themselves in a measure from the injurious effects of change of weather, smoke, cold, etc., frequent bathing and cleansing of the skin are absolutely necessary, and also the wearing of a woolen undershirt next the skin at all seasons.

The gases of coal which pour out of the furnace-door, if it is opened when the throttle is closed, have an especially injurious effect on the throat, lungs, etc. They should always see to it, therefore, that the blower is always started before the fire-door is opened, in order that these injurious gases, which have col-

* NOTE.—The greater part of this chapter is a translation from Prof. George Kosak's "Katechismus der Einrichtung und Betriebes der Locomotive."

lected during a halt, may be drawn forward and up the smoke-stack by the draft.

The steady, loud clatter which the engine makes while running has an injurious influence on the nervous system. The runner should therefore endeavor to lessen these shocks of the engine as far as possible by keeping watch over it and keeping its parts accurately adjusted. In order to keep himself fresh and strong in his service, which is extremely exhaustive to body and mind, the runner must try to strengthen himself by regular, temperate living, and eating abundant nourishing food. The common use of strong drinks, which undermines the mental and physical strength of men, should be avoided by a person occupying the exhaustive and responsible position of a locomotive runner. If in ordinary life a drunken man is unfit for any simple work, how shall a drunken runner or fireman undertake the difficult management of so great, so delicate and so costly a machine as a locomotive? How can hundreds of men quietly trust their lives and limbs to such a man, whom no one can help despising? Rightfully, therefore, conscientious railroad managers place the greatest stress on the *sobriety* of the runners and firemen, and instantly discharge from their service those who give themselves up to a passion for drink.

Owing to the demands which their daily labor makes upon their strength and endurance, locomotive runners should be careful not to increase the drain by dissipation, irregular hours or overwork. There seems to be something about the power of endurance of the human frame analogous to the capacity of a bar of iron or steel to resist strains. So long as the strains do not exceed the elastic limit, that is if the bar recovers its original length when the strain is removed, it will bear millions of such strains without becoming weaker; but if it is strained so hard that it is permanently stretched, then comparatively few applications of the force will rupture the bar. In a similar way, if the strain or fatigue which a man endures is no more than he will recover from after the ordinary rest, he can endure an almost unlimited number of such strains, but if the fatigue exceeeds his "elastic limit," then he soon becomes permanently injured thereby. It often happens that an excessive amount of work is unavoidable, but when it can be avoided it should be by those who wish to preserve their health and strength.

In order to save themselves from great injuries, runners and firemen should always act with the greatest caution, and never rush carelessly into danger. They should never adopt the principle of foolhardy and thoughtless people, who by the consciousness of continual danger fall into the habit of carelessly "trusting to their luck," etc. On the contrary, they should always face the danger with their eyes open and with the greatest conscientiousness. Many try to show great courage by scorning the danger, and some such even wish to meet a little in order to be able to show their pluck. These should bear in mind that they have a great responsibility laid upon them, and that it is not alone their own well-being or life which is at stake in case of any mishap, but that by their careless behavior they may wound or kill the helpless people who are committed to their care, cause incalculable misery by robbing families of their sole support and of their children; and bring great sorrow and mourning to their fellow-men. The thought of the curse and the despair of the survivors may give sleepless hours even to a locomotive runner who knows himself to have been without any fault regarding an accident; how much more must it be with him who cannot give himself this assurance? There are not wanting instances in which the runner who caused such an accident by his thoughtlessness, driven to despair by his own heavily-burdened conscience, went miserably to ruin.

QUESTION 562. *What requirements and duties should every locomotive runner fulfill?*

Answer. Every locomotive runner should fulfill the following requirements and duties:

1. He should have an exact knowledge of the engine intrusted to him, and a general knowledge of the nature and construction of steam engines generally. Likewise, he should be perfectly familiar with the management of the boiler, the running of the engine, and the way of keeping the working parts in good condition; also, with the forms and peculiarities of the line of road on which he runs, the rules which govern the running of trains and with the signal system adopted.

2. *Health* and *bodily strength* he must have in abundant measure in his position, which is exhausting and in which he is exposed to all sorts of weather.

3. He should have a good, plain common-school education, and be ready at reading, writing and arithmetic.

4. He should always carry out *exactly* and *cheerfully* the regulations of the service, or the instructions given him by special orders from the officers over him.

5. *Faithfulness, frankness* and *honesty*, which characterize an upright man in ordinary life, and also the strictest *temperance* in the use of strong drink, he should possess in a high degree in his very responsible position.

6. He should have acquired a certain degree of skill in putting together and taking apart locomotives, and also in repairing separate parts of them. It is desirable that he should always be present when his own engine is taken apart, put together or repaired, in order that he may acquire a thorough knowledge of its condition and learn to understand properly the importance of its various parts.

7. In caring for his engine he must preserve perfect cleanliness and order, and in using fuel he must manifest the greatest care and rigid economy.

8. Whenever there is danger, coolness and self-possession are indispensably necessary, and any thoughtlessness or recklessness is to be strictly avoided.

9. Towards his superior officers his behavior should be respectful and obliging; towards those under him, patient and kindly, and at all times he should avoid profanity and all intemperate language. He should endeavor, as far as possible, to instruct the fireman who accompanies him and make him familiar with the construction and management of the engine, and should see that he does his work strictly in accordance with his instructions.

It is the *fireman's* duty to follow the runner's instructions strictly, and in case of any sudden disability of the runner he must stop the engine in accordance with the instructions given him, and then give the proper signals for help, until another runner arrives. In the meanwhile the engine is to be kept at a halt with all the usual precautions.

10. The runner should try to keep himself informed of the progress and improvement of locomotives by reading suitable books and technical periodicals, and when possible acquire some skill in geometrical and mechanical drawing, in order to accustom himself to accurate work and sound and systematic thinking.

QUESTION 563. ***What studies should mechanics, locomotive runners and firemen take up, and what technical books should they read?***

Answer. As already stated, they should know how to read and write their own language, and understand arithmetic and have some knowledge of geography. Every locomotive runner and fireman has a good deal of spare time, a part of which he can devote to study, and all of them, even if they have not had the advantage of early education, could by industry and perseverance acquire a knowledge of "reading, writing and ciphering." The assistance of a good teacher should always be procured, if possible. With so much knowledge, some book on natural philosophy can be read to advantage, and then some book on mechanics. The following list of books is given, which the student will do well to read in the order in which they are named. It should always be remembered, however, that the mere buying of books contributes very little knowledge to the owner. It is the reading and ***understanding*** them which "increases knowledge."

LIST OF BOOKS FOR MECHANICS, LOCOMOTIVE RUNNERS, FIREMEN, ETC.

A Hand Book of the Steam Engine, by John Bourne; published by Longmans, London; $2.00.

A Catechism of the Steam Engine, by John Bourne; published by Longmans, London; $2.00.

Lessons in Elementary Physics, by Balfour Stewart; published by Macmillan & Co., New York; $1.50.

Experimental Mechanics, by Prof. Ball; published by Macmillan & Co., New York; $6 00.

The New Chemistry, by Prof. J. P. Cooke; published by Appleton & Co., New York; $2 00.

Elementary Treatise on Heat, by Balfour Stewart; published by Macmillan & Co, New York; $3.00.

Combustion of Coal, by C. Wye Williams; published by Lockwood & Co., London; $1.20.

A Treatise on Steam Boilers, by Robert Wilson; published by Lockwood & Co., London; $3.00.

Link-Valve Motion, by Wm. S. Auchincloss; published by D. Van Nostrand, New York; $3.00.

The Conservation of Energy, by Balfour Stewart; published by Appleton & Co., New York; $1.50.

Richards' Steam Engine Indicator, by Charles T. Porter; published by Longmans, London; $2.50.

PLATES.

PLATE IV.

DIMENSIONS, WEIGHT, ETC.,

OF

FOUR-WHEELED SWITCHING LOCOMOTIVE,

BY THE HINKLEY LOCOMOTIVE WORKS, BOSTON, MASS.

Gauge of Road	4 ft. 8½ in.
Number of Driving-Wheels	4
Number of Front Truck-Wheels	None.
Number of Back Truck-Wheels	None.
Total Wheel Base	6 ft. 9 in.
Distance between Front and Back Driving-Wheels	6 ft. 9 in.
Total Weight of Locomotive in working order	48,000 lbs.
Total Weight on Driving-Wheels	48,000 lbs.
Diameter of Driving-Wheels	50 in.
Diameter of Truck-Wheels	None.
Diameter of Cylinders	15 in.
Stroke of Cylinders	22
Outside Diameter of smallest Boiler ring	44¾ in.
Size of Grate	3 × 3⅔ ft.
Number of Tubes	121
Diameter of Tubes	2 in.
Length of Tubes	10½ ft.
Square Feet of Grate surface	11
Square Feet of Heating surface in Fire-Box	71
Square Feet of Heating surface in Tubes	580
Total Feet of Heating surface	651
Exhaust Nozzles — single or double	Double.
Diameter of Nozzle	2¾ in
Size of Steam Ports	10 × 1¼ in.
Size of Exhaust Ports	2¼ in.
Throw of Eccentrics	4½ in.
Outside Lap of Valve	¾ in.
Inside Lap of Valve	None.
Size of Main Driving-axle Journal	6½ × 7 in.
Size of other Driving-axle Journal	6½ × 7 in.
Size of Truck-axle Journal	None.
Diameter of Pump Plunger	1⅞ in.
Stroke of Pump Plunger	22 in.
Capacity of Tank	1,200 gallons.

Plate IV.

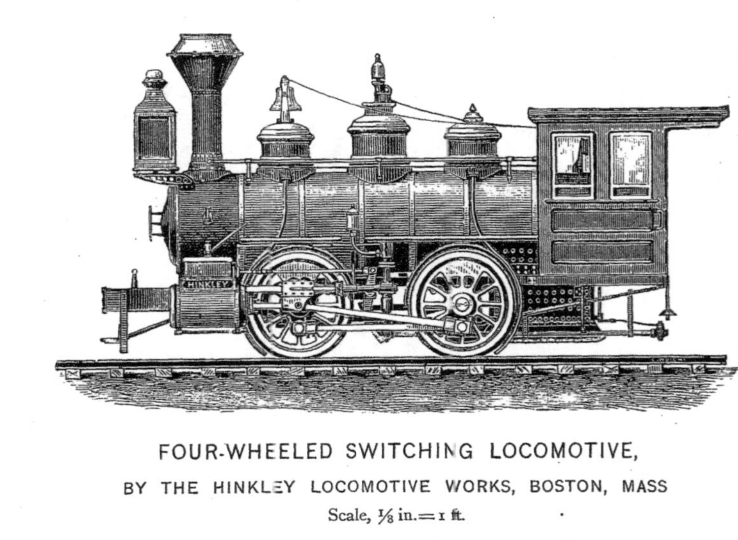

FOUR-WHEELED SWITCHING LOCOMOTIVE,

BY THE HINKLEY LOCOMOTIVE WORKS, BOSTON, MASS

Scale, 1/8 in. = 1 ft.

A

PLATE V.

DIMENSIONS, WEIGHT, ETC.,

OF

EIGHT-WHEELED "AMERICAN" LOCOMOTIVE

BY THE BALDWIN LOCOMOTIVE WORKS, PHILADELPHIA.

Gauge of Road	4 ft. 8½ in.
Number of Driving-Wheels	4
Number of Front Truck-Wheels	4
Number of Back Truck-Wheels	None.
Total Wheel Base	21 ft. 9 in.
Distance between centres of Front and Back Driving-Wheels	96 in.
Total Weight of Locomotive in working order	65,000 lbs.
Total Weight on Driving-Wheels	42,000 lbs.
Diameter of Driving-Wheels	60¾ in.
Diameter of Truck-Wheels	28 in.
Diameter of Cylinders	16 in.
Stroke of Cylinders	24 in.
Outside Diameter of smallest Boiler Ring	48 in.
Size of Grate	65 × 34½ in.
Number of Tubes	144
Diameter of Tubes	2 in.
Length of Tubes	10 ft 11 in.
Square Feet of Grate surface	15.5
Square Feet of Heating surface in Fire-Box	100.6
Square Feet of Heating surface in Tubes	825.4
Total Feet of Heating surface	926
Exhaust Nozzles — single or double	Double.
Diameter of Nozzle	2¾ to 3¼ in.
Size of Steam Ports	1¼ × 15 in.
Size of Exhaust Ports	2½ × 15 in.
Throw of Eccentrics	5½ in.
Outside Lap of Valve	¾ in.
Inside Lap of Valve	1-32 in.
Size of Main Driving-axle Journal	7 in. dia. × 8 in.
Size of other Driving-axle Journal	7 in. dia. × 8 in.
Size of Truck-axle Journal	4½ × 7½ in.
Diameter of Pump Plunger	2 in.
Stroke of Pump Plunger	24 in.
Capacity of Tank	2,000 gallons.

Plate V.

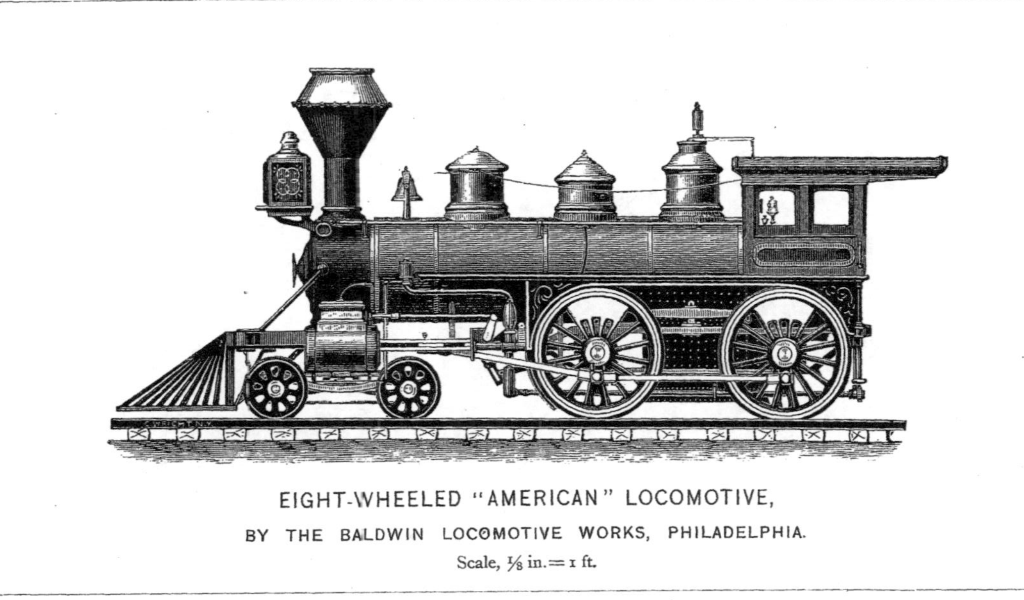

EIGHT-WHEELED "AMERICAN" LOCOMOTIVE,

BY THE BALDWIN LOCOMOTIVE WORKS, PHILADELPHIA.

Scale, ⅛ in. = 1 ft.

PLATE VI.

DIMENSIONS, WEIGHT, ETC., OF EIGHT-WHEELED "AMERICAN" LOCOMOTIVE

BY THE GRANT LOCOMOTIVE WORKS, PATERSON, N. J.

Gauge of Road	4 ft. 8½ in.
Number of Driving-Wheels	4
Number of Front Truck-Wheels	4
Number of Back Truck-Wheels	None.
Total Wheel Base	21 ft. 9 in.
Distance between centres of Front and Back Driving-Wheels	8 ft.
Total Weight of Locomotive in working order	62,000 lbs.
Total Weight on Driving-Wheels	42,000 lbs.
Diameter of Driving-Wheels	61 in.
Diameter of Truck-Wheels	28 in.
Diameter of Cylinders	16 in.
Stroke of Cylinders	24 in.
Outside Diameter of smallest Boiler Ring	48 in.
Size of Grate	60 × 34 in.
Number of Tubes	140
Diameter of Tubes	2 in.
Length of Tubes	11 ft.
Square Feet of Grate surface	14
Square Feet of Heating surface in Fire-Box	98
Square Feet of Heating surface in Tubes	805
Total Feet of Heating surface	903
Exhaust Nozzles — single or double	Double.
Diameter of Nozzle	3¼ to 3¾ in.
Size of Steam Ports	1¼ × 14 in.
Size of Exhaust Ports	2½ × 14 in.
Throw of Eccentrics	5 in.
Outside Lap of Valve	¾ in.
Inside Lap of Valve	None.
Size of Main Driving-axle Journal	6½ dia. × 7¾ in.
Size of other Driving-axle Journal	6½ dia. × 7¾ in.
Size of Truck-axle Journal	4½ dia. × 8 in.
Diameter of Pump Plunger	2 in.
Stroke of Pump Plunger	24 in.
Capacity of Tank	2,000 gallons.

Plate VI.

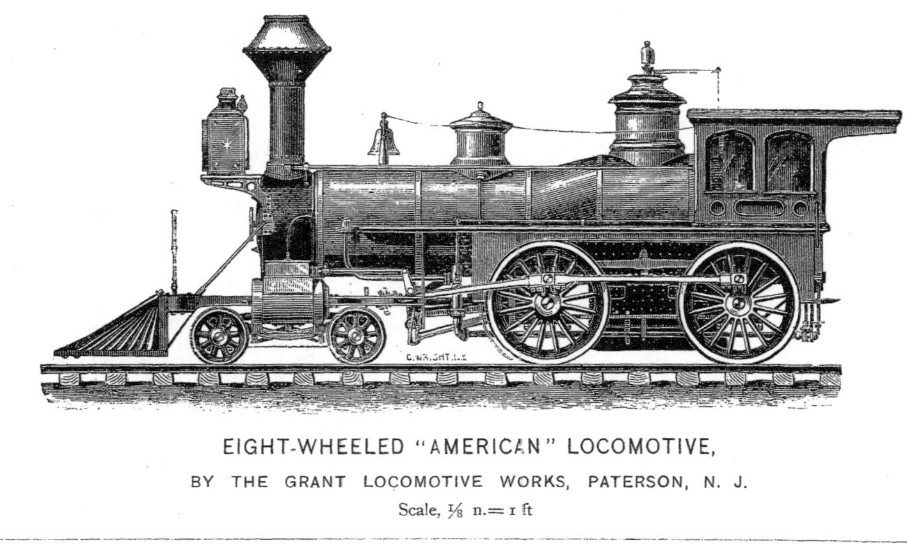

EIGHT-WHEELED "AMERICAN" LOCOMOTIVE,
BY THE GRANT LOCOMOTIVE WORKS, PATERSON, N. J.
Scale, 1/8 n. = 1 ft

PLATE VII.

DIMENSIONS, WEIGHT, ETC., OF

EIGHT-WHEELED "AMERICAN" LOCOMOTIVE

BY THE

DANFORTH LOCOMOTIVE AND MACHINE CO., PATERSON, N. J.

Gauge of Road	4 ft. 8½ in.
Number of Driving-Wheels	4
Number of Front Truck-Wheels	4
Number of Back Truck-Wheels	None.
Total Wheel Base	21 ft. 2 in.
Distance between centres of Front and Back Driving-Wheels,	7 ft. 9 in.
Total Weight of Locomotive in working order	60,200 lbs.
Total Weight on Driving-Wheels	38,350 lbs.
Diameter of Driving-Wheels	5 ft. 7⅝ in.
Diameter of Truck-Wheels	2 ft. 6 in.
Diameter of Cylinders	15 in.
Stroke of Cylinders	24 in.
Outside Diameter of smallest Boiler Ring	3 ft. 10 in.
Size of Grate	56 × 34½ in.
Number of Tubes	136
Diameter of Tubes	2 in.
Length of Tubes	11 ft.
Square Feet of Grate surface	13.5
Square Feet of Heating surface in Fire-Box	86
Square Feet of Heating surface in Tubes	775
Total Feet of Heating surface	861
Exhaust Nozzles — single or double	Double.
Diameter of Nozzle	2¾ in.
Size of Steam Ports	1¼ × 13½ in.
Size of Exhaust Ports	2½ × 13½ in.
Throw of Eccentrics	5½ in.
Outside Lap of Valve	⅞ in.
Inside Lap of Valve	⅛ in.
Size of Main Driving-axle Journal	6½ in.
Size of other Driving-axle Journal	6½ in.
Size of Truck-axle Journal	4½ in.
Diameter of Pump Plunger	2⅛ in.
Stroke of Pump Plunger	24 in.
Capacity of Tank	1,800 gallons.

Plate VII.

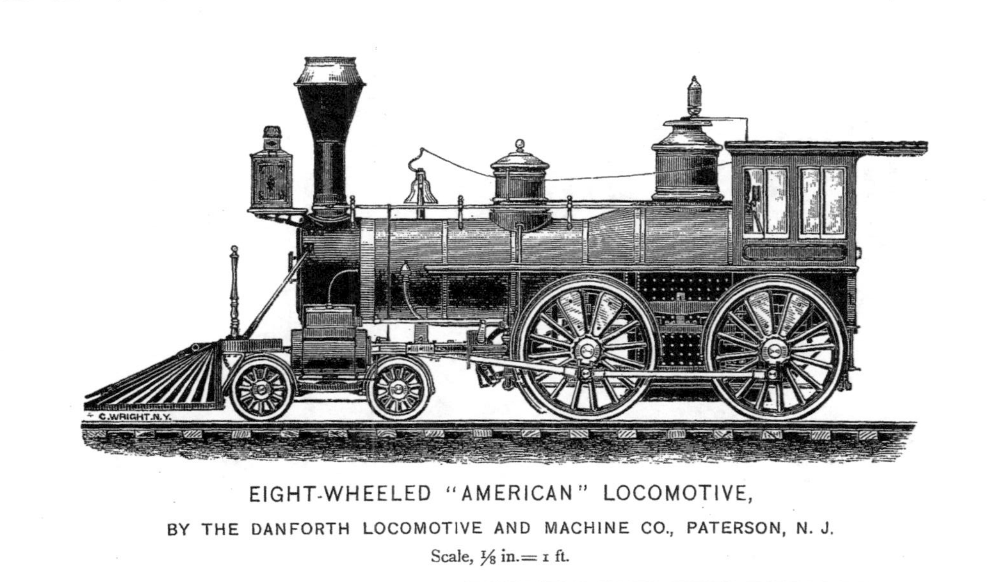

EIGHT-WHEELED "AMERICAN" LOCOMOTIVE,

BY THE DANFORTH LOCOMOTIVE AND MACHINE CO., PATERSON, N. J.

Scale, $\frac{1}{8}$ in. = 1 ft.

PLATE VIII.

DIMENSIONS, WEIGHT, ETC., OF EIGHT-WHEELED "AMERICAN" LOCOMOTIVE

BY THE MASON MACHINE WORKS, TAUNTON, MASS.

Gauge of Road	4 ft. 8½ in.
Number of Driving-Wheels	4
Number of Front Truck-Wheels	4
Number of Back Truck-Wheels	None.
Total Wheel Base	22 ft.
Distance between centres of Front and Back Driving-Wheels	8 ft.
Total Weight of Locomotive in working order	62,000 lbs.
Total Weight on Driving-Wheels	40,000 lbs.
Diameter of Driving-Wheels	5 ft. 6 in.
Diameter of Truck-Wheels	2 ft. 9 in.
Diameter of Cylinders	1 ft. 5 in.
Stroke of Cylinders	2 ft.
Outside Diameter of smallest Boiler Ring	3 ft. 10 in.*
Size of Grate	66 × 35¾ in.
Number of Tubes	155
Diameter of Tubes	2 in.
Length of Tubes	11 ft. 2 in.
Square Feet of Grate surface	16.38
Square Feet of Heating surface in Fire-Box	105
Square Feet of Heating surface in Tubes	906
Total Feet of Heating surface	1011
Exhaust Nozzles — single or double	Single.
Diameter of Nozzle	3¾ in.
Size of Steam Ports	15 × 1¼ in.
Size of Exhaust Ports	15 × 2¾ in.
Throw of Eccentrics	4½ in.
Outside Lap of Valve	⅞ in.
Inside Lap of Valve	1-16 in.
Size of Main Driving-axle Journal	6½ × 7½ in.
Size of other Driving-axle Journal	
Size of Truck-axle Journal	3¼ × 6½ in.
Diameter of Pump Plunger	1¾ in.
Stroke of Pump Plunger	24 in.
Capacity of Tank	2,250 gallons.

* The Boiler is made conical, 46 in. diameter at the Smoke-Box and 50 in. at the Fire-Box.

Plate VIII.

EIGHT-WHEELED "AMERICAN" LOCOMOTIVE,

BY THE MASON MACHINE WORKS, TAUNTON, MASSACHUSETTS.

Scale, ⅛ in. = 1 ft.

PLATE IX.

DIMENSIONS, WEIGHT, ETC., OF EIGHT-WHEELED "AMERICAN" LOCOMOTIVE

BY THE HINKLEY LOCOMOTIVE WORKS, BOSTON, MASS.

Gauge of Road	4 ft. 8½ in.
Number of Driving-Wheels	4
Number of Front Truck-Wheels	4
Number of Back Truck-Wheels	None
Total Wheel Base	21 ft. 4½ in.
Distance between centres of Front and Back Driving-Wheels	7 ft. 6 in.
Total Weight of Locomotive in working order	63,000 lbs.
Total Weight on Driving-Wheels	41,000 lbs.
Diameter of Driving-Wheels	68 in.
Diameter of Truck-Wheels	30 in.
Diameter of Cylinders	16 in.
Stroke of Cylinders	24 in.
Outside Diameter of smallest Boiler Ring	46 in.
Size of Grate	3 ft. × 5 ft.
Number of Tubes	150
Diameter of Tubes	2 in.
Length of Tubes	11 ft.
Square Feet of Grate surface	15
Square Feet of Heating surface in Fire-Box	100
Square Feet of Heating surface in Tubes	755
Total Feet of Heating surface	855
Exhaust Nozzles — single or double	Double.
Diameter of Nozzle	3 in.
Size of Steam Ports	14 × 1¼ in.
Size of Exhaust Ports	2⅜ in.
Throw of Eccentrics	5 in.
Outside Lap of Valve	13-16 in.
Inside Lap of Valve	None.
Size of Main Driving-axle Journal	7 × 7 in.
Size of other Driving-axle Journal	7 × 7 in.
Size of Truck-axle Journal	4½ × 7 in.
Diameter of Pump Plunger	1⅞ in.
Stroke of Pump Plunger	24 in.
Capacity of Tank	2,000 gallons.

Plate IX.

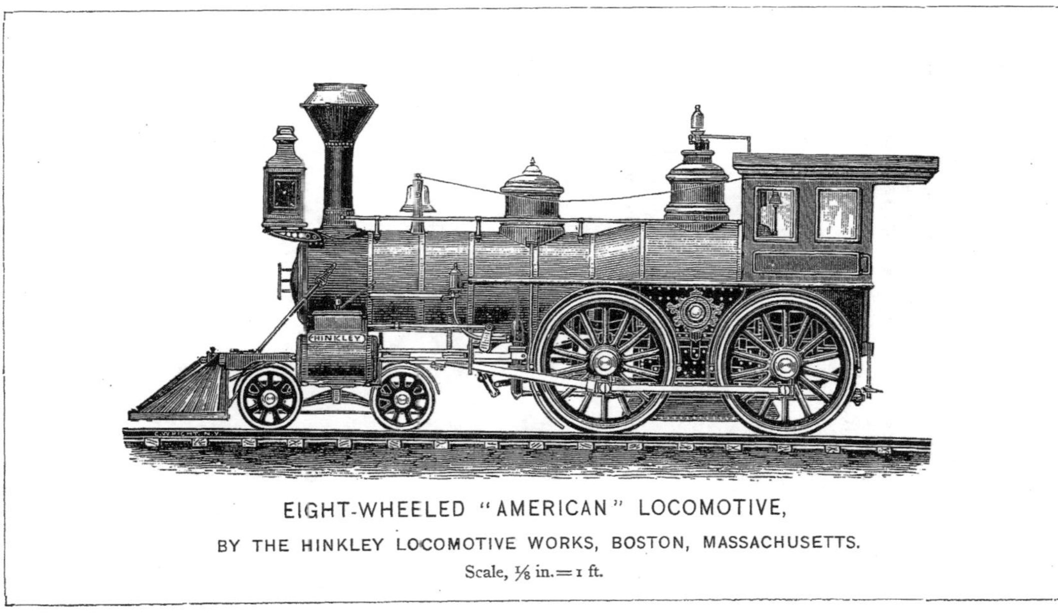

EIGHT-WHEELED "AMERICAN" LOCOMOTIVE,

BY THE HINKLEY LOCOMOTIVE WORKS, BOSTON, MASSACHUSETTS.

Scale, ⅛ in. = 1 ft.

Plate x.

DIMENSIONS, WEIGHT, ETC.,
OF
TEN-WHEELED LOCOMOTIVE,

By the Baldwin Locomotive Works, Philadelphia.

Gauge of Road	4 ft. 8½ in.
Number of Driving-Wheels	6
Number of Front Truck-Wheels	4
Number of Back Truck-Wheels	None.
Total Wheel Base	23 ft. 6 in.
Distance between centres of Front and Back Driving-Wheels	88 in.
Total Weight of Locomotive in working order	78,000 lbs.
Total Weight on Driving-Wheels	58,000 lbs.
Diameter of Driving-Wheels	54 in.
Diameter of Truck-Wheels	26 in.
Diameter of Cylinders	18 in.
Stroke of Cylinders	24 in.
Outside Diameter of smallest Boiler Ring	50 in.
Size of Grate	60 × 34½ in.
Number of Tubes	152
Diameter of Tubes	2 in.
Length of Tubes	12 ft. 9 in.
Square Feet of Grate surface	14.37
Square Feet of Heating surface in Fire-Box	94
Square Feet of Heating surface in Tubes	1014
Total Feet of Heating surface	1108
Exhaust Nozzles — single or double	Double.
Diameter of Nozzle	3 to 3½ in.
Size of Steam Ports	1¼ × 16 in.
Size of Exhaust Ports	2½ × 16 in.
Throw of Eccentrics	5½ in.
Outside Lap of Valve	¾ in.
Inside Lap of Valve	1-32 in.
Size of Main Driving-axle Journal	7 in. dia. × 8 in.
Size of other Driving-axle Journal	7 in. dia. × 8 in.
Size of Truck-axle Journal	4¼ × 7½ in.
Diameter of Pump Plunger	2 in.
Stroke of Pump Plunger	24 in.
Capacity of Tank	2,200 gallons.

Plate X.

TEN-WHEELED LOCOMOTIVE,

BY THE BALDWIN LOCOMOTIVE WORKS, PHILADELPHIA,

Scale, ⅛ in. = 1 ft.

PLATE XI.

DIMENSIONS, WEIGHT, ETC., OF "MOGUL" LOCOMOTIVE,

BY THE BALDWIN LOCOMOTIVE WORKS, PHILADELPHIA.

Gauge of Road	4 ft. 8½ in.
Number of Driving-Wheels	6
Number of Front Truck-Wheels	2
Number of Back Truck-Wheels	None.
Total Wheel Base	22 ft. 8 in.
Distance between centres of Front and Back Driving-Wheels	96 in.
Total Weight of Locomotive in working order	77,000 lbs.
Total Weight on Driving-Wheels	66,000 lbs.
Diameter of Driving-Wheels	52 in.
Diameter of Truck-Wheels	30 in.
Diameter of Cylinders	18 in.
Stroke of Cylinders	24 in.
Outside Diameter of smallest Boiler Ring	50 in.
Size of Grate	66 × 34½ in.
Number of Tubes	161
Diameter of Tubes	2 in.
Length of Tubes	11 ft. 3 in.
Square Feet of Grate surface	16
Square Feet of Heating surface in Fire-Box	102.7
Square Feet of Heating surface in Tubes	948
Total Feet of Heating surface	1051
Exhaust Nozzles—single or double	Double.
Diameter of Nozzle	3 to 3½ in.
Size of Steam Ports	1¼ × 16 in.
Size of Exhaust Ports	2½ × 16 in.
Throw of Eccentrics	5½ in.
Outside Lap of Valve	¾ in.
Inside Lap of Valve	1-32 in.
Size of Main Driving-axle Journal	7 in. dia. × 8 in.
Size of other Driving-axle Journal	7 in. dia. × 8 in.
Size of Truck-axle Journal	5 in. dia. × 8 in.
Diameter of Pump Plunger	2 in.
Stroke of Pump Plunger	24 in.
Capacity of Tank	2,200 gallons.

Plate XI.

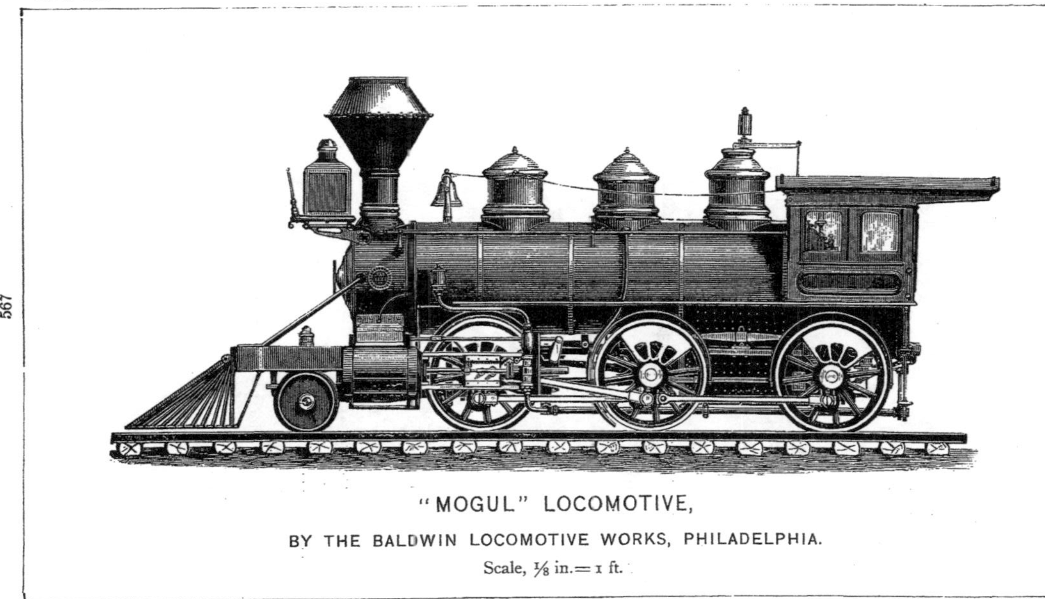

"MOGUL" LOCOMOTIVE,

BY THE BALDWIN LOCOMOTIVE WORKS, PHILADELPHIA.

Scale, ⅛ in. = 1 ft.

PLATE X

DIMENSIONS, WEIGHT, ETC.,

OF

"CONSOLIDATION" LOCOMOTIVE,

BY THE

DANFORTH LOCOMOTIVE AND MACHINE CO., PATERSON, N. J.

Gauge of Road	4 ft. 8½ in.
Number of Driving-Wheels	8
Number of Front Truck-Wheels	2
Number of Back Truck-Wheels	None.
Total Wheel Base	23 ft. 2 in.
Distance between centres of Front and Back Driving-Wheels	15 ft. 7 in.
Total Weight of Locomotive in working order	96,550 lbs.
Total Weight on Driving-Wheels	86,430 lbs.
Diameter of Driving-Wheels	4 ft. 2 in.
Diameter of Truck-Wheels	2 ft. 7 in.
Diameter of Cylinders	20 in.
Stroke of Cylinders	24 in.
Outside Diameter of smallest Boiler Ring	4 ft. 2 in.
Size of Grate	120 × 34¾ in.
Number of Tubes	165
Diameter of Tubes	2¼ in.
Length of Tubes	13 ft. 9¼ in.
Square Feet of Grate surface	29
Square Feet of Heating surface in Fire-Box	139
Square Feet of Heating surface in Tubes	1370
Total Feet of Heating surface	1509
Exhaust Nozzles—single or double	Double
Diameter of Nozzle	3½ in.
Size of Steam Ports	1½ × 15½ in.
Size of Exhaust Ports	2¾ × 15½ in.
Throw of Eccentrics	5½ in.
Outside Lap of Valve	⅝ in.
Inside Lap of Valve	None.
Size of Main Driving-axle Journal	6¾ in.
Size of other Driving-axle Journal	6¾ in.
Size of Truck-axle Journal	5 in.
Diameter of Pump Plunger	2¼ in.
Stroke of Pump Plunger	24 in.
Capacity of Tank	2,400 gallons.

Plate XII.

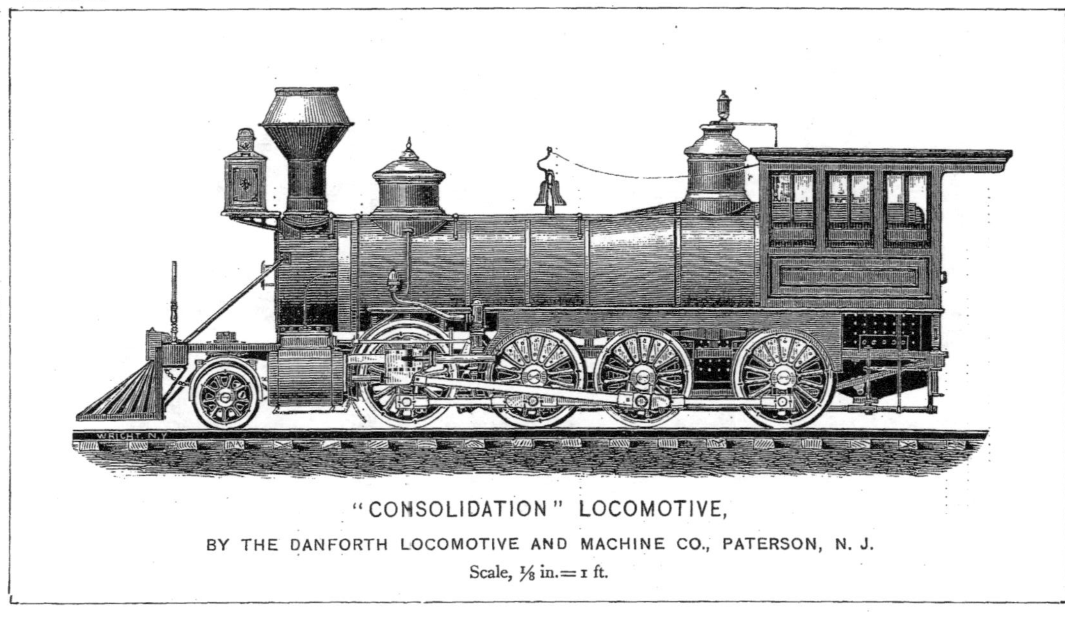

"CONSOLIDATION" LOCOMOTIVE,

BY THE DANFORTH LOCOMOTIVE AND MACHINE CO., PATERSON, N. J.

Scale, 1/8 in. = 1 ft.

PLATE XIII.

DIMENSIONS, WEIGHT, ETC., OF

DOUBLE-END TANK LOCOMOTIVE,

BY THE

ROGERS LOCOMOTIVE AND MACHINE WORKS, PATERSON, N. J.

Gauge of Road	4 ft. 8½ in.
Number of Driving-Wheels	6
Number of Front Truck-Wheels	2
Number of Back Truck-Wheels	2
Total Wheel Base	24 ft. 7½ in.
Distance between centres of Front and Back Driving-Wheels	12 ft.
Total Weight of Locomotive in working order	84,000 lbs.
Total Weight on Driving-Wheels	68,000 lbs.
Diameter of Driving-Wheels	40¼ in.
Diameter of Truck-Wheels	26 in.
Diameter of Cylinders	15 in.
Stroke of Cylinders	20 in.
Outside Diameter of smallest Boiler Ring	46¼ in.
Size of Grate	34 × 48 in.
Number of Tubes	132
Diameter of Tubes	2 in.
Length of Tubes	9 ft. 9¼ in.
Square Feet of Grate surface	11.7
Square Feet of Heating surface in Fire-Box	67
Square Feet of Heating surface in Tubes	608
Total Feet of Heating surface	675
Exhaust Nozzles—single or double	Double.
Diameter of Nozzle	2⅛ to 2⅜ in.
Size of Steam Ports	13¾ × 1 3-16 in.
Size of Exhaust Ports	13¾ × 2 7-16 in.
Throw of Eccentrics	4¾ in.
Outside Lap of Valve	⅝ × 1-64 in.
Inside Lap of Valve	1-16 in.
Size of Main Driving-axle Journal	6 × 7½ in.
Size of other Driving-axle Journal	6 × 7½ in.
Size of Truck-axle Journal	4½ × 8 in.
Diameter of Pump Plunger	1⅞ in.
Stroke of Pump Plunger	20 in.
Capacity of Tank	1,600 gallons.

Plate XIII.

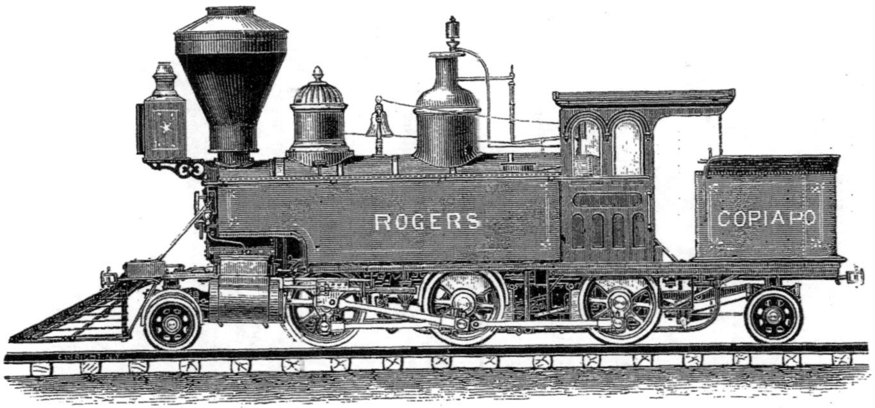

DOUBLE-END TANK LOCOMOTIVE,

BY THE ROGERS LOCOMOTIVE AND MACHINE WORKS, PATERSON, N. J.

Scale, ⅛ in. = 1 ft.

PLATE XIV.

DIMENSIONS, WEIGHT, ETC.,
OF
DOUBLE-END TANK LOCOMOTIVE,
BY THE
ROGERS LOCOMOTIVE AND MACHINE WORKS, PATERSON, N. J.

Gauge of Road	4 ft. 8½ in.
Number of Driving-Wheels	4
Number of Front Truck-Wheels	2
Number of back Truck-Wheels	4
Total Wheel Base	25 ft. 8½ in.
Distance between centres of Front and Back Driving-Wheels	6 ft. 6 in.
Total Weight of Locomotive in working order	75,000 lbs.
Total Weight on Driving-Wheels	40,000 lbs.
Diameter of Driving-Wheels	48¾ in.
Diameter of Truck-Wheels	30 and 26 in.
Diameter of Cylinders	15 in.
Stroke of Cylinders	22 in.
Outside Diameter of smallest Boiler Ring	43⅝ in.
Size of Grate	34 × 50 in.
Number of Tubes	139
Diameter of Tubes	2 in.
Length of Tubes	8 ft. 10½ in.
Square Feet of Grate surface	11.84
Square Feet of Heating surface in Fire-Box	82
Square Feet of Heating surface in Tubes	711
Total Feet of Heating surface	793
Exhaust Nozzles—single or double	Double.
Diameter of Nozzle	2⅜ to 2⅝ in.
Size of Steam Ports	13¾ × 1 3-16 in.
Size of Exhaust Ports	13¾ × 2 7-16 in.
Throw of Eccentrics	4¼ in.
Outside Lap of Valve	⅝ × 1-64 in.
Inside Lap of Valve	1-16 in.
Size of Main Driving-axle Journal	6 × 7½ in.
Size of other Driving-axle Journal	6 × 7½ in.
Size of Truck-axle Journal	4½ × 7½ in.†
Diameter of Pump Plunger	1⅞ in.
Stroke of Pump Plunger	22 in.
Capacity of Tank	1,000 gallons.

† Above is the Front Truck-axle Journal. That of the Back Truck-axle is 4¼ × 7½ in.

Plate XIV.

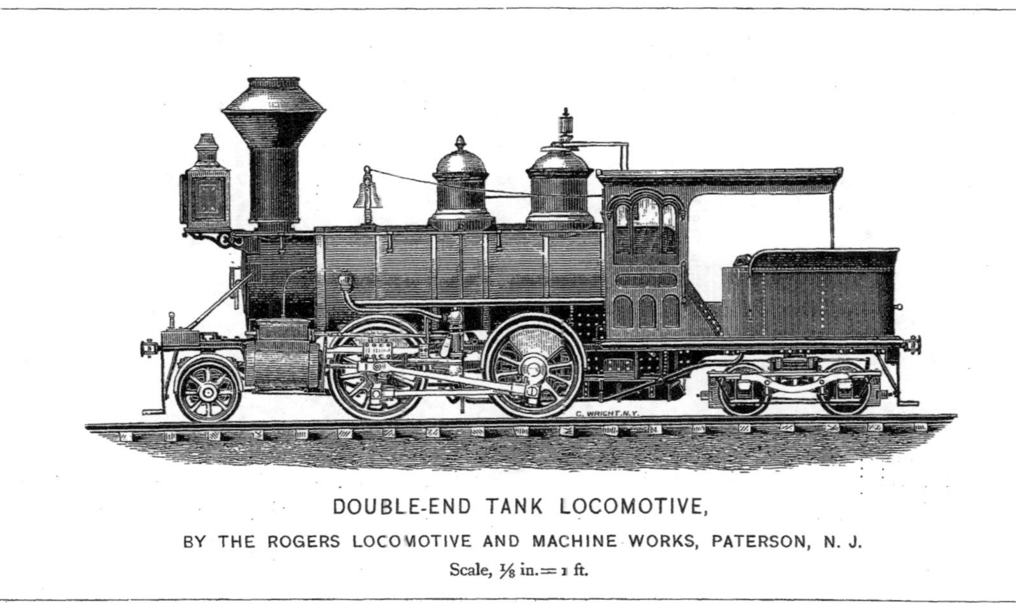

DOUBLE-END TANK LOCOMOTIVE,

BY THE ROGERS LOCOMOTIVE AND MACHINE WORKS, PATERSON, N. J.

Scale, ⅛ in. = 1 ft.

PLATE XV.

DIMENSIONS, WEIGHT, ETC.,

OF

IMPROVED TANK LOCOMOTIVE,

DESIGNED BY

M. N. FORNEY, 73 BROADWAY, NEW YORK.

Gauge of Road	4 ft. 8½ in.
Number of Driving-Wheels	4
Number of Front Truck-Wheels	4
Number of Back Truck-Wheels	None.
Total Wheel Base	20 ft. 9 in.
Distance between centres of Front and Back Driving-Wheels	6 ft. 8 in.
Total Weight of Locomotive in working order	60,000 lbs.
Total Weight on Driving-Wheels	44,000 lbs.
Diameter of Driving-Wheels	50 in.
Diameter of Truck-Wheels	26 in.
Diameter of Cylinders	14 in.
Stroke of Cylinders	20 in.
Outside Diameter of smallest Boiler Ring	46 in.
Size of Grate	54 × 36⅝ in.
Number of Tubes	139
Diameter of Tubes	2 in.
Length of Tubes	10 ft. 1½ in.
Square Feet of Grate surface	14
Square Feet of Heating surface in Fire-Box	78
Square Feet of Heating surface in Tubes	734
Total Feet of Heating surface	812
Exhaust Nozzles—single or double	Double.
Diameter of Nozzle	2¾ in.
Size of Steam Ports	12 × 1¼ in.
Size of Exhaust Ports	12 × 2½ in.
Throw of Eccentrics	5 in.
Outside Lap of Valve	¾ in.
Inside Lap of Valve	1-32 in.
Size of Main Driving-axle Journal	6 × 7 in.
Size of other Driving-axle Journal	6 × 7 in.
Size of Truck-axle Journal	3¾ × 7 in.
Diameter of Pump Plunger	4 in.
Stroke of Pump Plunger	5 in.
Capacity of Tank	1,500 gallons.

Plate XV.

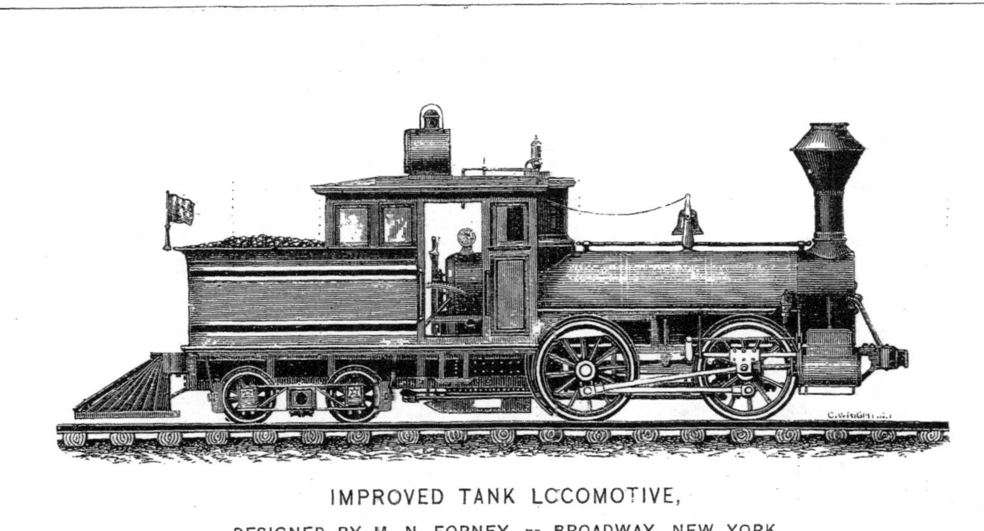

IMPROVED TANK LCCOMOTIVE,

DESIGNED BY M. N. FORNEY, 73 BROADWAY, NEW YORK.

Scale, ⅛ in. = 1 ft.

PLATE XVI.

DIMENSIONS, WEIGHT, ETC.,
OF
DOUBLE-TRUCK NARROW-GAUGE TANK LOCOMOTIVE,

BY THE MASON MACHINE WORKS, TAUNTON, MASS.

Gauge of Road	3 ft.
Number of Driving-Wheels	4
Number of Front Truck-Wheels	4
Number of Back Truck-Wheels	4
Total Wheel Base	19 ft. 6 in.
Distance between centres of Front and Back Driving-Wheels	5 ft.
Total Weight of Locomotive in working order	
Total Weight on Driving-Wheels	24,000 lbs.
Diameter of Driving-Wheels	2 ft. 9 in.
Diameter of Truck-Wheels	2 ft. 6 in.
Diameter of Cylinders	10 in.
Stroke of Cylinders	1 ft. 3 in.
Outside Diameter of smallest Boiler Ring	3 ft.
Size of Grate	41½ × 31 in.
Number of Tubes	81
Diameter of Tubes	2 in.
Length of Tubes	8 ft. 2 in.
Square Feet of Grate surface	8.93
Square Feet of Heating surface in Fire-Box	56
Square Feet of Heating surface in Tubes	346
Total Feet of Heating surface	402
Exhaust Nozzles—single or double	Single.
Diameter of Nozzle	2½ in.
Size of Steam Ports	9½ × 1⅛ in.
Size of Exhaust Ports	9½ × 2½ in.
Throw of Eccentrics	3¾ in.
Outside Lap of Valve	¾ in.
Inside Lap of Valve	1-16
Size of Main Driving-axle Journal	5 × 7 in.
Size of other Driving-axle Journal	
Size of Truck-axle Journal	3½ × 6½ in.
Diameter of Pump Plunger	
Stroke of Pump Plunger	
Capacity of Tank	800 gallons.

Plate XVI.

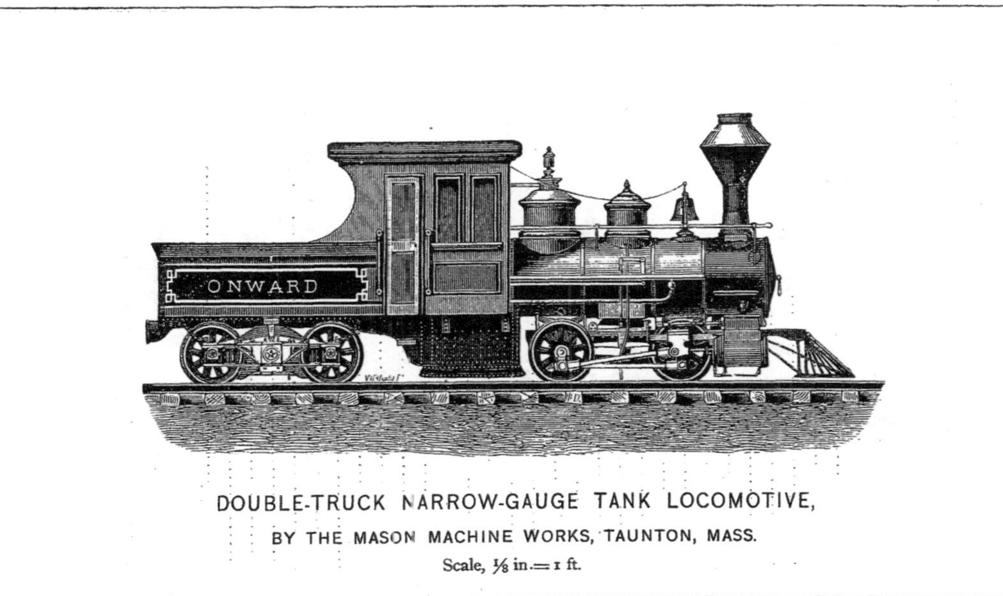

DOUBLE-TRUCK NARROW-GAUGE TANK LOCOMOTIVE,
BY THE MASON MACHINE WORKS, TAUNTON, MASS.
Scale, ⅛ in. = 1 ft.

PLATE XVII.

DIMENSIONS, WEIGHT, ETC.,
OF
DOUBLE-TRUCK TANK FREIGHT LOCOMOTIVE

BY THE MASON MACHINE WORKS, TAUNTON, MASS.

Gauge of Road	4 ft. 8½ in.
Number of Driving-Wheels	6
Number of Front Truck-Wheels	6
Number of Back Truck-Wheels	6
Total Wheel Base	31 ft.
Distance between centres of Front and Back Driving-Wheels	8 ft.
Total Weight of Locomotive in working order	
Total Weight on Driving-Wheels	66,000 lbs.
Diameter of Driving-Wheels	3 ft. 6 in.
Diameter of Truck-Wheels	2 ft. 6 in.
Diameter of Cylinders	1 ft. 4 in.
Stroke of Cylinders	2 ft.
Outside Diameter of smallest Boiler Ring	4 ft.
Size of Grate	66 × 48⅜ in.
Number of Tubes	154
Diameter of Tubes	2 in.
Length of Tubes	11 ft. 6 in.
Square Feet of Grate surface	22.17
Square Feet of Heating surface in Fire-Box	126
Square Feet of Heating surface in Tubes	927
Total Feet of Heating surface	1053
Exhaust Nozzles—single or double	Single.
Diameter of Nozzle	Variable.
Size of Steam Ports	15 × 1¼ in.
Size of Exhaust Ports	15 × 2¾ in.
Throw of Eccentrics	8 in.*
Outside Lap of Valve	¾ in.
Inside Lap of Valve	1-16 in.
Size of Main Driving-axle Journal	6½ × 10 in.
Size of other Driving-axle Journal	
Size of Truck-axle Journal	4 × 8 in.
Diameter of Pump Plunger	
Stroke of Pump Plunger	
Capacity of Tank	2,530 gallons.

* This engine has Walschacrt's valve gear, which is worked by a crank of 8 inches throw.

Plate XVII.

DOUBLE-TRUCK TANK FREIGHT LOCOMOTIVE,

BY THE MASON MACHINE WORKS, TAUNTON, MASSACHUSETTS.

Scale, ⅛ in. = 1 ft.

PLATE XVIII.

DIMENSIONS, WEIGHT, ETC., OF

DOUBLE-END LOCOMOTIVE,

BY THE GRANT LOCOMOTIVE WORKS, PATERSON, N. J.

Gauge of Road	4 ft. 8½ in.
Number of Driving-Wheels	4
Number of Front Truck-Wheels	2
Number of Back Truck-Wheels	2
Total Wheel Base	19 ft. 9 in.
Distance between centres of Front and Back Driving-Wheels	7 ft.
Total Weight of Locomotive in working order	52,000 lbs.
Total Weight on Driving-Wheels	42,000 lbs.
Diameter of Driving-Wheels	56 in.
Diameter of Truck-Wheels	28 in.
Diameter of Cylinders	14 in.
Stroke of Cylinders	22 in.
Outside Diameter of smallest Boiler Ring	42 in.
Size of Grate	73 × 34 in.
Number of Tubes	124
Diameter of Tubes	2 in.
Length of Tubes	7 ft. 10 in.
Square Feet of Grate surface	16.5
Square Feet of Heating surface in Fire-Box	80.8
Square Feet of Heating surface in Tubes	468.5
Total Feet of Heating surface	549.3
Exhaust Nozzles—single or double	Double.
Diameter of Nozzle	2½ to 3⅞ in.
Size of Steam Ports	14 × 1⅛ in.
Size of Exhaust Ports	14 × 2¼ in.
Throw of Eccentrics	5 in.
Outside Lap of Valve	¾ in.
Inside Lap of Valve	None.
Size of Main Driving-axle Journal	6 dia. × 7¾ in.
Size of other Driving-axle Journal	6 dia. × 7¾ in.
Size of Truck-axle Journal	4½ dia. × 8 in.
Diameter of Pump Plunger	3½ in.
Stroke of Pump Plunger	5 in.
Capacity of Tank	1,600 gallons.

Plate XVIII.

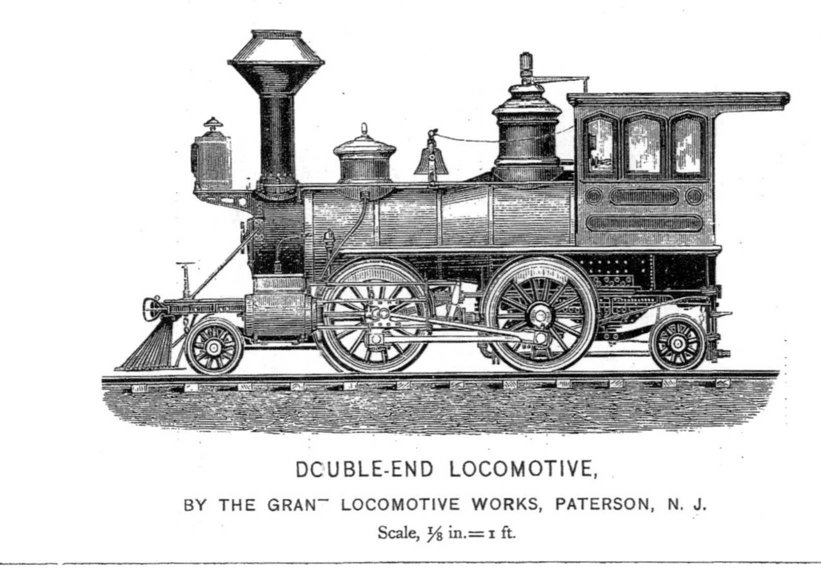

DOUBLE-END LOCOMOTIVE,

BY THE GRANT LOCOMOTIVE WORKS, PATERSON, N. J.

Scale, ⅛ in. = 1 ft.

PLATE XIX.

DIMENSIONS, WEIGHT, ETC., OF LOCOMOTIVE FOR THE N. Y. ELEVATED R. R.

DESIGNED BY D. W. WYMAN, SUPERINTENDENT.

Gauge of Road	4 ft. 10 in.
Number of Driving-Wheels	4
Number of Front Truck-Wheels	None.
Number of Back Truck-Wheels	None.
Total Wheel Base	5 ft.
Distance between centres of Front and Back Driving-Wheels	5 ft.
Total Weight of Locomotive in working order	8,000 lbs.
Total Weight on Driving-Wheels	8,000 lbs.
Diameter of Driving-Wheels	30 in.
Diameter of Truck-Wheels	None.
Diameter of Cylinders	7 in.
Stroke of Cylinders	10 in.
Outside Diameter of smallest Boiler Ring	28 in.
Size of Grate	28 × 28 in.
Number of Tubes	140
Diameter of Tubes	1¼ in.
Length of Tubes	3 ft.
Square Feet of Grate surface	5½ ft.
Square Feet of Heating surface in Fire-Box	25 ft.
Square Feet of Heating surface in Tubes	126 ft.
Total Feet of Heating surface	151 ft.
Exhaust Nozzles—single or double	Double.
Diameter of Nozzle	2 in.
Size of Steam Ports	6 × ⅝ in.
Size of Exhaust Ports	6 × 2 in.
Throw of Eccentrics	2½ in.
Outside Lap of Valve	⅝ in.
Inside Lap of Valve	1-32 in.
Diameter of Main Driving-axle Journal	3 in.
Size of other Driving-axle Journal	
Size of Truck-axle Journal	
Diameter of Pump Plunger	1⅜ in.
Stroke of Pump Plunger	10 in.
Capacity of Tank	109 gallons.

Plate XIX.

LOCOMOTIVE FOR THE NEW YORK ELEVATED RAILROAD,

DESIGNED BY D. W. WYMAN, SUPERINTENDENT

Scale, ⅛ in. = 1 ft.

PROPERTIES OF SATURATED STEAM.

Total pressure per sq. inch, measured from a vacuum...	Pressure above the atmosphere	Sensible temperature in Fahrenheit degrees..............	Total heat in degrees from zero of Fahrenheit.	Weight of one cubic foot of steam........	Relative volume of the steam compared with the water from which it was raised......
Lb.	Lb.	Deg.	Deg.	Lb.	
1	..	102.1	1144.5	.0030	20582
2	..	126.3	1151.7	.0058	10721
3	..	141.6	1156.6	.0085	7322
4	..	153.1	1160.1	.0112	5583
5	..	162.3	1162.9	.0138	4527
6		170.2	1165.3	.0163	3813
7	..	176.9	1167.3	.0189	3298
8	..	182.9	1169.2	.0214	2909
9	..	188.3	1170.8	.0239	2604
10	..	193.3	1172.3	.0264	2358
11	..	197.8	1173.7	.0289	2157
12	..	202.0	1175.0	.0314	1986
13	..	205.9	1176.2	.0338	1842
14	..	209.6	1177.3	.0362	1720
14.7	0.	212.0	1178.1	.0380	1642
15	.3	213.1	1178.4	.0387	1610
16	1.3	216.3	1179.4	.0411	1515
17	2.3	219.6	1180.3	.0435	1431
18	3.3	222.4	1181.2	.0459	1357
19	4.3	225.3	1182.1	.0483	1290
20	5.3	228.0	1182.9	.0507	1229
21	6.3	230.6	1183.7	.0531	1174
22	7.3	233.1	1184.5	.0555	1123
23	8.3	235.5	1185.2	.0580	1075
24	9.3	237.8	1185.9	.0601	1036
25	10.3	240.1	1186.6	.0625	996
26	11.3	242.3	1187.3	.0650	958
27	12.3	244.4	1187.8	.0673	926
28	13.3	246.4	1188.4	.0696	895
29	14.3	248.4	1189.1	.0719	866
30	15.3	250.4	1189.8	.0743	838
31	16.3	252.2	1190.4	.0766	813
32	17.3	254.1	1190.9	.0789	789
33	18.3	255.9	1191.5	.0812	767
34	19.3	257.6	1192.0	.0835	746
35	20.3	259.3	1192.5	.0858	726
36	21.3	260.9	1193.0	.0881	707
37	22.3	262.6	1193.5	.0905	688

PROPERTIES OF SATURATED STEAM - CONTINUED.

Total pressure per sq. inch, measured from a vacuum.........	Pressure above the atmosphere........	Sensible temperature in Fahrenheit degrees..............	Total heat in degrees from zero of Fahrenheit	Weight of one cubic foot of steam........	Relative volume of the steam compared with the water from which it was raised........
Lb.	Lb.	Deg.	Deg.	Lb.	
38	23.3	264.2	1194.0	.0929	671
39	24.3	265.8	1194.5	.0952	655
40	25.3	267.3	1194.9	.0974	640
41	26.3	268.7	1195.4	.0996	625
42	27.3	270.2	1195.8	.1020	611
43	28.3	271.6	1196.2	.1042	598
44	29.3	273.0	1196.6	.1065	585
45	30.3	274.4	1197.1	.1089	572
46	31.3	275.8	1197.5	.1111	561
47	32.3	277.1	1197.9	.1133	550
48	33.3	278.4	1198.3	.1156	539
49	34.3	279.7	1198.7	.1179	529
50	35.3	281.0	1199.1	.1202	518
51	36.3	282.3	1199.5	.1224	509
52	37.3	283.5	1199.9	.1246	500
53	38.3	284.7	1200.3	.1269	491
54	39.3	285.9	1200.6	.1291	482
55	40.3	287.1	1201.0	.1314	474
56	41.3	288.2	1201.3	.1336	466
57	42.3	289.3	1201.7	.1364	458
58	43.3	290.4	1202.0	.1380	451
59	44.3	291.6	1202.4	.1403	444
60	45.3	292.7	1202.7	.1425	437
61	46.3	293.8	1203.1	.1447	430
62	47.3	294.8	1203.4	.1469	424
63	48.3	295.9	1203.7	.1493	417
64	49.3	296.9	1204.0	.1516	411
65	50.3	298.0	1204.3	.1538	405
66	51.3	299.0	1204.6	.1560	399
67	52.3	300.0	1204.9	.1583	393
68	53.3	300.9	1205.2	.1605	388
69	54.3	301.9	1205.5	.1627	383
70	55.3	302.9	1205.8	.1648	378
71	56.3	303.9	1206.1	.1670	373
72	57.3	304.8	1206.3	.1692	368
73	58.3	305.7	1206.6	.1714	363
74	59.3	306.6	1206.9	.1736	359
75	60.3	307.5	1207.2	.1759	353

PROPERTIES OF SATURATED STEAM—CONTINUED.

Total pressure per sq. inch, measured from a vacuum..........	Pressure above the atmosphere..........	Sensible temperature in Fahrenheit degrees..............	Total heat in degrees from zero of Fahrenheit..............	Weight of one cubic foot of steam........	Relative volume of the steam compared with the water from which it was raised........
Lb.	Lb.	Deg.	Deg.	Lb.	
76	61.3	308.4	1207.4	.1782	349
77	62.3	309.3	1207.7	.1804	345
78	63.3	310.2	1208.0	.1826	341
79	64.3	311.1	1208.3	.1848	337
80	65.3	312.0	1208.5	.1869	333
81	66.3	312.8	1208.8	.1891	329
82	67.3	313.6	1209.1	.1913	325
83	68.3	314.5	1209.4	.1935	321
84	69.3	315.3	1209.6	.1957	318
85	70.3	316.1	1209.9	.1980	314
86	71.3	316.9	1210.1	.2002	311
87	72.3	317.8	1210.4	.2024	308
88	73.3	318.6	1210.6	.2044	305
89	74.3	319.4	1210.9	.2067	301
90	75.3	320.2	1211.1	.2089	298
91	76.3	321.0	1211.3	.2111	295
92	77.3	321.7	1211.5	.2133	292
93	78.3	322.5	1211.8	.2155	289
94	79.3	323.3	1212.0	.2176	286
95	80.3	324.1	1212.3	.2198	283
96	81.3	324.8	1212.5	.2219	281
97	82.3	325.6	1212.8	.2241	278
98	83.3	326.3	1213.0	.2263	275
99	84.3	327.1	1213.2	.2285	272
100	85.3	327.9	1213.4	.2307	270
101	86.3	328.5	1213.6	.2329	267
102	87.3	329.1	1213.8	.2351	265
103	88.3	329.9	1214.0	.2373	262
104	89.3	330.6	1214.2	.2393	260
105	90.3	331.3	1214.4	.2414	257
106	91.3	331.9	1214.6	.2435	255
107	92.3	332.6	1214.8	.2456	253
108	93.3	333.3	1215.0	.2477	251
109	94.3	334.0	1215.3	.2499	249
110	95.3	334.6	1215.5	.2521	247
111	96.3	335.3	1215.7	.2543	245
112	97.3	336.0	1215.9	.2564	243
113	98.3	336.7	1216.1	.2586	241

PROPERTIES OF SATURATED STEAM—CONTINUED.

Total pressure per sq. inch, measured from a vacuum........	Pressure above the atmosphere........	Sensible temperature in Fahrenheit degrees........	Total heat in degrees from zero of Fahrenheit	Weight of one cubic foot of steam........	Relative volume of the steam compared with the water from which it was raised........
Lb.	Lb.	Deg.	Deg.	Lb.	
114	99.3	337.4	1216.3	.2607	239
115	100.3	338.0	1216.5	.2628	237
116	101.3	338.6	1216.7	.2649	235
117	102.3	339.3	1216.9	.2674	233
118	103.3	339.9	1217.1	.2696	231
119	104.3	340.5	1217.3	.2738	229
120	105.3	341.1	1217.4	.2759	227
121	106.3	341.8	1217.6	.2780	225
122	107.3	342.4	1217.8	.2801	224
123	108.3	343.0	1218.0	.2822	222
124	109.3	343.6	1218.2	.2845	221
125	110.3	344.2	1218.4	.2867	219
126	111.3	344.8	1218.6	.2889	217
127	112.3	345.4	1218.8	.2911	215
128	113.3	346.0	1218.9	.2933	214
129	114.3	346.6	1219.1	.2955	212
130	115.3	347.2	1219.3	.2977	211
131	116.3	347.8	1219.5	.2999	209
132	117.3	348.3	1219.6	.3020	208
133	118.3	348.9	1219.8	.3040	206
134	119.3	349.5	1220.0	.3060	205
135	120.3	350.1	1220.2	.3080	203
136	121.3	350.6	1220.3	.3101	202
137	122.3	351.2	1220.5	.3121	200
138	123.3	351.8	1220.7	.3142	199
139	124.3	352.4	1220.9	.3162	198
140	125.3	352.9	1221.0	.3184	197
141	126.3	353.5	1221.2	.3206	195
142	127.3	354.0	1221.4	.3228	194
143	128.3	354.5	1221.6	.3250	193
144	129.3	355.0	1221.7	.3273	192
145	130.3	355.6	1221.9	.3294	190
146	131.3	356.1	1222.0	.3315	189
147	132.3	356.7	1222.2	.3336	188
148	133.3	357.2	1222.3	.3357	187
149	134.3	357.8	1222.5	.3377	186
150	135.3	358.3	1222.7	.3397	184
155	140.3	361.0	1223.5	.3500	179

PROPERTIES OF SATURATED STEAM—CONTINUED.

Total pressure per sq. inch, measured from a vacuum........	Pressure above the atmosphere.........	Sensible temperature in Fahrenheit degrees.....	Total heat in degrees from zero of Fahrenheit.................	Weight of one cubic foot of steam.......	Relative volume of the steam compared with the water from which it was raised........
Lb.	Lb.	Deg.	Deg.	Lb.	
160	145.3	363.4	1224.2	.3607	174
165	150.3	366.0	1224.9	.3714	169
170	155.3	368.2	1225.7	.3821	164
175	160.3	370.8	1226.4	.3928	159
180	165.3	372.9	1227.1	.4035	155
185	170.3	375.3	1227.8	.4142	151
190	175.3	377.5	1228.5	.4250	148
195	180.3	379.7	1229.2	.4357	144
200	185.3	381.7	1229.8	.4464	141
210	195.3	386.0	1231.1	.4668	135
220	205.3	389.9	1232.3	.4872	129
230	215.3	393.8	1233.5	.5072	123
240	225.3	397.5	1234.6	.5270	119
250	235.3	401.1	1235.7	.5471	114
260	245.3	404.5	1236.8	.5670	110
270	255.3	407.9	1237.8	.5871	106
280	265.3	411.2	1238.8	.6070	102
290	275.3	414.4	1239.8	.6268	99
300	285.3	417.5	1240.7	.6469	96

Table of Hyperbolic Logarithms.

Num.	Logarithms.	Num.	Logarithms.	Num.	Logarithms.	Num.	Logarithms.
1.01	.0099	1.46	.3784	1.91	.6471	2.36	.8586
1.02	.0198	1.47	.3852	1.92	.6523	2.37	.8628
1.03	.0295	1.48	.3920	1.93	.6575	2.38	.8671
1.04	.0392	1.49	.3987	1.94	.6626	2.39	.8712
1.05	.0487	1.50	.4054	1.95	.6678	2.40	.8754
1.06	.0582	1.51	.4121	1.96	.6729	2.41	.8796
1.07	.0676	1.52	.4187	1.97	.6780	2.42	.8837
1.08	.0769	1.53	.4252	1.98	.6830	2.43	.8878
1.09	.0861	1.54	.4317	1.99	.6881	2.44	.8919
1.10	.0953	1.55	.4382	2.00	.6931	2.45	.8960
1.11	.1043	1.56	.4446	2.01	.6981	2.46	.9001
1.12	.1133	1.57	.4510	2.02	.7030	2.47	.9042
1.13	.1222	1.58	.4574	2.03	.7080	2.48	.9082
1.14	.1310	1.59	.4637	2.04	.7129	2.49	.9122
1.15	.1397	1.60	.4700	2.05	.7178	2.50	.9162
1.16	.1484	1.61	.4762	2.06	.7227	2.51	.9202
1.17	.1570	1.62	.4824	2.07	.7275	2.52	.9242
1.18	.1655	1.63	.4885	2.08	.7323	2.53	.9282
1.19	.1739	1.64	.4946	2.09	.7371	2.54	.9321
1.20	.1823	1.65	.5007	2.10	.7419	2.55	.9360
1.21	.1962	1.66	.5068	2.11	.7466	2.56	.9400
1.22	.1988	1.67	.5128	2.12	.7514	2.57	.9439
1.23	.2070	1.68	.5187	2.13	.7561	2.58	.9477
1.24	.2151	1.69	.5247	2.14	.7608	2.59	.9516
1.25	.2231	1.70	.5306	2.15	.7654	2.60	.9555
1.26	.2341	1.71	.5364	2.16	.7701	2.61	.9593
1.27	.2390	1.72	.5423	2.17	.7747	2.62	.9631
1.28	.2468	1.73	.5481	2.18	.7793	2.63	.9669
1.29	.2546	1.74	.5538	2.19	.7839	2.64	.9707
1.30	.2623	1.75	.5596	2.20	.7884	2.65	.9745
1.31	.2700	1.76	.5653	2.21	.7929	2.66	.9783
1.32	.2776	1.77	.5709	2.22	.7975	2.67	.9820
1.33	.2851	1.78	.5766	2.23	.8021	2.68	.9858
1.34	.2926	1.79	.5822	2.24	.8064	2.69	.9895
1.35	.3001	1.80	.5877	2.25	.8109	2.70	.9932
1.36	.3074	1.81	.5933	2.26	.8153	2.71	.9969
1.37	.3148	1.82	.5988	2.27	.8197	2.72	1.0006
1.38	.3220	1.83	.6043	2.28	.8241	2.73	1.0043
1.39	.3293	1.84	.6097	2.29	.8285	2.74	1.0079
1.40	.3364	1.85	.6151	2.30	.8329	2.75	1.0116
1.41	.3435	1.86	.6205	2.31	.8372	2.76	1.0152
1.42	.3506	1.87	.6259	2.32	.8415	2.77	1.0188
1.43	.3576	1.88	.6312	2.33	.8458	2.78	1.0224
1.44	.3646	1.89	.6365	2.34	.8501	2.79	1.0260
1.45	.3715	1.90	.6418	2.35	.8544	2.80	1.0296

Table of Hyperbolic Logarithms—Continued.

Num.	Logarithms.	Num.	Logarithms.	Num.	Logarithms.	Num.	Logarithms.
2.81	1.0331	3.26	1.1817	3.71	1.3110	4.16	1.4255
2.82	1.0367	3.27	1.1847	3.72	1.3137	4.17	1.4279
2.83	1.0402	3.28	1.1878	3.73	1.3164	4.18	1.4303
2.84	1.0438	3.29	1.1908	3.74	1.3190	4.19	1.4327
2.85	1.0473	3.30	1.1939	3.75	1.3217	4.20	1.4350
2.86	1.0508	3.31	1.1969	3.76	1.3244	4.21	1.4374
2.87	1.0543	3.32	1.1999	3.77	1.3271	4.22	1.4398
2.88	1.0577	3.33	1.2029	3.78	1.3297	4.23	1.4422
2.89	1.0612	3.34	1.2059	3.79	1.3323	4.24	1.4445
2.90	1.0647	3.35	1.2089	3.80	1.3350	4.25	1.4469
2.91	1.0681	3.36	1.2119	3.81	1.3376	4.26	1.4492
2.92	1.0715	3.37	1.2149	3.82	1.3402	4.27	1.4516
2.93	1.0750	3.38	1.2178	3.83	1.3428	4.28	1.4539
2.94	1.0784	3.39	1.2208	3.84	1.3454	4.29	1.4562
2.95	1.0818	3.40	1.2237	3.85	1.3480	4.30	1.4586
2.96	1.0851	3.41	1.2267	3.86	1.3506	4.31	1.4609
2.97	1.0885	3.42	1.2296	3.87	1.3532	4.32	1.4632
2.98	1.0919	3.43	1.2325	3.88	1.3558	4.33	1.4655
2.99	1.0952	3.44	1.2354	3.89	1.3584	4.34	1.4678
3.00	1.0986	3.45	1.2387	3.90	1.3609	4.35	1.4701
3.01	1.1019	3.46	1.2412	3.91	1.3635	4.36	1.4724
3.02	1.1052	3.47	1.2441	3.92	1.3660	4.37	1.4747
3.03	1.1085	3.48	1.2470	3.93	1.3686	4.38	1.4778
3.04	1.1118	3.49	1.2499	3.94	1.3711	4.39	1.4793
3.05	1.1151	3.50	1.2527	3.95	1.3737	4.40	1.4816
3.06	1.1184	3.51	1.2556	3.96	1.3726	4.41	1.4838
3.07	1.1216	3.52	1.2584	3.97	1.3787	4.42	1.4838
3.08	1.1249	3.53	1.2612	3.98	1.3812	4.43	1.4883
3.09	1.1281	3.54	1.2641	3.99	1.3837	4.44	1.4906
3.10	1.1314	3.55	1.2669	4.00	1.3862	4.45	1.4929
3.11	1.1346	9.56	1.2697	4.01	1.3887	4.46	1.4914
3.12	1.1378	3.57	1.2725	4.02	1.3912	4.47	1.4973
3.13	1.1410	3.58	1.2753	4.03	1.3937	4.48	1.4996
3.14	1.1442	3.59	1.2781	4.04	1.3962	4.49	1.5018
3.15	1.1474	3.60	1.2809	4.05	1.3987	4.50	1.5040
3.16	1.1505	3.61	1.2837	4.06	1.4011	4.51	1.5062
3.17	1.1537	3.62	1.2864	4.07	1.4036	4.52	1.5085
3.18	1.1568	3.63	1.2892	4.08	1.4060	4.53	1.5107
3.19	1.1600	3.64	1.2919	4.09	1.4085	4.54	1.5129
3.20	1.1631	3.65	1.2947	4.10	1.4109	4.55	1.5151
3.21	1.1662	3.66	1.2974	4.11	1.4134	4.56	1.5173
3.22	1.1693	3.67	1.3001	4.12	1.4158	4.57	1.5195
3.23	1.1724	3.68	1.3029	4.13	1.4182	4.58	1.5216
3.24	1.1755	3.69	1.3056	4.14	1.4206	4.59	1.5238
3.25	1.1786	3.70	1.3083	4.15	1.4231	4.60	1.5260

Table of Hyperbolic Logarithms—Continued.

Num.	Logarithms.	Num.	Logarithms.	Num.	Logarithms.	Num.	Logarithms.
4.61	1.5282	5.06	1.6213	5.51	1.7065	5.96	1.7850
4.62	1.5303	5.07	1.6233	5.52	1.7083	5.97	1.7867
4.63	1.5325	5.08	1.6253	5.53	1.7101	5.98	1.7884
4.64	1.5347	5.09	1.6272	5.54	1.7119	5.99	1.7900
4.65	1.5368	5.10	1.6292	5.55	1.7137	6.00	1.7917
4.66	1.5390	5.11	1.6311	5.56	1.7155	6.01	1.7934
4.67	1.5411	5.12	1.6331	5.57	1.7173	6.02	1.7950
4.68	1.5432	5.13	1.6351	5.58	1.7191	6.03	1.7967
4.69	1.5454	5.14	1.6370	5.59	1.7209	6.04	1.7984
4.70	1.5475	5.15	1.6389	5.60	1.7227	6.05	1.8000
4.71	1.5496	5.16	1.6409	5.61	1.7245	6.06	1.8017
4.72	1.5518	5.17	1.6428	5.62	1.7263	6.07	1.8033
4.73	1.5539	5.18	1.6448	5.63	1.7281	6.08	1.8050
4.74	1.5560	5.19	1.6463	5.64	1.7293	6.09	1.8066
4.75	1.5581	5.20	1.6486	5.65	1.7316	6.10	1.8082
4.76	1.5602	5.21	1.6505	5.66	1.7334	6.11	1.8099
4.77	1.5623	5.22	1.6524	5.67	1.7351	6.12	1.8115
4.78	1.5644	5.23	1.6544	5.68	1.7369	6.13	1.8131
4.79	1.5665	5.24	1.6563	5.69	1.7387	6.14	1.8148
4.80	1.5686	5.25	1.6582	5.70	1.7404	6.15	1.8164
4.81	1.5706	5.26	1.6601	5.71	1.7422	6.16	1.8180
4.82	1.5727	5.27	1.6620	5.72	1.7439	6.17	1.8196
4.83	1.5748	5.28	1.6639	5.73	1.7457	6.18	1.8213
4.84	1.5769	5.29	1.6658	5.74	1.7474	6.19	1.8229
4.85	1.5789	5.30	1.6677	5.75	1.7491	6.20	1.8245
4.86	1.5810	5.31	1.6695	5.76	1.7509	6.21	1.8261
4.87	1.5830	5.32	1.6714	5.77	1.7526	6.22	1.8277
4.88	1.5851	5.33	1.6733	5.78	1.7544	6.23	1.8293
4.89	1.5870	5.34	1.6752	5.79	1.7561	6.24	1.8309
4.90	1.5892	5.35	1.6770	5.80	1.7578	6.25	1.8325
4.91	1.5912	5.36	1.6789	5.81	1.7595	6.26	1.8341
4.92	1.5933	5.37	1.6808	5.82	1.7613	6.27	1.8357
4.93	1.5953	5.38	1.6826	5.83	1.7630	6.28	1.8373
4.94	1.5973	5.39	1.6845	5.84	1.7647	6.29	1.8389
4.95	1.5993	5.40	1.6863	5.85	1.7664	6.30	1.8405
4.96	1.6014	5.41	1.6882	5.86	1.7681	6.31	1.8421
4.97	1.6034	5.42	1.6900	5.87	1.7698	6.32	1.8437
4.98	1.6054	5.43	1.6919	5.88	1.7715	6.33	1.8453
4.99	1.6074	5.44	1.6937	5.89	1.7732	6.34	1.8468
5.00	1.6094	5.45	1.6956	5.90	1.7749	6.35	1.8484
5.01	1.6114	5.46	1.6974	5.91	1.7766	6.36	1.8500
5.02	1.6134	5.47	1.6992	5.92	1.7783	6.37	1.8515
5.03	1.6154	5.48	1.7011	5.93	1.7800	6.38	1.8531
5.04	1.6174	5.49	1.7029	5.94	1.7317	6.39	1.8547
5.05	1.6193	5.50	1.7047	5.95	1.7833	6.40	1.8562

Table Showing the Value and Properties of Various Kinds of Coal.

Designation of Coal.		Weight per cubic foot by experiment	Cubic feet of space required to stow a ton	Volatile combustible matter in 100 parts	Fixed carbon in 100 parts	Earthy matter in 100 parts	Pounds of steam to 1 of coal from 212°	Total waste in the state of ashes and clinker from 100 of coal	Weight of clinker alone from 100 of coal	Av. weight in lbs. of unburnt coke left on grate after each experiment	Steam from 212° from 1 of combustible matter
Beaver Meadow, slope No. 3	Pa.	54.93	40.78	2.38	88.94	7.11	9.21	11.96	1.01	112 4	10.462
Beaver Meadow, slope No. 5	Pa.	56.19	39.86	2.66	91.47	5.15	9.88	6.74	0.60	61.2	10.592
Forest improvement	Pa.	53.66	41.75	3.07	90.75	4.41	10.06	6.97	0.81	40.2	10.807
Peach Mountain	Pa.	53 79	41.64	2.96	89.02	6.13	10.11	6.97	3.03	26.6	10.871
Lehigh	Pa.	55.32	40.50	5.28	89.15	5.56	8.93	7.22	1.08	36.1	9.626
Lackawanna	Pa.	48 89	45.82	3.91	87.74	6.35	9.79	8.93	1.24	57.2	10.764
Lyken's Valley	Pa.	48.56	46.13	6.88	83.84	9.25	9.46	12.24	4.40	18.0	10.788
Beaver Meadow (Navy Yard)	Pa.	55.08	40.65	.....	.....	8.10	9.08	8.10	1.40	107.1	9.881
Natural coke of Virginia	Va.	46.64	48.03	12.44	75.08	11.83	8.47	18.46	5.31	60.9	10.389
Coke of Midlothian coal	Va.	32 70	68.50	.....	.....	16.55	8.63	16.54	10.51	53.2	10.343
Coke of Neff's (Cumberland) coal	Md.	31.57	70.95	.....	.....	13 34	9.00	13.34	3.55	43.7	10.381
Mixture 1-5 Cumb. and 4-5 Beaver Meadow		54.29	41.26	.....	....	8.88	8.86	8.88	4.91	9.5	9.725
Mixture 1-5 Cumb. and 4-5 Beaver Meadow		54.51	41.09	.....	.....	8.18	9.18	8.18	3.09	16.0	9.997
New York and Maryland Mining Company's	Md.	53.70	4[illegible].71	12.31	73.50	12.40	9.78	12.71	5.43	10.1	11.208
Neff's Cumberland	Md.	54.29	41.26	12.67	74.53	10.34	9.44	10.96	4.53	6.1	10.604
Easby's "coal in store"	Md.	53.47	41.90	14.98	76.26	8.08	10.02	8.38	1.33	18.2	10.935
Atkinson & Templeman's	Md.	52.92	42.33	15.53	76.69	7.33	10.70	7.96	2.12	5.1	11.624

Easby & Smith's	Md.	51.16	43 78	15.52	74 29	9.30	9.96	9.69	3.04	5.3	11.034
Cumberland (Navy Yard)	Md.	53.29	42.04	14.87	70.85	14.98	.....	14.53	2.29	13.5	.....
Dauphin & Susquehanna	Pa.	50.54	44.32	13.82	74.24	11.49	9.34	16.36	3.50	23.7	11.171
Blossburg	Pa.	53.05	42.22	14.78	73.11	10.77	9.72	11.20	3.40	13.7	10.956
Lycoming Creek	Pa.	55.38	40.45	13.84	71.53	13.96	8.91	16.92	3.26	46.2	10.724
Quin's Run	Pa.	50.34	44.50	17.97	72.79	8.41	10.27	8.94	1.31	14.7	11 275
Karthaus	Pa.	52.54	42.63	19.53	73.77	7.00	9.09	7.89	3.66	52.5	9.887
Cambria County	Pa	53.46	41.90	20.52	69.37	9.15	9.24	9.75	3.48	14.8	10.239
Barr's Deep Run	Va.	53.17	42.13	19.78	67.96	10.47	9.02	11.07	4.78	6.4	10.142
Crouch & Snead's	Va.	53.59	41.80	24.38	59.98	14.28	8.34	14.34	5.37	6.0	9 740
Midlothian (900 feet shaft)	Va.	50.52	44 34	27.28	61.08	10.47	8.58	10.70	6.47	5.9	9.611
Creek Company's coal	Va.	46.50	48.17	32.47	60.30	8.57	8.42	8.64	4.41	10.5	9.211
Clover Hill	Va.	45.49	49.25	32.21	56.83	10.13	7.67	10.60	3.86	11.5	8 588
Chesterfield Mining Company's	Va.	45.55	49.18	32.63	58.79	8.63	9.00	9.07	4.19	10.5	9.896
Midlothian (average)	Va.	54.04	41.45	29.86	53.01	14.74	8.29	14.83	8.82	6.4	9.741
Tippecanoe	Va.	45.10	49.67	34.54	54.62	9.37	7.75	9.72	4.03	11.2	8.583
Midlothian (new shaft)	Va.	47.90	46.76	35.77	56.40	9.44	8.75	10.26	4.21	17.1	9 751
Midlothian (screened)	Va.	45.72	48.99	34.70	54.06	9.66	8.94	10.27	3.33	14.8	9.970
Midlothian (Navy Yard)	Va.	54.47	41.13	29.12	56.11	14.14	.....	.....	4.42	43.2	.....
Pictou (from New York)	N. S.	53.55	41.83	27.83	56.98	13.39	8.41	13.37	6.13	5.7	9.710
Sidney	N. S	47.44	47.22	23.81	67.57	5.49	7.99	6.01	2.24	5.9	8.497
Pictou (Cunards)	N. S.	49.25	45.48	25.97	60.74	12.51	8.48	12.06	6.19	3.7	9.648
Liverpool	Eng.	47.88	46.78	39.96	54.90	4.62	7.48	5.04	1.86	11.1	8 255
Newcastle	Eng.	50.82	44.08	35.83	57.00	5.40	8.66	5.68	3.14	10.7	9.178
Scotch	Scotland	51.09	43.84	39.19	48.81	9.34	6.95	10.10	5.63	5.7	7.719
Pittsburg	Pa	46.81	47.85	36.76	54.93	7.07	8.20	8.25	0.94	9.9	8.942
Cannelton	Ind.	47.65	47.01	33.99	58.44	4.97	7.34	5.12	1.64	6.4	7.734
Dry Pine Wood		21.01	106.02	.....	.....	0.30	4.69	0.30	.....	.....	4.707

Table of Resistances of Railroad Trains with Different Grades and Speeds.

Rise of gradient, feet per mile.	Resistance due to ascent alone in lbs. per ton (2,000 lbs.) of train.	Total resistance, lbs. per ton, at rate of 5 miles per hour.	10 miles per hour.	15 miles per hour.	20 miles per hour.	25 miles per hour.	30 miles per hour.	35 miles per hour.	40 miles per hour.	45 miles per hour.	50 miles per hour.	60 miles per hour.	70 miles per hour.
0..........		6.1	6.6	7.3	8.3	9.6	11.2	13.1	15.3	17.8	20.6	27.0	34.6
5..........	1.8	7.9	8.4	9.1	10.1	11.4	13.0	14.9	17.1	19.6	22.4	28.8	36.4
10..........	3.7	9.8	10.3	11.0	12.0	13.4	14.9	16.8	19.0	21.5	24.3	30.7	38.3
15..........	5.6	11.7	12.2	12.9	13.9	15.2	16.8	18.7	21.9	24.4	27.2	33.6	41.2
20..........	7.5	13.6	14.1	14.8	15.8	17.1	18.7	20.6	22.8	25.3	28.1	34.5	42.1
25..........	9.4	15.5	16.0	16.7	17.7	19.0	20.6	22.5	24.7	27.2	31.0	37.4	45.0
30..........	11.3	17.4	17.9	18.6	19.6	21.9	22.5	24.4	26.6	29.1	31.9	38.3	45.9
35..........	13.2	19.3	19.8	20.5	21.5	22.8	24.4	26.3	28.5	31.0	33.8	40.2	47.8
40..........	15.1	21.2	21.7	22.4	23.4	24.7	26.3	28.2	30.4	32.9	35.7	42.1	49.7
45..........	17.0	23.1	23.6	24.3	25.3	26.6	28.2	30.1	32.3	34.8	37.6	44.0	51.6
50..........	18.9	25.0	25.5	26.2	27.2	28.5	30.1	32.0	34.2	36.7	39.5	45.9	53.5
60..........	22.7	28.8	29.3	30.0	31.0	32.3	33.9	35.8	38.0	40.5	43.5	49.9	57.5
70..........	26.5	32.6	33.1	33.8	34.8	36.1	37.7	39.6	41.8	44.3	47.1	53.5	61.1
80..........	30.3	36.4	36.9	37.6	38.6	39.9	40.5	42.4	44.6	47.1	49.9	56.3	63.9

90..........	34.0	41.0	40.6	41.3	42.3	43.6	45.2	47.1	49.3	51.8	54.6	61.0	68.6
100..........	37.8	43.9	44.4	45.1	46.1	47.4	49.0	51.9	54.1	56.6	59.4	65.8	73.4
110..........	41.6	47.7	48.2	48.9	49.9	51.2	52.8	54.7	56.9	59.4	62.2	68.6	76.2
120..........	45.4	51.5	52.0	52.7	53.7	55.0	56.6	58.5	60.7	63.2	66.0	72.4	80.0
130..........	49.2	55.3	55.8	56.5	57.5	58.8	60.4	62.3	64.5	67.0	69.8	76.2	83.8
140..........	53.0	59.1	59.6	60.3	61.3	62.6	64.2	66.1	68.3	70.8	73.6	80.0	87.6
150..........	56.8	62.9	63.4	64.1	65.1	66.4	68.0	69.9	72.1	74.6	77.4	83.8	91.4
160..........	60.6	66.7	67.2	67.9	68.9	70.2	71.8	73.7	75.9	78.4	81.2	87.6	95.2
170..........	64.3	70.4	70.9	71.6	72.6	73.9	75.5	77.4	79.6	82.1	84.9	91.3	98.9
180..........	68.1	74.2	74.7	75.4	76.4	77.7	79.3	81.2	83.4	85.9	88.7	95.1	102.7
190..........	71.9	78.0	78.5	79.2	80.2	81.5	83.1	85.0	87.2	89.7	92.5	98.9	106.5
200..........	75.7	81.8	82.3	83.0	84.0	85.3	86.9	88.8	91.0	93.5	96.3	102.7	110.3
210..........	79.5	85.6	86.1	86.8	87.8	89.1	90.7	92.6	94.8	97.3	100.1	106.5	114.1
220..........	83.3	89.4	89.9	90.6	91.6	92.9	94.5	96.4	98.6	101.1	103.9	110.3	117.6
230..........	87.1	93.2	93.7	94.4	95.4	96.7	98.3	100.2	102.4	104.9	107.7	114.1	121.7
240..........	90.8	96.9	97.4	98.1	99.1	100.4	102.0	103.9	106.1	108.6	111.4	117.8	125.4
250..........	94.6	100.7	101.2	101.9	102.9	103.2	105.8	107.7	109.9	112.4	115.2	121.6	129.2
260..........	98.4	104.5	105.0	105.7	106.7	107.0	108.6	110.5	112.7	115.2	118.0	124.4	132.0
270..........	102.2	108.3	108.8	109.5	110.5	111.8	113.4	115.3	117.5	120.0	122.8	129.2	136.8
280..........	106.0	112.1	112.6	113.3	114.3	115.6	117.2	119.1	121.3	123.8	126.6	133.0	140.6
290..........	109.8	115.9	116.4	117.1	118.1	119.4	121.0	122.9	125.1	127.6	130.4	136.8	144.4
300..........	113.6	119.7	120.2	120.9	121.9	123.2	124.8	126.7	128.9	131.4	134.2	140.6	148.2

INDEX.

THE FIGURES BELOW REFER TO THE NUMBERS OF THE PAGES.

Advertisements.

CENTRAL FLUE SYSTEM

OF ANNEALING CAR WHEELS.

USED EXCLUSIVELY BY

BALTIMORE CAR WHEEL COMPANY.

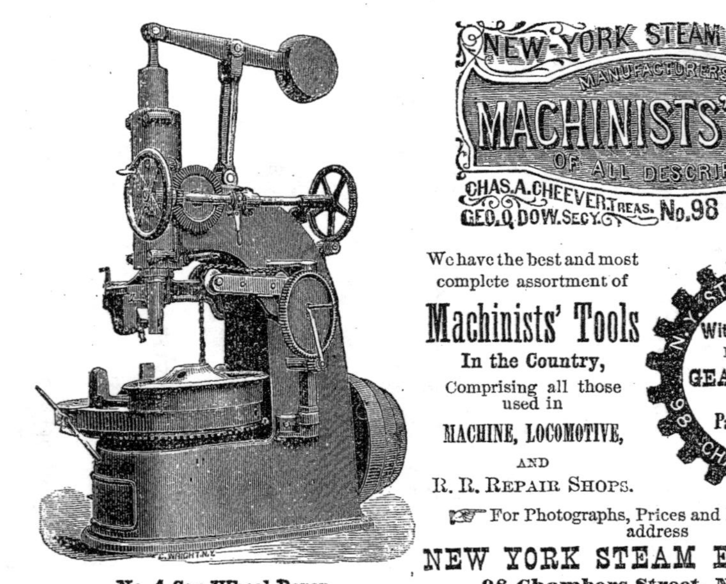
No. 4 Car Wheel Borer.

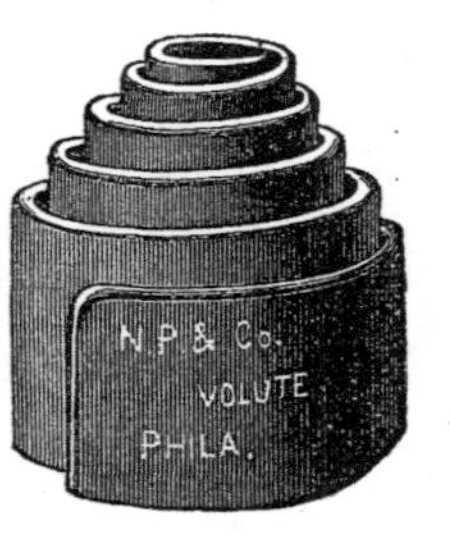

N.P.& Co.
VOLUTE
PHILA.

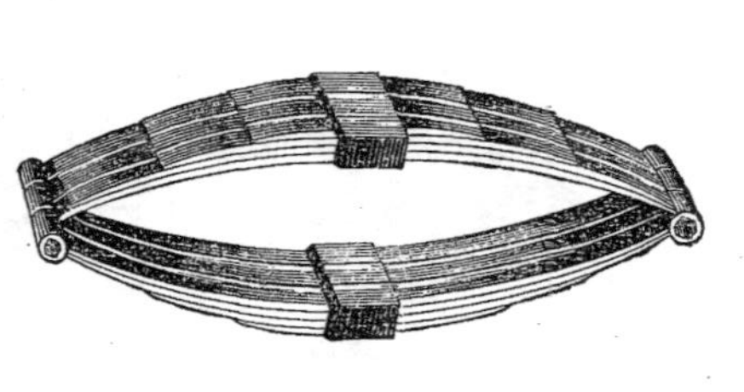

N P & Co.
NEST SPIRAL
PHILA.

www.ingramcontent.com/pod-product-compliance
Lightning Source LLC
LaVergne TN
LVHW021052110826
845150LV00001B/53